MOON HANDBOOKS

T3-ANT-749

SILICON VALLEY

The Children's Discovery Museum

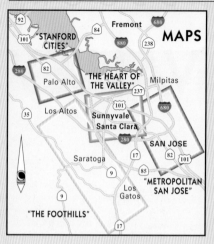

MAPS

"STANFORD CITIES"
"THE HEART OF THE VALLEY"
"METROPOLITAN SAN JOSE"
"THE FOOTHILLS"

Fremont
Milpitas
Palo Alto
Los Altos
Sunnyvale
Santa Clara
SAN JOSE
Saratoga
Los Gatos

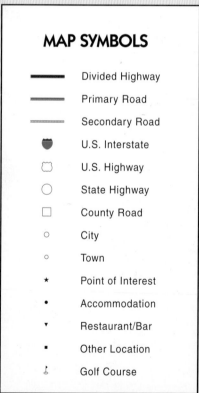

MAP SYMBOLS

▬▬▬	Divided Highway
▬▬▬	Primary Road
▬▬▬	Secondary Road
🛡	U.S. Interstate
▢	U.S. Highway
◯	State Highway
▢	County Road
⊙	City
○	Town
★	Point of Interest
•	Accommodation
▾	Restaurant/Bar
▪	Other Location
⚑	Golf Course

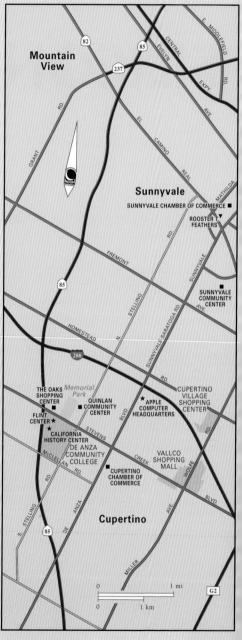

Mountain View

Sunnyvale

SUNNYVALE CHAMBER OF COMMERCE ▪
ROOSTER T. FEATHERS ▾

SUNNYVALE COMMUNITY CENTER ▪

FREMONT
HOMESTEAD

Memorial Park

THE OAKS SHOPPING CENTER ▪
FLINT CENTER ★
CALIFORNIA HISTORY CENTER ★
DE ANZA COMMUNITY COLLEGE

QUINLAN COMMUNITY CENTER ▪

★ APPLE COMPUTER HEADQUARTERS

CUPERTINO VILLAGE SHOPPING CENTER

VALLCO SHOPPING MALL

CUPERTINO CHAMBER OF COMMERCE ▪

Cupertino

0   1 mi
0   1 km

G2

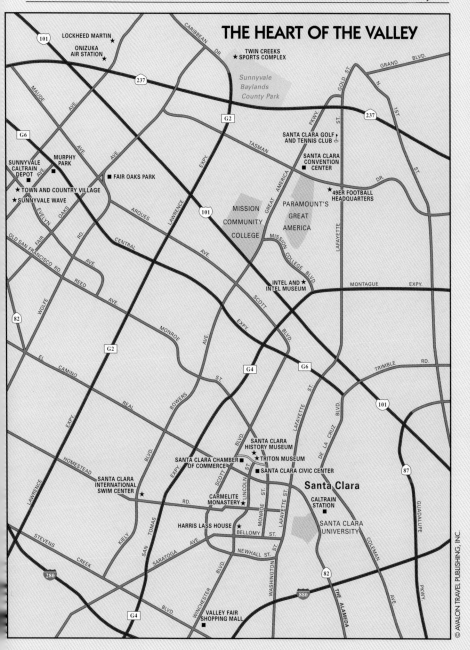

THE HEART OF THE VALLEY

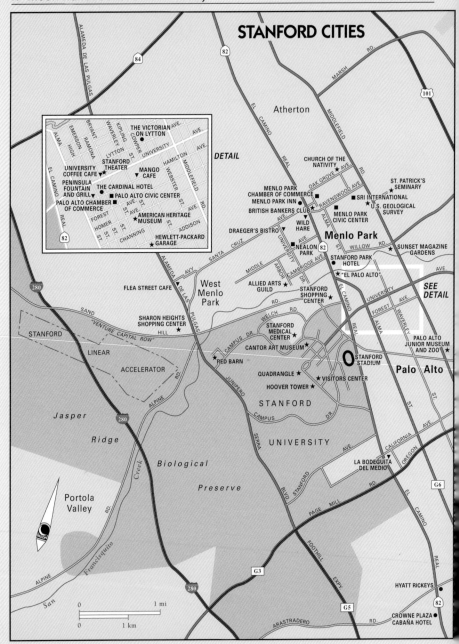

STANFORD CITIES

DETAIL

- THE VICTORIAN ON LYTTON
- UNIVERSITY COFFEE CAFE
- STANFORD THEATER
- MANGO CAFE
- PENINSULA FOUNTAIN AND GRILL
- THE CARDINAL HOTEL
- PALO ALTO CIVIC CENTER
- PALO ALTO CHAMBER OF COMMERCE
- AMERICAN HERITAGE MUSEUM
- HEWLETT-PACKARD GARAGE

ALMA EMERSON HIGH BRYANT RAMONA WAVERLEY KIPLING COWPER ST. UNIVERSITY AVE. AVE.

LYTTON HAMILTON WEBSTER ST. MIDDLEFIELD AVE. AVE.

EL CAMINO REAL FOREST AVE. ST. HOMER ST. CHANNING ST. ADDISON AVE.

Atherton

CHURCH OF THE NATIVITY

ST. PATRICK'S SEMINARY

MENLO PARK CHAMBER OF COMMERCE MENLO PARK INN

SRI INTERNATIONAL

U.S. GEOLOGICAL SURVEY

BRITISH BANKERS CLUB

MENLO PARK CIVIC CENTER

DRAEGER'S BISTRO

WILD HARE

Menlo Park

NEALON PARK

SUNSET MAGAZINE GARDENS

STANFORD PARK HOTEL

EL PALO ALTO

SEE DETAIL

FLEA STREET CAFE

West Menlo Park

ALLIED ARTS GUILD

STANFORD SHOPPING CENTER

PALO ALTO JUNIOR MUSEUM AND ZOO

SHARON HEIGHTS SHOPPING CENTER

"VENTURE CAPITAL ROW"

STANFORD

LINEAR

ACCELERATOR

STANFORD MEDICAL CENTER

CANTOR ART MUSEUM

STANFORD STADIUM

Palo Alto

RED BARN

QUADRANGLE

VISITORS CENTER

HOOVER TOWER

Jasper

Ridge

S T A N F O R D

U N I V E R S I T Y

LA BODEGUITA DEL MEDIO

Biological

Preserve

Portola Valley

PAGE MILL

HYATT RICKEYS

CROWNE PLAZA CABAÑA HOTEL

ARASTRADERO

San Francisquito Creek

ALPINE SAND HILL RD. JUNIPERO SERRA CAMPUS DR. STANFORD BLVD. FOOTHILL EXPY. EL CAMINO REAL CALIFORNIA OREGON AVE.

0   1 mi

0   1 km

84 82 101 280 G6 G3 G5 82

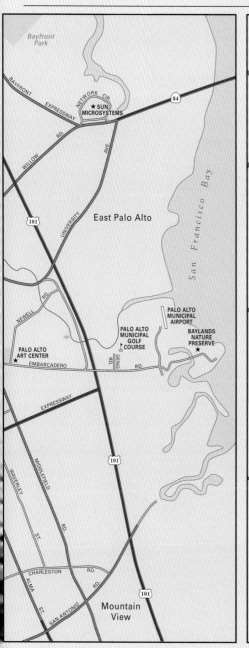

Bayfront Park

BAYFRONT EXPRESSWAY

NETWORK CIR

★ SUN MICROSYSTEMS

84

BAYFRONT RD.

WILLOW RD.

UNIVERSITY AVE.

101

East Palo Alto

San Francisco Bay

PALO ALTO MUNICIPAL AIRPORT

PALO ALTO MUNICIPAL GOLF COURSE

BAYLANDS NATURE PRESERVE ★

NEWELL RD.

PALO ALTO ART CENTER ■

EMBARCADERO

RUNNYMEDE

GENG RD.

EXPRESSWAY

101

MIDDLEFIELD RD.

WAVERLEY ST.

ST.

ALMA ST.

CHARLESTON RD.

SAN ANTONIO RD.

101

Mountain View

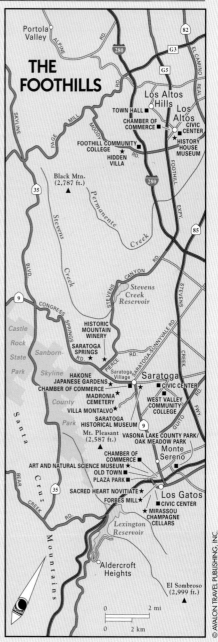

Portola Valley

ALPINE RD.

PAGE MILL RD.

280

82

G3

G5

EL CAMINO REAL

THE FOOTHILLS

Los Altos Hills

TOWN HALL ■

CHAMBER OF COMMERCE ■

Los Altos

CIVIC CENTER ■

HISTORY HOUSE MUSEUM ■

FOOTHILL COMMUNITY COLLEGE ★

HIDDEN VILLA ★

MOODY RD.

FOOTHILL EXPY.

280

Black Mtn. (2,787 ft.) ▲

SKYLINE BLVD.

35

Stevens Creek

Permanente Creek

85

Stevens Canyon RD.

Stevens Creek Reservoir

CONGRESS SPRINGS

9

HISTORIC MOUNTAIN WINERY ★

SARATOGA SPRINGS ★

Castle Rock State Park

Sanborn-Skyline County Park

Santa Cruz Mountains

PIERCE RD.

SARATOGA-SUNNYVALE RD.

STEVENS CREEK

Saratoga Village

HAKONE JAPANESE GARDENS ★

CHAMBER OF COMMERCE ■

MADRONIA CEMETERY ★

VILLA MONTALVO ★

SARATOGA HISTORICAL MUSEUM ★

Mt. Pleasant (2,587 ft.) ▲

Saratoga

CIVIC CENTER ■

WEST VALLEY COMMUNITY COLLEGE

QUITO RD.

9

VASONA LAKE COUNTY PARK/ OAK MEADOW PARK

Monte Sereno

CHAMBER OF COMMERCE ■

ART AND NATURAL SCIENCE MUSEUM ★

OLD TOWN ■

PLAZA PARK ■

SACRED HEART NOVITIATE ★

FORBES MILL ★

BEAR CREEK RD.

35

Los Gatos

CIVIC CENTER ■

MIRASSOU CHAMPAGNE CELLARS ■

Lexington Reservoir

Aldercroft Heights

El Sombroso (2,999 ft.) ▲

0   2 mi

0   2 km

© AVALON TRAVEL PUBLISHING, INC.

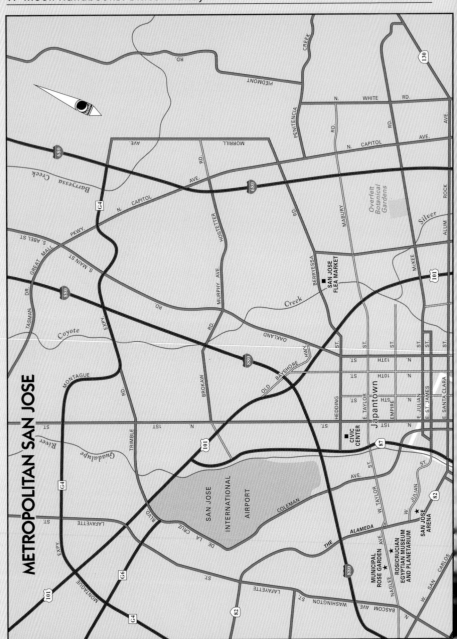

METROPOLITAN SAN JOSE

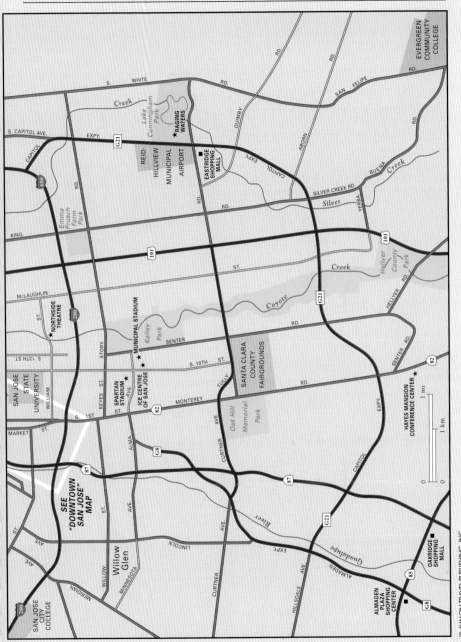

EVERGREEN COMMUNITY COLLEGE

SAN FELIPE RD.

S. WHITE RD.

Creek

Lake Cunningham Park

★ RAGING WATERS

S. CAPITOL AVE.

EXPY.

QUIMBY RD.

ABORN RD.

CAPITOL EXPY.

BUENA

Creek

REID-HILLVIEW MUNICIPAL AIRPORT

■ EASTRIDGE SHOPPING MALL

CAPITOL

RD.

RD.

SILVER CREEK RD.

Silver

YERBA

Emma Prusch Farm Park

KING

RD.

Creek

ST.

Coyote

Hellyer County Park

HELLYER RD.

KING

McLAUGHLIN

★ NORTHSIDE THEATRE

ST.

MUNICIPAL STADIUM

Kelley Park

SENTER

RD.

G21

SENTER RD.

SAN JOSE STATE UNIVERSITY

WILLIAM

STORY

S. 10TH ST.

Santa Clara County Fairgrounds

82

S. 19TH ST.

KEYES ST.

SPARTAN STADIUM

ICE CENTRE OF SAN JOSE

TULLY

MONTEREY

RD.

HAYES MANSION CONFERENCE CENTER ★

1 mi

MARKET ST.

S. 1ST

ALMA

Oak Hill Memorial Park

AVE.

CAPITOL EXPY.

1 km

SEE "DOWNTOWN SAN JOSE" MAP

87

ST.

AVE.

CURTNER

87

0

G8

G21

AVE.

LINCOLN

River

(Guadalupe)

OAKRIDGE SHOPPING MALL ■

Willow Glen

WILLOW

MINNESOTA

CURTNER

EXPY.

ALMADEN

HILLSDALE AVE.

85

ALMADEN PLAZA SHOPPING CENTER ■

G8

SAN JOSE CITY COLLEGE

280

MERIDIAN

AVE.

© AVALON TRAVEL PUBLISHING, INC.

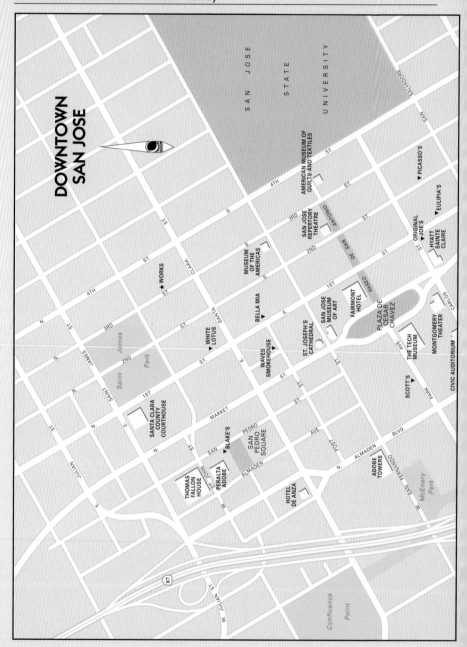

DOWNTOWN SAN JOSE

SAN JOSE STATE UNIVERSITY

★ WORKS

MUSEUM OF THE AMERICAS

AMERICAN MUSEUM OF QUILTS AND TEXTILES

SAN JOSE REPERTORY THEATRE

▶ PICASSO'S

▶ EULIPIA'S

ORIGINAL JOE'S

HYATT SAINTE CLAIRE

▶ BELLA MIA

WHITE LOTUS ▶

SAN JOSE MUSEUM OF ART

FAIRMONT HOTEL

PLAZA DE CESAR CHAVEZ

WAVES SMOKEHOUSE

ST. JOSEPH'S CATHEDRAL

Saint James Park

SANTA CLARA COUNTY COURTHOUSE

THE TECH MUSEUM

MONTGOMERY THEATER

SCOTT'S

CIVIC AUDITORIUM

THOMAS FALLON HOUSE

PERALTA ADOBE

BLAKE'S ▶

SAN PEDRO SQUARE

ADOBE TOWERS

HOTEL DE ANZA

McEnery Park

Confluence Point

87

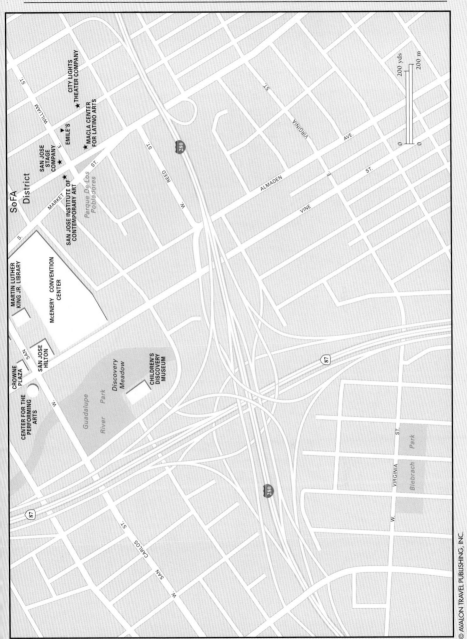

SoFA District

★ CITY LIGHTS THEATER COMPANY
★ EMILE'S
★ MACLA CENTER FOR LATINO ARTS
SAN JOSE STAGE COMPANY
SAN JOSE INSTITUTE OF CONTEMPORARY ART ★
MARKET ST.
Parque De Los Pobladores
WILLIAM ST.
2ND ST.
REED ST.
W.
S.
2ND

MARTIN LUTHER KING JR. LIBRARY
McENERY CONVENTION CENTER
CROWNE PLAZA
SAN JOSE HILTON
CENTER FOR THE PERFORMING ARTS

Guadalupe River Park
Discovery Meadow
CHILDREN'S DISCOVERY MUSEUM

SAN CARLOS ST.
W.

87

87

2ND

VIRGINIA ST.
ALMADEN AVE.
VINE ST.

VIRGINIA ST.
Biebrach Park
W.

200 yds
200 m
0
0

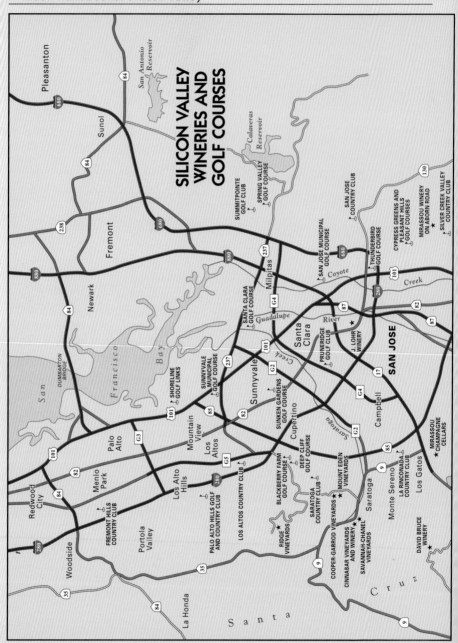

SILICON VALLEY
WINERIES AND
GOLF COURSES

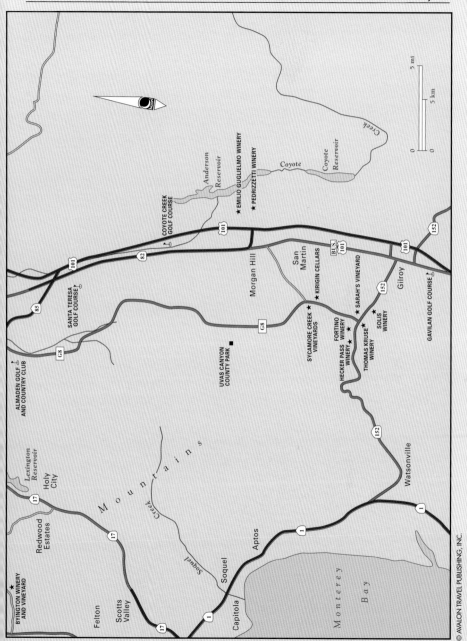

5 mi

5 km

0

0

Creek

Coyote Creek

Anderson
Reservoir

Coyote
Reservoir

★ EMILIO GUGLIELMO WINERY

★ PEDRIZZETTI WINERY

Coyote

COYOTE CREEK
GOLF COURSE

101

82

101

BUS.
101

101

152

San
Martin

Morgan Hill

★ KIRIGIN CELLARS

Gilroy

152

★ SARAH'S VINEYARD

GAVILAN GOLF COURSE

85

SANTA TERESA
GOLF COURSE

G8

★ SYCAMORE CREEK
VINEYARDS

G8

★ FORTINO
WINERY

HECKER PASS
WINERY ★

THOMAS KRUSE
WINERY ★

★ SOLIS
WINERY

ALMADEN GOLF
AND COUNTRY CLUB

UVAS CANYON
COUNTY PARK ■

152

Watsonville

Lexington
Reservoir

Holy
City

17

M o u n t a i n s

Creek

1

Redwood
Estates

17

Aptos

1

Soquel

Soquel

Felton

Scotts
Valley

Capitola

17

1

BYINGTON WINERY
AND VINEYARD

M o n t e r e y

B a y

Chitactac Adams County Park

MOON HANDBOOKS

SILICON VALLEY

INCLUDING SAN JOSE, PALO ALTO & SOUTH VALLEY

SECOND EDITION

MARTIN CHEEK

AVALON
TRAVEL

Moon Handbooks: Silicon Valley
Including San Jose, Palo Alto & South Valley
2nd edition

Martin Cheek

Published by
Avalon Travel Publishing
5855 Beaudry St.
Emeryville, CA 94608, USA

Please send all comments, corrections,
additions, amendments, and critiques to:

Moon Handbooks: Silicon Valley
AVALON TRAVEL PUBLISHING
5855 BEAUDRY ST.
EMERYVILLE, CA 94608, USA
email: atpfeedback@avalonpub.com
www.travelmatters.com

Printing History
1st edition—2000
2nd edition—February 2002
5 4 3 2 1

ISBN: 1-56691-370-5
ISSN: 1535-4369

Editor: Kim Marks
Series Manager: Erin Van Rheenen
Copy Editor: Leslie Miller
Graphics: Melissa Sherowski
Production: Jacob Goolkasian
Map Editor: Naomi Adler Dancis
Cartographers: Mike Morgenfeld, Chris Folks, Chris Alvarez
Indexer: Valerie Sellers Blanton

Front cover photo: © Richard Cummins

Distributed by Publishers Group West

Printed in Hong Kong by Prolong Press, Ltd.

ABOUT THE AUTHOR
Martin Cheek

Martin Cheek lives in Morgan Hill, California, "the Mushroom Capital of the World," which is in the South Valley region of Silicon Valley. His love of writing and knowledge of Silicon Valley first came together at San Jose State University, where he worked for various Silicon Valley-based publications while earning a bachelor's degree in newspaper journalism.

After college, Martin reported for the *Los Gatos Weekly-Times*. He also worked as a reporter for the high-tech news service Edittech International and served as that company's European Bureau Chief in London for more than two years. He was managing editor of the now-defunct *Triumph Magazine*, a Silicon Valley lifestyle publication.

When he's not writing, Martin enjoys hiking, biking, weight-lifting, fishing, swimming, good conversations and cooking dinner for friends.

For Pauline
Because you took me places I'd never been

In an alcove overlooking the Guadalupe River in downtown San Jose's Discovery Meadow, there lies a sandstone rock, a gift from the city of Dublin. Carved on it are words by Arthur O'Shaughnessy, a poet of the Emerald Isle, that capture well the spirit of Silicon Valley:

We are the music makers
And we are the dreamers of dreams,
Wandering by lone sea-breakers
And sitting by desolate streams.
World losers and world-forsakers
On whom the pale moon gleams
Yet we are the movers and shakers
Of the world forever it seems.

Contents

THE CITIES OF THE VALLEY **64**

SPECIAL TOPICS

ACCOMMODATIONS 226

Campbell; Cupertino; Gilroy; Los Gatos; Menlo Park; Milpitas; Morgan Hill;
Palo Alto; Downtown San Jose; Greater San Jose; Santa Clara; Saratoga;
Sunnyvale

SPECIAL TOPICS

FINE DINING, POTABLES, AND NIGHTLIFE .239

Campbell; Cupertino; Los Altos; Los Gatos; Menlo Park; Milpitas; Mountain
View; Palo Alto; San Jose; Santa Clara; Saratoga; South Valley; Sunnyvale
WINERIES, BREWPUBS, AND NIGHTCLUBS 255
Wineries; Brewpubs; Nightclubs

SPECIAL TOPICS

RESOURCES 267

Map Contents

Abbreviations

AI—artificial intelligence
GUI—graphical user interface
HP—Hewlett-Packard
IPO—initial public offering
PARC—Xerox's Palo Alto Research Center
PC—personal computer (usually refers specif-
    ically to the IBM Personal Computer)
R&D—research and development

RAM—random-access memory
ROM—read-only memory
SETI—Search for Extraterrestrial Intelligence
SLAC—Stanford Linear Accelerator
VC—venture capitalist

Keeping Current

Silicon Valley is a place of never-ending change. Where an orchard bloomed yesterday, an industrial park is under construction today. There's a dynamic vitality to this region that makes it such an exciting and interesting place to explore. But this vitality is also the dread of travel book writers. While researching this book, the author had to keep a continuous vigil on the valley's changing scene. So, if you note outdated information or want to suggest ways to make *Moon Handbooks: Silicon Valley* a better book, please drop the author a line at:

Moon Handbooks: Silicon Valley
c/o Avalon Travel Publishing
5855 Beaudry St.
Emeryville, CA 94608
email: atpfeedback@avalonpub.com
(please put "*Moon Handbooks: Silicon Valley*" in the subject line of your message)

Note from the Author

No business or organization described in this book paid for or bribed the author with other compensations to get into this guidebook. The joy of research and writing was reward enough.

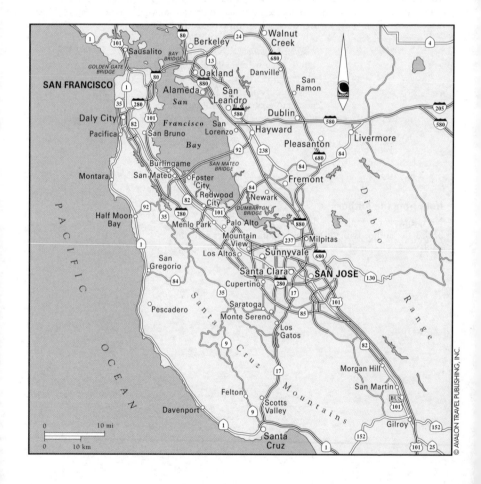

Introduction

A well-known photograph taken at Stanford University soon after the 1906 earthquake depicts a fallen statue with its head buried in the sidewalk. The statue is—ironically—of a *geology* professor named Louis Agassiz. Upon seeing the statue's condition, the university's president joked, "I prefer Agassiz in the abstract rather than in the concrete."

The photo serves as a metaphor for Silicon Valley. In a geologic sense, this valley was formed by the force of earthquakes raising the Diablo and Santa Cruz Mountains bordering it. In a human sense, the valley was built by the force of individuals who came here to make their mark and improve their lives. From the sophisticated trading system between ancient Ohlone Indian villages, to the modern-day trading of technology stocks, the Silicon Valley has long been a center of commerce.

It was the high-tech boom of the 1990s, however, that brought it all to a fever pitch. Thousands of people arrived, lured by the prospect of well-paying jobs and the opportunity to be on the cutting edge of their professions. But the dawn of the 21st century brought an economic upheaval that, like an earthquake, changed people's lives dramatically. Hit with layoffs and dropping stock values, many people found themselves in a financial free fall reminiscent of Agassiz's fall from his pedestal.

Still, the spirit of optimism persists. People in the valley believe in the future and know that economic ups and downs—along with earthquakes—are an unavoidable part of life here. They pick themselves up, make a few jokes, and go about the business of rebuilding their lives.

In good times and bad, Silicon Valley is a dynamic place. Within a matter of mere decades, the ideas, inventions, and innovations produced here have dramatically affected every aspect of society and virtually revolutionized the worlds of business, education, entertainment, and politics. The microchip, the personal computer, and the Internet are only three of the region's many notable creations. And the people and organizations here continue to indulge their curiosity and their wonder, to ask why, and to search for answers and solutions. It is here that NASA's Hubble Space Telescope was largely developed,

Stanford University, Palo Alto

the quest to send humans to Mars is being actively pursued, and the Search for Extraterrestrial Intelligence Institute seeks evidence that *we are not alone*. Biotechnologists in this valley are mapping human genetic code, and the atomic scientists at Menlo Park's Stanford Linear Accelerator are dissecting the tiniest particles of physical matter. In addition to which, of course, the engineers and companies that inhabit this region are in constant hot pursuit of ways to make the electronic devices we all take for granted faster, smarter, smaller, more efficient, more communicative, easier to use, easier to carry, less expensive, and just in all conceivable ways better.

Silicon Valley is the planet's preeminent center for technological advances. What happens here today has an impact on just about every aspect of our lives, whether we feel that impact tomorrow, next week, or a year from now. This valley is the epicenter from which the revolutionary ripples of the Information Age radiate around the globe. You could make a case that Silicon Valley's influence is felt everywhere in the world that there's a computer, fax machine, or other high-tech marvel; into outer space, wherever a satellite orbits the globe; in fact, anywhere humans apply the tools of technology in their never-ending quest for better lives. The area's scientists, engineers, and researchers are working on projects that will profoundly affect how we experience—and perhaps even whether we survive—the 21st century.

Throughout the United States and the rest of the world, there *are* other regions that are developing their own high-tech industries. The Seattle area is home to more than 2,500 high-tech firms—most notably the "Big M," Microsoft; Salt Lake City hosts more than 2,000 firms; Washington, D.C., more than 3,000. Boston, home of the Massachusetts Institute of Technology, has more than 3,600; North Carolina has the high-tech Research Triangle; Austin, Texas, supports digital cowboys such as Dell Computer; Champaign-Urbana, Illinois, is the hot spot for supercomputer research at the National Center for Supercomputer Applications, among others. And outside the United States, there's Cambridge, England, with more than 1,100 high-tech firms;

Tel Aviv, Israel, with 1,000; and Bangalore, India, site of the famous Indian Institute of Science. These are all important technology centers, but Silicon Valley seems to be the one that has perfected the intricate combination of infrastructure, climate, universities, venture capital, lifestyle, megasuccess stories, major research institutions, and risk-taking attitude. It's that risk-taking attitude that really exemplifies the Silicon Valley culture. The people here live on the edge—both in a geologic sense and in a personal sense. And that's what makes life here an adventure. You never know what's going to come next.

GEOGRAPHY

Officially, there is no such place as Silicon Valley. Though more than two million people live and work in this area, you won't find it on any authoritative map of the United States. Nevertheless, most people have a general idea that Silicon Valley is somewhere in California's Bay Area. In the 1980s, the TV show *Good Morning America* even asked this teaser question before a commercial break: "Where Is Silicon Valley?" The answer, when they came back, was, "San Francisco." Well, *close*.

With the rise of technology, the world now has a much better idea where Silicon Valley is located. But there is still debate as to exactly where the boundaries lie. Some broad definitions say that Silicon Valley includes Berkeley, San Francisco, Santa Cruz, and Monterey because these cities have a strong connection to the high-tech world. The Peninsula (the stretch of Bay Area land extending from Menlo Park to San Francisco) also has its share of technology firms (especially Oracle in Redwood City). And the East Bay also could be considered Silicon Valley—a sign in the city of Newark proclaims it as "the gateway to Silicon Valley." But the bottom line is, defining the geography of Silicon Valley is a purely subjective undertaking.

For the purposes of this book (and in general agreement with the boundary definition of the Silicon Valley Chamber of Commerce), Silicon Valley occupies about 1,325 square miles in what is officially known as the Santa Clara Valley, which curls around the southern tip of San Francisco Bay, approximately 50 miles south of San Francisco, between the Santa Cruz Mountains and the Diablo Range. With the single exception of the city of Menlo Park (which is vitally important for its venture capital backing of high-tech firms), the region is contained entirely within Santa Clara County, extending south from the Bay about 50 miles, to Gilroy, just north of the county boundary, the Pajaro River.

Although the valley can be carved up in a variety of ways, "The Cities of the Valley" chapter moves from north to south, while the maps at the front of this book reflect the following city groupings:

The Stanford Cities

The western leg of Silicon Valley is topped by Menlo Park and Palo Alto. In many important respects, these two wealthy, quiet cities were the birthplace of Silicon Valley—the cradle of this burgeoning civilization—and they still play very significant roles. Predominantly residential, they are also vital centers of shopping and fine dining.

The Gateway to Silicon Valley

Across the bay, the eastern leg of the U ends at Milpitas, in the East Bay. Milpitas is home to a sizable concentration of high-tech manufacturing companies, which makes it an extremely vital contributor to the region's economic base.

The Heart of the Valley

The cities of Mountain View, Sunnyvale, Santa Clara, Cupertino, and Campbell constitute the physical and psychic heart of the region. Roughly equally divided between residential and high-tech industrial areas, these cities are home to many of the valley's best-known companies as well as a large proportion of its employees.

San Jose—The Silicon Capital

The region's largest city—with the highest population and most expansive geographic boundaries—is San Jose, the self-proclaimed "capital of Silicon Valley." Once a rather run-down agricultural center, the city has embraced its new role as the gentrified, cosmopolitan hub of a region of global importance.

The Foothill Communities

Lying along the eastern foothills of the Santa Cruz Mountains at the valley's western edge, the very wealthy communities of Los Altos Hills, Los Altos, Saratoga, Monte Sereno, and Los Gatos provide beautiful settings from which magnificent homes look out onto panoramic vistas.

The South Valley

Comprising the communities of Morgan Hill, San Martin, and Gilroy, this area (also known as South County) offers a glimpse at the region's fast-disappearing agricultural past. Even now, a growing number of high-tech workers make their homes here—and there can be little doubt that this is the site of future expansion of Silicon Valley.

GEOLOGY AND WEATHER

Since long before the first humans ever set foot here, geology and weather have worked together to create the Mediterranean-like climate in Silicon Valley.

Millions of years ago, the area lay underwater. But the gradual, unceasing pressure of plate tectonics slowly pushed it above the surface, where it became dry land. Evidence of this includes fossils of marine creatures found locally—such as at Alum Rock Park. The area's terrain consists of a broad flat valley with numerous creeks flowing from the surrounding mountains into the southern end of the San Francisco Bay. Over the eons, these creeks washed rich soil from the mountains and helped make the valley a natural paradise consisting of grassy plains dotted with oaks and other flora.

Two mountain ranges border the valley. Resembling rumpled bedsheets, these were built up by the force of earthquakes along geologic fault lines such as the San Andreas Fault (which borders the Pacific Plate and the North American Plate) on Silicon Valley's western ridge. The Santa Cruz Mountains (a northern spur of the Santa Lucia Range) border Silicon Valley on its western

© MARTIN CHEEK

Mt. Hamilton

landmark peak here, topped by the white domes of the Lick Observatory. The mountain was named for the Reverend Hamilton, who, in 1861, was the first to reach the summit during an official U.S. Geodetic Survey expedition (the surveyors didn't know that the landform had already been named Mt. Isabel). Farther north, near Milpitas, is Mission Peak, identifiable by the TV and radio antennas at its summit. On the other side of the Diablo Range is California's massive Central Valley (comprising the San Joaquin and Sacramento Valleys), the state's agricultural heartland.

Climate

Silicon Valley's blessed weather is due to several factors. Most of the year, a mountainous volume of air called the Pacific high pressure system sits along the coast, forming a meteorological wall that prevents strong storms from reaching the area. In the winter months, this slips south toward the equator, letting in colder storms from the Gulf of Alaska.

The heating of California's Central Valley also plays a role in creating the temperate climate. As the valley east of the Diablo Range heats up, its air expands, thus dropping its pressure. When this pressure drops below that of the Pacific high pressure zone, nature—abhorring a vacuum—moves air from the Pacific to the Central Valley to equalize the pressure. This air cools as it moves across thousands of miles of ocean, and when it reaches California, it serves as a natural air conditioner for Silicon Valley. Often, the water-laden air condenses along the coast, forming San Francisco's famous fog. One reason Silicon Valley doesn't receive the same fog is that the redwood trees covering the Santa Cruz Mountains have evolved their needlelike leaves to gather the moisture in the air, then let it drip down to the roots.

edge. On the sunset side of this is a big puddle known as the Pacific Ocean. A prominent peak here is the 4,085-foot Loma Prieta (Black Hill), which provides extensive vistas of the Santa Clara Valley and Monterey Bay. Overlooking the Almaden Valley at San Jose's southern end sits a mountain with an immense structure at its summit. This is Mt. Umunhum (oo-MOON-oom—believed to be an Ohlone Indian word for "hummingbird"). The prominent construction is a closed U.S. Air Force radar station once used to watch for approaching Soviet bombers.

Along the east is the Diablo Range, named for Mt. Diablo, a prominent peak near the East Bay city of Walnut Creek. Mt. Hamilton is the

JUST ADD WATER

A great metropolis can never come into existence without the magical ingredient of water. London and Paris were created by their rivers. New York, New Orleans, and San Francisco would not be world-famous cities without their bays. And, if it weren't for the massive aqueduct projects, Los Angeles would certainly remain a dried-up desert village today. The same can be said about Silicon Valley. Water as much as high-tech industry created it. In fact, the chip-making business could never have existed here without water. Highly purified tap water is used to cleanse the chips during manufacturing.

In the early years of valley settlement, water obviously played an important role in the developing orchard business. Farmers dug artesian wells, which allowed the precious liquid to pour out of the ground due to the subsiding pressure of the land. By the 1890s, as these wells began to lose their pressure and dry up, farmers simply dug deeper wells and used pumping stations to bring up the water so vital for their crops.

In the 20th century, people began to notice a problem caused by this constant pumping of the groundwater supply. A geological phenomenon called subsidence was causing the land to sink severely. Imagine an air mattress, on top of which lies a heavy board. If the air is allowed to leak out, the board sinks lower and lower. Similarly, land sinks as water is drawn from the geological stratums. By the 1960s, San Jose had sunk by 10 feet and Alviso, by San Francisco Bay, had dropped 13 feet. With this descending land, bay water began to creep up, drowning small villages such as Drawbridge, which is now a ghost town along the Amtrak tracks near Alviso.

With the drought years of the 1920s and 1930s, the valley's population realized the necessity of conserving water. In 1929, a water conservation district was formed, which built six dams in Santa Clara County in the next six years. These dams caught the rain runoff from winter storms, thus also helping to ease the problems of flooding that had plagued the valley since the days of the Spanish missionaries.

Compounding the need for water was the valley's population surge following World War II. Rain would simply not provide enough water for the growing population and industry. Viewing the success of the Los Angeles aqueduct system, the county and state (funded in part by federal dollars) began building the South Bay Aqueduct, a $50 million pipeline which moved water from the Sacramento–San Joaquin River Delta. On July 1, 1965, Governor Edmund G. Brown dedicated the opening of this project by pouring mercury from a vial into a small tank. This closed an electric circuit, which caused a pump to pull water into the pipeline.

In the northern valley, cities such as Palo Alto and Menlo Park also began to receive water from San Francisco's Hetch Hetchy aqueduct, which transported water from the Sierras. A third aqueduct for the valley was the more than $500 million San Felipe Project. This 35-mile system of pipes conveyed water from San Luis Reservoir along Pacheco Pass in Merced County just south of Silicon Valley. It opened in 1987, just in time for the valley's big population boom of the 1990s.

Today, most Silicon Valley residents take their showers, water their yards, wash their cars, and turn on the tap with little thought of the engineering marvels that make their lives in the valley possible.

History

Despite their many brilliant innovations, Silicon Valley engineers and scientists have yet to develop time travel technology. But if they ever do invent a machine that can transport us to the region's past, the visit would help us understand the events that have shaped today's Silicon Valley. Its human chronology is an epic story filled with colorful personalities and dramatic history.

Some archaeologists estimate that humans first set foot in the valley as far back as 10,000 years ago, during the end of the last great ice age. Those original settlers found a fertile plain region of creeks and bay wetlands bordered by the rugged redwood-covered mountains on the west and the more gentle foothills on the east. Oak trees blanketed much of the valley, and the mild climate and abundance of food made it a perfect home for these first inhabitants.

Over the centuries, the natives came to call themselves the Ohlone (the People). They developed a relatively peaceful society of small villages (numbering 50–250 people) situated near meandering creeks throughout the valley. The villages contained half-sphere huts made of willow stalks driven into the ground and latticed with branches, redwood bark, and dirt. During the warm months, men and children went naked while women wore skirts of deerskin and grasses. In the winter, the Ohlone wore robes and cloaks made from soft seal and otter fur. They took their food from the land, hunting for fish, deer, rabbit, and waterfowl. And, like today's residents, they traveled across the western mountains to enjoy seafood, including mussels and abalone caught in Monterey Bay. Acorns from the abundant oaks made up their staple food. In the fall, women gathered the acorns, ground them in stone mortars with pestles, and soaked the resulting meal in water to leach out the toxic tannic acid.

The Ohlone worshiped various nature gods with religious dances and seasonal festivals. These deities included the sun, the eagle, and the hummingbird, as well as the coyote, which they believed had created the world. They developed a sophisticated trading system between villages, using shells from the *saxidomus nuttali* clam as currency. Little did the Ohlone know their simple and peaceful lives would dramatically change when, on November 6, 1769, strange men with pale complexions first journeyed into the valley.

Spanish Exploration

On that day, the Spanish explorer Gaspar de Portolá and his men became the first Europeans to see the beauty of the valley. They called it Llaño de los Robles (Plain of the Oaks). They had come to explore the land for colonization.

Concerned about Russian and other foreign encroachment of its lands in Alta California, the Spanish Empire decided to establish token settlements to protect its New World conquests. In 1602, the explorer Sebastián Vizcaíno had explored the California coast by ship and discovered Monterey Bay. But the Spanish did nothing about this information until 1769, when officials sent Portolá overland to establish a base on this

© MARTIN CHEEK

replica of an Ohlone hut

© MARTIN CHEEK

Santa Clara Mission cemetery

large bay. Due to Vizcaíno's exaggerated details in his report, Portolá mistakenly passed his destination and traveled too far north, giving him the opportunity to become the first white man to discover the San Francisco Bay. His expedition crossed the mountains and set up camp beneath an exceptionally tall redwood that they called *el palo alto*. (The landmark tree still stands, in the city of Palo Alto.) Portolá observed some of the Ohlone in a nearby village, describing them in his expedition journal as "barbarous heathens who are very affable, mild, and docile, and very generous."

The Spanish government planned to protect its territory by converting Alta California's inhabitants into *gente de razon* (people of reason). It intended to civilize the Ohlone and turn them into Spanish citizens by setting up missions and instructing them in the ways of the Christian religion. In 1775, Juan Bautista de Anza and his group of Spanish settlers traveled through the valley intent on finding a location to establish a mission. They traveled along a well-trod Ohlone trail that the Spanish eventually turned into a road called El Camino Real (The Royal Road). A mission site was selected in the middle of the valley close to the Guadalupe River as a water source. On January 12, 1777, the Franciscan padres conducted the first mass at the Mission Santa Clara de Asis, named after Saint Clare of Assisi. The land surrounding the mission eventually became known as the Santa Clara Valley.

First Californian City

Shipping a constant supply of grain and necessities from Mexico to the Santa Clara Valley proved a difficult undertaking. The Spanish government realized they needed to establish a civilian settlement to provide food and basic goods, or the mission would fail. On November 29, 1777, ground was broken near a small creek for a frontier outpost. It was named El Pueblo de San Jose de Guadalupe, after the patron saint of California. The colony's founding date makes it the earliest civilian settlement in California. The *pobladores* (citizens of the pueblo) enjoyed the valley's fertile soil and Mediterranean climate, which reminded them of Spain. A problem occurred, however, because of the pueblo's location (in an area near where the Santa Clara County government building stands today, on Hedding Street). During the winter rainy season, the gentle Guadalupe River turned into a raging torrent. A dam collapsed, and the rising water destroyed adobe buildings and washed away cropland. By the end of 1797, the pueblo began the process of moving to a new location, which is now downtown San Jose (in the area between the Children's Discovery Museum and San Pedro Square). Meanwhile, the Spanish missionaries and settlers planted fruit trees and vineyards, raised cattle, and taught the Ohlone how to farm grain, corn, and other crops. An agricultural heritage was established in the valley.

A major change in the region's political climate came in early 1821, when Mexico gained its independence from Spain. The next year, Californios (inhabitants of Mexican and Spanish descent) took an oath of allegiance to Mexico, thus ending Spanish dominion in its West Coast frontier. To establish settlements and help occupy its new territory, the Mexican government began giving large land grants of up to 76 square miles to soldiers and settlers. The "ranchos" created from these grants were owned by families that would play important roles in the valley's history.

In its 25-year possession of California, the Mexican government did little to strengthen its hold on the territory. There was much confusion among the Californios about who was in power. This created an atmosphere of political turmoil in the Santa Clara Valley and surrounding area. Foreigners came and explored California, including in 1827 an American named Jedediah Smith, who provided the U.S. government with

JOHN CHARLES FRÉMONT—THE VALLEY'S FIRST ENGINEER

One of the most prominent engineers ever to leave his mark on the valley first set foot here a century prior to the dawn of the Age of Silicon and never had a single thing to do with computers. John Charles Frémont, one of the Old West's most colorful and influential personalities, first saw the valley in early 1846, during the turbulent end of Mexico's rule of California. The brilliant and egotistical adventurer found his way here as the leader of the United States Army Corps of Topographical Engineers, a squad of explorers surveying America's uncharted frontier.

John C. Fremont

NEVADA HISTORICAL SOCIETY, RENO

Born in 1813 in Savannah, Georgia, the illegitimate child of a Virginia socialite and a poor French refugee, Frémont grew up to become an ambitious man with a knack for social climbing. His wife Jessie was the daughter of Senator Thomas Hart Benton, the expansionist Democratic leader of the Senate for more than 30 years, and Frémont was quite helpful in advancing his father-in-law's "Manifest Destiny" ideas. When Frémont returned from his various survey expeditions, Jessie helped him write best-selling books that promoted the settlement of the West. So popular were these guides that Frémont became known as "The Great Pathfinder"—although in reality he merely followed trails that others had blazed or discovered.

Frémont had a huge impact on the Bay Area's history. It was he who gave the entrance to San Francisco Bay the poetic name of "the Golden Gate," now also the name of the famous bridge spanning the gap. While he and his troops were encamped for the winter at Rancho Laguna Seca, near what is now San Jose's village of Coyote, Frémont formulated plans for helping America seize the bountiful Alta California territory from Mexico. He visited the nearby New Almaden Quicksilver Mines and reported to the federal government about this tremendous mineral treasure house. And it was Frémont who, in an act of defiance of Mexico's rule, first raised the American flag in California. That incident took place at Hawks Peak, in the Gabilan Mountains, near San Juan Bautista, about 40 miles south of San Jose. The summit is now called Fremont Peak, and a marker and flagpole at the state park mark the historic spot.

Frémont also helped initiate the Bear Flag Revolt by organizing a volunteer battalion that helped in the American conquest of California. After statehood, he served as one of California's first two U.S. senators and in 1856 ran unsuccessfully as the Republican Party's first presidential candidate (he lost to James Buchanan). During the Civil War, he served as a general for the Union Army in Missouri, but because in August 1861 he emancipated slaves of that state without federal approval, President Lincoln stripped him of the command. His later years were spent in poverty, living off money from his wife's writings. He died in 1890 in New York while working on a magazine article. But the famous name of the Great Pathfinder lives on throughout the Silicon Valley (for one example, the city of Fremont, just north of Milpitas, is named in his honor) and the American West.

an extensive report on the riches of Mexico's western territory. By the 1840s, the famous explorer Captain John C. Frémont and his men began mapping California—a pretense they used to spy on the region. The Mexican government feared the aspirations of Americans and their doctrine of Manifest Destiny, a belief that God intended the United States to, among other things, extend to the Pacific Ocean. Mexico strengthened its military presence in California, causing more political tension. Seeking to expand west, the U.S. government finally declared war on Mexico in 1846. In that year, California's population included about 800 U.S. citizens. On January 2, 1847, a clash occurred between the Californios and the U.S. Navy and Marines in rain-muddied fields two miles from the Santa Clara Mission. The Battle of Santa Clara (really more of a skirmish) was the only military campaign fought in Northern California during the Mexican-American War.

Gold Changes the Valley

On January 24, 1848, in the town of Coloma (near what is today Sacramento), gold was discovered on the grounds of a sawmill owned by John Sutter, a German rancher claiming to be Swiss who had fled to California to escape debts in his homeland.

On February 2 of that same year, the hostilities with Mexico came to an end with the signing of the Treaty of Guadalupe Hidalgo, which granted the United States possession of Texas, New Mexico, and California.

The discovery of gold and the reduction of tensions with Mexico sparked a rush of new immigrants to the territory. The Santa Clara Valley reaped vast financial rewards from the Gold Rush, but not from the grueling work of mining the precious element—a number of citizens gained great wealth by selling food and supplies to the miners.

The element mercury, or quicksilver, also reaped windfalls for the Santa Clara Valley during this time. In 1845, a Mexican cavalry officer named Andres Castillero discovered that the red rock found in the valley's western foothills was actually cinnabar, an ore containing mercury and

sulphur. The New Almaden Quicksilver Mines were quickly established, named after Almaden, a rich mine in Spain that had been worked since ancient Roman times. By 1848, between 100 and 150 pounds of mercury were extracted each day from ore taken from the mines. Because this valuable element was used in the amalgamation process of mining gold and silver, New Almaden played a crucial role in stimulating the California Gold Rush of 1849.

In 1850, California entered the union as the 31st state, and San Jose became the state's first capital. The new state was run by officials known as "the Legislature of a Thousand Drinks," for their habit of consuming alcoholic beverages after work. At the end of that first year, the rainy season hit the valley, and legislators decided to seek a drier climate in which to create laws.

But thousands of the "forty-niners" found the climate and lifestyle much to their liking—and ideal for farming and ranching. Many of them had spent their winters in the temperate Santa Clara Valley, when the Sierras were covered with snow, and after they grew tired of the gold-fields, they made their homes here. The valley's population began to grow with new settlers from throughout the world. They set up businesses in San Jose and surrounding villages. Many of them also bought land from the Mexican ranchos and began to establish what in the coming decades would become the orchards and vineyards that would make the region a bountiful agricultural paradise.

Agricultural Boom

In the 1850s, wheat became the region's principle crop. Year after year, the rich soil produced bountiful crops, ground at local flour mills. But gold miners were paying exorbitant amounts for fresh plums, pears, apples, and cherries. Two French brothers, Louis and Pierre Pellier, recognized the economic potential of growing fruit in the valley. In 1853, they set up the Pioneer Horticultural Society to promote this fledgling industry.

In 1855, San Jose was the site of California's first State Agricultural Fair, and the valley's orchards won many of the blue ribbons. In 1856, Pierre traveled back to France and returned with

MONKEYS PICKING FRUIT: THINKING TOO DIFFERENT?

Innovation has long been a tradition in Silicon Valley, resulting in some brilliant ideas that have virtually revolutionized the world. Other brilliant ideas have, alas, only *seemed* brilliant—and have ended in disaster. An unverifiable but charming rural legend from the area's turn-of-the-19th-century agricultural days holds that a Bascom Avenue prune farmer named Martin B. Seely lamented the rising cost of hiring farm hands to pick the d'Agen plums from the trees in his orchard. This was at a time before practical mechanized picking machines. Seely had read about how monkeys in tropical regions had been trained to harvest coconuts and other fruit, and he reasoned that primates might be just as useful for picking the plums that he dried into prunes.

From Panama, Seely imported 500 monkeys. He split them into groups of 50, placing a human foreman in charge of each group. The monkeys scampered into the trees and did indeed nimbly pick the juicy purple fruit. But it turns out that they were hungry, and they ate the entirety of Seely's harvest as they went through the orchard.

fine specimens of cherry, pear, and plum trees. But the true agricultural treasure he brought the region's farmers was cuttings of the petit prune d'Agen. The Pellier brothers certainly didn't realize it at the time, but by grafting those first cuttings to a tree in their nursery off San Jose's San Pedro Square, they were cultivating the prune industry that would come to dominate the valley.

By 1868, so fruitful had the valley become that environmentalist John Muir wrote: "It was bloom time of the year . . . The landscapes of the Santa Clara Valley were fairly drenched with sunshine, all the air was quivering with the songs of the meadowlarks, and the hills were so covered with flowers that they seemed to be painted."

Paralleling today's Silicon Valley, during the 1800s the people of the region welcomed modern tools to help them work more efficiently. New technology during this era played an important role in making Santa Clara Valley an agricultural powerhouse. On January 16, 1864, the region's first railroad line was completed when the San Francisco & San Jose Railroad Company laid its last rail. This provided valley farmers with the means to bring their wheat and fruit crops far more quickly to the ships in the San Francisco Bay. "Networking" isn't really a new concept in the valley. From the 1860s to the turn of the century, the network wasn't fiber-optic lines between computers but rather railroad lines between agricultural villages. Many of modern Silicon Valley's cities originated as railroad stops for an iron network crisscrossing the region. In 1869, the transcontinental railroad was completed, a feat just as important to American commerce as the Internet has become today. A branchline from San Jose to Sacramento connected Santa Clara Valley directly to the burgeoning markets of newly arriving European immigrants on the East Coast.

Innovation played just as important a role in the area's culture in the 1800s as it does today. While the railroads blessed the valley with lucrative markets, local minds came up with new ways to process and pack fruit. By the 1870s, fruit had far surpassed wheat as an economic commodity. During this time, a local farmer named John Quincy Adams Ballou experimented with methods of drying fruits such as apricots and prunes. A new industry was born. Local farmer John Z. Anderson figured out a way to refrigerate railcars with ice, thus providing the East with fresh California fruit. Local innovators also developed canning techniques. With new processing and packaging machinery, the mass production of canned goods provided a way to enjoy fruit throughout the year.

Wine had been produced by the Santa Clara Valley missionaries, who had used it for holy sacrament. But it had never been developed as a commercial product in the region. That changed when a Frenchman named Pierre Mirassou saw that the valley's Mediterranean cli-

THE VALLEY ORIGINS OF ORCHARD SUPPLY HARDWARE

Farming has always been a high-risk enterprise. In addition to the whims of the weather, farmers also have to deal with the variable market forces which can jeopardize their livelihood.

The farmers of the Santa Clara Valley quickly realized the need to band together to combat the unpredictability of economic factors. For example, in 1872, the San Jose–San Francisco Railroad raised its freight rates dramatically, cutting substantially into the local farmers' profits. So they formed the San Jose Farmers Club and Protection Association and hired a steamer to transport their produce from Alviso to the auctions in San Francisco. The price of shipping a small container of fruit dropped from $1 to $.60, a major savings for the farmer.

Two years later, the Farmers Union Corporation was founded by valley growers to supply equip-ment and seeds at discounted bulk rates. During the next several decades, valley farmers united in other associations to give them more power in negotiating with railroads for freight prices as well as obtaining better rates for packing and storage costs.

In 1931, during the bleak years of the Great Depression, Santa Clara County's orchardists formed another cooperative venture to buy equipment cheaply. Called Orchard Supply Hardware, the first store was located on 10th St. in San Jose. In 1946, the successful cooperative moved to 720 W. San Carlos St. by the railroad tracks. This store is still open.

In 1980, the cooperative's members sold the venture to W. R. Grace Company. Today, Orchard Supply Hardware is a nationally recognized chain with more than 75 stores serving customers with home repair and do-it-yourself products.

mate could produce wine as high in quality as that in his native homeland. His winery (which still operates) helped spark the growth of commercial vineyards in the region. Labels such as Paul Masson and Almaden Vineyards became highly respected wines surpassing many French vineyards. With the cornucopia of agricultural goods spilling forth, it was little wonder the world soon began referring to the area as "the Valley of Heart's Delight."

Victorian Era

The new railroad spanning the continent carried thousands of new settlers to California seeking to escape the hardships caused by the Civil War. The valley's population continued to expand and diversify. Among the new residents were Chinese laborers who had helped build the Central Pacific Railroad from Sacramento over the Sierras, linking with the Union Pacific in Utah. Although they were supposed to return to their Asian homeland, many of the Chinese brought their families across the Pacific Ocean and settled in the Santa Clara Valley. They toiled cheaply, providing a hard-working farm labor force. By 1870, more than one-third of San Jose's population was Chinese. They even had their own independent Chinatown section on the east side of downtown San Jose's Plaza. Much of the white population resented this Asian race's growth in the area, and on the night of May 4, 1887, a fire of unknown origin broke out among the wooden shanties, burning Chinatown to the ground. The ashes still smoking, its residents were relocated to another part of San Jose.

With its newfound wealth, the valley entered a modern world. Small agricultural railroad stops grew into villages and towns. Flower gardens and towering palm trees surrounded many fine Victorian homes and public buildings. Everyone talked about the extraordinary mansion built by an eccentric widow named Sarah Winchester. She ordered her workmen never to stop building. Locals gossiped that the petite, frail woman feared the ghosts of people killed by her father-in-law's invention, the Winchester repeating rifle.

San Jose quickly became the Santa Clara Valley's dominant city, a role it keeps to this

THE STANFORDS

In a quiet grove on the northeastern corner of Stanford University there stands a Grecian-style marble mausoleum with two stolid cherubim keeping watch at the entrance. This is the final resting place of Leland Stanford, his wife Jane, and their only child, Leland Jr. No other family had a bigger impact on making Silicon Valley what it is today.

One of six sons of a tavern owner, Leland Stanford was born in 1824 in Watervliet, New York, near Albany. He and his brothers cut wood to sell to the Mohawk and Hudson Railroad, but Leland also went off and studied law at a firm in Albany and was admitted to the bar. In 1849, his brothers went to California, while Leland married Jane Eliza Lathrop, the beautiful daughter of an Albany merchant. Leland and Jane moved to Wisconsin, where Leland practiced law until his office burned down in 1852. That year, he joined his brothers in California and invested in a gold mine. Three years later, he went back to Albany for his wife. They returned to California and made their home in Sacramento, where Leland started a wholesale grocery business. With his business savvy, the business increased his wealth substantially. In 1860,

he stumped for Abe Lincoln, and later visited the president in Washington.

In 1861, Leland ran for the governorship of California as a Republican Party candidate and won (during the Civil War, he worked hard to keep California in the Union). In June of that year, he also became president of the Central Pacific Railroad, the western link of a dream to connect the eastern seaboard and California with a railroad spanning the continent. When completed, that railroad enabled the rapid western expansion of the United States.

Stanford was one of the Big Four, a group of Sacramento businessmen who aggressively pushed the risky western link of the transcontinental railroad. The others were Charles Crocker, Mark Hopkins, and Collis Huntington. On May 10, 1869, at Promontory Junction in the Utah Territory, Stanford swung a silver mallet to drive the famous last spike into a hole drilled into a laurel tie. He missed, but the telegraph operator tapped out the single word "Done," setting off celebrations when the message reached San Francisco and the East Coast. That last laurel tie was de-

day. By 1879, three years after its invention, the telephone came into service in the area. Its installers little realized how sophisticated communications technology would become in the region in the next century. By 1888, San Jose had the first electric streetcar west of the Mississippi, a Victorian version of the Light Rail. Citizens affectionately called the railcars "galloping bathtubs." On July 2, 1892, a large fire destroyed much of the downtown's business district, but this loss cleared the way for modern buildings.

Turn of the 20th Century

In 1900 the valley was a peaceful and prosperous place. Its inhabitants could hardly predict the turmoil the new century would bring. President McKinley visited San Jose in 1901 and gave a rousing speech in St. James Park. (Three months

later, he would be shot by an anarchist at the Buffalo Pan-American Exposition.) In 1903, Sid Grauman opened his Unique Theater in San Jose, presenting "moving pictures" and vaudeville acts to local citizens. He discovered one comic talent working as a singing waiter in San Jose, a hefty fellow who went down in Hollywood lore as Fatty Arbuckle. On April 18, 1906, the San Andreas Fault slipped, causing a violent earthquake that rocked 450 miles of California's coastland. San Francisco suffered the most damage, particularly from a devastating fire, but the Santa Clara Valley also was severely hit. Agnews State Hospital collapsed, killing more than 100 patients and staff. The Unique Theater also was destroyed, prompting the owner to move to Los Angeles and build his famous Grauman's Chinese Theater. But most locals stayed and persevered in the job of rebuilding the valley.

stroyed in the great fire that followed the San Francisco earthquake of 1906. The 18-ounce golden spike, valued in 1869 at $350 and removed from the track as soon as the ceremony was complete, is in the possession today of Stanford University.

Making San Francisco their new home, the Stanfords built a magnificent Victorian mansion on Nob Hill (it, too, burned in the 1906 fire). Seeking a country retreat in the scenic Peninsula area—as many California millionaires did—in 1876 they purchased 650 acres of El Rancho San Francisquito land. This was in the foothills west of the double-trunk redwood where the explorer Portolá had first camped in the valley. The Stanfords named the ranch Palo Alto Farm in honor of that landmark tree and began raising race horses there. Their horses wound up setting 19 world records.

Leland Jr. died tragically of typhoid fever in 1884. His grieving parents decided to endow $20 million to build a world-class university in his name. They would establish it on Palo Alto Farm, which had now grown into an 8,000-acre property. Leland Stanford, Jr., University opened on October 1, 1891.

On June 21, 1893, Leland himself died. The country was in a financial crisis, the estate was troubled with legal problems, and the future of Stanford University was uncertain. Strong, independent Jane Stanford struggled to keep the university open. A close friend of Susan B. Anthony and Elizabeth Cady Stanton, Jane Stanford was a pioneer of women's rights who (unusually for the Victorian period) admitted women to the university. She succeeded in keeping Stanford University from closing, and during its first 100 years, it blossomed into an internationally renowned institution.

At the age of 76, shortly before midnight on February 28, 1905, Jane Stanford died after a lingering pain. Her death was controversial—the first doctor said she had been poisoned with strychnine. A final analysis found that the probable cause of death was chronic myocarditis, a partial blockage of the vessels carrying blood to the heart. Every year, on the anniversary of its October 1 founding, the university celebrates Founder's Day with a dignified memorial at the Stanfords' mausoleum.

In 1908, drivers in the Great Race to Paris passed through San Jose, helping to stimulate the horseless-carriage craze. The dirt roads of that time eventually became some of the highways and interstates of modern Silicon Valley. In 1917, the valley got its first traffic signal, a glimpse of the massive traffic infrastructure to come.

The United States entered the Great War, "the war to end all wars," and many of the valley's men were soon fighting and dying in the trenches of France and Germany. The Great Flu Epidemic of 1918–19 took the lives of hundreds of residents. And although the 1920s were a relatively calm and prosperous time for Santa Clara Valley, when the Great Depression hit, the tranquillity soon ended. Workers struck against orchard growers for better wages. In turn, the orchard growers struck against the canneries for better prices on their crops. FDR's New Deal had its impact on the area, bringing new developments such as construction of a massive airship hanger on Moffett Field. In 1938, General Motors bought the valley's extensive streetcar lines and tore them out to force people to use automobile transportation. The salvaged iron was sold to Imperial Japan, perhaps much of it used to build weapons, fighter planes, and military ships.

The storm clouds of approaching global war grew darker. Little did the people of the valley know that their simple and peaceful lives would dramatically change when on December 7, 1941, the American fleet in Pearl Harbor was devastated in a surprise Japanese attack. World War II would play a major role in transforming Santa Clara Valley from a region of agricultural abundance to one of high-tech wonders. The Valley of Heart's Delight had begun its metamorphosis into Silicon Valley.

UNDERESTIMATING TECHNOLOGY: EVEN THE EXPERTS AREN'T IMMUNE

Benjamin Franklin is said to have once been discussing his discovery of the principle of electricity with a friend when the friend asked, "But, sir, what is its use?" Franklin replied, "What's the use of a baby?" In the same spirit, here are a few choice observations by people who, you'd think, would have known better.

"I think there is a world market for maybe five computers."—Thomas Watson, founder and chairman of IBM

"Computers in the future may weigh no more than 1.5 tons."—*Popular Mechanics,* boldly going out on a limb in a 1949 article predicting the progress of science

"I have traveled the length and breadth of this country and talked with the best people, and I can assure you that data processing is a fad that won't last out the year."—a farsighted Prentice Hall business book editor, 1957

"But what is it good for?"—an engineer at IBM's Advanced Computing Systems Division after examining a microchip, 1968

"There is no reason anyone would want a computer in their home."—Ken Olson, founder, president, and chairman of Digital Equipment Corporation, 1977

BRAVE NEW WORLD: INVENTING SILICON VALLEY

In 1884, a 15-year-old boy died of typhoid fever while vacationing with his parents in Italy. This tragedy triggered a series of events that would come to invent Silicon Valley. The boy was the son of railroad baron Leland Stanford. In his memory, Stanford and his wife endowed $20 million to establish a university on the 8,000-acre site of their horse farm on the Santa Cruz Mountains foothills. Stanford University opened on October 1, 1891, and quickly became a cauldron of knowledge and innovation on which much of today's high-tech world is based.

The university stressed a practicality in learning, encouraging its students to apply their knowledge to improve society. A town grew on the east side of the university grounds, and locals named it Palo Alto after the historic tree that explorer Portolá camped under in 1769. Palo Alto and Stanford University developed a symbiotic relationship, and many of the graduates made their homes in the town and established businesses there. From the start, Stanford students excelled in science and technology. Before the turn of the century, they had developed and were testing a high-potential oil switch that made it possible for copper-wire lines to carry 40,000 volts of electricity over long distances. This paved the way for our modern electric world. But it was Stanford's research in the new field of radio that planted the seeds of Silicon Valley.

Wireless World

In 1909, Stanford president David Starr Jordan paid engineering graduate Cyril Elwell $500 to develop wireless technology. This early stab at venture capitalism set in motion work on improved radio communications. In a small house at 1451 Cowper St. in Palo Alto, Elwell set up a workshop, and before too long, two 75-foot antennas in the garden transmitted "The Blue Danube Waltz" to receiving stations as far away as Mountain View. That same year, Stanford radio researcher Dr. Charles Herrold broadcast the world's first commercial radio transmissions from the top of San Jose's seven-story Garden City Bank building. By 1911, Elwell started the Federal Telegraph Company in Palo Alto, and Lee de Forest, inventor of the audion (a three-element vacuum tube), was appointed the firm's research director. De Forest became known as the founder of modern electronics due to his brilliant contributions to the field. The Santa Clara Valley had become a hotbed of electronic research and development.

Among the Federal Telegraph employees was Frederick Terman, who had recently earned degrees in chemistry and electrical engineering at Stanford. Future generations would call him "the father of Silicon Valley." Terman's experience at Federal made him aware of the important link between academic research and the business world. In 1927, he took a part-time position at Stanford as an electrical engineering professor. He also started a new radio engineering laboratory at the university, where he became the world's leading authority on electronics. As a professor in the 1930s, he encouraged his students to stay in the area and start up technology-based businesses. Among them were two friends, William Hewlett and David Packard, who started up a small garage-based company in Palo Alto manufacturing audio-oscillators. Hewlett-Packard Company's big break came in 1939 when Walt Disney helped boost the young firm by buying eight sets for sound production in making the animated film *Fantasia*. Another two pupils, Russell and Sigurd Varian, invented a new electron tube called a klystron, which helped in developing radar and microwave technology. (In 1948, the brothers formed a company called Varian Associates, which became an important supplier of semiconductor manufacturing equipment.) By the end of the 1930s, the Palo Alto area had emerged as the West Coast home for electronics innovations.

With the advent of World War II, science began to play a crucial role in building weapons and defense systems. For the war effort, the U.S. government needed sophisticated electronics such as vacuum tubes, two-way radios, radar systems, and microwave telephones. The Stanford-spawned companies in the Bay Area supplied much of this equipment. Terman worked for the Defense Department developing radio technology. By the war's end, he realized the new role of the government's involvement in high-tech research and development. He saw the expansion of science and technology in the postwar world and knew universities such as Stanford would play crucial roles in modern innovations. In 1946, he helped found the Stanford Research Institute. The not-for-profit laboratory in Menlo Park con-

SILICON VS. SILICONE

In the world's high-tech capital, you do not want to confuse the element sili*con* with the compound sili*cone*.

The term "Silicon Valley" was first coined by editor Don Hoeffler in a series of articles he wrote in 1971 for the trade journal *Electronic News*. It was a clever, shorthand way of conveying the (accurate) impression that this valley was home to the world's highest concentration of semiconductor manufacturers—the primary ingredient in whose semiconductors (the formal name of computer chips) is a crystalline form of the element silicon.

Silicon (Si in the periodic table, atomic number 14) is a brittle, tetravalent, nonmetallic element. After oxygen, it is the most abundant element in the earth's crust—commonly found in sand, gravel, and quartz. It was first isolated in 1823 by Jöns Berzelius, a Swedish chemist. (Surprisingly, it was named *before* actually being discovered when, in 1817, Scottish chemist Thomas Thompson theorized its chemical properties on the periodic table by analogy with boron and carbon.) In the manufacturing process, silicon is formed into round, thinly sliced wafers. These wafers are then chemically etched to create microscopically small integrated circuits containing more than a million components. Under a powerful microscope, this etching resembles a map of a city, with streets and freeways for electrons to travel through, routed by on-off switches (tiny transistors).

Sili*cone*, on the other hand, is a chemical compound made by substituting silicon for carbon in compounds of oils, greases, resins, synthetic rubber, and other substances. Silicone is used for industrial purposes, such as plumbing and construction, in addition to its much more famous role in plastic surgery.

ducted research under business and industrial sponsorship. Research here laid the groundwork for such modern inventions as the mouse, ink-jet printing, and the modem.

© MARTIN CHEEK

The Knight-Ridder Building stands where the Garden City Bank Building was once located and where Stanford radio researcher Dr. Charles Herold in 1909 broadcast the world's first commercial radio transmissions.

The Santa Clara Valley underwent dramatic social changes after the war as well. Many veterans who had passed through the area to fight in the Pacific returned to make their homes in the friendly climate. The population of farm towns such as Milpitas, Sunnyvale, and Campbell grew significantly, foreshadowing the eventual loss of the valley's agricultural heritage. And at the University of Pennsylvania, a monstrous machine was being built that would have major consequences for the quiet valley's future. The Electronic Numerical Integrator and Computer (ENIAC) held 18,000 vacuum tubes and calculated in binary code. It was the world's first electronic computer, and its creation symbolized the beginning of the end of Santa Clara County's farm-based economy.

In 1950, New York–based business giant IBM saw Santa Clara Valley as a source of exciting electronic developments. It sent one of its most brilliant scientists, Reynold Johnson, inventor of the Scantron testing machine, to create a research lab in San Jose. The lab at 99 Notre Dame Ave. conducted research on a technology called "source recording," which led to the magnetic disk drives crucial to storing data in today's computers. In 1953, IBM built a $32 million plant in south San Jose to make disk drives and other components. This marked a turning point in establishing Santa Clara Valley as the world's most important high-tech center. Just as the Gold Rush had drawn settlers to California, the dawning Information Age drew businesses and workers to the intellectual gold mine of the Santa Clara Valley. Seeking to tap into that creativity, so many major industries were establishing bases here that in 1954 Frederick Terman pushed for the concept of the Stanford Industrial Park. This high-tech park on university property led to further expansion in the area by companies such as GTE, General Electric, Lockheed, and Hewlett-Packard. It served as the prototype for industrial parks that would soon be scattered across the valley.

One company at Stanford Industrial Park that had a profound effect on inventing Silicon Valley was Shockley Semiconductor Laboratory. It was started by the eccentric scientist William Shockley, who back in 1947 had participated in inventing a device called the transfer resistor, or transistor. This major breakthrough replaced bulky vacuum tubes and paved the way for practical computers. By 1960, more than 40 firms were established at Stanford Industrial Park.

Santa Clara County's economy was now clearly becoming dependent on high-tech industries. Family farms and orchards still existed in the valley, but they were quickly vanishing, replaced by industrial parks, suburbs, and shopping malls. Quiet country roads built for horse-drawn carriages soon were transformed into freeways built for rush-hour traffic. The valley's culture changed, the tempo of life shifting into a higher gear. Between 1958 and 1963, nearly 80 percent of all new manufacturing jobs in the valley were in the electronics fields.

During this time of major changes, political power struggles heated up among the valley's towns and cities. San Jose leaders decided the city needed to become the next Los Angeles, little realizing the impact of transforming the city into a sprawling urban jungle. They spent millions of public dollars incorporating land to build their dream metropolis, swallowing up small communities such as Alviso and stretching the city's borders far south into unincorporated agricultural land. Today's drivers along U.S. 101 near Cochrane Rd. can see the San Jose city limit sign in a desolate area of the county. Towns such as Campbell, Cupertino, Santa Clara, Milpitas, and Los Altos quickly incorporated before San Jose could absorb them as suburbs.

The valley's growing electronics industry also experienced power struggles. Lacking good management skills (to put it diplomatically), William Shockley drove eight of his key researchers to quit Shockley Semiconductor in 1957 and form their own electronics firm. Led by Robert Noyce, the "Traitorous Eight" founded Fairchild Semiconductor, a division of an East Coast–based camera manufacturer. The firm developed the first commercially practical integrated circuit (a very complex series of transistors on a silicon chip). But by 1968, Fairchild was struggling against two hard-hitting competitors: Texas Instruments and Motorola. With morale low, company stars Robert Noyce, Andy Grove, and Gordon Moore quit to start up a new electronics company. Reflecting its intellectual roots, they named it Intel. In 1971, they came out with the microprocessor, essentially a computer on a chip, calculating in binary code through extremely fast on-off switches. They had managed to pack the computing power of the room-sized ENIAC into a device that can be held on a fingertip.

In 1970, copier manufacturer Xerox Corporation opened a facility near Stanford called the Palo Alto Research Center (PARC). From this lab came brilliant innovations in computing, such as the laser printer, easy word-processing programs, portable computers, and the Post-Script language used by printing devices. With these developments, Xerox could easily have grown into the world's foremost computer company. But short-sighted executives did little to capitalize on the inventions. Many frustrated PARC researchers left, taking their ideas and forming their own companies. In 1971, Don Hoeffler, editor of trade journal *Electronics News*, realized how important electronics had become to the Santa Clara Valley. In an article, he coined the term "Silicon Valley" after the silicon wafers used in producing computer chips. The nickname quickly caught on as a way to identify the electronics mecca.

Computers took an important leap into the consumer electronics market in 1972, when Nolan Bushnell founded a company in Sunnyvale called Atari. Its hit game Pong (an electronic version of ping-pong) proved addicting to players, making Bushnell a multimillionaire. More important, it sowed the seeds for public acceptance of computers in daily life. In the mid-1970s, the only "hobby" computer was the Altair 8800. A kit that sold for $500, it contained no software, and about the only thing it did was light up rows of lights. In March 1975, a hobby club was formed that met in an auditorium at Menlo Park's Stanford Linear Accelerator. Called the Homebrew Computer Club, among its founding members was a bearded engineer named Steve Wozniak, who at one meeting showed off a machine he called a personal computer. The next year, his friend Steve Jobs joined "the Woz," starting a company based out of Jobs's parents' Cupertino garage. Marketing genius Jobs wanted to ensure the public wouldn't feel threatened by the device, so he gave it the nontechnical moniker Apple Computer. The launch of Apple triggered a revolution in personal computer development, changing not only the city of Cupertino but the entire valley as well. The race was on to bring computers to ordinary people.

Boom Time

Following the success of Apple, Hewlett-Packard introduced a personal computer in 1980, but the flash point really came in 1981, when megafirm IBM began selling its IBM PC. With IBM's entrance into the market, the personal computer gained credibility. No longer was it just a hobby for nerds—these machines were designed for the masses. The PC revolution began a new era of prosperity for Silicon Valley. Start-ups by university graduates grew quickly, bringing to the area millions of dollars in revenue and a flood of new residents. In 1982, Scott McNealy helped found Sun Microsystems, which sold networked workstations. He based the company on what he had learned at Stanford building the Stanford University Network (SUNet). That same year, John Warnock and Charles Geschke left Xerox PARC to found a company targeted at the booming desktop publishing business. Their Adobe Systems software used the PostScript language to transfer font data from PCs to printers. In 1984, husband and wife Leonard Bosack and Sandra Lerner started Cisco Systems to market routers. Bosack had invented the internetworking device at Stanford so that he could send romantic messages across departmental networks to then-girlfriend Lerner. Also that year, Apple came out with a computer that the public absolutely fell in love with because its graphical user interface and other innovative features made it easy to use. The Macintosh demonstrated that computers could be tools that didn't require a Ph.D. to operate.

Redevelopment

The land grab by San Jose in the 1950s and 1960s came back to haunt the city. Local government leaders had spent so much time, energy, and money expanding San Jose's boundaries that the quality of life had fallen significantly. By the early 1970s, so many department stores and businesses had left downtown San Jose for suburban malls such as Santa Clara's Valley Fair that the city center became an ugly wasteland known for prostitution and drug dealing. In the early 1980s, Mayor Thomas McEnery realized that the city's downtown was its destiny. He pushed a controversial proposal to use the city's newfound wealth from the booming high-tech industry to give San Jose a billion-dollar facelift. The dramatic changes included the construction of the Children's Discovery Museum, the Fairmont Hotel, and the Arena stadium. By the end of the 1980s, the redevelopment was luring tourists, business travelers, and sports teams (including the San Jose Sharks ice hockey team) downtown. Other Silicon Valley communities such as Mountain View and Cupertino followed suit, creating major

redevelopment projects to improve their civic image. A $500 million Light Rail system was also built during this time, bringing back to the valley the popular transit line stretching from Almaden Valley to Santa Clara.

The rapid population growth of Silicon Valley in the 1980s catapulted San Jose to its new status as the nation's 11th most populous city. With more than 891,600 residents in 1989, it surpassed San Francisco in population. By the end of the decade, San Jose grandly declared itself "the Capital of Silicon Valley." But for all its prosperity, a temporary setback occurred on October 17, 1989, literally sending a shockwave sweeping through Silicon Valley. The Loma Prieta Fault slipped, causing a 6.9 earthquake. The Loma Prieta earthquake destroyed many homes, particularly in and around Los Gatos. As had happened after the 1906 earthquake, the rebuilding started immediately, and soon impressive new structures rose to replace those that had fallen.

Growing Prestige

The Silicon Valley of the 1990s had recast itself as a metropolis for the future. Washington politicians Bill Clinton and Al Gore began wooing the valley's industry executives, realizing the money base and political influence their companies represented. Computers were transforming the world's commerce, education, politics, and social structure, and much of that change came from the hard work and innovative ideas of people in high-tech companies scattered throughout the valley. The early 1990s saw a slump as many companies downsized, a euphemism for laying off large chunks of the workforce. But many of these workers started their own businesses, helping to fuel more growth in the industry. By 1993, the world was being introduced to the Internet, a revolution as important as Gutenberg's printing press. With the touch of a button, anyone with a PC and a phone line could tap into a vast communications network containing everything from up-to-the-minute news broadcasts to information on virtually every topic imaginable. Multitudes of people began communicating by email, buying products online, and starting their own websites. The world was

SILICON VALLEY AND THE MOVIES

With the booming increase in the use of computers in film production, the bond between Hollywood and Silicon Valley is getting stronger by the day, and the valley is rapidly gaining a reputation as "Hollywood North." Movies such as James Cameron's *Titanic* and Steven Spielberg's *Jurassic Park* would not be the same without the rendering software and processing power created by companies such as Silicon Graphics in Mountain View. Industry experts estimate that by 2010, highly advanced digital cameras will render obsolete the use of actual film in filmmaking. And movie theaters will use digital media developed in Silicon Valley to show movies to audiences.

But Silicon Valley's involvement in the movie industry is nothing new. The germinal core technology that made possible the entire process of creating moving images was born in 1877 at Leland Stanford's Palo Alto Farm when photographer Eadweard Muybridge created his famous series of 24 sequenced photos of a trotting horse.

East of Fremont, Niles Canyon beat Hollywood as America's movie capital in the early years of the 20th century. Studios there churned out more than 500 movies between 1911 and 1916, attracting even the luminary likes of Charlie Chaplin, as well as the cast and crew of countless westerns featuring Bronco Billy Anderson. Many early movie stars spent their off-camera hours enjoying San Jose attractions.

More recently, Hollywood has used San Jose's theaters as venues for audience-testing some of its biggest blockbusters, including *E.T.* and *Stars Wars,* prior to general release.

Directors have used many of Silicon Valley's locations in their films. Part of the 1971 cult-classic black comedy *Harold and Maude* was shot at the St. Thomas Aquinas Church at 745 Waverly St. in Palo Alto. A rally scene in Robert Redford's 1972 political satire *The Candidate* was filmed at San Jose's Eastridge Mall. Clint Eastwood and Charlie Sheen spent a lot of time in San Jose filming their 1990 dud action movie *The Rookie.* That same film also used the closed-during-construction portion of Highway 87 south of I-280 for car chase scenes,

and Terminal A at San Jose International Airport was the setting for Eastwood's pursuit of the bad guy up the down escalator. Parts of James Cameron's 1991 *Terminator II* were filmed around Silicon Valley—most spectacularly at a derelict office building in Fremont, which received a thorough facelift and immaculate landscaping before being destroyed in a huge, explosive shootout.

Scenes for Paramount Pictures' 1994 *Beverly Hills Cop III* were shot at Great America, which happens to be owned by Paramount Pictures. The theme park was also a backdrop, that same year, for Macaulay Culkin's *Getting Even with Dad* (*not* a Paramount picture), which also filmed scenes at Raging Waters. In 1997, John Travolta and Dustin Hoffman spent a lot of time in the St. James Park area in downtown San Jose filming *Mad City,* which used the Scottish Rite Temple building as the museum taken hostage by the security guard played by Travolta. And in 1998, the scene in Ron Howard's *EDtv* in which actor Matthew McConaughey drives a Zamboni machine was filmed during a Sharks ice hockey game at the San Jose Arena.

Several scenes of the short-lived TV series *Star Man* were filmed at the Lick Observatory on Mt. Hamilton. And movie director Robert Altman spent a lot of time in the Palo Alto area preparing a television series of his own. Tentatively called *Killer Apps,* based on Silicon Valley's sometimes ruthless business world, the series was canceled before production started.

In 2001, Silicon Valley was the subject of two critically praised documentaries. "Secrets of Silicon Valley" is a 60-minute film examining the dark side of the valley such as the high cost of housing and the expanding breach between the high-tech elite and temporary workers on computer company assembly lines. The film "Startup.com" documents one year (and the demise) of a fledgling Internet firm.

San Jose puts on a respectable local film festival every February and March called Cinequest, 408/995-5033, website: www.cinequest.com. Over 100 independent films, many by Bay Area filmmakers, are showcased at downtown theaters.

now hooked up, and Silicon Valley fed consumers' need for faster and better computer equipment.

Booming sales of computer products in the mid-1990s meant more prosperity than Silicon Valley had ever experienced. Just like the Gold Rush had done a century and a half earlier, the Silicon Rush raised the quality of life. Venture capitalists (many located along Menlo Park's Sand Hill Rd.) pumped funds into start-ups based on daring ideas. Technology stocks rose rapidly, creating paper millionaires and billionaires across the valley overnight. Real estate prices shot up outrageously as residents poured into the area, lured by its halcyon days. Million-dollar mansions mushroomed in the foothills. Construction workers couldn't build homes fast enough.

In 1998 and 1999, "Y2K" doomsayers promulgated widespread concern about the "millennium bug," the glitch in some computer systems and software using the computer-standard two-digit date that would cause them to misread the "00" abbreviation of the year 2000 as 1900. The unforeseeable results could have affected virtually any computer-dependent system, from banking, credit, and automated payment to air traffic control, global navigation, and satellite communication. But in the valley, people pretty much laughed off the threat. Of course, Y2Kers were just highly verbal alarmists. Life as we knew it did not cease to exist at the stroke of midnight, December 31, 1999. Satellites did not fall from the sky, nor did the world's financial systems suddenly rewind a century and recalculate interest at 1900 rates.

However, the years 2000 and 2001 did see an economic downturn for Silicon Valley as well as for the rest of the United States. Overinflated high-tech stocks fell drastically, and many people in the valley who had made millions from stock options now were faced with selling their homes due to their sudden losses.

Still, with the vigor of its past successes, Silicon Valley begins the third millennium with great optimism. Certainly, Stanford, Santa Clara University, and San Jose State University will continue training students who will invent the next

generation of technologies. And new start-ups will continue to spring up, marketing these high-tech developments and changing people's lives. Well into the 21st century, the area undoubtedly will continue to reign as the United States' leading center of international high-tech trade.

THE PEOPLE

Silicon Valley has a reputation of being a land of instant millionaires, a place inhabited by daring entrepreneurs who have reaped fortunes from the harvest of high-tech discoveries and inventions. Although most people think of the region only in terms of its technology and business success, Silicon Valley is much more than code, chips, and multimillion-dollar real estate. It's also a place of people.

The common stereotype of a Silicon Valley citizen is a computer or engineering geek with a pocket protector and taped-up glasses who inhabits a world of cubicles. Admittedly, such people do exist here. But a visit to Silicon Valley reveals a healthy diversity of cultures and lifestyles. Various people of Hispanic, Asian, Native American, Pacific, African, and European ancestry have imprinted the area with a kaleidoscope of ethnic color. The Spanish and Mexicans laid down the valley's cultural foundation during the mission and pre–Gold Rush era. California was granted statehood in 1848, and the valley's agricultural industry and towns and cities developed with the arrival of French, German, Irish, Chinese, Portuguese, Japanese, and other immigrants. In the 20th century's last quarter, as the region more or less abandoned its agricultural roots for high-tech, other Asian cultures—including Indians, Vietnamese, and Koreans—added to the valley's vibrant mix of cultures. And as newcomers arrive daily from all around the world to make their homes here, Silicon Valley's way of life continues to evolve in directions that can only be imagined at the start of the third millennium.

Not everything is perfect for people in this paradise, of course. The fast-paced lifestyle is highly stressful, driven by intense corporate competition. It's not uncommon for workers to put in

WILLIAM SHOCKLEY—BRILLIANT WEIRDO

If Leland Stanford might be considered the grandfather of Silicon Valley, William Shockley might be considered its slightly wacko uncle. Shockley won the Nobel Prize for co-inventing the transistor—the basis for computer chip technology, the cornerstone of the modern high-tech industry. He had a brilliant scientific mind—and the ego to go with it. He also had some habits and opinions which were a little . . . well, weird.

The son of a Stanford University professor, Shockley was born in 1910 and lived in Palo Alto from 1913 to 1922. It was 25 years later, on December 16, 1947, that Shockley—working with W. H. Brattain and John Bardeen at Bell Laboratories in New York—brought eight years of scientific research to a successful conclusion with the development of the technological wonder they named the transistor (short for "transfer resistor").

In 1956, the year he won the Nobel Prize, he returned to Palo Alto to start Shockley Semiconductor Laboratories, a company established to commercialize transistor technology. He formed a team of ambitious young scientists and engineers recently graduated from Stanford. However, he had never run a company before and had to ask David Packard how to hire a secretary and where to buy pencils. He treated his employees rudely, showing his distrust of them pretty clearly by forcing them to take lie detector tests. In September 1957, tired of his poor management and arrogant behavior, eight of his top engineers quit the company. Led by Robert Noyce, who had been a favorite of Shockley's, this cadre worked out of their garages and living rooms to form their own company. Eventually, they received financial backing from a company called Fairchild Camera and Instruments and formed Fairchild Semiconductors in Mountain View. Shockley never forgave the "Traitorous Eight."

Harry Farrell, a former *San Jose Mercury News* reporter, tells in his enjoyable memoir, *San Jose and Other Places,* of how Shockley would record all his telephone calls for posterity, the beeping of the recording machine so pronounced as to interrupt conversations. Farrell also describes Shockley's obsessive documentation of virtually every aspect of his existence in filing cabinets in his house on the Stanford University campus. "In them," writes Farrell, "Shockley's whole life was documented, indexed, crossfiled, annotated and decimalized."

The inventor of the transistor kept views which today would be considered politically incorrect. He espoused a theory that white people are inherently intellectually superior to blacks, and wrote lengthy treaties on his theory of "dysgenics," which he defined as "the retrogressive evolution through the excessive reproduction of the genetically disadvantaged." For the benefit of society, he suggested a voluntary sterilization plan whereby people who did not fit the ideal genetic profile would be paid not to breed. And Shockley had run the numbers: "At a rate of $1,000 for each point below 100 I.Q., $30,000 put in trust for a 70 I.Q. moron potentially capable of producing 20 children might return $250,000 to taxpayers in reduced costs of mental retardation care." At the other end of the spectrum, Shockley led by example by donating his sperm to a Southern California sperm bank whose mission was to inject sperm samples from Nobel laureates into super-intelligent women in hopes of producing perfect babies.

Obviously, his co-invention of the transistor and his fostering—albeit inadvertently—of the birth of Fairchild Semiconductors give Shockley, who died in 1989, claim to a significant impact on Silicon Valley. But his racial views made him a considerable embarrassment in the area.

success
depended
on others

© MARTIN CHEEK

kids playing in the fountain at the Tech Museum

HOW GREEN IS THE VALLEY?

Silicon Valley is a place driven by money. During the economic boom of the late 1990s, the region was in some ways the 20th century's answer to El Dorado. The number of stock-option millionaires at high-tech firms was growing every day and by 1999, at least 13 billionaires called the valley home. According to a market research survey commissioned by the *San Jose Mercury News,* in 1999, an estimated 65,000 households in Santa Clara County (about one in every nine in the region) was worth more than a million bucks—*not* counting the value of their homes.

But reality started to hit hard in 2000 and 2001 as the economic boom reached its pinnacle and started its downturn. The high-tech companies once flying so high saw their stock value suddenly take a nosedive. Dot-com firms—once the darling of Wall Street—started to drop into oblivion. Even such premier companies as Cisco Systems and 3COM announced massive layoffs. Engineers in their 20s and 30s who had become stock-option millionaires in the boom years suddenly found themselves needing to sell off their luxury mansions in a hurry.

As in the Gold Rush of 1849, *most* people do *not* strike it rich today in Silicon Valley (though many clearly do quite nicely, working for very handsome salaries in companies offering world-class benefits packages in order to lure the cream of the crop). Much of what you've heard about the ease with which people get rich in this valley is pure myth. That myth is kept alive by headline stories of fantastically successful public stock offerings, such as that of VA Linux Systems, Inc., a Sunnyvale-based firm whose value on December 9, 1999, soared from an initial $30 a share to $242.38 a share, a record-breaking rise of 708 percent. Cases like these, however, are exceptional, and even VA Linux eventually dropped below its initial IPO value.

While every high-tech company aspires to huge success in its start-up years, it won't necessarily achieve it. Competition is ferocious here. Many new firms fall by the wayside, never hitting anywhere near the big time. Stock options are a

12 or more hours a day at their jobs, and burnout is a widespread affliction. The exponential growth continues to increase traffic on the network of freeways crisscrossing the valley—another source of tension during commute hours. The computer industry's cycles of boom and bust create an atmosphere laced with uncertainty for employees. And the extensive construction of new suburbs, shopping centers, and industrial parks have paved over and put in jeopardy much of the rich soil and water resources that once made this region an American agricultural hub.

Even so, Silicon Valley's ethnic diversity and relative racial harmony has made it an area esteemed for an exceptionally high quality of life. It overflows with excellent restaurants run by world-renowned chefs, many of these eateries serving internationally award-winning wines produced by the valley's many vineyards such as J. Lohr and Mirassou, America's oldest wine-making family. The various ethnic groups also contribute to the valley's cultural scene with a multitude of annual festivals, such as Campbell's Scottish Highland Games, San Jose's Vietnamese Spring Festival, and Mountain View's Affribean Parade.

popular incentive at high-tech companies, given to employees to urge them to work harder for potential future gains. People can hit the jackpot once they're vested (a couple of years ago, about one out of every 10 employees at Cisco Systems was a millionaire thanks to stock options). But more often than not, the stock fizzles on Wall Street, the company founders, its products are rendered obsolete by an even hotter company, and the options end up worth little, if anything. Due to that uncertainty, stock options have been called "Silicon Valley lottery tickets."

All this wealth has created in Silicon Valley a social structure of haves and have-nots. And, as with every Gold Rush, one of the downsides is high prices—especially the hyperinflation of real estate. For example, an ordinary four-bedroom, ranch-style home in San Jose's Cambrian Park district (which originally sold for less than $30,000 in the 1950s) can go for as much as $600,000–800,000 in today's market. Rent for a nice but unexceptional two-bedroom apartment can start at $1,500 a month. With the additional expenses of living in Silicon Valley, even workers making more than $100,000 in salary have a hard time getting established. And those in the lower-paying service industries—such as teachers and cops—find it all but impossible to live here. They buy homes in cheaper outlying regions such as Modesto, Tracy, Hollister, and Salinas—and join the long caravans of commuters.

The money mania has created an ostentatious lifestyle among the valley's nouveau rich. People have always tried to keep up with the Joneses, but with the inflow of people moving here looking for big, quick bucks, Silicon Valley's society in recent years has come to seem greedier than the norm. Salaries, bonuses, and rewards from the stock market have become common touchstone comparisons (not that this is peculiar to Silicon Valley, but it's quite pronounced here). People buy fancy cars and clothes to project success, but many a rich-looking resident in a hot new BMW is heavily in debt. The valley's social scene is also influenced by the money obsession. It's not unusual to be asked, along with your marital status and history of sexually transmitted diseases, what your net worth is.

In fiscal good times or bad, money is definitely the driving force in today's Silicon Valley.

A User's Guide: The Basics

Silicon Valley has undergone dramatic image changes in the last two decades. Gradually, it has moved out of the shadow of San Francisco, its more cosmopolitan sister to the north, and become an area considered just as sophisticated and well known worldwide. San Francisco is a compact, European-style city, built in an era when most people walked to their destinations. Much of Silicon Valley's sprawling growth occurred in the post–World War II years, when Americans' love affair with cars began in earnest.

San Francisco draws travelers with its grand vistas, waterfront landmarks, and legendary cable cars and bridges. Silicon Valley's major share of visitors come here for business meetings, trade shows, and conferences. But an increasing number of adventurous

travelers—particularly from electronics-savvy countries like Germany and Japan—often come here on their vacations to tour the region so famous for its cutting-edge style.

Silicon Valley has frequently been compared to the Renaissance city of Florence. Like the hometown of Leonardo da Vinci and Michelangelo, it's a place filled with innovation and adventure, daring and genius, risk and reward, success and failure. These qualities have brought the region onto the world stage in a relatively short period of time. More and more travelers are making pilgrimages here to see how, in a few decades, a once-sleepy agricul-

Tech Museum, San Jose

© MARTIN CHEEK

MOVERS AND SHAKERS: GOOD NAMES TO KNOW

Although the flow of power changes with time, here are some names worth knowing to understand who the major players in Silicon Valley are—or have been recently:

Media

Rob Elder—editor of *San Jose Mercury News*

Dan Pulcrano—publisher of *Metro*, a popular weekly tabloid, as well as a number of local newspapers throughout the valley

Leigh Weimers—widely read society columnist for the *San Jose Mercury News*; considered "Mr. Silicon Valley"

Politics

Rod Diridon—former chairman of Santa Clara County Board of Supervisors, influential in building the area's transportation infrastructure such as the Light Rail

Ron Gonzales—first Hispanic mayor of San Jose

Susan Hammer—mayor of San Jose during the 1990s; continued Tom McEnery's redevelopment program

Tom McEnery—mayor of San Jose during the 1980s; initiated the city's redevelopment program

Frank Taylor—for almost 20 years the principal architect of downtown San Jose's redevelopment program (left the position in early 1999)

At press time, the congressional representatives of the area are:

Mike Honda (Democrat)
15th District (including Campbell, Los Gatos, Monte Sereno, Santa Clara, Saratoga, and south San Jose), 408/244-8085 or, in Washington, D.C., 202/225-2631

Anna Eschoo (Democrat)
14th District (including Cupertino, East Palo Alto, Los Altos, Los Altos Hills, Menlo Park, Mountain View, Palo Alto, and Sunnyvale), 408/245-2339 or, in Washington, D.C., 202/225-8104

Zoe Lofgren (Democrat)
16th District (including Gilroy, Morgan Hill, downtown and northern sections of San Jose, and San Martin), 408/271-8700 or, in Washington, D.C., 202/225-3072

Fortney "Pete" Stark (Democrat)
13th District (including Alviso, Fremont, Milpitas, and Newark), 510/494-1388 or, in Washington, D.C., 202/225-5065

Technology

Larry Ellison—co-founder and CEO of database software company Oracle in Redwood City

Bill Gates—co-founder and CEO of Microsoft; works in Redmond, Washington, lives in Seattle, but always a major topic of conversation in Silicon Valley

Andrew Grove—co-founder and former CEO of Intel

Steve Jobs—co-founder and CEO of Apple Computer

Michael S. Malone—author and commentator on Silicon Valley's technology, culture, and business

Scott McNealy—co-founder and CEO of Sun Microsystems

Regis McKenna—eponymous founder of public relations firm that pioneered the marketing of major high-tech corporations such as Apple Computer

David Packard—highly revered co-founder of Hewlett-Packard; with his family, set up the Packard Foundation, which has contributed millions of dollars to various Bay Area organizations

Arthur Rock—important venture capitalist who helped finance such companies as Fairchild, Apple, and Intel

Stephen Wozniak—co-founder of Apple Computer, now largely a philanthropist and technology teacher in local schools tural region was transformed into an ultramodern world capital for the new millennium.

POINTS OF INTEREST

A surprisingly large number of special-interest museums and other attractions are scattered throughout the Silicon Valley region, allowing visitors to learn about such topics as quilting, railroads, donuts, airplanes, lace making, map-making, and, of course, technology. One of the best is the Rosicrucian Museum, in San Jose's Rose Garden district. It contains the West Coast's finest collection of Egyptian artifacts. Many of these attractions are free (sometimes requesting a small donation), staffed with friendly docents ready to answer any questions pertaining to the exhibits.

Being a place where information is a popular commodity, Silicon Valley also has a number of world-renowned research centers. The United States' best collection of works by Ludwig van Beethoven can be found at San Jose State University, and an excellent comprehensive medical library is open to the public at the Stanford Shopping Center in Palo Alto.

The valley also abounds with historical museums and sites containing exhibits that tell the stories of human drama, sordid scandals, and political wheeling and dealing that have shaped the region's and the nation's development. Among the best is the San Jose Historical Museum, at Kelley Park, which has re-created a turn-of-the-19th-century village.

And, of course, in the quiet streets and busy boulevards of Silicon Valley's many cities and towns, you can see the buildings in which the electronics and biotechnology industries' most influential companies are shaping tomorrow's history. However, most of these complexes have tight security and won't allow casual visitors beyond the reception area (though that may not be such a bad thing, given the lack of spectacle inherent in people—even busy, brilliant people—sitting at desks solving problems on computers). But there are a few exceptions; among the office buildings of interest to travelers is chip-maker Intel's Santa Clara head-

quarters, which contains a popular microprocessor museum.

ENTERTAINMENT

Silicon Valley plays just as hard as it works. After being on the job for long hours, its citizens can choose from a multitude of places to relax and socialize with friends. The area offers a variety of venues satisfying all tastes in nightlife entertainment. The South of First Area (SoFA) in downtown San Jose has quite a few popular nightclubs, many of which draw a younger crowd, such as students from nearby San Jose State University. Sunnyvale's historic 100 block of S. Murphy Ave. as well as downtown areas of Los Gatos and Mountain View also attract residents who want to "paint the town."

Besides nightclubbing, the area also offers many entertainment opportunities for those who enjoy the performing arts. The valley's first professional dramas were performed in the summer of 1859, when actor James Stark built a theater on San Jose's 1st St. and performed as the Cardinal Duke in a play called *Richelieu*. During the 19th century, residents watched a tremendous number of excellent productions from local and traveling performers. In 1870, San Jose built its first Opera House, which put on many fine performances until it burned down in 1881. Well-known actors including Edwin Booth and W. E. Sheridan performed in San Jose's theaters during this time. In the postwar years, the valley's performing arts took a dive in popularity as they competed with television, but the 1980s saw a renewed interest in such cultural pursuits.

With the continued influx of wealth into the area, Silicon Valley plays host to many well-received professional and amateur dance, music, and theater productions. Opera San Jose is a world-class company of professional singers and musicians, and the San Jose Symphony is one of the nation's most prestigious orchestras. Dance companies include the San Jose Ballet Company, which under the direction of Dennis Nahat has produced several world premiere performances. The area has also begun to gain worldwide recognition as a burgeoning center for drama, with such esteemed groups as Mountain View's TheatreWorks and the San Jose Repertory. For cinema buffs, art films can be viewed at downtown San Jose's Camera One and Camera Three theaters. Or, for classic movies from Hollywood's Golden Age, the beautifully decorated Stanford Theater movie palace in downtown Palo Alto makes a wonderfully romantic place to spend an evening.

Visual Arts

For many years, Silicon Valley was considered a barren wasteland for fine art, but that view has changed dramatically in the last few years. With the economic boom, a significant number of residents and corporations bought works of art, creating a major growth industry for local art museums and commercial galleries. Many local cities are also investing in paintings and sculptures, and public works can be viewed throughout the valley. Nonprofit arts organizations endow more than $70 million a year to promote art in the area. Accomplished artists exhibit at the many public galleries, such as the San Jose Museum of Art and Santa Clara's Triton Museum of Art. Palo Alto has a thriving art community highlighted by its recently reopened Iris and B. Gerald Cantor Center for Visual Arts at Stanford University and its city-funded Palo Alto Art Center. And San Jose State University's art department has developed a reputation as one of the most creative in the country, putting on outstanding student exhibitions in its various galleries.

RECREATION

Blessed with more than 300 days of sunshine each year, Silicon Valley is also a great place for outdoor recreation. It has an abundance of public parks, open preserves, and gardens. These range from those along the bay lands, such as Mountain View's Shoreline Park, to those in the foothills, such as Henry Coe State Park in Morgan Hill and Ed R. Levin County Park in Milpitas. Additional recreational opportunities include a slew of excellent golf courses, riding stables, tennis courts, and aquatic centers. If you're more daring in your outdoor pursuits, you can hang glide from Mission Peak or climb sheer cliffs at parks such as Saratoga's Castle Rock State Park (for a somewhat safer climbing experience, visit the indoor rock-climbing training center at Santa Clara's Planet Granite). All of the cities have recreation departments, which provide such classes as martial arts and swing dancing, and you need not be a resident of that city to get involved. Many cities such as Cupertino and Santa Clara also have excellent sports centers open for public use, and the various community colleges also provide classes and facilities for those interested in trying out new athletic endeavors.

With Pong and Pacman getting their starts here, Silicon Valley is the birthplace of the immensely popular computer game industry. But that doesn't mean children here spend all their free time playing Nintendo. The area's mild climate and its multitude of outdoor activities make it a great place to be a kid. From farm heritage centers such as Los Altos Hills' Hidden Villa to fa-

Italo Scanga's Figure Holding the Sun greets visitors to the San Jose Museum of Art.

FRY'S: ELECTRONICS STORE OR THEME PARK?

In a search for the essence of Silicon Valley business, it's all but mandatory to make a stop at Fry's Electronics. This locally owned chain of stores is simultaneously revered and despised by its customers. It originated as a valley supermarket chain started by Charles Fry. But in 1985, Fry's three sons, Randy, John, and David, dumped the vegetables and replaced them with virtually every electronic gadget and gizmo conceivable—promising to sell them at "guaranteed low prices." The chain has become a valley institution, where families often bring the kids on the weekends. At some Fry's locations, shoppers don't even need to leave for lunch—theme cafés serve meals inside the stores.

Any Fry's will provide a crash course in electronic products—wander through one for an hour or so, and you'll get a fairly clear sense of Silicon Valley's obsession with technology. In this gadget wonderland you can find everything from simple resistors for under a buck to flat-screen digital televisions for $15,000. Fry's stocks a bizarre agglomeration of merchandise, including major kitchen appliances, toothpaste, networking software, Gummi bears, fax machines, video games, beef jerky, motherboards, and toilet paper.

Each store is designed in a kitschy amusement park style that contrasts strangely with the cutting-edge high-tech wares: the Palo Alto store has a Wild West theme, Sunnyvale's store takes you back to Babylonia, San Jose's store is a faux Mayan temple, and Campbell's store is the Egyptian temple of Luxor.

San Jose Mercury News columnist Mike Cassidy has called Fry's a "living Silicon Valley Smithsonian." Considering that many of the products you'll see probably will be outdated or at least superseded within a year or so, you are indeed walking through a kind of living museum.

Stores are open Mon.–Fri. 8 A.M.–9 P.M., Sat. 9 A.M.–9 P.M., and Sun. 9 A.M.–7 P.M. Fry's locations in Silicon Valley:
- Campbell: 600 E. Hamilton Ave. (just off Hwy. 17), 408/364-3700
- Palo Alto: 340 Portage Ave., 650/496-6000
- San Jose: 550 E. Brokaw Rd. (west of I-880), 408/487-1000
- Sunnyvale: 1077 E. Arques Ave., 408/617-1300

cilities such as Raging Waters or Happy Hollow Park and Zoo, there are many options for family outings. Attractions such as Paramount's Great America, the Children's Discovery Museum, and the hands-on Tech Museum also make Silicon Valley a fun place for kids to live and visit. Unlike the adult-oriented attractions of nearby San Francisco, Silicon Valley provides more family-oriented leisure activities.

The area's numerous annual festivals and events draw large crowds, especially the highly popular art and wine festivals held in the summer in various cities. Sports fans will find that Silicon Valley is fast becoming a nationally recognized site for professional athletics, including the NHL Sharks ice hockey team, which plays in the San Jose Arena. The valley also has produced quite a few Olympians. Bruce Jenner trained for the 1976 Montreal Olympics decathlon event at San Jose City College, Mark Spitz is among the large number of gold-medal winners from the Santa Clara International Swim Club, and figure skaters such as Peggy Fleming and Rudy Galindo lived and trained in the area. The San Jose Arena has been the site of international figure-skating championships as well as Final Four basketball games.

SHOPPING

With so many residents enjoying an increased standard of living, it just seems logical that there will be plenty of places to spend all that cash. Have no fear that Silicon Valley's inhabitants and visitors can satisfy that primal urge to hunt and gather (armed with a Visa card instead of a spear). Such a variety of retail stores exist throughout Silicon Valley that it's easy to believe shopping is the residents' major activity. In the last few years, many of the large shopping centers and malls have undergone multimillion-dollar renovations due to heightened competition to attract customers. Along with the megastores, smaller specialty shops scattered throughout the valley sell more unique items. And a couple of immense flea markets provide a fun day out for those hungry for secondhand bargains.

The valley is a cornucopia of antique dealers, most notably along Lincoln St. in San Jose's Willow Glen district. The South County region also has a fine selection of antique shops, many found along the downtown streets of Morgan Hill and Gilroy. An excellent area for window shopping is downtown Los Gatos. The downtown shopping districts in Menlo Park, Los Altos, and Palo Alto are also fun places to browse among interesting boutiques and one-of-a-kind shops. The seemingly endless supply of shopping centers, emporiums, and retail stores has made Silicon Valley a shopper's dream.

Festivals and Events

Throughout the year, Silicon Valley holds various community celebrations and events. Almost every weekend brings some opportunity to get out and explore the region's cultural diversity. From the International Auto Show at the McEnery Convention Center in January, to downtown San Jose's charming Christmas in the Park in December, every month holds its treasure of seasonal events. Some border on the quirky, such as Rubberama, a gathering of rubber stamp fanatics. Others are pure hometown Americana, such as the numerous Independence Day events or the local Christmas tree lightings. Many events highlight Silicon Valley's mixture of ethnic groups, including its Hispanic, Italian, African-American, Vietnamese, and Portuguese populations. Among the more popular events are the art and wine festivals sponsored by many chambers of commerce during the summer months—expect huge crowds at these gatherings.

The festivals listed below are suitable for the entire family, and admission to the majority of them is free. If there is a charge, it's usually less than $10. Parking at some of the huge events, such as those in downtown San Jose, can become a big hassle—best avoided by taking the Light Rail train or other forms of public transportation.

For the latest schedules for the area's performing arts, gallery shows, festivals, nightclub acts, and movies, there are two good printed sources. The best one is *Metro* (www.metroactive.com), a free tabloid-sized publication that calls itself "Silicon Valley's Weekly Newspaper." It also provides theater and movie reviews, published every Thursday. You can find it in fire-engine red boxes in downtown areas throughout the valley. (Many local libraries also stock it in their free-to-the-public sections near their entrances.) Another source is the "Eye" section of the *San Jose Mercury News.* This insert, published every Friday, provides reviews and schedules for Silicon Valley performances and events. Various websites also provide up-to-date information on many events. The best ones to try include San Jose Living (www.sanjose.org), Silicon Valley online (www.silvalonline.com/content), and Just Go (www.justgo.com/bayarea).

JANUARY

San Jose International Auto Show

Get a close-up look at the latest models and concept cars, and meet local celebrities all under one roof. Many automakers use the show for their big debuts—such as Volkswagen's introduction of its resurrected Beetle at the 1998 show. Adults $7, children 6–12 $3.50, children under 6 free. McEnery Convention Center, downtown San Jose. For more information, call 800/521-3833.

Martin Luther King Day

Several Silicon Valley festivities mark the national holiday honoring the American civil rights leader, and past years have included a free gospel night at Emmanuel Baptist Church and a Freedom Train Ride to San Francisco from San Jose's Diridon Station. For more information, call 408/292-3157.

Chinese New Year

On the last weekend of the month, Milpitas brings in the new year Chinese style with festivities including a traditional dragon dance and firecrackers. Free. Milpitas Square Shopping Center. For more information, call 408/262-2613.

East-West Shrine Bowl

This annual tradition at Stanford Stadium is the United States' oldest all-star football game, dating back to 1925. Proceeds benefit the 22 Shriners Hospitals dedicated to caring for children. Tickets range from $8 to $20 at the 50-yard line. Stanford University, Palo Alto. For more information, call 650/372-9300, website: www.shrinebowl.com.

Westech Career Expo

This is Silicon Valley's most popular job fair. Potential employees meet representatives from more than 285 high-tech companies ranging from 3Com to Zilog Corporation. Free. Santa Clara Convention Center. For more information, call 408/970-8800, website: www.vjf.com.

FEBRUARY

Vietnamese Spring Festival

Taking place around the Tet New Year, this cultural celebration of the valley's Vietnamese population includes traditional music and food, dances, games for kids, a Miss Vietnamese Pageant, and a colorful 50-foot dragon leading a parade. Admission charged. Parkside Hall, Civic Auditorium, and Almaden Walkway, downtown San Jose. For specifics, call 408/262-3411.

Gem and Mineral Show

For rock hounds and those interested in collecting beautiful gems, this annual event is hosted by the Santa Clara Valley Gem and Mineral Society. Admission charged. Santa Clara County Fairgrounds, San Jose. For specifics, call 408/494-3100.

Santa Clara Valley Kennel Club Dog Show

An assortment of man's best friends can be viewed at Silicon Valley's largest dog show. Admission charged. Santa Clara County Fairgrounds, San Jose. For more information, call 408/494-3100.

MARCH

Mercury News Press Run

Silicon Valley's biggest race, this 10K run/5K walk starts and ends in downtown San Jose's Plaza de César Chávez, passing through the Rose Garden district. Besides possible shinsplints, the thousands of participants get the customary race T-shirt. Money raised goes to health services for local families. For more information, call 408/920-5755.

Modern Bridal Fair

For those about to take the matrimonial leap, this annual fair provides a one-stop shopping opportunity for every wedding necessity except the groom. Admission charged. Santa Clara County Fairgrounds. For more information, call 408/494-3247.

APRIL

Campbell Spring Carnival

Thrilling rides, greasy junk food, and games of chance highlight this annual tradition, a favorite of Campbell residents. Free. Campbell Community Center. For information, call 408/866-2105.

American Indian Pow Wow & Arts Festival

Native American arts and crafts as well as cultural traditions, dance, and music mark this festival. Free. De Anza Community College, Cupertino. For specifics, call 408/864-5448.

Japanese Cultural Festival

As the cherry blossoms come into bloom, Cupertino holds an annual Japanese cultural festival sponsored by its sister city of Toyokawa. Visitors experience traditional Japanese food, music, dance, and ceremonies. Free. Memorial Park, Cupertino. For more specifics, call 408/257-7424.

National Library Week

Special games and programs oriented toward children encourage reading at many local Silicon Valley library branches. Free. Various locations. For specifics, call 408/277-4846.

MAY

Prune Festival

Despite the festival's name, there are paltry few prune-themed attractions. But thousands come anyway to wine-taste and stroll through more than 150 arts and crafts booths. Free. Downtown Campbell. For more specifics, call 408/378-6252.

À la Carte & Art

Esteemed chefs in the Mountain View area provide cooking demos and serve samples at food booths. Upscale wine-tasting, microbreweries, 200 arts and crafts vendors as well as children's entertainment make this increasingly popular festival a pleasant spring outing. Free. Downtown Mountain View. For information, call 650/964-3395.

Memorial Day

San Jose Historical Museum holds an annual remembrance of California's past with various activities. Some years have included Civil War Days and a Gold Rush festival. Admission charged. Kelley Park, San Jose. For more information, call 408/287-2290.

Affribean Parade

Reggae music, traditional African and Caribbean dance, and zesty costumes lend a party atmosphere to this parade growing in popularity. Free. Downtown Mountain View. For specifics, call 650/964-2056.

Cinco de Mayo Celebration

Centered in Discovery Meadow, this festival spreads across much of San Jose's downtown during the weekend nearest May 5. It features Aztec and Mexican dancing and music, but the Hispanic heritage gets lost with too many food and trinket booths devoted to other cultures. Free. Downtown San Jose. For more information, call 408/258-0663.

Los Altos Mayfest

This festive weekend community event is a long-standing Los Altos tradition. The fun includes a pancake breakfast, the often comical Kiwanis Club Pet Parade through downtown, a fine arts show in Lincoln Park, and a flea market with more than 100 booths. Free. Downtown Los Altos. For more information, call 650/948-1455.

Rubber Stamp Festival

Rubber stamp enthusiasts flock to this event (known affectionately as "Rubberama"), where they can buy supplies and unusual stamp products. Civic Auditorium, San Jose. For information, call 408/272-0211, website: www.astampinthehand.com.

Mushroom Mardi Gras

Held every Memorial Day weekend, this family-oriented event honors Morgan Hill's status as the Mushroom Capital of the World. More than 40 food booths provide dishes including the wondrous fungus (the portabella mushroom sandwich is a must). Live entertainment on two stages and 200 crafts booths keep with the mushroom theme in the park setting. Adults $10, seniors and children $5. Family packages available. Community Park, West Edmundson and Monterey Rd., Morgan Hill. For more specifics, call 408/778-1786.

A USER'S GUIDE

Santa Clara County Fair

Breathe in the aroma of cotton candy, corn dogs, and livestock at the valley's annual two-week showing of its agricultural heritage. In recent years, the fair has tried to get high-tech hip with such attractions as a nerdy chicken mascot, but old-fashioned carnival rides and country music performers draw in the crowds. Admission charged. Santa Clara County Fairgrounds, San Jose. For further information, call 408/494-3247.

JUNE

Highland Games

If you're into bagpipes and kilts, be sure to attend this festival. Highland clans participate in sporting events such caber tosses, join in Celtic dances, and enjoy ethnic food such as haggis. Adults $8, seniors and youths 8–17 $6, wee'uns free. Campbell Community Center, Campbell. For more information, call 408/866-2138.

Firefighters Chili Cook-Off

Since 1981, this event has been a Silicon Valley favorite for tasting authentic firehouse-hot chili, cooked by more than 50 teams of Bay Area firefighters. It's a great family day out where kids can climb on fire trucks and learn about fire safety. Proceeds go to the burn unit of the Valley Medical Center. Usually held at Discovery Meadow, downtown San Jose. For specifics, call 408/295-6999.

Strawberry Festival

The sweet berries are the stars in this nonalcoholic festival that includes arts and crafts booths as well as live music. Treats include strawberry shortcakes, waffles, and chocolate-dipped strawberries. Proceeds benefit EMQ Children and Family Service, a valley mental health agency that originated from an orphanage funded by 19th-century philanthropist James Lick. Free. West Valley College, Saratoga. For more information, call 408/364-4081.

San Jose Greek Festival

Sometimes held in late May. Dine on Greek foods such as *souvlakia* and barbecued lamb, and watch ethnic dance groups wearing traditional Greek costumes perform to live music. Vendors offer Greek fisherman hats and other items. Adults $3, seniors and students $2, children under 6 free. St. Nicholas Greek Orthodox Church, 1260 Davis St., San Jose. For more information, call 408/246-2770.

Juneteenth Festival

Celebrate Lincoln's emancipation of the slaves with lively games, parades, music, food, and proclamations. Free. Location varies. For specifics, call 408/292-3157.

Sunnyvale Art and Wine Festival

With more than 500 art vendors, eight local wineries, and a number of local breweries, this is one of the largest art and wine festivals in Silicon Valley. Free. Downtown Sunnyvale. For specifics, call 408/736-4971.

Filipino Fiesta!

Many of Milpitas's residents emigrated from the Philippine islands, and this vibrant festival celebrates their culture with Filipino foods, art, music, and dancing until midnight to live bands. Free. Milpitas Community Center. For details, call 408/263-8160.

Nativity Carnival

An annual tradition in Menlo Park, this school-sponsored country fair provides carnival rides, live entertainment, and family dinners. Nativity School, corner of Oak Grove and Laurel Aves., Menlo Park. For more information, call 650/325-7304.

JULY

Fourth of July Street Fair and Fireworks Sky Concert

Milpitas celebrates Independence Day with a spirited party that includes food, live entertainment, and a hot rod show. After sunset, fireworks sparkle across the sky. Free. Great Mall of the Bay Area. For further information, call 408/942-2470.

Menlo Park Fourth of July Parade

Honor the country's birthday with an old-fashioned parade that marches down Santa Cruz Avenue. An arts and crafts fair, live entertainment, and food booths continue the celebration at Burgess Park. Free. For more information, call 650/858-3470.

San Jose Americas Festival

Held July 3–4, this multicultural celebration includes a variety of food, arts and crafts, and entertainment celebrating the diversity of San Jose's people. The festival ends with an ear-popping fireworks show. A headliner concert costs $7–10, but the rest is free. Discovery Meadow, San Jose. For specifics, call 408/294-2100, ext. 444.

Chinese Summer Festival

The Chinese played an important role in settling the valley during the 19th century. This cultural event honors their contribution with various family-oriented activities. Admission charged. Kelley Park's San Jose Historical Museum. For details, call 408/287-2290.

Gilroy Garlic Festival

The Garlic Capital celebrates the pungent bulb that made it world famous with Silicon Valley's biggest festival. Crowds come from all over the Bay Area to taste foods such as garlic ice cream and buy gifts such as garlic perfume. It's good-spirited fun, but a little garlic can go a long way. Traffic and parking can be a headache, so consider taking Caltrain to Gilroy, from whence a shuttle bus will take you to the festival. Christmas Hill Park, Gilroy. For details, call 408/842-1625.

Mariachi Conference & Festival

Put on your Mexican sombrero for this lively music festival featuring some of the best mariachi bands in the world. Free. Downtown San Jose. For specifics, call 408/292-5197.

Obon Festival

Japanese foods, San Jose's famous Taiko drum performers, and more than 500 Obon dancers (the largest such gathering in America) highlight this Buddhist remembrance of the dead. Held the second weekend of July. Free. Japantown, San Jose. For more specifics, call 408/293-9292.

Los Altos Arts and Wine Festival

More than 100,000 people pour into Los Altos's quaint downtown village to wander among the works of 400 artists. Three stages provide music, street performers entertain crowds, and an array of premium wines from the Santa Cruz Mountains is available for tasting. Free. Downtown Los Altos. For details, call 650/949-5282.

Armenian Picnic

More than 1,200 people come to this event, which includes traditional Armenian music and dancing. À la carte food booths sell items including authentic shish kebab, hummus, and *tan,* a yogurt drink diluted with water. Vasona County Park, Los Gatos. The event is sponsored by St. Andrew Armenian Church in Cupertino. For additional information, call 408/257-6743.

AUGUST

Milpitas Art and Wine Festival

This event features hundreds of artisans and dozens of food vendors, as well as live music and children's attractions. Free. Milpitas Town Center. For specifics, call 408/262-2613.

Cupertino Art and Wine Festival

Cupertino was once known for its world-famous vineyards, and the premium wine still flows at this annual festival. Free. Memorial Park. For more information, call 408/252-7054.

San Jose Jazz Festival

At the United States' largest free jazz festival, the crowds swell to hear big-name performers such as Spyro Gyra. Vendor booths sell souvenirs and food. Many participants bring folding chairs. Free. Plaza de César Chávez, San Jose. For more information, call 408/288-7557.

Tapestry in Talent Festival of the Arts

San Jose's wine-tasting and arts and crafts festival is a huge event, drawing artisans from around the country. Free. Downtown San Jose. For specifics, call 408/293-9728.

SEPTEMBER

Food Fest

Los Gatos hosts this celebration of international cuisine, providing tastes from local restaurants. Proceeds support nonprofit youth organizations. Free. Los Gatos Town Plaza. For specifics, call 408/354-9300.

SoFA Street Festival

This happening spotlights the numerous nightclubs, restaurants, and galleries of San Jose's South of First Area. Free. Downtown San Jose. For details, call 408/279-1775, website: www.sj-downtown.com.

Celebrate Saratoga!

Once a year, Saratoga Village is closed off for a popular street party. Food from the city's esteemed restaurants, wine- and beer-tasting, and live music predominate the festivities. Parking can be a problem, but free shuttles offer rides to parking lots. Free. Big Basin Way, Saratoga. For details, call 408/867-0753.

Chinese Moon Festival

A more reverent festival during the full moon period set among the statues, temples, and natural setting of the Chinese Cultural Garden. Free. Overfelt Gardens, San Jose. For specifics, call 408/251-3323.

Mexican Independence Day

Celebrate Mexico's independence from Spain. A much more low-key celebration than the overwhelming Cinco de Mayo event. Free. Downtown San Jose. For more information, call 408/295-9600.

San Pedro Square Brew Ha Ha

The name says it all—beer from local microbreweries and live comedy performances at San Pedro Square. Free. Downtown San Jose. For details, call 408/279-1775.

Santa Clara Art and Wine Festival

Visit more than 200 arts and crafts vendors, drink premium wines, play carnival games, and enjoy live entertainment on three stages. Free. Central Park, Santa Clara. For specifics, call 408/984-3257.

A Taste of Morgan Hill

A two-day street festival where Morgan Hill's eateries provide a sampling of their cuisine and chefs demonstrate recipes. Besides culinary delights, there's live music on three stages, arts and crafts vendors, grape stompings, and a classic car show. Free. Downtown Morgan Hill. For details, call 408/779-9444.

OCTOBER

Los Altos Fall Festival

This harvest fair includes more than 175 arts and crafts booths as well as food from Los Altos eateries. Music, entertainment, and the popular Children's Alley draw families. South Parking Plaza, Los Altos. For more details, call 650/948-1455.

Wildlife Festival

A fun educational event for kids who are keen on natural history and animals. Free. Alum Rock Park, San Jose. For more details, call 408/259-5477.

Oktoberfest

Put on your lederhosen and dust off your stein—Silicon Valley has two popular Oktoberfest celebrations. The city of Campbell's, held downtown, 408/378-6252 (admission charged), boasts an abundance of arts and crafts booths to browse through, but the traditional Teutonic ambiance somehow gets misplaced. For more of *that,* go to the Oktoberfest at Germania Hall, 408/292-0291, near San Jose's St. James Park (free).

World's Largest Haunted House

Featuring scary zombies, decapitated heads, and bloodthirsty vampires, this annual walk through a dark labyrinth full of unearthly surprises raises funds for local nonprofit organizations. Admis-

© MARTIN CHEEK

Contemporary dancers perform traditional Portuguese steps.

sion charged. Santa Clara County Fairgrounds, San Jose. For details, call 408/494-3100.

Italian American Cultural Festival

Silicon Valley's Italians put on a big Mediterranean-style party with lotsa pasta and wine as well as a grape-stomping competition. Free. Plaza de César Chávez, San Jose. For specifics, call 408/293-7122.

Portuguese Festival

Celebrating the valley's Portuguese heritage, this event includes oxen-drawn carts, folk dance, John Philip Sousa band music, and traditional foods such as linguiça sausages and octopus stew. Kelley Park's San Jose Historical Museum. For details, call 408/287-2290.

NOVEMBER

Founding of the Pueblo Celebration

Held in mid-month to celebrate San Jose's founding, this wonderful cultural event gives families a glimpse of life during the valley's frontier days. Kids can grind corn and cook tortillas, make corn husk dolls and adobe bricks, and listen to Ohlone and African-American storytellers. Entertainment includes Aztec dances. Tours are given of the Peralta Adobe and Thomas Fallon House. Free. San Pedro Square, San Jose. For more information, call 408/287-2290.

Harvest Festival

Many Silicon Valley residents like to kick off their Christmas shopping with this arts and crafts fair, which highlights the work of local artisans. Usually held the weekend after Thanksgiving, this huge festival includes one-of-a-kind, handmade gifts in a Victorian Christmas-like setting. Admission. McEnery Convention Center, San Jose. For specifics, call 707/778-6300.

DECEMBER

San Jose Holiday Parade

The Yuletide season officially begins in San Jose with the annual Holiday Parade, held early in December. The route starts at the San Jose Arena and ends at the Plaza de César Chávez. It includes spectacular holiday floats, marching bands, giant Santa balloons, and the usual roundup of local celebrities and officials waving from classic cars. Free. Downtown San Jose. For more information, call 408/277-3303.

Christmas in the Park

Plaza de César Chávez turns into a winter wonderland during the annual Christmas in the Park. It features more than 60 animated displays, including a Santa Claus train and a "growing" Christmas tree. Hundreds of small trees decorated by local schools and clubs fill up much of the park, and before you leave, it's a sure bet that at least one Christmas carol will get stuck in your head. This favorite holiday treat among valley residents is well worth seeing, especially for kids who want to visit Santa. It's open from 9 A.M. to midnight. Free. Downtown San Jose. For details, call 408/277-3303.

Tree Lighting Ceremonies

Many Silicon Valley communities hold public celebrations of the holidays. These free family-centered events often include an official Christmas tree lighting, holiday parades, carolers, and candlelight processions. Here is a sampling:

Campbell, at the Teddy Roosevelt Tree, W. Campbell Ave. and Winchester Blvd., 408/378-6252

A USER'S GUIDE

Santa Clara, at City Hall, 408/984-3266
Downtown Los Altos Festival of Lights Parade, 650/948-1455
Las Posadas in **downtown San Jose,** 408/467-9890
Milpitas Tree Lighting Community Sing-Along, Milpitas City Hall, 408/942-2310
Menlo Park Candlelight Procession, from various churches, coming together at Fremont Park, 650/854-5897
Los Gatos Christmas Parade, 408/354-9300
Palo Alto Christmas Lane Show, 650/324-3121

IT'S GEEK TO ME: A SILICON VALLEY GLOSSARY

Silicon Valley boasts an argot of slang, acronyms, and buzzwords all its own. Generated mainly by the valley's high-tech workers, this lingo is locally known as "Geek Speak." There's even a website (www.sabram.com/site/slang.html)—set up by Steve and Mette Sabram, two Silicon Valley software designers—dedicated to keeping its readers abreast of the latest additions to and changes in valley vocabulary. Many of the following terms come from that website.

assmosis—climbing the corporate ladder by kissing up to the boss instead of through talent or hard work

beepilepsy—an awkward pause or sudden spasm a person gets when his or her vibrating beeper suddenly goes off while the person is in the middle of a sentence

betamaxed—outmarketed; referring to VHS videotape standard's eclipsing of the higher-quality Beta standard in the 1970s, "betamaxing" is the process by which superior technology loses out in the market due to poor marketing or a competitor's aggressive marketing of an inferior product

bloatware—software with useless features—usually put in more as a marketing ploy—for which most users have absolutely no need

blow your buffer—lose your train of thought

booth bunnies—at trade shows, attractive women (usually temps, and usually lacking any but the most basic knowledge about computers) hired to attract geeks to booths

chips and salsa—hardware and software

code 18—a user-created error; refers to the fact that the user sits about 18 inches from the screen of the computer monitor.

curry—a product or technology that is so innovative and popular, it's as "hot" as the spice used in many Asian Indian foods

east coasting—using an uptight, old establishment mentality that is blind to innovation and won't take risks; refers to Silicon Valley's perception of the New York and Boston style of business administration. Also can be used of a person too focused on corporate hierarchy

The Evil Empire—Microsoft Corporation

five and dime—the 510 area code for telephone dialing (includes much of the East Bay including the cities of Berkeley and Oakland)

FM—"fuckin' magic"; used by telecom workers when a problem "magically" fixes itself; used to give customers the impression the problem came about due to interference from radio transmissions

grepping—conducting an extremely methodical search; comes from the Unix programming language acronym for "global regular expression print"

high dome—a very smart scientist or engineer, particularly one who has a Ph.D.

high visibility position—the company scapegoat, the person who is usually fired in a very public beheading when things go wrong—in troubled firms, this is often the CEO

keyboard plaque—the stuff that accumulates on computer keyboard keys over time due to being typed on with unwashed fingers

kludge (or kluge)—cobbled-together or jury-rigged

Business

More than 6,200 high-tech firms employing more than 250,000 workers are located in Silicon Valley. Along with Stanford University's human genome project, the area also has its share of hot biotech companies doing genetics research and development. For example, Menlo Park's Geron Corporation, a cell research firm, made headlines in May 1999 when it paid $25.9 million in stock for Roslin Bio-Med of Scotland, the firm that in April 1998 cloned the first mammal, a sheep named Dolly. But because this area has the world's highest concentration of electronics

engineering project, software code, or computer system; something hammered out without much planning or sophistication

meatspace (or carbon community)—the realm of humans, as opposed to technology

milker—a consultant who takes longer than necessary to do a job in order to "milk" the customer of extra money

nerd bird—a weekday commercial air flight from San Jose to Austin (Texas's major technology city) or vice versa, filled with engineers and techies

Nyetscape—derogatory nickname for AOL's web browser, as opposed to the better-designed Netscape

out of the garage—a start-up company that has moved into a professional office site or taken other formal establishing steps; refers to Silicon Valley's many companies, including Hewlett-Packard and Apple, which actually did begin in garages

PEBCAK—Problem Exists Between Chair And Keyboard; used by technical support staff to explain that the user is to blame for a problem

prairie dogging—office workers' practice of standing up and peering over their cubicle walls to investigate a commotion

percussive maintenance—giving a computer a hard whack in an effort to get it to work correctly

ponytails—creative or artistic types in a company who provide designs; most often found in entertainment-based companies, such as those producing video games

salmon day—a day when a person feels as if s/he has been swimming upstream all day

seagull manager—a company supervisor who dive-bombs into the office, squawks a lot, dumps dung over everything, and then flies off again, leaving behind a lot of ruffled feathers among the underlings

sneakernet—the transfer of data between two computers by copying the files onto a diskette and walking over to the receiving computer instead of transferring data over a network electronically

square-head girlfriend—a computer

telephone number salary—a salary that's over one million dollars; refers to the seven digits of a standard American telephone number without the area code

treeware—a hard-copy document, such as a book or a manual; also known as a "dead trees edition" or "a papyrus-based information storage system"

vaporware (or wonderware)—software that is hyped in trade publications or advertisements but has yet to be available in any form; usually a marketing ploy to try to get customers to wait and not buy a competitor's product which is available earlier

Waldo—a flashy demonstration of a prosaic product; refers to the "Where's Waldo?" children's cartoon books in which readers have to find a man in a bright red and white shirt hidden in pictures filled with considerable detail

wetware—the human brain

WOMBAT—Waste Of Money, Brains, And Time

World Wide Wait—derogatory nickname for the World Wide Web firms, high-tech is where the real multibillion-dollar action happens.

The valley has become such an economic powerhouse that it dramatically affects the diverse regions surrounding it. Commuters get up as early as 3 A.M. to drive from San Joaquin Valley towns such as Modesto, Stockton, or even Fresno (a three-hour commute each way), or to come up U.S. 101 from "bedroom communities" in San Benito and Monterey Counties or over Hwy. 17 from Santa Cruz.

Its considerable wealth and prestige as an international business capital has also earned Silicon Valley significant political influence with Washington power brokers. During much of the 1990s, President Clinton and Vice President Gore were frequent visitors who come to shake the money tree for campaign contributions. One of the area's more influential lobbying organizations is the bipartisan group Technology Network (or TechNet), founded in July 1997. It's made up of many of the valley's corporate chieftains united in promoting the high-tech agenda among political leaders.

The major high-tech companies have settled into various roles in the valley's business culture. Hewlett-Packard, Lockheed Martin, Varian, and IBM are the well-respected giants. Intel, AMD, National Semiconductor, and other chip manufacturers established in the 1960s and 1970s have also come into their own as maturing companies, with occasional "midlife crises" when they periodically try to reinvent themselves. Then there are the firms such as Adobe, Cisco, Silicon Graphics, Sun Microsystems, and 3Com, which rose up during the PC boom of the 1980s. These companies are slipping out of their risk-taking adolescence, entering a more thoughtful early adulthood. The 1990s and the turn of the millennium gave birth to a number of brash, rambunctious newcomers involved with the Internet, including YAHOO!, eBay, and Netscape.

Silicon Valley's dynamic business environment is a complex one with its own intrinsic culture. The following companies are considered some of the biggest and best-established corporations.

Adobe System's downtown headquarters is a local landmark.

MAJOR COMPANIES

3Com

Robert Metcalfe, one of the Xerox PARC inventors of Ethernet technology, founded this company, which specializes in providing networking products and services for voice, video, and data. In 1982, it sold the world's first network adapter for IBM PCs, thus laying the foundation for the network revolution of the late 1980s. It holds 470 patents. The three "Coms" are computer, communication, and compatibility.

5400 Bayfront Plaza, Santa Clara (off Great America Pkwy.), 408/326-5000, website: www.3com.com; established in 1979.

Adobe Systems

Started by former Xerox PARC researchers, Adobe revolutionized the world of publishing with its PostScript language. Now the world's second-largest desktop software company, it specializes in creating high-quality software for professional publishers, as well as Web and graphics designs. Some of its products have also been used to create special effects for TV and film. With Adobe's move to downtown San Jose, its twin-tower skyscraper headquarters became a prominent city landmark in the mid-1990s.

324 Park Ave., San Jose (corner of Almaden Blvd.), 408/536-6000, website: www.adobe.com; established in 1982.

Advanced Micro Devices

Commonly known as AMD, this semiconductor company was started by engineer Jerry Sanders after he quit Fairchild in the late 1960s. It's a tough competitor against Intel and lately has focused its efforts on developing future markets in manufacturing chips for mobile computing and telecommunications devices.

1 AMD Place, Sunnyvale (off Lawrence Expwy. and Duane Ave.), 408/732-2400, website: www.amd.com; established in 1969.

Agilent

In 1999, Hewlett-Packard spun off this company, which focuses on developing and selling test and measurement devices, semiconductor products, health-care equipment, and chemical analysis tools. With about 48,000 employees worldwide, it quickly grew into one of Silicon Valley's top high-tech firms.

395 Page Mill Rd. (near El Camino Real), 650/752-5300, website: www.agilent.com; established in 1999.

Altera

The first company to provide programmable logic devices. It also provides logic development software.

101 Innovation Dr., San Jose (at 1st St. and Montague Expwy.), 408/544-7000, website: www.altera.com; established in 1983.

Amdahl Corporation

A wholly owned subsidiary of Fujitsu Limited, this company was started by Gene Amdahl, chief architect of IBM's 360 Series computers, who left Big Blue in 1970. Today's Amdahl provides products and services for integrated enterprise computing, supporting such environments by blending MVS, Windows NT, and UNIX operating systems.

1250 E. Arques Ave., Sunnyvale (off Lawrence Expwy. S. between Kiefer and Oakmead), 408/746-6000, website: www.amdahl.com; established in 1970.

Apple Computer

The PC revolution started with Apple's introduction of its pioneering Apple II computer in the late 1970s. Its fortunes really took off in the next decade with the introduction of the Macintosh and its marketing in the education, publishing, and graphics markets. With a change of leadership and heavy competition from the IBM-compatible market, Apple's business suffered in the late 1980s and much of the 1990s, but under the renewed leadership of CEO Steve Jobs and its introduction of the popular iMac system in the late 1990s, Apple improved its economic outlook.

One Infinite Loop, Cupertino (next to De Anza Blvd. exit off I-280), 408/996-1010, website: www.apple.com; established in 1977.

Applied Materials

The world's top semiconductor equipment manufacturer, Applied Materials builds fabrication systems for making chips. In 1987, the company's Precision 5000 product came out, a single-wafer, multichamber processing system that was a turning point in the chip-making process. The model was considered so significant that there's one in the Information Age exhibit at the Smithsonian Institution.

3050 Bowers Ave., Santa Clara (off Central Expwy.), 408/727-5555, website: www.applied-materials.com; established in 1967.

Atmel Corporation

This company makes memory chips, integrated circuits, and flash memory products for communications and networking, consumer, computer, and peripheral applications. In the late 1990s, it entered the smartcard arena, providing chips for that emerging market.

2325 Orchard Pkwy., San Jose (at N. 1st and Brokow), 408/441-0311, website: www.atmel.com.

Cadence Design Systems

The world's largest supplier of software products and consulting and design services for electronic components, its customers include semiconductor, computer, and networking firms.

555 River Oaks Pkwy., San Jose (off Montague Expwy.), 408/943-1234, website: www.cadence.com; established in 1988.

WHITE HOUSE CONNECTIONS

Silicon Valley has shot up rapidly in political importance in the last two decades. The president of the United States occasionally comes to pay a visit, flying in on Air Force One and landing at Moffett Field in Mountain View. Bill Clinton was an expert schmoozer with the corporate executives here and raised a substantial amount of campaign funds. On his first visit after his public confession during the Monica Lewinsky scandal, he attended a $20,000-a-plate fundraiser at the then-newly constructed Tech Museum and spent the night at Steve Jobs's house. Clinton's daughter, Chelsea, graduated from Stanford University in 2001. (Ironically, one of her fellow students was Carolyn Starr, the daughter of independent counsel Kenneth Starr.) President George W. Bush is not as frequent a visitor to Silicon Valley, but he does make an appearance now and then.

But the region boasts an association with the White House that long predates the Clinton and Bush administrations. John C. Frémont launched his political career in San Jose in 1848, when the newly formed state legislature chose him to represent California as one of its two U.S. senators. Frémont went on to become the first Republican presidential candidate, losing the 1856 election to James Buchanan.

Because Abraham Lincoln decided that the federal government should take by force the British-owned New Almaden Quicksilver Mines, he so angered California's residents that he may have come close to losing the state's support against the Confederate cause. Luckily, the crisis passed when the owners sold the property a month later. The last letter Lincoln ever wrote described his desire to visit California, and it's almost certain that he would have visited the famous mines that played such a crucial role in helping the Union forces win the Civil War.

In 1879, former President U. S. Grant watched Leland Stanford's horse run a race at Agriculture Park, near San Jose's Alameda. In 1901, President William McKinley gave a speech in St. James Park (at the spot where the statue honoring him now

stands). In 1903, President Teddy Roosevelt passed through on his grand tour of the West, spending a night sleeping in his train car in the middle of a Campbell orchard.

Stanford University, of course, had a link to the White House long before Chelsea Clinton enrolled. Herbert Hoover entered as a freshman in 1891, graduating in engineering in 1895. While there, he organized the first "Big Game" with football rival U.C. Berkeley. Today, that event is a hallowed valley tradition. Hoover also lived on the Stanford campus and, in 1928, received the Republican Party's presidential nomination at Stanford Stadium.

After President Benjamin Harrison left the White House in 1893, he taught classes in constitutional and international law at Stanford. In 1940, a recent Harvard graduate named John F. Kennedy rented a cottage on campus for $60 a month while taking the class "Introduction to Business and Government" from Professor Theodore Kreps at the university.

In 1948, Harry Truman made a whistle stop in San Jose during his "Give 'Em Hell Harry Campaign." He almost bypassed the town, but John McEnery (father of former San Jose mayor Tom McEnery) went up to San Francisco and met Truman one morning while the Man from Missouri was shaving in his hotel bathroom, securing Truman's cordial promise to stop en route to Los Angeles. At the San Jose depot, Truman told a corny joke (which may have been the reason he lost Santa Clara County to Tom Dewey by 11,000 votes). Truman told the large crowd: "I heard yesterday about a man from Nebraska who was visiting in Palo Alto and asked a lady, 'How do I get to San Josie?' The lady explained to him that in Spanish, 'J' sounds like 'H,' and it was San Hosay. Then she asked him how long he would be in California, and he replied, 'Oh, till Hune or Huly.'"

In 1962, then–Vice President Lyndon Johnson visited San Jose, giving a speech at City Hall at 5 P.M.—quitting time for many civic workers. So paltry was the turnout that Mayor Robert Welch had to search the city's government offices for secretaries, janitors, and engineers to fill up the space. Even that wasn't enough to please LBJ, who threw a temper tantrum on his way to the hotel—and never returned to San Jose.

While campaigning in 1968, Richard Nixon held his first full-scale political rally at Buck Shaw Stadium at Santa Clara University. Nixon made a short visit to San Jose on October 29, 1970, during the peak of the Vietnam War demonstrations. When his motorcade reached the Civic Auditorium parking lot (a space now occupied by the McEnery Convention Center), about 2,000 peace marchers stormed his car. Nixon stood on the car hood and gave a V-sign, which antagonized the crowd. A rock flew through the air, hitting the car. More rocks, as well as eggs and vegetables, came flying at the president, and the Secret Service quickly got him into the limo and drove back to the airport. However, one car in the motorcade stalled, and demonstrators pelted it with rocks, breaking windows and injuring the passengers inside.

For more piquant tales of the presidency and Silicon Valley, read Harry Farrell's wonderful memoir, *San Jose and Other Famous Places: The Lore and Lure of the South Bay.*

Cisco Systems

With its line of end-to-end networking solutions products, Cisco's fortunes rose with the Internet's phenomenal growth in the 1990s. It's now the world's No. 1 manufacturer of networking hardware for the Internet, its product line including routers, LAN and ATM switches, dial-up access servers, and network management software. Early in 1999, Silicon Valley was rocked by the company's announcement that it planned to build a facility for more than 20,000 workers in the undeveloped Coyote Valley of south San Jose, thus opening up the South Valley area to high-tech development.

170 W. Tasman Dr., San Jose (off N. 1st St.), 408/526-4000, website: www.cisco.com; established in 1986.

Compaq Computer

Although its headquarters are in Houston, Texas, Compaq is developing a significant presence in Silicon Valley with several of its divisions. Its AltaVista Company in Palo Alto, a well-known World Wide Web search and navigation site, is expanding into the realm of Internet e-commerce. Its Tandem Division offers Unix-based and other platform products that provide business-critical computing for enterprise customers. Compaq also runs research laboratories and an Internet Exchange Center in Palo Alto. In 2000, to add to its marketing presence in Silicon Valley, the company paid the city of San Jose millions of dollars to change the name of the downtown Arena to "The Compaq Center."

10435 N. Tantau Ave., Cupertino, 408/725-6000, website: www.compaq.com; established in 1982.

Hewlett-Packard

Considered Silicon Valley's most philanthropic company, HP has also been one of the region's longest established and most successful high-tech pioneers. It's also one of the area's largest employers. HP was started in 1938 by Stanford graduates William Hewlett and David Packard, making test and measurement instruments for scientific analysis. In 1966, it entered the computer and peripheral equipment market and now makes products ranging from palmtops to supercomputers. HP leads the world in laser, inkjet, and color printer sales. It ranks among the top 10 U.S. exporters and has been listed as No. 5 among *Fortune* magazine's Most Admired Companies. In 1999, it split its computer and measurement equipment divisions into two separate companies, creating the new firm Agilent.

3000 Hanover St., Palo Alto (off Page Mill Rd.), 650/857-1501, website: www.hp.com; established in 1938.

IBM Corporation

Big Blue has made its presence felt in Silicon Valley since the early 1950s, when it established manufacturing and research facilities in South San Jose. In a plant tour in 1959, Soviet leader Nikita Khrushchev found it amusing when IBM board chairman Thomas Watson Jr. took him to the cafeteria, gave him a tray, and made him stand in line with the workers. Among other accomplishments, its engineers developed disk drive technology here, naming one series the "Winchester" in honor of rifle heiress Sarah Winchester. IBM has long been the computer industry's dominant player, getting its humble start in 1911 as the Computer-Tabulating-Recording Company, making time clocks and punch card tabulators for businesses.

5600 Cottle Rd., San Jose (off Hwy. 85), 408/256-1600, website: www.ibm.com; established in region in 1943.

Intel Corporation

By far the largest semiconductor manufacturer, this Fairchild spin-off was started by engineers Robert Noyce, Gordon Moore, and Andy Grove. Besides chips, the Silicon Valley powerhouse also makes products such as flash memory, server, and workstation components, as well as hubs and routers for the Internet and networking. Its headquarters has a small museum that gives visitors a glimpse into the company's history and how microprocessors are made.

2200 Mission College Blvd., Santa Clara (off U.S. 101 near Great America), 408/765-8080, website: www.intel.com; established in 1968.

KLA-TENCOR

Making automated photomask inspection systems, this company helps semiconductor manufacturers improve their yield in the wafer fabrication process. The present company was created in 1997 from a merger of KLA Instruments and Tencor Instruments.

160 Rio Robles, San Jose (off N. 1st St.), 408/434-4200, website: www.tencor.com; established in 1997.

Lockheed Martin Missiles & Space

Historically one of the valley's largest employers, Lockheed was founded by Los Gatos's Loughead brothers (they later changed their name), who brought the company here from its original location adjacent to Southern California's Van Nuys Airport. It builds satellites for military use as well as communications, global positioning (GPS), and weather surveillance. It is also the sole supplier for the U.S. Navy's Fleet Ballistic Missiles. Among the more well known projects it has helped develop are the International Space Station, the Hubble Space Telescope, the Lunar Prospector, and the Iridium communication system.

1111 Lockheed Martin Way, Sunnyvale (off N. Mathilda Ave.), 408/742-6688, website: www.lockheedmartin.com; established in 1958.

LSI Logic Corporation

This semiconductor manufacturer uses its CoreWare design system to create "systems on a chip," which are customized, application-specific integrated circuits. Customers include networking, wireless/telecom, computer, and workstation companies. LSI Logic targets high-volume markets such as consumer electronics, video games, DVD, and digital camera products.

1551 McCarthy Blvd., Milpitas (between Hwy. 237 and I-880), 408/433-8000, website: www.lsilogic.com; established in 1981.

National Semiconductor

Founded in Danbury, Connecticut, this company moved to Silicon Valley in 1968 and makes integrated circuit products spanning a wide range of uses from desktop and notebook computers to automobiles and consumer products. In 1997, it acquired Medimatics and entered the PC MPEG market, which provides multimedia video on the desktop. That same year, it merged with Cyrix Corporation, a supplier of PC microprocessors. In 1998, it acquired Gulbransen Corporation, gaining their digital audio technology, and ComCore Semiconductors, expanding its market into digital signal processing for high-speed networks.

AMERICAN DREAMERS: THE IMMIGRANTS OF SILICON VALLEY

Often overlooked in the phenomenal success story of Silicon Valley is the importance of the vast number of foreign-born people who have settled here and helped build the region's high-tech industry. Since the 1960s, these American dreamers have played an increasingly significant role.

The Cato Institute estimates that approximately one-third of the valley's engineers and scientists were born outside the United States. And one in every five of the region's high-tech companies was founded by immigrants—a market segment responsible for generating annual revenues of $27.9 billion and, since 1996, hiring about 67,500 American workers. Many of these immigrants come to the valley to study in the Bay Area's excellent universities and continue residing here after graduation when offered better-paying high-tech jobs than they can find in their homelands. In time, obviously, many of them go on to start their own companies—finding the business climate in the valley much more conducive to start-ups than their homelands, too (India in particular is known for horrendous bureaucracy in getting licenses and permits to start a business.) And some become so successful that, after selling their firms, they become venture capitalists, investing in the start-ups of other foreign-born engineers.

These engineers and scientists contribute to the ethnic diversity of the valley. They come from all parts of the globe, including Britain, France, Germany, and Iran. After the fall of communism, many Russian and Eastern European engineers came to Silicon Valley and quickly assimilated into the fast-paced culture. But it's the Indians and Chinese who make up the majority of the valley's immigrant engineers. One local quip says that the valley's reputation for being built on ICs doesn't necessarily mean "integrated circuits," but rather the skills of the Indian and Chinese engineers. University of California, Berkeley professor AnnaLee Saxenian conducted a study that found Indian and Chinese engineers served in senior executive positions in about 25 percent of Silicon Valley's new high-tech businesses.

Among the valley's immigrants, the term "H-1B" is well known. This is the name of a special visa issued by the U.S. government that allows foreigners skilled in high-tech to come to work in the United States. In 1999, Silicon Valley lobbyists pushed Congress to pass legislation expanding the H-1B immigrant quota from 65,000 to 115,000. This was a controversial issue in the valley. Labor unions protested, saying that the high-tech companies were only out to save a few dollars an hour by avoiding hiring Americans. The high-tech firms argued that the legal and regulatory costs of recruiting skilled immigrants eliminate any monetary savings and that native-born workers simply don't create a large enough pool of skilled workers. Thus, in the new millennium, Silicon Valley will see an increase in the number of immigrants pursuing the American dream in the world of high-tech.

2900 Semiconductor Dr., Santa Clara (off Kifer Rd.), 408/721-5000, website: www.national.com; established in 1959.

Netscape

This company merged with America Online in 1999. It was founded by James Clark, who also started Silicon Graphics, and Marc Andreessen, co-creator of Mosaic software, which allows people to navigate the World Wide Web. Netscape's Navigator product was the first commercially successful browser product for exploring the Internet. (Microsoft's Internet Explorer product later proved to be a hard-hitting competitor.) Netscape also produces client-server software as well as software for creating and publishing HTML documents, many of which are used for e-commerce websites.

501 E. Middlefield Rd., Mountain View (off Ellis St.), 650/254-1900, website: www.netscape.com; established in 1994.

THE GEEK SHALL INHERIT THE EARTH

Enough has been written about Bill Gates to fill an ocean with ink. And, because Gates—the man who dropped out of Harvard to start a company called Microsoft—has now become a software tycoon and one of the richest persons on the planet—this handbook will now add to that mass of words.

Gates makes his home in a charming little 50,000-square-foot, $53 million cottage on a five-acre lot adjoining Seattle's Lake Washington (near Microsoft's Redmond, Washington, headquarters). Considered by many the most powerful person in the computer industry, he holds massive influence over Silicon Valley's business environment. Some people consider him the epitome of the American dream and a brilliant role model for modern business in creating a company that affects the lives of billions of people. Other people revile his aggressive business tactics and his unhesitating willingness to ruthlessly crush competitors. They vilify him, believing he wants nothing less than to rule the world. Whatever the public's perception, Microsoft—with its Windows and NT operating systems running on more than 90 percent of the world's PCs—is *the* dominant software company.

Because Silicon Valley is the world's high-tech capital, Microsoft obviously plays a large role here. The company has a research center in Mountain View to attract the computing graduates that come out of the area's universities (particularly Stanford). Opened in the fall of 1999, the five-building campus houses more than 2,000 Microsoft employees in the heart of the Silicon Valley. Gates also donated a few extra million dollars to Stanford University, which named a computer department building after him, and $5 million more to the United Way of Santa Clara when that organization suffered a financial deficit in 1999.

The high-tech mogul has also bought a few Silicon Valley start-ups, acquiring those that fit certain niches in Microsoft's expansion plans—or that threatened to compete. He purchased WebTV, for example, and attempted to buy Intuit (the maker of the popular Quicken financial program) but was thwarted when the government ruled against the deal.

In the last few years, the local press eagerly and closely followed Gates's courtroom battle with the U.S. Department of Justice when Microsoft was sued primarily for antitrust violations incurred in its rather desperate attempt to corner the booming Internet market. Specifically, the company targeted and, apparently, took several aggressive steps to crush Navigator, Netscape's popular Web browser. The government alleged that Microsoft abused its Windows monopoly, strong-arming computer sellers, Internet service providers, and others in the industry into offering their customers Microsoft's Internet Explorer browser exclusively. On November 5, 1999, the judge in the case issued findings of fact that agreed in virtually every material way with the government's case: Microsoft does have a monopoly, it abused that monopoly power, and that abuse caused harm to both consumers and technical innovation. But appeals and other steps may drag the case out for years to come.

Gates stepped down as CEO of Microsoft and was replaced by fellow founder Steve Ballmer. Gates now retains his title as chairman and also chief software architect. And with the economic downturn and Gates giving millions of his dollars away to charity, his fortune fell in 2001 to a mere $54 billion, according to the *Sunday Times of London*. Thus, behind Wal-Mart Chairman Robson Walton with $65 billion, Gates became the second richest man in the world. But still, his presence is very much felt in Silicon Valley.

Nortel Networks

This company, which dates back to the late 19th century, builds networking systems on a global scale, focusing much of its development on Internet applications. In 1998, it expanded its operation by purchasing Bay Networks.

2305 Mission College Blvd. (off U.S. 101 near Great America), 408/988-5550, website: www.nortelnetworks.com; established in 1895.

Silicon Graphics

Remember all those cool dinosaurs roaming around in *Jurassic Park?* Silicon Graphics's powerful workstation computers brought them to digital life. SGI also makes some of the world's fastest server systems, and its powerful supercomputers are used in commercial and military applications for 3-D visualization of complicated data. It also creates software for Internet and entertainment applications.

1600 Amphitheater Pkwy., Mountain View (just off U.S. 101 near Shoreline Amphitheater), 650/960-1980, website: www.sgi.com; established in 1982.

Solectron Corporation

Designs and manufactures electronics products such as PCs and printers for a vast number of

© MARTIN CHEEK

A sculpture adorns the lawn of a Mountain View business park near Silicon Graphics's headquarters.

high-tech customers. The unusual name came about during the solar energy craze of the 1970s. Among the firm's first customers was a supplier of electronic controllers for solar energy equipment, prompting the combination solar + electron = Solectron.

777 Gibraltar Dr., Milpitas (off Milpitas Blvd.), 408/957-8500, website: www.solectron.com; established in 1977.

Sun Microsystems

With Scott McNealy as its down-to-earth CEO, this company still retains its youthful culture in its management style. Sun stands for Stanford University Network, showing its origins from that Palo Alto–based institution of higher education. It provides businesses with Unix-based, high-end computer workstations and is also considered one of the best Unix training companies. Its Java programming language, which serves as a multiplatform, is considered a strong contender against Microsoft's dominant Windows operating system.

901 San Antonio Rd., Palo Alto (off U.S. 101), 650/960-1300, website: www.sun.com; established in 1982.

Varian

A true Silicon Valley pioneer, Varian was started by brothers Russell and Sigurd Varian, Stanford graduates who built klystron vacuum tubes in the 1930s. In the decades following, the company expanded its line of businesses, developing health-care systems, instruments for precise scientific measurements, and semiconductor manufacturing equipment. As of April 1999, it divided its operations into three independent publicly traded companies. Varian Medical Systems is the world's largest supplier of oncology equipment used to fight cancer. Varian, Inc. makes scientific instruments, vacuum technology, and electronic components. Varian Semiconductor Equipment Association makes ion implantation systems.

Varian Medical Systems: 3100 Hansen Way, Palo Alto (off Page Mill Rd.), 650/493-4000; Varian, Inc.: 3120 Hansen Way, Palo Alto, 650/213-8000; Varian Semiconductor Equip-

CORPORATE HUMOR: A SAMPLING

The stress of long hours and tight deadlines give rise in Silicon Valley to a fair amount of inside humor. Email and the Internet make it possible to broadcast this humor far, wide, and fast. The pleasant surprise is that some of this material is actually funny.

One all-time favorite concerns Bill Gates and a prostitute, who ends up telling the multibillionaire that now she knows "why they call it 'Microsoft.'"

Also popular and milder is the one poking fun at the legendary arrogance of Oracle CEO Larry Ellison:

Q. What's the difference between Larry Ellison and God?

A. God doesn't think he's Larry Ellison.

But the targets aren't always so big.

Q. What's the difference between a computer salesperson and a used car salesperson?

A. Car salespeople know when they're lying.

There are also gigabytes' worth of variations on old formulae:

Q. How many managers does it take to change a lightbulb?

A. Three. Two hold the ladder and one screws the lightbulb into a faucet.

Acronyms are another popular target. The first versions of Windows NT were plagued by so many bugs that programmers declared the acronym stood not for the official "New Technology" but rather for "Not There." PCMCIA, a technology in which a credit card–sized contraption holds data, stands for "Personal Computer Memory Card International Association." But Silicon Valley wags have changed it to "People Can't Memorize Computer Industry Acronyms."

And the fun doesn't stop with mere jokes. Pranks are also popular. April Fools' Day is a dangerous time to be at Sun Microsystems, for instance. In 1988, employees turned CEO Scott McNealy's office into a golf course; in 1994, it was converted into a day care center. In 1993, Sun executive Andy Bechtolsheim's Porsche was dismantled and reassembled in his office.

Even conservative Hewlett-Packard is known to tolerate some lighthearted pranksterism. On one occasion, visitors from HP's Boise, Idaho, facility were greeted at the Palo Alto headquarters by a live sheep wearing sexy lingerie and black stockings—local employees had rented the bewildered animal, they said, in an effort to make the Boise employees "feel at home."

---

ment Association: Gloucester, Massachusetts, 978/282-2000; website: www.varian.com; established in 1938.

YAHOO!

Stanford engineering students David Filo and Jerry Yang turned their hobby of creating a customized database to locate material on the Internet into a multimillion-dollar Web browser company. The founders insist the firm's name came about because they considered themselves a couple of yahoo hicks, but another story goes that it's an acronym for "Yet Another Hierarchical Officious Oracle."

3420 Central Expwy., Santa Clara (between Lawrence Expwy. and Bowers Ave.), 408/731-3300, website: www.yahoo.com; established in 1994.

REAL ESTATE

Silicon Valley's real estate is among the highest priced in the United States. Basic three bedroom ranch homes start at around $450,000, and depending on location, prices can climb to well over $1 million. The valley's *median* house price is $500,000. The prices are especially jaw-dropping in prestigious communi-

THE FIGHT OVER LUIS MARIA PERALTA'S ESTATE

With the high sales turnover of homes in the area, title companies have had a thriving business in Silicon Valley. Today, the land deeds are very rarely disputed. This, however, was not the case during the era of American conquest of California. During that turbulent time many land grants and ranchos did not have thorough documentation of ownership and thus became the subject of lawsuits.

The feud over Luis Maria Peralta's will was one of the most brutal lawsuits in the valley's history. It serves as an illustration of how a fight over property can lead to a family's disintegration.

Peralta was one of the original pioneers of the pueblo San Jose (his humble adobe hut still stands in a history park in downtown's San Pedro Square district). Witnessed by attorney James Alexander Forbes, physician Dr. Divini, and Father John Nobili (the founder of Santa Clara College), Peralta signed his last will and testament on April 29, 1851. Four months later he died of influenza and was buried in the cemetery at Mission Santa Clara.

At the time of his death, Peralta's estate was worth $1,383,500—a fantastic sum in 1850s California. About $10,000 of this value was in San Jose land, the rest was made up of his Rancho San Antonio land in the East Bay. That property now comprises the cities of Oakland, Alameda, Berkeley, Emeryville, Piedmont, Albany, and part of San Leandro.

The will gave Peralta's San Jose land to his daughters Maria Josefa and Maria Guadalupe.

His Rancho San Antonio estate was divided up between his sons. Peralta might have had a premonition of the legal dispute to come because in his will, he included the sentence: "I command all my children that they remain in peace, succoring each other in your necessities, eschewing avaricious ambitions."

Disregarding this instruction, his two daughters brought to trial a suit saying that their father, during the time of writing his will, had been unduly influenced by his lawyer Forbes and the priest Nobili. They claimed their father had been of unsound mind while writing his will. The lawsuit was lengthy and brutal. Witnesses included some of the most respected pioneers of San Jose, and some of their testimony offered contradictory views of Peralta's alleged insanity.

Like the lawsuit in Dickens's novel *Bleak House,* the dispute dragged on for years in the Santa Clara County courts. Compounding the Peraltas' problems, American squatters began to settle on the San Antonio land, and the owners faced tough legal challenges to get them off. In 1859, the sisters' suit went to a tribunal of the California Supreme Court, which decided in favor of the sons.

It was a hollow victory. The lawyers for the disputing Peraltas were the only winners in the matter, receiving much of the land for payment of their legal services. Land not lost to squatters and lawyers was sold to pay court costs. Due to the foolish lawsuit, the vast rancho of Luis Maria Peralta was shrunk to a minuscule remnant of its legendary size.

---

ties with scenic vistas of the valley such as Los Altos Hills, Palo Alto, Los Gatos, Saratoga, and San Jose's Evergreen/Silver Creek district. If you're not making an annual income equivalent to the gross national product of a small nation, you can pretty much forget about ever buying a home here.

Well, okay, it's not quite that bad. Many middle-income families buy "starter homes" in the South Valley cities of Morgan Hill and Gilroy.

Those who don't mind a hellish daily commute go outside the region altogether to find homes in mushrooming housing subdivisions of bedroom communities such as Hollister, Modesto, and Tracy.

A good place to get a sense of Silicon Valley's real estate and rental market is to pick up the free publications *Homebuyers Journal, RE/MAX Real Estate Buyer's Guide, The Property Pages,* and *Apartments For Rent.* You'll find them at the exits of supermarkets and drugstores such as Safeway, Albertsons, and Longs. These monthly publica- tions provide a listing of homes for sale as well as apartment and condominium rentals.

Tips for the Traveler

WEATHER

One of the most important factors in determin- ing when to visit any destination is the weather. Here's some excellent news: Silicon Valley en- joys one of the world's best climates. It's blessed with warm days and cool nights, and doesn't suf- fer extreme temperature differences throughout the year.

The winter months can get chilly (by Cali- fornia standards). January averages a daily low of 41°F and a high of 58°F. In nondrought years, winter brings storms in from the Pacific Ocean. These often pound the area with torrents of rain, which can cause considerable flooding in the valley's creek regions. The mountains often get dusted with snow, giving a pseudo-Alpine look to their peaks. It's extremely rare that snow falls on the valley floor, but it did one afternoon in De- cember 1998—to residents' amazement. The slushy flakes melted the instant they hit the ground.

In spring, the rains taper to gentle showers, and the warm sunshine brings the blossoms out. April averages a daily low of 47°F and a high of 69°F. This is the best time to visit the valley's many parks because the wildflowers are in full bloom.

Summer has its spells of heat waves, during which the mercury shoots over the 100° mark. Unlike the humid heat of America's southern and eastern states, Silicon Valley heat is dry and more bearable. These heat waves generally take place between mid-July and mid-September and can last from several days to as long as a couple of weeks. July averages a daily low of 55°F and a high of 81°F.

The cooler fall weather usually starts in late September and lasts sometimes until Christmas. The region is blessed with mild Indian summer days during this period, although the nights can get brisk enough to require sweaters. October enjoys a daily low of 51°F and a high of 74°F.

Because Silicon Valley stretches over hundreds of square miles, it is home to a complex series of microclimates. The South Valley area generally becomes the hottest and driest. The temperature gets cooler as you approach the San Francisco Bay. Communities near the shoreline—such as Moun- tain View, Palo Alto, and Alviso—often get morn- ing fog and stay overcast for a while. Tornados are exceptionally rare in the region, but during the El Niño of 1998, a minor one did land on a Sunnyvale suburb, damaging several homes.

For updated **weather conditions,** call 415/364-7974.

DRESS

To really fit in and be taken for a local in Silicon Valley, you *are* required to wear a pocket pro- tector loaded with cheap ballpoint pens. At all times. The hems of your trousers must ride about six inches off the floor. You must wear white socks even with dark shoes. And if you wear glasses, they must be taped across the bridge (preferably with a Band-Aid).

Just kidding, of course. Like the rest of this state, Silicon Valley observes a dress code proba- bly best described as "California casual." You'll also see plenty of people wearing expensive, ele- gant clothes, but for daily activities, jeans or in- formal slacks (and shorts in hotter months) and T-shirts are completely acceptable for both men and women. On cool fall days, you'll also want a sweater or a heavy sweatshirt. And for cold win- ter days, an overcoat or a ski jacket is advisable.

Work clothes depend on the corporate envi- ronment and a person's position in the company. Generally speaking, employees in the older com- panies—particularly those in management and sales—tend to dress more conservatively to pre- sent a traditionally professional appearance. Employees in research and development divisions can usually get away with casual but neat attire. And "casual Fridays" are becoming a common practice, when employees dress down in more relaxed clothing such as jeans and T-shirts.

So long as you present a clean and neat appearance, fashion is not commonly a big deal when you go out. You won't need a tuxedo or elegant evening dress even at a fine restaurant, the symphony, or the opera.

COSTS, MONEY, AND BANKING

Expenses

Although Silicon Valley is one of the most affluent areas of the United States, prices here for most goods and meals are comparable to those found in the rest of the nation.

Lodging will most likely be your biggest expense. Exceptionally frugal travelers will find a well-run youth hostel at Sanborn County Park in Saratoga for less than $12 per night. Expect most hotels and motels to run from $90 on up depending on the quality of accommodations and time of week you stay. Many hotels provide special weekend packages starting at $99. If you have a difficult time finding cheap lodging within the San Jose area, try the South Valley motels in Gilroy and Morgan Hill.

For **meals,** the economical traveler should plan to budget about $25 a day for eating breakfast, lunch, and dinner at restaurants here. If you want to go cheaper, you can get your meals from supermarkets. Stores such as Safeway, Nob Hill, and Albertsons have deli sections that will prepare picnic lunches or foil-wrapped dinners.

For your **transportation** requirements, the cheapest option is to use the system of buses and trains that travel throughout the valley. A daily pass from the Valley Transit Authority (VTA) costs from $.80 for senior citizens to $4 for express routes for adults. Mass transit is not one of the valley's strong points, but if you're patient, you can eventually get where you're going if it isn't too far out of the way.

For your **entertainment** needs, many of the area's museums are free. At those museums that aren't, expect to pay from $5 to $10. Performing

arts can be cheap if you see productions at the numerous amateur and college theaters. Nightclubs charge a range of cover costs from free to about $10 or higher depending on where you go.

In the matter of **gratuities,** a respectable tip is 15 percent of the total price. For large parties (six people or more), many restaurants automatically add this amount onto the bill, so check before you pay. Tip bartenders $.50 to $1 per drink. Doormen, bellhops, and skycaps usually get $.50 to $1 per bag, depending on how heavy it is and the distance they carry it.

Credit Cards

The vast majority of the area's stores and restaurants accept major credit cards such as Visa, MasterCard, and American Express. However, it's a good habit before making reservations or dining at some restaurants—particularly small, family-run operations—to inquire what credit cards they accept.

Automatic Teller, Cashpoint, or Cash Card Machines

ATMs are plentiful in Silicon Valley, dispensing money 24 hours a day unless the computer servers are down (which seems to happen only when you need the cash the most). Most bank branches, including Wells Fargo and Bank of America, operate many conveniently located ATMs. If you use a machine at a bank other than your own, your account is usually charged a service fee ranging from $1 to $2. A growing number of supermarkets and retail stores—including Safeway, Albertsons, and Target—also have ATMs at their cash registers and generally don't charge a fee (though they may impose limits on the amount of cash back you can request).

Currency Exchange

Most of the valley's major banks will exchange foreign currency during business hours. They'll add a service charge for the privilege, however.

American Express provides foreign exchange services at two Silicon Valley travel agency locations—and charges a $3 fee. One is at the Valley Fair Mall at 5155 Stevens Creek Blvd., 408/244-

1015, and the other is at 250 University Ave., downtown Palo Alto, 650/327-3711.

Depending on the current exchange rate, if you need a large sum, you may save some money by obtaining a cash advance on your credit card. Your card company will charge a much smaller percentage than a bank will.

Traveler's Checks

It's a good idea to bring traveler's checks from your point of departure. These are the safest way to carry large amounts of money, and this form of currency is readily accepted in most area stores and restaurants. (Using better-known brands—American Express, Thomas Cook, or Master-Card—will ensure wider acceptance.)

TRAVELERS WITH DISABILITIES

Whether on business or vacation, travelers with disabilities will find Silicon Valley a welcoming, enlightened, and enjoyable destination. Federal and California state law mandates easy access to public facilities such as museums, office buildings, restaurants, and lodging sites. Public restrooms are required by law to provide toilet stalls that accommodate wheelchairs. Many of the region's modern buildings are designed with ramps, elevators, and push-button-operated doors. Many motels and hotels offer special rooms designed for the comfort of their guests with disabilities—inquire about these when you call for reservations.

Handicapped parking can be found near the entrances to most public buildings, including supermarkets, shopping malls, performance venues, and so on. Designated spaces are identified usually by the international emblem of a white wheelchair symbol on a blue background, appearing on a signpost or painted on the pavement in the space itself—and sometimes both. To park in any of these spaces, you need a special license plate or a dashboard sign available from the local Department of Motor Vehicles. If you get caught parking in a designated slot *without* proper authorization, you will receive a *very* expensive ticket (and the fine multiplies if you get caught more than once).

Travelers with disabilities may find it an unenjoyable challenge to visit some of the area's historic sites and structures. Century-old Victorians, for example, often feature steep staircases and other obstacles—and cannot be modified to accommodate visitor disabilities. Before visiting a historic home or site, call ahead to determine accessibility and see if they offer special arrangements.

Most disabled people will find that the system of buses and Light Rail trains provides easy access. If you have special needs, VTA provides door-to-door paratransit. You'll need proof of disability such as a certified document by a public transit operator. This excellent service is provided seven days a week from 5 A.M. to 2 A.M. It costs $2.20 for a one-way ticket. You must reserve a paratransit trip at least one day in advance by calling 408/436-2865.

A volunteer-staffed, 24-hour crisis line, 800/426-4263, provides counseling, support, information, and referrals for visitors with disabilities.

GAY AND LESBIAN TRAVELERS

Despite its relative proximity to San Francisco, Silicon Valley's traditional farming heritage may be one reason the region is more conservative than its northern neighbor in its social attitudes toward homosexuality.

In recent years, however, the valley *has* grown more accepting of the gay and lesbian lifestyle. Gay pride marches are held in downtown San Jose, and the Silicon Valley Gay Men's Chorus is a popular ensemble that performs at various venues here. Many high-tech corporations have started providing benefits for the same-sex partners of their employees. Even so, gay and lesbian civic and business leaders in Silicon Valley generally tend to be much lower-key than their counterparts in more-liberal San Francisco.

Most Silicon Valley residents are perfectly tolerant of gays and lesbians, though you may find flamboyance rather widely frowned upon.

If you're interested in specific Silicon Valley information and special events, call the Billy De-Frank Lesbian and Gay Community Center in San Jose, 408/293-2429, website: www.defrank.org.

EARTHQUAKE!

Bordering the infamous San Andreas fault, Silicon Valley is in the midst of earthquake country. Although that doesn't mean that the ground here is constantly shaking, the threat does loom in the back of the minds of the locals.

The world's most famous earthquake struck the Bay Area on April 18, 1906, at 5:13 A.M. Several miles underground at Point Reyes (north of San Francisco along the Marin coast), the North American and Pacific plates shifted, generating enough energy to shake the land for 60 seconds. Most of the damage took place in San Francisco, which was incinerated by the destructive fire following the earthquake. The rural Santa Clara Valley, however, also suffered loss of life and structures.

In San Jose, the bulk of the damage was concentrated in the downtown area. Among other public buildings, St. Patrick's Church was completely destroyed along with San Jose High School and portions of the California State Normal School. The U.S. Post Office along the plaza lost its tower. The city had fires, but not to the extent of San Francisco. The El Monte lodging house burned down, killing seven. Company B of the National Guard settled in St. James Park to guard the city from looters.

San Jose's total dead numbered 16. But the worst death toll took place near Santa Clara, where the Agnews State Hospital for the Insane collapsed, killing 112 people. About 1,000 terrified patients walked the grounds after the catastrophe and the more violent ones were tied to trees.

For the next seven decades, the valley was left unscathed by significant earthquakes. Then, on October 17, 1989, at 5:04 P.M., the earth vented its energy once more with a 6.9 quake. The epicenter was near a Santa Cruz Mountain peak called Loma Prieta just south of San Jose. Seismologists were unaware of this branch fault of the San Andreas, and named it Loma Prieta after the peak. The earthquake lurched the two plates about five feet across each other, and the Pacific plate was lifted by four feet. Santa Cruz, Hollister, Watsonville, Oakland, and San Francisco all suffered significant damage.

The town of Los Gatos was the worst hit in Silicon Valley. Showcase Victorians were demolished. About 1,000 homes and commercial buildings were damaged and 55 houses needed to be razed. The damage to the community totaled more than $500 million. Stanford University was also hit hard due to the fact of having a large number of unreinforced masonry buildings on its campus. Among the buildings damaged was the Stanford Art Museum. It has since been renovated and is now called the Iris and B. Gerald Cantor Center for the Visual Arts. Stanford's bill for damages totaled about $120 million.

No one can predict when another significant earthquake will hit Silicon Valley. But seismologists at Menlo Park's U.S. Geological Survey office are looking at the complexity of the region's fault systems. They use powerful computers to map out the Bay Area's fault lines and animate them to show how the force of an earthquake will impact the region. Perhaps with the development of faster computer chips and more sophisticated software, one day it might be possible to understand geological sciences enough to predict when the "Big One" will strike.

HAZARDS

Earthquakes

The majority of tremors that hit Silicon Valley are minor ones that do little damage. If you're visiting the region for only a short while, the chances are slim that you'll experience even a small earthquake. But it's wise to have a general knowledge of how to react in the event that a major earthquake does strike.

From the first instant you feel the primary waves of a quake, you usually have little time to do anything before the more powerful secondary wave comes. Don't run outside—falling walls or heavy objects can hit you. Move immediately to a safe area of the building. If possible, stand in a doorway or get under a strong desk. Stay away from large windows, pictures, bookcases, or mirrors that can come crashing down. Also, stay away from heavy furniture and appliances that can move, as well as masonry, such as brick walls or fireplaces. Hang on tight and try to ride it out.

After the earthquake, check for downed electric lines and gas and water main leaks. If you smell a sulfurous odor, immediately shut off the gas valve if you can (or report the leak to someone in authority). Do not touch downed electrical wiring—the current might still be running and could shock or kill you. Prepare for aftershocks; most likely, these will be smaller than the main quake, but they can still do additional damage—especially to structures weakened by the initial temblor.

Preparation is the key to surviving the aftermath of a devastating earthquake. If you're going to be in the area for any length of time, it's a good idea to assemble a small box containing a selection of basic supplies—a portable radio, flashlights, extra long-life batteries, a first-aid kit, a three-day supply of drinking water, canned food, and any required medication. If your family is with you, determine a place in advance where you should unite after an earthquake. Transportation and communication might be interrupted, so you may have to rely on your own survival skills until help can arrive.

For a good website to learn about recent earthquakes, try the U.S. Geological Survey's National Earthquake Information Center at www.neic.cr.usgs.gov.

Crime

Like all metropolitan areas, Silicon Valley has its share of crime. But compared with other regions, residents and visitors need not worry excessively about their security. In recent years, the FBI has ranked San Jose No. 1 in safety for a city of its size—a major turnaround from the 1970s and early 1980s, when crime was a serious problem. During that time, the intersection of King and Story Roads was the site of so many drug transactions that it was known as "PCP City." Before redevelopment, the derelict downtown was a South Bay center for prostitution and drug sales, and for a time, San Jose wore the unwelcome title of "Crack Capital."

Much of the cocaine drug use in the 1980s was by Silicon Valley professionals who used the stimulant to work long, stressful hours. Acid drugs were used by many lower-end workers with boring, repetitive jobs at high-tech factories. Local urban legends include horror stories of workers getting so high on drugs that they put their heads into vats of corrosive acid used for chip making.

Thanks to rehabilitative programs and changing social attitudes, drug use has diminished significantly in the past decade throughout the valley—as in much of the rest of the country.

Today, the majority of reported crime involves domestic violence (many of these incidents involving alcohol). Car theft is also prevalent due to the number of expensive sport utility vehicles and imported European cars present in the region. If you're driving in Silicon Valley, take commonsense precautions, such as always remembering to lock all doors and not leaving valuables easily visible in your vehicle.

Less often reported are the white-collar crimes happening in the corporate world. High-tech companies traffic heavily in the difficult-to-define area of "intellectual property," thus they are zealous in protecting their work and preventing it from being stolen. Companies generally have tight security systems, so if you are visiting these sites on business, expect to be required to sign in at a reception desk, wear a visitor's badge, and be escorted through the halls. In a kind of blending of past and present, hijacking also occasionally occurs, when trucks hauling chips and computer equipment are stopped and stolen. It sounds like a sort of charmingly archaic kind of crime, but *Tech-Week* magazine estimated that valley corporations lose about $1 million *a day* to such hijackers.

San Jose's low-income Eastside district still has a reputation for having some of the roughest neighborhoods. Hispanic and Vietnamese gang violence still erupts in this area, but the crime rate is steadily diminishing. Neighborhood Watch programs have helped significantly.

The region's cities all have their own police forces, and law enforcement officers are generally respected by citizens. Police corruption does occasionally surface here, but it's not as serious a problem as in other cities of comparable size. Overall, thanks in large part to the widespread affluence experienced by Silicon Valley in the 1990s, the towns and cities here have hired well-trained police officers who make the communities safe places to live and visit.

LIQUOR LAWS

To legally purchase and consume alcoholic beverages in California, a person must be 21 or older. Proof of age with a photo—such as a driver's license or passport—is often required at stores and bars. Most nightclubs "card" (check identification) at the door if a customer appears to be under the age of 30.

SMOKING

With the state's health-conscious lifestyle, it should come as no surprise that many Californians are nonsmokers. But it may come as a surprise to find California and Silicon Valley unfriendly to the point of hostility toward cigarette smoke. Throughout California, it is against the law to smoke in bars, restaurants, theaters, government buildings, and virtually all other public places unless special, completely separate facilities are provided. San Jose International Airport has one such area, a specially vented glass cage where smokers congregate while waiting for their flights. Some restaurants have also built special smoking rooms.

If you do have the cigarette habit, be courteous. If you're visiting a Silicon Valley home, ask permission before lighting up. Generally, nonsmoking residents here probably don't mind if you smoke but would prefer you do so outside.

Also, prepare yourself for the *price* of cigarettes here. With all the various taxes placed on tobacco products in California, a pack of cigarettes in Silicon Valley costs about $3.25.

For those thinking of trying to conquer nicotine addiction, call the California Smokers Helpline, 800/766-2888.

THE INTERNET: HOW WIRED IS WIRED?

Obviously, computers play a hugely critical role in Silicon Valley—they're the reason the valley exists in its present form, they're at the very least of professional interest and at the most extreme an obsession of most of the people living and working in the immediate area and for many miles around, and most things that happen in high technology happen here first.

But don't expect the place to look like something out of *The Jetsons* (or *Blade Runner,* either, for that matter). The cars still need to be driven by actual human beings, you still have to stop at a counter and pay for groceries when you leave a market, and people don't have computer chips surgically implanted in their brains so they can download data directly from the Internet into their neural storage systems. No, in most ways, the cities in the Silicon Valley look very much like most other major contemporary cities.

This is not to say that you won't see lots of computers and other high-tech gear in use in the valley—or that you'll be able to escape the ubiquity of www-dot-fillintheblank-dot-coms, which appear on every advertisement in every medium. Just don't expect to find modem jacks in the streetlight standards, email terminals instead of mailboxes on the corners, or anything like that. More surprisingly, Internet cafés and coffee shops are just about as rare here. They were made more or less obsolete by the proliferation of lap- and palmtop computers and wireless connectivity, in addition to the fact that virtually anyone who *needs* to use a computer while eating lunch or having coffee carries his or her own. If you didn't bring *your* own and you find yourself in need of a log-on, head for any of the local libraries— all have terminals available for public use. Or, if you want to seize the opportunity to go shopping for an upgrade, head instead to a Fry's Electronics store and browse among the hottest high-tech curry. (Just remember that, with chip capacity doubling every 18 months, the cutting-edge today is a doorstop in a year and a half.)

TELEPHONE
Primary Provider
Pacific Bell, 800/303-3000, is the primary provider of local telephone service. The quality of service is usually good.

Area Codes
The 408 code covers southern Santa Clara County, including San Jose; the 650 code covers the valley's northern cities, including Palo Alto and Menlo Park.

Emergency Calls
The emergency number for police, fire, and ambulance is 911.

Directory and Operator Assistance
For local telephone directory assistance, call 411. If you wish to find the number in another area code, dial 1, then the area code of the city you want to call, then 555-1212. If you don't know the area code, check the maps and lists at the front of the telephone directory or dial the operator (0).

Pay Phones
Public telephones charge a basic rate of $.35

per local call up to 12 miles away. For longer distances and additional minutes, a computerized operator will tell you how much change to put in the slot.

Calling Cards
Prepaid calling cards are available in many locations in a wide range of denominations. These are printed with a code number to punch into the phone; the costs of calls are deducted from the original denomination until the card runs out. If you expect to use pay phones extensively, calling cards eliminate the need to carry large amounts of cash in coins. Do be aware, however, that service charges can sometimes accrue, reducing the value of the card by more than merely the cost of a call. Also, the card does *not* pay for any hotel or motel surcharges for telephone use—those will appear on your room bill as usual.

News, Weather, Sports, and More
In the Silicon Valley calling area, Pacific Bell provides a free service called Local Talk, which gives users updated information 24 hours a day on various topics, including news, weather, sports, soap opera developments, horoscopes, and the lottery. To use the service, dial 408/494-0100 (the call is free if dialed locally) and, at the prompt, the four-digit message code. For example, world news is 1510, sports updates is 1715, the lottery is 7777, *All My Children* is 1050. Check the Pacific Bell Smart Yellow Pages for other message codes.

POSTAL SERVICE
The U.S. Postal Service operates offices in all of Silicon Valley's communities. The nearest branch offices can be located by calling 800/275-8777. This number also provides information on postal services, rates and fees, and ZIP codes. Although hours vary, generally post offices are open Mon.–Fri. from 9 A.M. to 5 P.M. and Saturdays 9 A.M.–3 P.M. Post offices are closed on Sundays except for the one at Eastridge Mall, 129 Tully Rd., open Sun. 11 A.M.–6 P.M. Check out the Postal Service website at www.usps.gov.

A number of Mail Boxes Etc. (website: www.mbe.com) stores throughout the valley provide many of the same services as the U.S. Postal Service. This includes private mailbox rental, parcel shipment, and receiving for UPS, FedEx, and other delivery companies (including the Postal Service).

If you only need stamps, many supermarkets and drugstores sell booklets of them at their checkout counters.

MEDIA

Television

If you can get cable, a wide variety of TV programs are available—everything from excellent biographies on A&E to Beanie Baby pitches on the Home Shopping Channel. **AT&T Cable Services** (formerly TCI), 408/452-3355, is the primary provider of cable and digital cable television. Their website is www.broadband.att.com.

The Sunday edition of the *San Jose Mercury News* contains a "Television" supplement containing the week's complete listing of show schedules.

Several stations provide local coverage:
•San Jose–based **KNTV** (Channel 11) is a former ABC affiliate that does a good job covering the South Bay's local news and weather. The station occasionally runs excellent documentaries analyzing the region's business issues and lifestyle, and has an entertaining weekly high-tech update show, *Tech Now!*, which usually airs on Saturday evenings. Website: www.kntv.com.
•**KTEH** (Channel 54) is Silicon Valley's Public Broadcasting System (PBS) station, providing viewers with educational TV. It has produced exceptional documentary series, including one on California's water resources, *Cadillac Desert,* one of the most-watched shows in PBS history. In June 2001, the station premiered its history documentary *Forgotten Journey* about the Stephens-Townsend-Murphy pioneers who settled in Santa Clara Valley. Website: www.kteh.org.
•**Bay TV** (Channel 35), connected with San Francisco's KRON (Channel 4), is a cable station focused on providing quality coverage of Silicon Valley and communities surrounding the San Francisco Bay Area. It does a superb job of producing local shows such as "Bay Cafe," a cooking show hosted by Chef Joey Altman of Menlo Park's Wild Hare Restaurant. Its "Take Issue" talk show is a usually excellent program hosted by Sue Kwon that looks at Bay Area topics Mon. through Thurs. nights. Website: www.baytv.com.
•**KICU** (Channel 36) broadcasts a lot of second-rate TV shows and low-rent movies (it occasionally cuts to commercials in the middle of dialogue). On Sat. and Sun. nights, it airs *Silicon Valley Business This Week,* which reviews local business developments. The station's *High School Sports Focus* does a weekly wrap-up of the South Bay's high school athletics. Website: www.kicu.com.

Radio

Residents listen to the radio frequently while on the road or as background music at work. This being the home of the world's first commercially broadcast radio station, the quality of most of the valley's radio channels is exceptional. Stations in English, Spanish, and Vietnamese are available to suit almost every taste in music and news. Telephone numbers listed below are the request and contest lines.
•**KAZA,** 1290 AM, 408/575-1290 (Spanish radio)
•**KBAY,** 94.5 FM, 408/370-7377; website: www.kbay.com (light rock)
•**KEZR,** Mix 106.5 FM, 408/287-5775; website: www.kezr.com (light rock)
•**KFJC,** 89.7 FM, 650/949-7260 (Foothill Community College)
•**KFOG,** 104.5, 97.7 FM, 800/300-5364; website: www.kfog.com (adult rock)
•**KFOX,** 98.5 FM, 800/788-4369; website: www.kfox.com (classic rock)
•**KGO,** 810 AM, 415/954-8100; website: www.kgoam810.com (news talk)
•**KRTY,** 95.3 FM, 408/575-5789; website: www.krty.com (country)
•**KSJO,** 92 FM, 408/575-1592; website: www.ksjo.com (rock)
•**KSJS,** 90.5 FM, 408/924-4548 (San Jose State University)

MEDICAL AND DENTAL NEEDS

For **medical referrals,** call 408/998-5700. For dental referrals, call 800/336-8478 (DEN-TIST).

ELECTRICITY

As throughout the United States, electricity in Silicon Valley is 110 volts alternating current. Outlet plugs are flat. If you need a special converter, it's best to find one in your own country. Electronics stores such as Fry's or Radio Shack carry some foreign converters, but there's no guarantee that they'll stock the one you need. The primary source of electric power in the region is **Pacific Gas & Electric,** 800/743-5000.

TIME ZONE

Like all of California, Silicon Valley is located in the **Pacific Time** zone, which is eight hours behind Greenwich Mean Time. It's three hours behind New York City, so when it's noon in the Big Apple, it's 9 A.M. here.

For Silicon Valley **current time,** call 408/767-8900.

The first Sunday in April, **daylight saving time** begins, and clocks are moved forward one hour. Six months later, on a Sunday in late October, daylight saving time ends, and clocks are moved back one hour.

MEASUREMENTS

The United States, almost alone among nations, does not use the metric system for measurements. Road distances are measured in miles, shorter distances in feet and inches. For help making conversions, turn to the guide at the back of this book.

Transportation

At the turn of the 19th century on the track at San Jose's long-gone Agricultural Park, road racer Barney Oldfield broke the world's automobile speed record by reaching a heart-pounding 60 miles an hour. At the height of rush hour today, of course, Barney would be pretty lucky to "achieve" about one-tenth of that; and outside of rush hour, he'd be hard pressed even to keep up with most of the drivers traversing the interstates and highways that form a web across Silicon Valley.

Because of its sprawling vastness, the region is extremely oriented toward the car (a statement that pretty much applies to most of California). According to several surveys, transportation is the No. 1 issue of concern for the area's residents. That's not surprising, really, in light of how much time so many locals spend in their vehicles, getting to and from work, home, and shopping centers.

But cars are more than just a form of transportation in the valley. They're also a measure of success. Sport utility vehicles are hugely popular here—the bigger, the more prestigious (although it's been estimated that over 90 percent of Silicon Valley drivers with SUVs have never had any real need to use their four-wheel drive on the urban streets and highways here). You'll also see plenty of BMWs and Porsches—especially in affluent areas such as Los Altos Hills, Saratoga, and Palo Alto.

Even so, if you don't own or drive a car, there *are* other ways of getting to the various destinations throughout the valley.

VALLEY TRANSPORTATION AUTHORITY

The Valley Transportation Authority (VTA) runs a fairly decent mass transit system comprising buses and an ultramodern Light Rail trolley system. However, the region it must serve is so expansive that getting to distant locations can sometimes become a major chore. Buses con-

CHARLEY PARKHURST'S SECRET

Winding through the Santa Cruz Mountains, Hwy. 17 can sometimes seem a treacherous route. But today's paved modern highway would seem an easy traverse compared to the dangerous dirt roads crossing these mountains in the mid-19th century. Passengers wishing to travel from San Jose to Santa Cruz often boarded stagecoaches piloted by drivers known as "whips."

Among these whips was one Charley Parkhurst. Famous for possessing great skill and strength in handling horses, Charley was a coarse and cold character, as adept and practiced in using profanity as he was at driving a stage over wild terrain. In 1858, during a stage run near Redwood City, Charley was kicked in the face by a horse, losing an eye and gaining a deformed jaw. Charley's lips were frequently stained with tobacco juice and—unusual for the profession—he never grew a beard. In fact, Charley possessed a big secret, and kept that secret until death. Although pretending to be a man, Charley was actually a woman.

Born Charlotte Parkhurst in 1812, she began the deception in her teenage years in Vermont by pretending to be a boy to obtain a job at a livery stable. She graduated to driving stagecoaches, eventually handling as many as six horses. Charley drove the overland stage for three years in the Council Bluffs area of Iowa, and perhaps would have stayed on longer if the Mormons there hadn't encouraged matrimonial union so vigorously. Obviously, Charley would have given up her unusual secret if she did marry some surprised young lady.

So she came out to California in the early 1850s and ran a stagecoach over Pacheco Pass in the southern Santa Clara Valley for a short while. Realizing her ability, the Danforth Porter line hired Charley to run the hazardous Santa Cruz–San Jose route. On a Concord stage pulled by six mustangs, Charley could take as many as 20 passengers safely across the mountain range.

The day of the stagecoach ended with the construction of a railroad crossing the Santa Cruz Mountains. Charley gave up her career as a whip to raise livestock on Bear Creek with a mountain man named Frank Woodward. She did this for a number of years, Frank never suspecting his business partner's true gender. Ailing for a short period, she died in December 1879 near Soquel. It was not until the undertaker began preparing the body that the truth came out about Charley Parkhurst's identity. When the deception that had taken place over all those years was revealed, Frank Woodward is said to have cussed a blue streak.

John V. Young provides an interesting footnote to the story in his book *Ghost Towns of the Santa Cruz Mountains.* Charley's name appears in 1866 on the register of voters in Santa Cruz County, and election records show that, under that name, she voted in the election of November 3, 1868. Young suggests that Charlotte Parkhurst can claim to be the first known case in the United States of a woman voting in a public election. This occurred over half a century before the ratification of the 19th Amendment to the Constitution.

---

nect with the valley's rail services as well as the San Jose International Airport. Services follow most major routes throughout the valley, from South Valley communities such as Morgan Hill and Gilroy to the northern cities of Menlo Park, Palo Alto, and Milpitas. VTA's fleet of 460 buses serves 4,600 stops along 72 routes, carrying over 42 million passengers each year.

If you decide to use the area's mass transit system, stop early in your visit at **VTA's Customer Service Center,** located on the corner of North 1st

and Santa Clara Sts. in downtown San Jose (just across the street from the towering Bank of America building). Here you can purchase tickets or a monthly pass. The VTA people will also gladly help you plan any local traveling, providing you with maps, schedules, brochures, and other information. (The center is also home to VTA's lost and found bureau.) It's open Mon.–Fri. 5:30 A.M.–8 P.M. and Sat. 7:30 A.M.–4 P.M.

Single-ride bus **fare** is $1.25 for adults, $.70 for ages 5–17, and $.40 for seniors and riders with

The Light Rail passes through downtown San Jose.

disabilities. A day pass costs $3 for adults, $1.75 for youths, and $1 for seniors and riders with disabilities. Express single rides are $2 for adults, $.70 for youth, and $.40 for seniors and riders with disabilities. Express day passes are $5. VTA tickets can be purchased throughout the valley at government agencies and many businesses, including Longs Drug Stores and selected supermarkets. Bus drivers don't carry change, so make sure you have the exact fare.

For its customers in wheelchairs or those with disabilities that don't allow them to independently use regular and Light Rail services, VTA provides **paratransit** door-to-door transportation. (Proof of disability—such as a certified document by a public transit operator—may be required.) This service is provided seven days a week from 5 A.M. to 2 A.M. and costs $2.20 for a one-way ticket. Reserve a paratransit trip at least one day in advance by calling 408/436-2865.

Bikes are allowed on Light Rail trains and some buses (those equipped with special racks—but the racks can carry only two bikes).

VTA's telephone number is 800/894-9908. Its website is www.vta.org.

Sam Trans, the San Mateo County mass transit service, accepts VTA passes at many of its stops, such as those connecting with Menlo Park and Palo Alto Caltrain stations, Stanford Shopping Center, and Page Mill Rd. at El Camino Real. Call 800/660-4287.

TRAINS

Amtrak

Amtrak serves Silicon Valley seven days a week, stopping at San Jose's Diridon Station, at 65 Cahill St., near the downtown Arena. Call the station at 408/287-7462 or Amtrak toll-free at 800/872-7245.

Caltrain

Caltrain is a good way to get around Silicon Valley's long distances by rail. It follows the route of the historic San Francisco-to-San Jose Railroad track completed in 1864. Over 6.8 million passengers every year ride to Caltrain's 32 stations between Gilroy and San Francisco including stops in San Jose, Sunnyvale, Santa Clara, Palo Alto, and Menlo Park. The ride takes about an hour and a half to get to San Francisco from San Jose. It does go through some unsightly industrial parts of Silicon Valley. From 9 A.M. to 2:30 P.M., a one-way ticket costs $4; it costs $5.25 at all other times. Weekend ticket costs vary, and some passes let you explore the Peninsula by getting on and off anywhere along the route. Call 800/660-4287 for departure times. Buy the ticket at the station with cash only (no credit cards accepted). The Caltrain website is www.transitinfo.org/Caltrain.

BART

In the 1970s, the original proposal for BART (Bay Area Rapid Transit) was to have this train line serve the entire San Francisco Bay Area, with a stop at San Jose. City government in the Silicon Valley failed to foresee the growth that would take place in the area in future years, and their short-sightedness cost the valley access to the system. If you want to get to San Francisco by BART, take VTA's bus 180 from San Jose's First and San Carlos Streets, directly to the Fremont station. A one-way ticket costs $4.05. The train ride takes about one hour and fifteen minutes. Call 510/441-2278. The website is www.transitinfo.org/Bart/

Light Rail

In the 19th and early 20th centuries, the northern portion of Santa Clara Valley had an excellent trolley car system. In the 1930s, this was dismantled by the powers that be, who thought the automobile was transportation's future. The 1980s saw a resurrection of the trolley, although on a much smaller scale. VTA's Light Rail service is a fast and efficient way to travel along a 21-mile corridor stretching from Almaden Valley through downtown San Jose along North 1st Street all the way to Santa Clara's Great America amusement park. A 7.5-mile extension was completed in 1999 that takes passengers from north San Jose to Mountain View, with stops at companies including Cisco Systems, Rolm Siemans, Lockheed Martin, Netscape, and Hewlett-Packard. Over 6.1 million passengers ride the system each year.

Light Rail trains operate seven days a week, 24 hours a day. During the day, trains run every 10 to 15 minutes on weekdays and every 15 minutes on weekends and holidays. During the evening, trains run every half hour. Automated vending machines sell tickets at each station. Single-ride fare is $1.25 for adults, $.70 for ages 5–17, and $.40 for seniors or riders with disabilities. Make sure you have proof of ticket purchase while you're riding the Light Rail or you can be fined. Security guards patrol both trains and stations, which are generally safe.

Altamont Commuter Express

A recent addition to the Silicon Valley rail system is the Altamont Commuter Express (ACE). It serves many of Silicon Valley's workers in Stockton, Modesto, and other cities in the San Joaquin Valley—where land is cheaper and homes are more affordable. The daily commute by car along I-680 is a horrific grind, but in 1998, ACE opened, stretching from Stockton through Altamont Pass to San Jose's Diridon Station. Depending on which zone you travel to, a one-way fare is $3–10, a monthly pass costs $59–279. Call 408/321-2300. The website is www.acerail.com.

Eco Pass

Many of the region's companies are members of a popular VTA program that provides workers with unlimited rides on VTA's buses and Light Rail for an entire year. Called Eco Pass, the employer company must purchase the tax-deductible pass for its workers. Call 408/321-7544.

PLANES

Silicon Valley receives its commercial airplane transportation from two major airports.

San Francisco International Airport

SFO is located about half an hour's drive north of San Jose along U.S. 101. Often, you can save a considerable amount on your ticket by flying into SFO instead of San Jose International (from SFO, Greyhound bus service takes passengers to the downtown San Jose bus terminal). Six terminals provide service for more than 40 commercial airlines. Call 650/876-2377. The website is www.sfoairport.com.

San Jose International Airport

A lot of travel hassle can be avoided by flying into San Jose International Airport (SJC), which is smaller and more manageable than the sometimes chaotic SFO. San Jose International currently has two terminals, although plans are in the development stages for a third. Located close to downtown, the airport is the fourth largest in California, its 13 major commercial carriers serving more than 10 million passengers a year. Call 408/277-4759, website: www.sjc.org.

Terminal A is the more modern and easily maneuverable of the two. At the bottom of the escalators in the baggage claim area, you'll find a helpful visitor's information booth staffed by personnel who'll answer your Silicon Valley travel questions or assist you in finding lodging. On-site car rentals are also at this area. Taxis and hotel shuttles are located just outside the baggage claim area. The older **Terminal C** is an ugly, uncomfortable building which will eventually be modernized. You'll find car rentals in the walkway leading to the baggage claim. A directory board to hotels and shuttle services is located at baggage claim, and taxis and shuttles pick up right across the street.

VTA provides a **free shuttle service** from San Jose International Airport to the Santa Clara

Caltrain Station and the Metro/Airport stop of the Light Rail from 6 A.M. to midnight. Service is every 10 minutes on weekdays and every 15 minutes on weekends. Board this shuttle on the departure side bus stop of Terminal A or across the street from baggage claim at Terminal C.

Smaller Airports and Flying Tours

Three smaller public airports operated by Santa Clara County offer other options. **Reid-Hillview Airport,** 408/929-2256, is located in San Jose's Eastside district, at 2350 Cunningham Avenue. Low-flying private pilots making landings at Reid-Hillview often worry customers at Eastridge Shopping Mall. **South County Airport,** 408/683-4741, is located in San Martin, at 13030 Murphy Ave., and is frequently used for touch-and-goes by the region's student pilots. **Palo Alto Airport,** 650/856-7833, is located next to the bay at 1925 Embarcadero Rd., east of U.S. 101.

If you would like to take a scenic fly-over of Silicon Valley, or a Bay Tour, **Nice Air,** 408/729-3383, based at Reid-Hillview Airport, can oblige.

AUTOMOBILES

"Rush hour" is more than a bit of a misnomer, since at peak commute times the entire freeway looks like a bumper-to-bumper parking lot. Generally speaking and depending on the area of the valley, Silicon Valley's commute is at its worst between 7 and 9 A.M. and 4 and 6 P.M.; though nothing is guaranteed, if you can travel to your destination outside of these hours, you'll usually have a less stressful drive. Certain areas tend to back up during peak hours. One of these is the hellish spot where U.S. 101 merges into I-880—right at the same place that 880 narrows to two lanes. Another area to watch out for during the morning commute is northbound 101 heading from Morgan Hill to the Hwy. 85 overpass. Expect backups here.

California motor vehicle law requires drivers and passengers to wear seat belts, and small children and infants must be placed in child-safe car seats.

Drinking and driving is a serious crime in California. The blood alcohol limit is .08. If you plan on drinking beyond that limit, make sure you have a designated driver or can find a taxi to take you home.

While driving, the Department of Motor Vehicles (DMV) requires that you carry in the vehicle written evidence of financial responsibility. This can include a valid liability insurance policy, a $35,000 surety bond, a DMV-issued self-insurance certificate, or a $35,000 cash deposit with the DMV. For further information, see their website at www.dmv.ca.gov.

For the most part, Silicon Valley drivers are courteous, and the "road rage" seen on Los Angeles highways occurs less frequently here. However, there are rude drivers who will cut others off, or weave dangerously in and out of lanes. Drive-by shootings do occur but are rare.

Diamond lanes are seen on many of the area's highways and expressways to encourage carpooling of at least two people in a vehicle. Carpool times are generally Mon. through Fri. 6–9 A.M. and 3–6 P.M. Single drivers can use it during non-carpool times. Motorcyclists can use the diamond lane any time. Be warned: if you're caught driving in a diamond lane by yourself during lane hours, the fine is a hefty $271—and that's just for your first offense; the cost goes up with subsequent violations.

VTA offers several services to encourage carpooling in the Silicon Valley. It provides a number of **Park & Ride** free parking lots at bus stops and Light Rail stations where commuters can meet a carpool or vanpool. The organization RIDES for Bay Area Commuters provides a free service by supplying a list of people who travel to nearby work locations. Groups of 10–15 commuters can get luxury vans. Call 800/755-7665.

For **road conditions,** call the California Highway Patrol at 800/427-7623.

Gasoline Prices

This can often be a sore point for Silicon Valley commuters, many of whom resent the fact that oil companies take advantage of the area's wealth by gouging buyers at the gas pump (by American standards, that is). Prices can fluctuate drastically; a gallon of regular unleaded fuel can cost from $1.50 to more than $2. Prices go up significant-

GRIDLOCK TORMENT

Longtime residents of the valley still talk about the days when quiet country lanes passed through serene orchards and fields. Those days are only memories now. The country lanes are now busy city streets and highways filled bumper-to-bumper with commuters during Silicon Valley's brutal rush hours.

Silicon Valley's population explosion caused by the abundance of jobs has created a gridlock hell for those who drive to work here. Weekday morning commute hours can be pure torture as cars barely roll forward. Commuters are forced to wake up earlier and earlier to face the increasingly dense morning traffic. Waking up at 3 or 4 A.M. is not exceptional in order to hit the road. And the rush hour for the return home can start as early as 3:30 P.M. for some regions.

It's only projected to get worse as more people move to Silicon Valley and the surrounding towns and cities. One study forecasts that traffic congestion will surge 177 percent in the next 20 years, particularly as San Benito and Monterey Counties to the south see dramatic growth of their populations because of more affordable housing. San Benito County has been hit particularly hard by Silicon Valley's surge. The two lanes of Hwy. 25 that run from the county's community of Hollister to U.S. 101 have turned into a "blood alley" route due to an increasing number of fatal head-on collisions.

Cutting through South Valley, U.S. 101 has also seen a significant increase in traffic congestion with the population explosion. Every workday morning, this route faces a bottleneck just north of Cochrane Road. Construction started in the summer of 2001 to expand this route to three lanes, but the increased traffic flow is projected to create more backups on Hwy. 85 and I-280 farther north.

The lack of an efficient mass transit system is a heated topic of discussion for those who live and/or work in the valley. Part of the problem has been local government's inadequate planning for the major population growth that hit Silicon Valley in the 1990s. People here are willing to pay for mass transit improvements. In the fall election of 2000, the county's voters approved a $6 billion tax plan to extend BART (Bay Area Rapid Transit) tracks from Fremont to San Jose. The plan will also extend Light Rail lines throughout the valley.

But with more and more people pouring in, many disgruntled residents are talking about calling it quits and moving to less-crowded regions. They reason that they might get a fat paycheck here, but what's the point of making gobs of money if so much of their day is spent stuck behind the steering wheel?

ly between Memorial Day and Labor Day. ARCO and Rotten Robbies generally sell good-quality gasoline at the lowest prices. Shell and BP are on the high end.

Freeways

Eight major freeway systems serve Silicon Valley. For the residents who use them daily, these ribbons of asphalt can often seem like old friends, each with its quirks and characteristics.
•**Interstate 280** (known as the Junipero Serra Freeway, after the Spanish missionary) is the most scenic freeway going through the Bay Area. It starts at the San Francisco side of the Oakland Bay Bridge. It makes its way past Daly City, then goes through natural foothill scenery on the west side of the bay. In Cupertino, it reenters urban terrain and generally becomes more congested. The freeway ends when it becomes I-680 at the U.S. 101 spaghetti junction.
•**Interstate 680** (called the Sinclair Freeway, for Joseph P. Sinclair, the district engineer for Caltrans from 1952 to 1954) skirts the Diablo Mountain range, passing through Milpitas and

turning sharply to the northeast near Mission San Jose in Fremont. It's a heavily traveled commute route which has, during Friday afternoon traffic stalls, driven grown men (at least one travel handbook author among them) to tears.

•**Interstate 880** (called the Nimitz, in honor of Admiral Chester W. Nimitz, who commanded the Pacific Fleet during World War II) skirts the eastern edge of Santa Clara, passing near San Jose International Airport (at the Coleman Ave. exit). It passes through a gauntlet of billboards in the homely industrial corridor of north San Jose and Milpitas, continues through Fremont, and roughly follows the east side of the bay until it becomes I-980 in Oakland.

•**Highway 17** begins in the coastal town of Santa Cruz, makes its winding, picturesque way up to the summit of the Santa Cruz Mountains and then down into the valley past Lexington Reservoir, through Los Gatos and Campbell. Where I-280 crosses it, at the Valley Fair Mall, Hwy. 17 becomes I-880.

•**Highway 85** provides a good shortcut to avoid much of the valley's congested highways. This well-designed freeway starts at U.S. 101 in south San Jose, making a graceful curve as it cuts through Hwys. 87 and 17 and I-280 until it reunites with U.S. 101 up by Mountain View.

•**Highway 87** starts from Hwy. 85 near Oakridge Mall, traveling north. Around Alma Ave., the highway foundation is slowly sinking into the ground, creating a roller-coaster effect for several hundred feet. After passing under I-280, it becomes the Guadalupe Pkwy., passing the Civic Center on Hedding Ave. and the San Jose Airport and coming to an end as it merges into U.S. 101.

•**U.S. 101,** the Bayshore Freeway, stretches the length of the West Coast from Los Angeles to northwest Washington, where it makes a loop around the Olympic Peninsula to intersect with I-5 near Olympia. In the Silicon Valley, it passes through the western edge and is considered the main route to Gilroy and Morgan Hill. From downtown San Jose to East Palo Alto, it passes through unscenic industrial territory.

Renting a Car

If you plan to do a lot of traveling within Silicon Valley and don't think you have the patience to wait for buses and trains (or have specialized destinations that aren't served by those modes), you'll certainly enjoy your visit much more driving around in a car. A number of car rental agencies operate branches at the airport and some major hotel chains. A current driver's license is required, and foreign visitors must possess both a valid driver's license from their home country and a current International Driver's License. Price differences between car rental agencies can be considerable, so if you're on a budget, call several, asking for competitive quotes. Major agencies at San Jose International Airport are:

Alamo, 408/288-4658; website: www.goalamo.com
Avis, 408/993-2360; website: www.avis.com
Budget, 408/286-7850; website: www.budgetrentacar.com
Hertz, 408/437-5700; website: www.hertz.com
Enterprise, website: www.pickenterprise.com

TAXIS

Unlike major cities such as San Francisco, Chicago, and New York, it's rare in Silicon Valley to just step to the curb and hail a cab. Usually you or your hotel concierge must call the cab company, which will dispatch a car to come pick you up. Taxis rides aren't cheap in Silicon Valley, but the drivers are usually cordial. Rates are $1.80 at the flagdrop and an additional $1.80 per mile. At San Jose International Airport, the flagdrop is $3.55. If you hire a cab at the airport, you'll pay from $12 to $15 to get to downtown San Jose.

Alpha Cab Express Service, 408/295-9500
American Cab, 408/727-2277
Checker Cab, 408/293-1199
Rainbow Cab Company, 408/271-9900
United Cab, 408/971-1111
Yellow Cab, 408/293-1234

LIMOUSINES

In Silicon Valley, it's no big deal to see a stretch limousine on the freeway. Around here, limos are often used as transportation for some business executives, and you can always imagine that sitting behind those tinted windows is computer gazillionaire Steve Jobs or Larry Ellison talking on the cell phone about some multimillion-dollar deal. (Of course, it's actually more likely a group of teenage kids heading to the high school prom.) If you're in a group of up to 15 people that might like to take a special trip to the Napa wine country or the Monterey coast, a limousine will definitely make your trip a memorable one. Charter rates start at about $45 per hour.

Here are several limo companies that provide special rates for package trips:

New West Limousine, 408/867-1004

Cloud 9 Limousines, 408/999-0999
Krystal Limousines, 408/292-9393 or toll-free 888/292-9393
Expresso Limousines, 408/982-5466 or toll-free 800/675-6654

NATIONAL BUS LINES

Greyhound Bus Lines, 800/231-2222, serves two Silicon Valley terminals. Downtown San Jose Greyhound bus station, 408/295-4151, is located at 70 South Almaden Ave. near the Plaza de César Chávez. Gilroy's Greyhound stop, 408/847-7610, is located at the Gilroy Caltrain station.

A USER'S GUIDE

The Cities of the Valley

Although the world knows it mainly for high-technology developments, Silicon Valley still exists very much on the human level—a place composed of communities where people live and work. And each of the region's cities has its own particular persona, a definitive character that makes it a unique part of the valley. To fully appreciate—let alone understand—Silicon Valley, you need to treat yourself by visiting these communities and seeing how each one works in conjunction with the others to create the dynamic economy and distinctive culture of this region. This chapter presents a profile of each of the cities that make up Silicon Valley.

Wallace Stegner, local hero and founder of the world-renowned Stegner Writing Program at Stanford University, once wrote, "Local history is the best history, the history with more of ourselves in it than other kinds." It may come as a surprise that these cities have pasts that actually predate the innovations in that famous Palo Alto garage that gave rise to Hewlett-Packard and, in turn, the computer industry. But they do—in some cases much more colorful pasts than would seem possible for suburbs on the fringes of the technology industry. Therefore, each profile includes a sketch of the city's history. It also includes a driving-walking tour that showcases each city's natural beauty, architectural gems, intriguing people, and important historic events.

Joseph D. Grant County Park

© MARTIN CHEEK

Menlo Park

Two loud horn blasts and the heavy throbbing of a diesel engine reverberate through downtown Menlo Park as the Caltrain locomotive ambles to a stop. These familiar sounds are heard here daily—a fitting reminder of its origins as a railroad town. The only Silicon Valley community not located within Santa Clara County, Menlo Park is an economically vibrant city with a strong historic connection to Stanford University. With a population of just over 32,000 people, the community is home to so many venture capital companies, high-tech workers, and Stanford professors and researchers that it is a driving force in Silicon Valley's success. A healthy number of software start-ups and biotechnology companies have put down stakes here, and with the boom in Silicon Valley, Menlo Park has achieved a good residential/industrial mix. Revenues coming in from the growing number of successful companies basing their operations here have helped fund redevelopment throughout the city, especially the downtown area.

Menlo Park is located on the southern tip of San Mateo County. It's bordered on the west by the Stanford University–owned foothill lands that make up the Jasper Ridge Biological Preserve. To the north is the millionaires' enclave of Atherton. To the east it borders San Francisco Bay marshlands and East Palo Alto. And to the south it's separated from Palo Alto and the Stanford campus by San Francisquito Creek, the city's southern boundary.

Geographically, Menlo Park's official city limits are broken into two sections divided by the unincorporated community of West Menlo Park. The smaller Sharon Heights district makes up the western segment, which includes beautiful homes set around the Sharon Heights Golf and Country Club. In this district are the facilities for Stanford University's two-mile-long linear accelerator, a scientific wonder designed to break down atoms to their most elementary particles. And along Sand Hill Rd., known as "Venture Capital Row," are a number of companies that have sustained the growth of Silicon Valley's

© MARTIN CHEEK

The Menlo Park train station, built in 1867, is still in operation.

CITIES OF THE VALLEY

high-tech companies by providing important financial backing.

The heart of Menlo Park is made up of mature neighborhoods filled with a bounty of oak, poplar, and other large trees. This section also contains Menlo Park's downtown business district, which stretches along Santa Cruz Ave. a few blocks from El Camino Real, the bustling thoroughfare running like a thread almost clear to San Francisco in the north. The downtown area is well supplied with pricey restaurants and upscale boutiques. Just west of downtown is the Menlo Park Civic Center and the landmark Caltrain depot. In the Middlefield-Willow Rd. area are various organizations, including St. Patrick's Seminary, *Sunset* Magazine headquarters, the United States Geological Survey's western branch, and SRI International, one of Silicon Valley's most significant research facilities. Rural land of the Bayfront Park and San Francisco Bay National Wildlife Refuge borders Menlo Park's northeastern corner, but high-tech businesses have been settling into this area. Near the Dumbarton Bridge, where Willow Rd. meets Hwy. 84, Sun Microsystems has built a vast campus with an interesting village-like architectural style.

Menlo Park puts on several community events throughout the year, including a Fine Arts Festival and an old-fashioned Fourth of July Parade. Cultural activity centers around the Menlo Park

VENTURE CAPITAL ROW

Forget Las Vegas. That's a place strictly for amateurs. If you want to take part in some *serious* gambling action, the high-stakes stuff that changes the course of history, you've got to head to Menlo Park's Sand Hill Road. Known as Venture Capital Row, this district has the world's highest concentration of venture capital companies. They're all gambling on (or, as they prefer to put it, investing in) the future success of Silicon Valley's brightest high-tech start-ups. In boom times or downturns, venture capitalists (VCs) are the financial engine that run the area's economy.

Want some figures? In 1998, VCs invested a whopping $4.55 billion into area start-ups—an average of $5.8 million *per company* in 786 Silicon Valley businesses seeking financial backing. E-commerce and Internet companies were the blazing hot bets, and more than $1.3 billion was placed in various online companies such as eBay, the thriving Web auction house. In 1998, Silicon Valley received about one-third of all venture capital investments made in the nation, according to accounting firm PricewaterhouseCoopers LLP. The runner-up, receiving $561 million (15 percent), was the Boston–New England area. In the fourth quarter of 1998, the money pie was divided into the following portions in Silicon Valley (figures coming from the *San Jose Mercury News*). Internet companies received about one-third of all venture capital invested, communications companies got about 29 percent, software firms 12 percent, biotech and medical product makers another 12 percent, semiconductors 8 percent, and computer peripherals 4 percent. Of course, with the economic downturn at the start of the new millennium, a lot of this venture capital money (especially the dollars spent on dot-com companies) never gave the investors much return.

It's debatable, but some consider the first true Silicon Valley venture capitalist to be David Starr Jordan, the first president of Stanford University. In 1909, Jordan invested $500 in Cyril Elwell's Poulsen Wireless Telephone and Telegraph Company. In more recent years, the undisputed "King of VC" is Arthur Rock, a name not well known outside of Silicon Valley. He has been instrumental in quite a few deals that have shaped the course of technology. As a Boston-based investor in 1957, Rock helped William Shockley's "Traitorous Eight" get the backing to form Fairchild Semiconductors, a firm that has spun off more than 50 high-tech companies in the valley. To get Intel going in 1968, Rock made a few phone calls and, within half an hour, found the seed money to build what is now the largest semiconductor manufacturer in the world. In 1976, he met with Mike Markkula and two computer nerds in their 20s—Steve Jobs and Steve Wozniak—who wanted to build a company with the unlikely name of Apple Computer.

Start-ups looking for initial financial backing expect to be turned down quite a few times. Even successes such as Cisco Systems and Silicon Graphics got numerous negative responses from VCs who didn't believe they had a chance. Investors interested in high-tech can be found throughout Silicon Valley and in the financial districts of San Francisco, New York, Boston, Los Angeles, and other major cities. Along Menlo Park's Venture Capital Row, here are some of the major players:
- Institutional Venture Partners, 650/854-0132
- Interwest Partners, 650/854-8585
- Mayfield Fund, 650/854-5560
- McCown De Leeuw & Co., 650/854-6000
- Mohr Davidow Ventures, 650/854-7236
- U.S. Venture Partners, 650/854-9080

Players Guild, which puts on plays at the Burgess Theatre, and the historic Allied Arts Guild, a complex designed in the classical style of Spain's Granada. For train buffs, near the railroad station is a building housing the West Bay Model Railroad Association (open to the public twice a month), a large collection of railroad miniatures. The city also has nine small public parks.

HISTORY

The territory that Menlo Park now sits upon was once part of a Mexican land grant called Rancho de las Pulgas (Ranch of the Fleas). According to legend, it received this name when during a 1769 expedition, explorer Portolá's band of men found an abandoned Indian hut and spent the night in it. Their sleep was cut short when fleas started biting the men, and they ran out cursing the tiny pests. The area experienced little development until November 26, 1835, when Mexico's governor of California Jose Castro granted the land to the widow and heir of Don Luis Antonio Arguello. Arguello was the first native-born governor of California, serving from 1823 to 1825.

In 1854, 1,700 oak-covered acres were sold to two Irish brothers-in-law, Dennis J. Oliver and D. C. McGlynn, who built two houses here, intending to raise cattle. Across the entrance to their estate, they built an arching wood gateway, upon which they inscribed in foot-tall letters the words "Menlo Park." This was an anglicized version of the Gaelic "Menlough," their hometown in the Irish county of Galway. Although the two left the area after living here only a few years, the gateway became a local landmark, weathering the elements for almost seven decades until it was accidentally destroyed when a car hit it on July 7, 1922.

In 1863, the San Francisco–San Jose railroad was in the process of being built, and a major part of the project was a bridge fording the San Francisquito Creek (next to the spot where Portolá's men camped under the landmark tree *el palo alto*). The temporary end of the line, where bridge-building materials and food were delivered, was near the spot where the Menlo Park

gateway stood. Thus, the railroad designated this station Menlo Park. Upon completion of the bridge, the railroad had an inauguration ride on October 17, 1863, transporting 500 of San Francisco's most prominent citizens down the line for an elaborate ceremony in what is now Palo Alto. Among the celebrants that day was Governor Leland Stanford, who got his first view of the land that would eventually become his horse farm and later a world-famous university.

Menlo Park's first station house, a virtual shack, stood for only a few years. It was later placed on a flat car and taken to serve as the station house in the town of Belmont farther north along the line. In 1867, a Victorian gingerbread-style station was built to more adequately take care of the needs of the bustling railroad's passengers. This structure became the seed from which the community of Menlo Park sprung. As more people moved into the area, there popped up a few small houses, stores, saloons, and boardinghouses. For Catholic worship, the small Church of the Nativity was built in 1872, the city's first church. Two years later, the Presbyterian residents built a frame structure church on what is now Santa Cruz Ave., just west of El Camino Real. Menlo Park was officially incorporated on March 23, 1874, to allow for improvements to the road, but this incorporation lapsed after two years and was not renewed until half a century later.

Mansions

Among the town's original residents was an Ohioan named Milton S. Latham, who had come to California in 1850 during the Gold Rush. In 1859, he was elected governor of the state. He left that office after five days, the shortest term of any California state governor, to serve in the U.S. Senate. Latham filled the vacancy left by Senator David C. Broderick, a Union sympathizer slain in a pistol duel with David C. Terry, California's Chief Justice of the Supreme Court and a pro-Southerner. (This dramatic fight took place in what's now Daly City and was seen as a forerunner to the bloodshed of the approaching Civil War.) For his retirement years, Latham bought land near the Menlo Park station from John T. Doyle in 1871. In an area now occupied by the city's Civic Center, he built an elaborate 50-room country estate with intricate water fountains placed in a beautifully landscaped garden. He became the first of many of California's newly rich inhabitants to settle in Menlo Park. Bankrupt from his extravagant spending, he died in 1883.

The town's serene setting in the coastal mountain range and its perfect climate drew many of San Francisco's wealthy here as well as to nearby Atherton. Some of 19th-century Bay Area's most important families, including those of railroad barons Leland Stanford and Mark Hopkins, followed in Latham's footsteps, creating country estates where they could retreat during the summer. Here in this oak-dotted paradise, they built magnificent mansions rivaling the finest on the East Coast. Among Menlo Park's early visitors was inventor Thomas Edison. Local legend has it that Edison was so impressed by the area's beauty, he later christened his own New Jersey "invention factory" Menlo Park after the California town. Edison would later be known as "the Wizard of Menlo Park" (the New Jersey one).

By the 1890s, Menlo Park was a community of about 400 people and growing in prominence in California. Its depot served as the stop for students and faculty heading to the recently opened Stanford University. On April 29, 1891, President Benjamin Harrison stepped off his special train at Menlo Park's depot to the awaiting Stanford procession of six carriages that took him and his party to lunch at the newly built campus. As the railroad brought more people to the area, residents started a Town Improvement Club to renovate the community. Concrete sidewalks were constructed on once-muddy streets, and pipes were laid to bring running water into homes. In the 1890s, San Francisco archbishop Patrick W. Riordan noticed a shortage of parish priests for the growing number of churches in his archdiocese. Menlo Park resident Kate Johnson donated 86 acres of her farmland along Middlefield Rd. to build a new seminary campus. Designed in a spacious Romanesque style by Charles I. Devlin, the red brick St. Patrick's Seminary was dedicated by Riordan and more

than 100 priests on August 24, 1898. By the turn of the 19th century, the town had become a center of religious instruction.

Camp Fremont

During World War I, 1,300 acres of land in Menlo Park's eastern section became home to more than 43,000 U.S. soldiers who were training to fight in Europe. Called Camp Fremont after the explorer John C. Frémont, the army base made up of tents and barracks stood for a year and a half. The town's atmosphere changed considerably as it found itself playing host to thousands of soldiers. The military considered making Camp Fremont a permanent installation, but with the war's end in 1919, the camp was quickly disbanded and Menlo Park went back to its quiet affluence.

In the mid-1920s, with a population of almost 2,000 people, it was time for a second incorporation, and Menlo Park planned to include the adjacent community of Atherton as part of its boundaries. Atherton's residents, however, wanted their community to remain a separate entity. The two communities' representatives made a mad dash to the San Mateo County Courthouse in Redwood City to file their respective papers, but the Atherton people won the race by a few minutes, thus preventing Menlo Park from incorporating their land. Menlo Park residents voted for incorporation for the second time on November 15, 1927.

With the postwar boom, Menlo Park's population grew substantially. In 1945, its population was 4,182. The next year, that number had risen to 7,180 people. Also in 1946, the seeds were planted to make Menlo Park a vibrant community vitally important in the development of what would later be known as Silicon Valley. That year Stanford University joined with business executives in establishing Stanford Research Institute in Menlo Park. Now known as SRI International, this nonprofit laboratory had the mission of bringing newfound technologies into the commercial market.

Starting in the 1970s with the onslaught of high-tech in Silicon Valley, Menlo Park's close proximity to Stanford allowed it to reap much of the economic benefits from the research done there. A considerable amount of that financial bounty has come from venture capital companies setting up offices throughout the city, most notably along Sand Hill Road.

TOUR

A tour of Menlo Park begins in the Sharon Heights district in the foothills and ends with a look at the bayfront area where the Sun Microsystems facility is located. Take I-280 north and get off at the Sand Hill Rd. exit. Head east down this foothills road known as **Venture Capital Row;** on your right, you'll pass the entrance to the **Stanford Linear Accelerator,** 650/926-3300, a two-mile-long site where scientists send atoms hurtling at speeds approaching light to break them up into their most elementary particles. Take a look from Sand Hill Rd. at sparkling San Francisco Bay, as well as the top of Stanford University's Hoover Tower. On your left across from Stanford Hills Park is the **Sharon Heights Shopping Center,** 650/854-5053. The Sharon Heights district was named after a magnificent 32-room mansion built here after the 1906 earthquake by Frederick Sharon, son of Comstock silver king William Sharon. Now gone, the estate had immense grounds requiring 30 full-time gardeners and 70 part-time helpers.

Turn left at the stoplight intersection onto Santa Cruz Ave. and follow this briefly through the unincorporated area of **West Menlo Park.** At one point here, the road divides at a stoplight, the left lane is the Alameda de las Pulgas (Way of the Fleas), which heads into a small shopping and residential area. But continue along Santa Cruz Ave. as it curves to the right. At Oakdell Ave., you'll be returning into Menlo Park. Turn right on Oakdell, and follow it for several blocks through an older neighborhood until it ends at Olive Street. Turn right at Olive, drive a short distance to Middle Ave. and turn left here. Follow Middle Ave. for about seven blocks until the Arbor Rd. intersection; turn right onto Arbor Road. Follow Arbor a short distance until you reach a stop sign. On your right immediately after the stop, you'll see the historic **Allied Arts**

Guild, 650/322-2405, on Arbor Road. Originally built in 1929 as an artists' community, it has evolved into a collection of art shops in a gardenlike setting. Among the working studios still here is one run by sculptor **Robert Browne,** 650/325-6832, an artist whose work often shows a mischievous sense of humor. His *From Trilobites to Gigabytes* work provides an interesting look at evolution and the development of high-tech. The **Allied Arts Guild Restaurant,** 650/324-2588, serves food prepared by volunteers of the Palo Alto Auxiliary, and proceeds go to fund the Lucile Salter Packard Children's Hospital at Stanford. Expect to spend at least one hour browsing through the guild shops.

Head down Arbor Rd. back to Middle Ave. and turn right at the stop sign. Two blocks after passing **Nealon Park** on your left, you'll reach the stoplight intersection of El Camino Real. Turn left here, and travel four blocks north along this route to the stoplight intersection of Santa Cruz Ave., where you will turn left and enter Menlo Park's downtown shopping district. You'll find many parking lots on side streets, but these can fill up quickly during busy shopping days such as holidays and weekends. This downtown area can bustle with a vitality at these times as shoppers come to browse the upscale boutiques as well as eat at its fine bistros. One of these eateries, **The Left Bank,** 650/473-6543, with its French decor and music, makes you feel as if you're visiting a well-run Parisian café. Also downtown you'll find several rug dealers, including **St. Clair Gallery,** 650/321-8495, which sells exquisite handmade rugs. Among the more interesting art shops to visit is **Folk Art International,** 650/329-9999, at 871 Santa Cruz Ave., which contains an extensive collection of antiques and finely crafted art pieces from Africa, Asia, and Latin America. It's worth browsing through the large store and gallery for its collection, which includes jewelry, masks, and puppets.

Take a walk across El Camino Real, and at the southeastern corner you'll find the brick Federal-style **British Bankers Club Building,** 650/327-8769, erected in 1926. Now a pub and restaurant, it was originally built as the American Trust Bank. Later, it served as the growing town's

SMASHING ATOMS AT SLAC

Silicon Valley is a place of extremes. The Hubble Space Telescope, built in Sunnyvale's Lockheed Martin Missiles & Space plant, has been used to peer across vast celestial distances and see stars forming in galactic clouds. On the opposite end of the size spectrum, Menlo Park's Stanford Linear Accelerator is a tool used by scientists searching for the smallest particles of matter.

Known by the rather unprepossessing acronym of SLAC, the multimillion-dollar laboratory was conceived in the mid-1950s by Dr. Wolfgang K. H. Panofsky. He suggested building a two-mile-long laboratory to "smash atoms" in an effort to discover *their* component pieces. SLAC was founded in 1962, and the 426-acre facility, set on foothill land belonging to Stanford University, was completed in 1966. Two years later, SLAC scientists discovered evidence for quarks, which make up hadrons—particles that "feel" the strong nuclear force. (These particles were named by physicist Murray Gell-Mann, quoting a line from James Joyce's *Finnegan's Wake:* "Three quarks for Muster Mark!")

In the 1970s, SLAC scientists discovered the psi particle, and the tau and charm leptons—particles with a half-integral spin that "feel" the *weak* nuclear force. In 1975, it was in an auditorium on the premises that the Homebrew Computer Club, which met there frequently, bore witness to Steve Wozniak's first unveiling of a machine he called a personal computer, the Apple I.

SLAC is a National Historic Engineering Landmark. Exhibits in a small visitor center open to the public showcase much of the theoretical and experimental research done here on particle physics. On display is a cosmic ray detector that demonstrates how high-energy particles striking Earth's upper atmosphere produce muon particles—which are counted as they hit the display. A Nobel Prize exhibit presents reproductions of medals awarded for various discoveries made at SLAC by scientists Burton Richter, Richard Taylor, and Martin Perl. For kids, one of the more fascinating exhibits is the replicated *paleoparadoxia* fossils, which were discovered on October 2, 1964, during construction of the accelerator. This extinct creature was a large, plant-eating marine mammal that lived in the area 10 to 20 million years ago.

SLAC, 2575 Sand Hill Rd. (just east of I-280), provides free, guided two-hour tours (10 A.M. and 1 P.M.) several times a week. These tours are extremely popular, so make a reservation far in advance by calling the public affairs office, 650/926-2204, website: www.slac.stanford.edu. Admission and parking are both free. Open Mon.–Fri. 8 A.M.–5 P.M.

city hall, library, and police station. The nearby **Wessex Bookstore,** 558 Santa Cruz Ave., 650/321-1333, was the original site of the Menlo French Laundry. According to a local legend, before a presidential visit by William McKinley, Jane Stanford ordered her servant to send the fine linens across the country to New York City to be laundered. Misinterpreting the order, the servant instead took the tablecloths to this local laundry shop. Jane found the local laundry had done such an excellent job that she continued using its services for the rest of her life.

Where Santa Cruz Ave. ends at Merrill St., you'll find the historic Menlo Park railroad station. This dignified Victorian, at 1100 Merrill St.,

now serves as the **Menlo Park Chamber of Commerce,** 650/325-2818, which will provide you with information on community events. Built in 1867, the structure is considered California's oldest station still in use. Leland Stanford, Mark Hopkins, and other men of wealth and their wives would step off the train and pass through this station to reach their waiting horse-drawn carriages.

After returning to your car, drive east along Santa Cruz Ave. back to El Camino Real and turn right at the stoplight. Go one block to the next stoplight at Ravenswood Ave. and turn left here. After crossing the Caltrain tracks, you'll see on your right the **Menlo Park Civic Center.**

On the basement floor of the public library here, the Menlo Park Historical Association keeps its small **History Room,** 650/858-3368. Friendly historical association volunteers help visitors find information on Menlo Park's history. It's open Tues. and Wed. from 10 A.M.–2 P.M. The Civic Center complex was built on land owned by Mark Hopkins, one of the "Big Four" railroad tycoons who encouraged Leland Stanford to move to this area. His magnificent estate is now gone except for the **gatehouse,** which you can observe on your right at 555 Ravenswood. It was once part of the 380-acre estate originally owned by William Eustance Barron, a Gold Rush–era pioneer who made his wealth from the New Almaden mercury mines south of San Jose.

At the southeastern corner of Ravenswood and Laurel Dr., you'll see a complex of buildings belonging to **SRI International,** a nonprofit organization that created much of the technology that began Silicon Valley. Turn left on Laurel and drive through a quiet residential block. At the stop sign on Oak Grove, take a moment to view on your left the tree-enshrouded 12-acre **Vallombrosa** (Shady Valley), once belonging to the estate of Edward Hopkins, a nephew of Mark Hopkins. In 1947, the grounds became a retreat for the Archdiocese of San Francisco. Turn to your right and continue driving a short distance along Oak Grove. On your left, the charming white steepled building at 210 Oak Grove Ave. is the **Church of the Nativity,** 650/323-7914. Built in a Victorian Gothic style, it has been dubbed "the Roamin' Catholic Church" because it was moved several times before finally coming to this spot. Early in its history, the area's Irish-Catholic population used it as a school as well as for religious and social purposes. The church welcomes visitors.

Continue along Oak Grove Ave., and you will enter for a short time the city limits of Atherton. This wealthy community is home to many of the valley's corporate executives, including Oracle CEO Larry Ellison. At the stoplight, turn right on Middlefield Rd. and continue along it, passing the eastern boundaries of SRI's property. On your right at 345 Middlefield Rd., you'll come to the western region office of the **U.S.**

Geological Survey, 650/329-4390. Here, the public is welcome to visit the **Earth Science Information Center,** which has mapmaking and geology displays. You can buy maps for about $4 and pick up free booklets and other literature on geological topics such as earthquakes and volcanoes. Plan to spend about 20 to 30 minutes here.

Continue south along Middlefield Road. The property on your left belongs to **St. Patrick's Seminary.** At the intersection of Willow Rd., you'll find the headquarters of *Sunset* Magazine, 650/321-3600. The immensely popular monthly publication is known as the West's premier home and lifestyle magazine. Founded in 1898 as a Southern Pacific Railroad marketing tool to lure East Coast tourists to the rugged West, it was named after a train called the Sunset Limited, which had a route from New Orleans to Los Angeles. Among its early celebrated writers were Jack London, Mark Twain, Dashiell Hammett, and western novelist Zane Grey. In 1990, the magazine was bought from the Laurence Lane family by Time Warner, and now is read by about 6 million people. Here at its California ranch-style complex, take a stroll through the famous **gardens** bordering the San Francisquito Creek. From the front lobby desk, pick up a brochure that describes the garden's flora, from major western climate zones such as the Arizona desert and Washington rainforest. The gardens are best visited during spring, when the tulips come out. Admission is free; plan to spend about 45 minutes here.

Take Willow Rd. east through a commercially zoned area for about three-quarters of a mile. On your left, you'll see the **U.S. Veterans Hospital.** Cross the U.S. 101 overpass and take its northbound entrance heading toward San Francisco. Drive along U.S. 101 for about 1.5 miles and take the Marsh Rd. exit, keeping to the far right lane and heading toward the bay. After crossing the stoplight intersection at Bayfront Expwy., enter **Bayfront Park,** 650/366-6609. Built on landfill, this small park provides walks along levees crossing through tidal lands as well as breathtaking vistas from its hills. To the southeast is the Dumbarton Bridge, heading into Newark, and to the northeast is the San Mateo Bridge. Plan to spend about an hour exploring this city park, but bring a jacket or sweater as it can get windy in the afternoons.

At the stoplight just outside the park entrance, turn left onto Bayfront Expwy., and take this scenic route that follows tidal lands on your left. About a mile from the park, you'll come to a stoplight intersection for Willow Road. The large townlike complex of office buildings on your left belongs to **Sun Microsystems.** Turn right at Willow Rd. and follow it west for about half a mile back to U.S. 101. The northbound entrance heads to San Francisco and the southbound leads to San Jose.

© MARTIN CHEEK

Menlo Park's lovely Church of the Nativity has been relocated so many times that it's sometimes called "the Roamin' Catholic Church."

POINTS OF INTEREST

United States Geological Survey

Map fans will enjoy a stop at the USGS's Silicon Valley base. On the ground floor is the Earth Science Information Center, where visitors can learn about geologic, hydrologic, cartographic, and biologic topics. The center also has general information areas providing aerial and satellite imagery and digital maps. A large rack here contains a treasure trove of free pamphlets informing the public on such topics as dinosaurs, the stones used to build national monuments, and volcanoes in the United States. The center is a popular Christmas gift shopping site for locals, who come here during the holidays to buy detailed maps (most priced at $4). These maps cover many locations throughout the western United States. A small museum off the entrance lobby provides various exhibits on natural science and cartography. Also open to the public is a reference library containing an immense collection of material focusing on earth science.

345 Middlefield Rd. (across from Seminary Dr.), 650/853-8300; public events calendar recording 650/329-5000; website: www.usgs.gov; free parking in lots behind buildings; admission free; open Mon.–Fri. 8 A.M.–4 P.M.

Church of the Nativity

Menlo Park's most historic religious structure has earned its nickname of "the Roamin' Catholic

Church." The Victorian Gothic Revival building was constructed in 1872 at the corner of Middlefield and Ringwood Rds., then moved five years later to Santa Cruz Avenue. The following year it was relocated to its present spot on Oak Grove Avenue. The beautiful church features a 1,200-pound bell, which was first rung on Christmas Day 1881, and a stained-glass rose window added in 1900. Pope Pius IX blessed the church's hand-wrought crucifix. In 1977, the church was listed on the National Register of Historic Places.

210 Oak Grove Ave. (between Marcussen Dr. and Middlefield Rd.), 650/323-7914; parking in church lot; admission free; God's house open 24 hours a day.

Allied Arts Guild

Set in a quiet, tree-lined neighborhood near the San Francisquito Creek, this California landmark was built by Garfield and Delight Merner, Menlo Park residents who, while on vacation in Spain, were enchanted by the historic Granada. Inspired, in 1929 they had architect Gardner Dailey and artist Pedro de Lemos design a Spanish classical building and grounds that would serve as an arts guild. Stone and brick pathways take visitors through patios and courtyards decorated with murals, statues, and water fountains. The gardens feature roses, citrus trees, and flowerbeds brilliant with annuals and peren-

SRI INTERNATIONAL

After World War II, in light of an increasing reliance on science and technology in the postwar world, Stanford University administrators such as Frederick Terman saw a need for more efficient ways of channeling university lab research—primarily discoveries in the areas of electronics, chemistry, and physics—to the business world for dissemination into the commercial market. In 1946, Stanford developed a then-unique nonprofit organization for connecting commerce with research. Called the Stanford Research Institute (later abbreviated as SRI International), the organization is headquartered in Menlo Park and has become one of the United States' most important research facilities.

Many of the discoveries coming out of SRI have had an effect on daily life and can be found in most homes and businesses. Its first success, in 1946, was the development of dodecyl benzene, a petrochemical product used in creating economical household detergents. In the 1950s, the organization won an Academy Award for its invention of the Technicolor electronic printer timer, which enhanced the color quality in movies. That same decade, it created a prototype system for automatic checking and account bookkeeping called ERMA (Electronic Recording Method of Accounting).

During the 1960s, SRI researchers helped develop the ARPANET, the foundation network for what would later become the Internet. SRI's Menlo Park node received the first message across this embryonic communications network. The organization also worked on developing the first liquid crystal display (LCD) and the acoustic modem—originally invented to help deaf people communicate over the phone but later used to let computers communicate with each other across transmission lines.

In 1970, SRI officially separated from Stanford University. Among its developments during this decade were pen-input computing (which recognizes handwritten words and symbols), packet-switched radio, and ultrasonic imagery, in which ultrasound waves are used to form X-ray-like pictures. During the 1980s, SRI developed the stealth technology used in such weapons as the Air Force's F-117. Its Sarnoff Corporation, a for-profit subsidiary, developed high-definition television technology. The 1990s have seen SRI developing such technologies as telepresence surgery (where doctors can use computers and robotics to remotely operate on a patient). Its medical advances include Tirapazamine, a drug used to combat cancer.

Today, about 2,700 engineers and scientists work in SRI's various research facilities. Its clients include Charles Schwab, Hitachi, Toshiba, and Sanyo. Its discoveries in electronics and pharmaceuticals have started 15 spin-off companies, among them Genetrace Systems, which provides proprietary genetic analysis. In the 1990s, more than $1 billion was spent on U.S. government-sponsored SRI projects ranging from military technology for the Department of Defense to research for the National Cancer Institute. Website: www.sri.com.

nials. Today, while there are few actual working artists here, visitors can browse through a number of boutiques and antique shops as well as enjoy a buffet lunch at the restaurant staffed by volunteers.

75 Arbor Rd. (near stop-sign intersection of Cambridge Ave.), 650/322-2405, website: www.alliedartsguild.org; parking on street and in lot; admission free; open Mon.–Sat. 10 A.M.–5 P.M.

Sunset Magazine Gardens

Visitors from throughout the world stop to stroll through the spacious gardens located at the headquarters of "The Magazine of Western Living." Built in 1952, the main building was designed by architect Cliff May, considered "the father of the California ranch-style home." From the lobby receptionist, pick up a free brochure detailing a walking tour and step through the sliding-glass door into the gorgeously landscaped 15-acre garden designed by Thomas Church. A well-kept 1.2-acre lawn serves as the stunning centerpiece. Surrounding this, flora growing in various sections reflect the West's major climate regions, including California's Central Valley, the Pacific Northwest, and the Southwest desert. Take a peek at the 3,200-square-foot test garden for plant projects to be featured in upcoming editions.

80 Willow Rd. (at Middlefield Rd.), 650/321-3600, website: www.sunsetmagazine.com; parking on street; admission free; open weekdays except major holidays 9 A.M.–4:30 P.M.

Bayfront Park

Set along the San Francisco Bay, this wilderness-like setting was a landfill area developed into a public park in 1981. It's a popular place for jogging and walking dogs along trails meandering through marshlands. The park's grass-swept hills make perfect places for flying kites on bay breezes.

Unhewn stones clustered on a three-quarter-mile trail represent Native American pictographs. Placed here by Menlo Park artist S. C. Dunlap during the park's construction, they are meant to create a "visual poem" (explained in a free brochure at the trailhead). Made with 505 tons of rocks, it's considered the world's largest sculpture of its kind. Vistas include the Dumbarton and San Mateo Bridges.

End of Marsh Rd. (from U.S. 101, take Marsh Rd. exit one block east to the Bay), 650/366-6609; free admission; open daily 7 A.M.–sunset.

Filoli Center

Most of Menlo Park's celebrated mansions no longer exist, but if you want to get a sense of what they might have been like, visit the Filoli Mansion in nearby Woodside. Designed in 1916 by architect Willis Polk, the spectacular 43-room Georgian mansion served as the home of William Bourne, a Gold Rush millionaire. The estate's unusual name comes from a combination of letters from his motto "Fight, Love, and Live." Located in the foothills a couple of miles from Menlo Park, the estate and its surrounding 16-acre garden has been the setting for movies such as Warren Beatty's *Heaven Can Wait* and the TV series *Dynasty*. Wander through the ornately decorated rooms, where volunteers explain the mansion's history, then stroll through the well-tended botanical gardens. The best time to visit is spring, but a variety of flowers are in bloom through much of the year.

Cañada Rd. in Woodside (from Menlo Park, take I-280 north to Edgewood Rd. exit; after 200 yards, turn right on Cañada Rd. and drive 1.25 miles—house will be on your left), 650/364-8300, website: www.filoli.org; admission $10 for adults, $1 for children under 12; open Tues.–Sat. 10 A.M.–3 P.M. Docent-led tours by reservation.

Palo Alto

Palo Alto is Silicon Valley's college town. Its history and that of Stanford University are closely intertwined, going back to the late 19th century, when Leland and Jane Stanford founded their esteemed institution of higher education. Perhaps because of the university's influence, the more than 62,000 people who live in the city are some of the best educated in the nation. About 80 percent of its high school graduates go on to college. One-third of its adults over 25 years of age have at least one graduate degree, and 65 percent have four years or more of college education. Many of Silicon Valley's high-tech companies sprang from the discoveries and inventions conceived by the university's brilliant minds. Palo Alto can truly call itself "the birthplace of Silicon Valley."

But despite the broad shadow the university casts upon the city, Palo Alto is more than just Stanford University. It is a city of well-kept neighborhoods, many of which are set among natural surroundings of creeks and trees. The community has successfully integrated its flourishing business environment with quiet residential streets of middle- and upper-class homes. Its 26 square miles contain 34 parks, public gardens, and nature preserves totaling 4,100 acres. The city's terrain ranges from the marshlands along the San Francisco Bay in the east to the foothills and Skyline Ridge of the Santa Cruz Mountains on the west. It is bordered on the south by Los Altos, on the north by Menlo Park, and on the northeast corner by East Palo Alto (a separately incorporated community that's part of San Mateo County).

Palo Alto also has more than its share of historic homes and sites. Among its more impressive buildings is the John A. Squire House at 900 University Ave., a magnificent Greek Revival building modeled after the University of Virginia's Pavilion designed by Thomas Jefferson. The Palo Alto Historical Association has made the structure its headquarters. The 15-room Hoover House, at 623 Mirada Ave. on top of Stanford's San Juan Hill, was originally built for

© MARTIN CHEEK

CITIES OF THE VALLEY

Hoover Tower, at Stanford University in Palo Alto

the university's most famous graduate, Herbert Hoover. He lived here before and after his presidency, and heard the news of his 1928 election victory from the residence. Also on Stanford's campus is Leland Stanford's Red Barn, which stands at the end of Electioneer Road. At this still rural site, the fundamentals of moving pictures were discovered.

As one of Silicon Valley's more affluent cities, Palo Alto has a thriving retail core as well as corporate businesses. Its University Ave. area is Silicon Valley's most bustling downtown district. Pedestrians and automobile traffic constantly flow among the restaurants and shops. Placed in the midst of such an intellectually fertile community, the downtown is especially known for its quality bookstores. Another of Palo Alto's major retail centers is the Stanford Shopping Center, adjacent to Stanford University's campus.

The city enjoys a thriving cultural life, both locally and internationally. Palo Alto keeps sister city relations with, among others, Oaxaca in Mexico, Enschede in the Netherlands, Linkoping in Sweden, and Albi in France. Contributing to its artistic endeavors is the Palo Alto Art Center, known throughout the valley for its excellent exhibits and community art classes. Its citizens enjoy dramatic arts performances frequently presented at the Lucie Stern Theatre, home of the Palo Alto Players as well as the Palo Alto Children's Theatre and the West Bay Opera Company. The city also serves as a home for the American Heritage Museum, which gives visitors a fascinating history of technical developments such as radios, telephones, and other modern conveniences.

Palo Alto has the Bay Area's premier medical center, Stanford Hospital, known worldwide for its excellence in health research and patient care. Along its bayland region, the city operates a municipal airport as well as a golf course. More than 60 high-tech and biotech firms are based in the Stanford Research Park area along Page Mill Road. Among the major firms and research centers here that have contributed to developing technological wonders are Hewlett-Packard, Varian Associates, and Xerox PARC.

HISTORY

For many centuries, the Ohlone Indians lived in the Palo Alto area, and archaeologists have discovered one of their massive mounds at Hewlett-Packard's headquarters along Page Mill Road. This now-demolished mound measured 30 feet high and 600 feet long, built by centuries of depositing shells and human remains. An Ohlone village was situated on what is now the city's Marion and Webster Sts. intersection. These early inhabitants stayed in the area because they found the climate favorable and food sources abundant. They gathered acorns from the oak trees and often fished for salmon in the nearby creek.

On November 6, 1769, Gaspar de Portolá and his men became the first European explorers to enter the Santa Clara Valley. Here in what would later become the Palo Alto–Menlo Park boundary, they discovered a majestic double-trunked redwood standing near a meandering creek. They named the creek San Francisquito and the unusual tree *el palo alto* (the tall tree). Over time, it became a prominent landmark for travelers venturing into the valley. With the development of the missions in the Bay Area, the creek served as a dividing line for Mission Dolores and Mission Santa Clara boundaries, and now functions as the northern border of Santa Clara County. The Spanish originally planned to build a mission at this scenic location, but when they saw that the creek dried up during summer months, they changed the location to what is now the city of Santa Clara. The land surrounding *el palo alto* served as mission sheep pastures tended by Christianized natives.

In 1839, California's Mexican governor Juan Alvarado granted 1,471 acres of land to Antonino Buelna for helping him in a political revolt that brought Alvarado to power. This property is where Stanford University campus now sits. Buelna called it Rancho San Francisquito after the creek flowing through it. Here, he built a three-room adobe house, making it his home until his death three years later. His widow continued living on the ranch for another decade, dealing with American squatters and lawyers over messy property disputes.

Uncle Jim's Cabin

With the American settlement of California, Scotch Canadian James Otterson opened a tavern in 1853 along the San Jose to San Francisco Rd. (now El Camino Real). It was ideally situated at a crossing with another road leading to the burgeoning lumber mills in the Santa Cruz Mountains. The tavern, called Uncle Jim's Cabin, became a social center from which a small community grew. That same year, an attorney named Elisha Crosby purchased 250 acres of land from Mexican land-grant owner Secundino Robles to start his Mayfield Farm. Two years later, as the rural village grew, a post office located in the tavern was named Mayfield after Crosby's farm.

In 1863, several of the squatters on the land of Rancho San Francisquito sold 650 acres of their

HEWLETT-PACKARD: NICE GUYS CAN FINISH FIRST

In a one-car wooden garage set back behind an ordinary house in Palo Alto's Professorville district, an electronics empire was born. Out of this humble origin comes the story of a couple of nice guys who built Silicon Valley's most respected company. William Hewlett and David Packard had become close friends in 1930 as freshman electrical engineering students at Stanford University. Encouraged by their professor Frederick Terman, the two young men stayed in Palo Alto after graduating, and in 1938 started an electronics company, working part-time from the tiny garage.

Their firm's first product was a measurement device called an audio oscillator, which used negative-feedback principles Hewlett had discovered while a student. Their first big sale was to Walt Disney Studios, which wanted oscillators to monitor sound while making the innovative animated film *Fantasia*. The cartoon studio first considered buying similar oscillators from General Radio Company for $400 each, but when Hewlett informed Bud Hawkins, Disney's chief sound engineer, that their model cost less than $100, Disney bought eight units for $71.50 each.

The ambitious friends formed a partnership on January 1, 1939, naming their company Hewlett-Packard (the order of the names determined by a coin flip). Working hard (and using the kitchen oven to dry the paint on their oscillator panels), Hewlett and Packard moved out of the garage the following year and into a rented office on the corner of El Camino Real and Page Mill Rd., next to Tinker Bell's Fix-it Shop. That year, with three employees and eight products, they made $34,000 in sales. World War II affected the business when Hewlett was called up (he worked in the Army Signal Corps laboratories in Fort Monmouth, New Jersey), but during the war, HP built microwave signal generators for Naval Research and also radar-jamming devices.

In the postwar years, HP grew substantially, developing innovative products using its signal generator technology.

During the 1940s and 1950s, the company developed the "HP Way" of doing business—a more humane method of management in which employees were trusted and highly respected. For example, HP was among the first high-tech firms to provide its workers with flexible hours and profit-sharing incentives. The HP Way has made the company one of the most desirable places to work in Silicon Valley, even today. With its corporate philanthropy programs, HP was also innovative in returning some of its profits to society. Today the company annually gives many millions of dollars in money and equipment to educational and charitable organizations. In addition, the private Packard Foundation—started in 1964—has provided money for such philanthropical causes as the Lucile Salter Packard Children's Hospital at Stanford University and the Monterey Bay Aquarium.

HP has evolved with Silicon Valley, taking advantage of many of the technological developments throughout the years. In the 1960s, it entered the medical measurement field when it bought Sanborn Company, based in Waltham, Massachusetts. In 1965 it acquired F&M Scientific Corporation, gaining entry into the analytical instrumentation field. In 1966, it brought out its first computer, and in the last three decades its R&D programs have introduced many significant innovations. Among the most profitable has been its printing devices—today HP leads the market with its ink-jet and laser printer products for desktop computers.

In 1989, the garage at 367 Addison Ave., where Hewlett and Packard started their company, was designated a California Historical Landmark. A plaque in front of the house describes the site as "the birthplace of Silicon Valley."

CITIES OF THE VALLEY

property to George Gordon, a wealthy Englishman living in San Francisco. Gordon wanted to develop the property into a country estate near the town of Mayfield, by that time becoming a prominent valley community. His mansion stood where Stanford Children's Hospital is located now. (The wood from Gordon's Victorian home was burned in 1965 in Stanford University's traditional "Big Game" bonfire.) By 1867, Mayfield village had grown into a town of 1,700 people and boasted its own railroad stop. In a display of patriotism during the post–Civil War years, William Paul, a Scot known as the "father of Mayfield," christened local streets after important Union figures such as Sherman, Grant, Sheridan, and Lincoln. Many of these names continue today as Palo Alto routes.

Gordon died in 1869, and the executors of his estate sold the property in 1876 to Leland Stanford. The railroad tycoon and former California governor established a large horse ranch here where he bred horses specifically for racing. Stanford called his stables the Palo Alto Farm after the tree that Portolá's expedition had camped under. A decade later, Leland and Jane Stanford started to build on the horse farm the university honoring their adolescent son who had succumbed to typhoid two years earlier in Italy.

The Stanfords wanted an alcohol "dry" town nearby to keep the university's reputation unsoiled, but the citizens of Mayfield refused their requests to give up their saloons and brewery. Seeking to establish a clean-and-sober community for professors and students to live in close to the campus, Leland Stanford asked Timothy Hopkins, the adopted son of railroad baron Mark Hopkins, to buy 740 acres of the Rafael Soto Ranch. This land adjacent to the university's northeast corner was subdivided in 1889 to create a community then called University Park. One enterprising real estate developer bought 120 acres next to Stanford's land and named his development Palo Alto after the world-famous horse farm. Leland Stanford filed a lawsuit, and so the name Palo Alto was dropped and replaced with College Terrace. Later, Timothy Hopkins would change the name of the small college town

of University Park to Palo Alto in honor of the Stanfords' farm.

Professorville

The city's connection with Stanford University has always been a strong one. Palo Alto essentially came into existence as a town to service the university. By the turn of the 19th century, many professors had built themselves fine homes in the area south of the community's downtown district. This area became a prestigious neighborhood of wood-shingled homes. Called Professorville, some of its finest homes were designed by well-known architects such as R. B. Maybeck and Charles Hodges. Today, this historic section of Palo Alto is bordered by Ramona, Addison, Waverly, and Kingsley Streets.

Palo Alto quickly grew into a community resembling an eastern college town. Many of the streets are named after classical authors such as Seneca, Webster, and Poe. As for the nearby town of Mayfield, it suffered a lingering death as incoming residents preferred moving into the more upscale, modern community of Palo Alto. As the less affluent rival city, Mayfield's bars and saloons attracted some of the university's student population, but with competition from Palo Alto's growing commercial areas, the once thriving town's days were numbered. On January 1, 1905, it banned saloons in an attempt to gain some respectability, but that didn't help. In 1925, Mayfield was officially annexed to Palo Alto and its identity was lost forever. Now replacing the former town's site are affluent neighborhoods and businesses located east of El Camino Real between California Ave. and Page Mill Road.

With high-tech's rise in importance, Stanford University brought some of the world's best minds to Palo Alto. These people have stayed in the area to found some of Silicon Valley's most important businesses. Among the city's early entrepreneurs were William Hewlett and David Packard, two of the university's engineering students who in 1939 established their firm of Hewlett-Packard in a single-car garage on Addison Street. During the years following World War II, Stanford University realized the importance of connecting businesses with the research coming from its laboratories. Thus it established the Stanford Research Park in the Page Mill Rd. area, where companies could set up camp. Among the organizations that established operations here at the world's first industrial park were Varian Associates, Loral Space Systems, and several genetics and pharmaceutical companies. In the late 1960s, Xerox Corp. opened its Xerox PARC facilities here, which have created many innovations for the computer age and helped plant the seeds for many of Silicon Valley's most influential companies. With the massive computer boom in the 1980s and 1990s, Palo Alto saw an increasing number of start-up companies form within its borders, many of them created by Stanford students. Today's Palo Alto is a community well connected with Stanford University, the source of its creation, but the city has also matured to form a strong identity of its own.

TOUR

This Palo Alto tour highlights the bayland area, Professorville and downtown districts, and, of course, Stanford University. Begin from U.S. 101, taking the Embarcadero Rd. exit and heading east for about one mile, passing the **Palo Alto Municipal Golf Course,** 650/856-0881, on your left. Next to this is the **Palo Alto Municipal Airport,** 650/856-7833, where small airplanes land and take off into bay breezes. At the stop sign, turn left and follow Embarcadero Rd. into the **Palo Alto Baylands Nature Preserve,** 650/329-2506, open 8 A.M.–sunset. On the left you'll pass the city's duck pond, and on the right the historic yacht harbor house, now no longer serving that purpose because silt has made the former harbor unusable for boating. Park in the parking lot at the end of the road and take a stroll here, breathing in the salty air of the surrounding marshlands.

The building on stilts over the marsh is the **Lucy Evans Nature Center,** 650/329-2506, which contains exhibits on the plant and animal life inhabiting this section of the bay. A boardwalk from the center allows visitors to take in the vista of the Dumbarton Bridge in the north. The large white mounds you see in the

east are mountains of salt from the Cargill Salt Flats near Newark. Expect to spend about half an hour to an hour at the center and preserve.

Following Embarcadero Rd. back along the route you first followed, you'll pass an office building of **Regis McKenna** on your right along the golf course. One of Silicon Valley's major public relations firms, it helped in the all-important marketing of start-ups such as Apple Computer. After the stoplight intersection, cross the overpass above U.S. 101, driving into a residential area filled with handsome older homes. About a mile from the freeway, you will see on your right the rust-brown modern sculpture in the lawn area by the **Palo Alto Art Center,** 650/329-2366. Turn right on Newell Rd., park in the parking lot and enter this free art gallery and cultural facility. Plan to spend about 20 to 30 minutes viewing the fine art.

Getting back onto Embarcadero Rd., you'll pass Rinconada Park on your right at the corner of Middlefield Road. Continue driving on, and soon you'll find yourself in a neighborhood of pristine turn-of-the-century homes. This is Professorville, whose borders roughly consist of Waverly, Addison, Ramona, and Kingsley Streets. Turn to your right on Waverly and drive down several blocks until you get to the stop sign at Addison. Turn left here, and two houses down on your right you'll see 367 Addison Avenue. Park along the street and make a short stop at one of Silicon Valley's sacred high-tech shrines—the **garage** where Hewlett-Packard started. You'll find here a historical marker explaining the significance of this important site to Silicon Valley's development.

From the famous garage, continue driving west on Addison for two blocks to Emerson Street. Turn right here, and on your right at the corner office building at 913 Emerson St., you'll see the site where Cyril Elwell started his **Federal Telegraph Company** in 1909. This is where his employee Lee de Forest did his early experiments in electronics. Here between 1911 and 1913, de Forest invented the three-element and radio vacuum tube, the first vacuum tube amplifier and oscillator. These technologies were the building blocks that led to the invention of the microchip.

Continue driving down Emerson St. for about five blocks until you reach University Avenue. You're now in **downtown Palo Alto,** and on any day of the week here, you'll feel the vibrant pace of the city's heart. Parking can be sometimes tricky to find here; there are two-hour parking lots along the side streets in the likely event that you can't find a parking space on University Avenue.

Take about an hour or so to walk through the downtown area (two hours if you decide to enjoy a leisurely lunch). This busy district is an excellent place for people watching and window-shopping, with plenty of coffeehouses, restaurants, bookstores, and art galleries. **The Stanford Theater,** 221 University Ave., 650/324-3700, is a gem of an old-fashioned movie palace renovated with funds from the Packard Foundation. Residents often enjoy a delightful evening out by dining at one of the nearby restaurants and then catching one of the art deco theater's classic films. A Wurlitzer organ often plays during intermissions. During your downtown visit, you can find visitors information at the **Palo Alto Chamber of Commerce,** 650/324-3121, two blocks down Bryant St. west of University at 325 Forest Avenue.

After exploring the downtown area, head west on University Ave. and take a right on Alma Street. Drive four blocks, then park along Alma St. near the corner of Poe St. and take a short stroll to the small park at this corner. Follow the bike path leading to the iron pedestrian bridge crossing San Francisquito Creek. To the left of this bridge is the 113-foot *el palo alto,* California's first living landmark. Early Stanford students use to climb up the tree and tie banners on top. On admission day in 1909, one student named Vincent Levesque climbed to the top and got stuck. He had to wait until his friends built a bonfire and threw him a rope to get down. Originally the tree had twin trunks called St. Peter and St. Paul, but one broke off during a winter storm in 1886.

After visiting this site, continue northward along Alma St., crossing the Caltrain tracks and merging onto El Camino Real. Here, get in the far left lane and continue driving so that you enter the city of Menlo Park for a short distance. Make a U-turn at the Cambridge Ave. intersection and return south on El Camino Real, entering the **Stanford Shopping Center,** 800/722-9332, on your right. Park here and visit the collection of restaurants, upscale shops, and department stores, including Bloomingdale's and Macy's. Depending on your shopping habits, plan to spend about an hour roaming through this lavish shopping center.

From the shopping center, follow the parking lot to its southern boundary where it exits onto Quarry Rd. and turn right. Follow Quarry Rd. past the **Stanford Medical Center** until it curves into Campus Drive. Turn left at the stop sign here and follow Campus Dr. to the visitor's parking lot in front of the **Cantor Art Center,** 650/723-4177, on your right. The museum, shut down after experiencing extensive damage in the 1989 Loma Prieta earthquake, reopened 10 years later, with a new modern wing displaying modern art and cultural artifacts. Just outside the museum is a **sculpture garden** displaying some magnificent bronze works by Auguste Rodin; it's the largest collection of the artist's work outside of France. Plan to spend at least an hour at the free museum.

A full visit to Stanford University requires quite a bit of walking. One of the best ways to see the campus highlights is to take the free campus tour that starts at the **Visitors Center,** 650/723-2560, located inside the Memorial Auditorium on the east side of the fountain plaza. On the opposite side stands **Hoover Tower,** the university's largest landmark, which locals sometimes mischievously call "Hoover's Last Erection." On most days, Stanford students give two free walks lasting about one hour (usually at 11 A.M. and 3:15 P.M.). Call to check what time they start for the day of your visit. The tour guide will describe to you many of Stanford's traditions, including its longtime rivalry with U.C. Berkeley and the midnight freshman kiss-fest ceremony, at which incoming students get smooches from Stanford seniors under the light of a full moon. This ritual takes place in the **Quadrangle,** an immense courtyard gathering spot designed in a Romanesque style. In the Quad, the historic heart of the university, you'll also find the serene Spanish-style **Stanford Memorial Chapel,** with its breathtaking Renaissance-inspired artworks. The tour will also take you to the Quad's far western corridor, the dividing point between Stanford's "Fuzzyland" (the southern humanity classrooms) and "Techyland" (the northern science classrooms).

After finishing the tour, return to your car parked in front of the art museum and head back onto Campus Dr., turning left and following this road west. Continue for about a mile until you reach Electioneer Rd., then turn right here. Drive the short distance to the impressive Victorian barn and stables. Built in 1870, it's known simply as the **Red Barn.** It was in this area that Leland Stanford bred horses for racing and from which Stanford University gets its nickname "The Farm." The bronze statue here is of Stanford's finest breeding horse, Electioneer. Legend has it that Stanford made a bet with two men that at some point during its run, all four hooves of a trotting horse are lifted from the ground. He hired noted photographer Eadweard Muybridge to take pictures of a horse running. It took Muybridge five years to develop a camera with a fast enough shutter to achieve motion photography experiments. Finally, in 1877, he lined up 24 still cameras attached to trip wires along the racetrack and had a rider take a horse across them. The horse set the shutters off, creating a series of photographs. When these were placed inside a drum and revolved at high speed, it gave the illusion of a horse running. Stanford won the bet—some of the pictures showed all four hooves off the ground at the same time. Later, Thomas Edison visited Stanford's farm, and his viewing of these "moving pictures" eventually led to the development of cinematography.

From the Red Barn, go back to Campus Dr., turning right at the stop sign and continuing on to the stoplight at Junipero Serra Boulevard. Turn left here, and follow the Boulevard to the next stoplight, where you will turn left onto Campus Drive. Follow the drive for about two miles as it wanders past buildings containing the university's dormitories, classrooms, and administration offices. At Galvez St. on the campus's eastern section, turn right and continue past the coliseum-like **Stanford Stadium,** which you'll see on your right. Galvez St. merges onto Arboretum Road. Follow this road east to El Camino Real, where you will turn right. Immediately to your right you'll see one of the last surviving **El Camino Mission Bells,** of which hundreds once dotted the 700-mile path connecting California's missions.

Continue traveling about 1.5 miles down El Camino Real. On your left where California Ave. intersects this heavily traveled street is the site where **Uncle Jim's Cabin** once stood. A historical plaque marking the spot reads: "In 1853, James Otterson built a hotel near this corner. It was the first building in what was to become Mayfield. Travelers between San Francisco and San Jose stopped here as did lumbermen coming down from the hills to the bay." The small shopping district along California Ave. was once downtown Mayfield.

Drive a short distance farther to Page Mill Rd., and turn right at the stoplight intersection. Here, you are entering Stanford Research Park, the valley's first industrial park. Among the major high-tech and biotech companies with headquarters in the Park are **Varian Associates** and **Hewlett-Packard. Xerox PARC** also has its research facilities here, creating much of the electronic age's gadgets and technologies, and *The Wall Street Journal* keeps a Silicon Valley–based office here.

Where Page Mill Rd. crosses the Foothill Expwy., you'll pass over the **Hetch Hetchy Aqueduct,** carrying water from the Sierra Mountains near Yosemite to the city of San Francisco. Because it's located underground, you can't actually see this aqueduct that is so important for San Francisco's survival. After this point, the industrial park quickly ends, and you'll begin driving through scenic foothill country belonging to Stanford University. In a mile or so, Page Mill Rd. reaches I-280. The southbound entrance leads to San Jose; the northbound entrance heads toward San Francisco.

POINTS OF INTEREST

American Heritage Museum

Technology isn't a newcomer to the Santa Clara Valley, and a visit to this fascinating museum will prove it. This downtown Palo Alto museum is located in the historic Williams House and Gardens. It features numerous electrical and mechanical contraptions from the 19th century and early 20th century. A print shop and a radio repair shop showcase developments in mass communication before the computer age. Special exhibits change throughout the year, providing a glimpse at artifacts from toys to toasters. The museum also includes a library and gift shop.

351 Homer Ave. (downtown Palo Alto between Waverly and Bryant Sts.), 650/321-1004; parking on street; admission free; website: www.moah.org; open Fri.–Sun. 11 A.M.–4 P.M.

Stanford University

The heavyweight of Silicon Valley institutions, with eight Nobel laureates on its faculty, the campus's official name is Leland Stanford Jr. University (the campus switchboard occasionally gets calls from people who mistakenly believe it's a junior college). Frederick Law Olmsted, the designer of New York's Central Park and Chicago's Jackson Park, laid out the campus's semi-arid landscape, liberally sprinkled with oaks and eucalyptus trees. The formal Palm Drive leads up the Quadrangle, built of sandstone in a combination of Romanesque and mission revival styles. The Memorial Church in the Quad is popular for weddings among Stanford alumni and students.

You could spend an entire day visiting the various attractions on the 8,180-acre campus stretching from El Camino Real into the Santa Cruz foothills. The university also maintains Hopkins Marine Station, near the Monterey Bay Aquarium in Pacific Grove, and overseas centers in Berlin; Moscow; Paris; Rome; Oxford, England; Kyoto, Japan; and Santiago, Chile. Start out at the **visitors information center** in Memorial Auditorium (east of the fountain in front of the prominent Hoover Tower). Free one-hour walking tours begin from here at 11 A.M. and 3:15 P.M.

© MARTIN CHEEK

on the campus quad, strikingly beautiful Stanford Memorial Chapel

on most days. **Hoover Tower** has at its ground level small museums dedicated to Stanford alumni Herbert Hoover and his wife, Lou. Take the elevator to the tower's observation deck for a splendid view of Silicon Valley and the San Francisco Bay (admission is charged).

Exhibits of special interest at Stanford include the **Earth Sciences Mineral Collection** on the 2nd floor of the Mitchell Building, and the **Anthropology Museum** in Building 110 in the Quad. Set in a shady grove not far east of the Quad is the **Stanford New Guinea Sculpture Garden,** a fascinating collection of South Sea totem poles, and wood and stone sculptures. The gardens were installed in 1994 when, at the invitation of a Stanford art student, 10 artists from Papua New Guinea carved these beautiful native works. If you want to visit the Victorian stables where Eadweard Muybridge discovered the principles of moving pictures, head to the **Red Barn** (not to be confused with the Stanford Barn at Stanford Shopping Center) located at the end of Electioneer Rd. just off Campus Dr. West. Much of Stanford's land is taken up by the **Jasper Ridge Biological Preserve** (you can see "The Dish," a landmark giant radio telescope, from I-280 here), and occasional docent-led tours pro-

INNOVATION CENTRAL: XEROX PARC

Thomas Edison had his "invention factory" in Menlo Park, New Jersey, and Palo Alto has something similar. Instead of inventing the light bulb and the phonograph, Xerox's Palo Alto Research Center (PARC) invents technologies for the digital age. Established in 1970, this research facility laid the foundation for the personal computer revolution.

Xerox could have been the king of the computer world right now if its officers had only realized the significance of much of the work done by its PARC researchers. The facility was started in the belief that the paperless office would arrive by 1990—a premise in which photocopier giant Xerox had much at stake. So in the Palo Alto foothills, it set up this state-of-the-art facility and gave free reign to about 50 of the world's most brilliant scientists and engineers to perform research relating to people working in the office environment. One of its better-known researchers during this time was Doug Engelbert, who had worked at the Stanford Research Institute before coming to PARC. Among other PARC inventions that changed the world, Engelbert developed the graphical user interface and the mouse cursor device.

The early 1970s were a high-water mark in PARC's fertile history. During this period, the facility invented the world's first high-speed computer network using Ethernet technology (invented by a team led by Bob Metcalfe). It linked a computer to another PARC invention, the laser printer. At a time when computers were still basically limited to exorbitantly expensive, room-size mainframes only corporations could afford or use, PARC researchers Butler Lampson and Chuck Thacker came out with the Alto, the world's first workstation. It came with a hard disk and a black-and-white bit-mapped screen (which has points that light up to form words and images). The computer cost about $10,000 in materials and would have sold for $25,000—a lot of money in 1973. So Xerox decided not to explore its potential as a commercial product.

Apple Computer's Steve Jobs visited the facility and borrowed many of Alto's innovations, using them himself in his Lisa computer. These ideas included the mouse, the WYSIWYG (what-you-see-is-what-you-get) screen, and the GUI. These features later came out in the immensely popular Macintosh computer, which, of course, made Apple gobs of money.

Unfortunately for Xerox, it tended to alienate its PARC researchers by deciding to not do much with the technologies developed here. Many of these frustrated researchers wound up quitting to form companies of their own. Among them were John Warnock and Chuck Geschke, who started a company using technology Warnock had invented at PARC, called Interpress, a language program that allowed printers to understand computer instructions. They named their company after Adobe Creek, which flowed through Warnock's Los Altos Hills backyard. Adobe is now headquartered in downtown San Jose in two towering office buildings.

Yet, Xerox PARC continues to be in the business of inventing. One of its more intriguing developments, headed for commercial application in the 21st century, is "electronic paper," a rubbery material called Gyricon. The invention of scientist Nicholas Sheridon, the substance contains millions of microscopic plastic balls floating in oil-filled pockets. Each sphere is half black and half white, and digital information turns them around so that people can read text or draw on the "paper" with an electronic stylus. The material can be used to download books, newspapers, email, or other sources of information.

Business values are also creeping into PARC, which was originally intended purely as a research facility. The PARC 2000 project has established five main research directions for the facility, each connected with Xerox's long-term business goals. For example, the company is actively pursuing licensing agreements for many of its innovations and intends to form spin-off firms for potential products coming out of the center.

L'AFFAIRE DU FRANÇAIS MYSTÉRIEUX, PETER COUTTS

CITIES OF THE VALLEY

In the spring of 1875, everyone in the village of Mayfield was puzzling over the mysterious Frenchman. This handsome and aristocratic character, calling himself Monsieur Peter Coutts, had bought the farm of town founder William Paul, just west of the village. Coutts christened it Ayrshire Farm, after the cattle he planned to raise there. He hired a hundred local men and set them to work building a grand estate including houses and chalets, a 50-foot-tall clock tower, stables for his racehorses, a race track (including viewing stands), a wine cellar, kennels for his beagles, and a dozen brick barns to house his cattle. Polite but reserved, Coutts never talked about his past, fueling speculation among the townspeople and farmers as to Monsieur Coutts's true identity.

Among the estate's prominent landmarks was a 30-foot-tall brick tower designed in the style of a Norman fortress. Unlike most Norman fortresses, however, it had no door or other means of ingress. Coutts hired Cornish miners to dig a two-mile network of irrigation tunnels leading to his prominent landmark. No one in town could fathom the purpose of the structure they dubbed "Frenchman's Tower." Some speculated that it imprisoned Coutts's wife, who had perhaps been driven insane by some horrible tragedy. And the tunnels might have been built so that Coutts could quickly escape from whatever pursuers were after him to retrieve the alleged fortune in gold he had stolen.

When all was ready, Coutts's invalid wife Marie, his young son and daughter, and governess Mlle. Eugenie Clogenson came to live with him in the nine-room "Escondite Cottage" (Spanish for "hiding place"). Locals said (incorrectly) that it was fashioned after Marie Antoinette's Le Petit Trianon in Versailles. Work on the estate continued for the next six years. Coutts bought more property, expanding his farm to 1,242 acres and spending an astonishing $40,000 a year developing his cattle ranch. And then in 1880, with a sudden haste and no announced reason, Coutts and his family left his farm and returned to Europe. This mysterious departure only added to the mystery surrounding the enigmatic Frenchman.

Two years later, Senator Leland Stanford purchased the property for $140,000 to expand his own Palo Alto Farm, which would eventually, of course, become Stanford University. David Starr Jordan, the university's first president, lived in Escondite Cottage, and the Stanfords often visited the home and pondered about the Frenchman who had once lived there. It wasn't until the 1920s that Monsieur Coutts's real identity was discovered. His real name was Paulin Caperon, and he had made a fortune in banking in Paris. He had published an anti-royalist newspaper called *La Liberté*, and, facing the political wrath of Napoleon III, fled France for California, where he assumed his alternative identity.

His cottage is still located on Escondido Rd. at Stanford University. Much of his former farm now is the site of Silicon Valley's high-tech corporations along Page Mill Rd. such as Hewlett-Packard. And one street off this well-traveled thoroughfare is named Peter Coutts Road.

For more details on the compelling story of Peter Coutts, read Pamela Gullard and Nancy Lund's excellent book *History of Palo Alto: The Early Years*.

vide visitors with the natural history of the area.

Stanford University Campus (take El Camino Real to University Ave., turn left at Palm Dr. to Main Quad), 650/723-2560, website: www.stanford.edu; open daily.

Stanford Museum of Art: Cantor Art Center

Recently reopened after major renovations from structural damage caused by the 1989 earthquake, this museum received a new name that's a mouthful: the Iris and B. Gerald Cantor Center for Visual Arts. It's Silicon Valley's best place to view art and artifacts. Among the 18 galleries in this 10,000-square-foot museum originally built in 1891 are a changing exhibition of works by 19th- and 20th-century artists, including Georgia O'Keeffe, Henry Moore, and Roy Lichtenstein. Other galleries present fine examples of Asian, African, Oceanian, ancient Mediterranean, and ancient American artifacts. One gallery offers a fascinating look at the Stanford family through various objects and artworks they once owned. Around the corner from this room, look for "Little Leland's Last Breakfast" by David Gilhooly, a satirical poke at the typical Victorian's overzealous remembrance of the deceased. The adjacent Rodin Sculpture Garden displays many examples of the French artist's works, including his dramatic *Gates of Hell.*

Stanford University Campus (at Lomita Dr. and Museum Way), 650/723-4177; parking metered on weekdays and free on weekends; admission free; open Wed., Fri., Sat., and Sun. 11 A.M.–5 P.M., Thurs. 11 A.M.–8 P.M.

Palo Alto Art Center

Formerly known as Palo Alto Cultural Center, a rotation of gallery exhibits can be viewed at this city-run facility. Workshops in visual and performing arts for children and adults are given here as well as occasional lecture series. A small shop sells artwork and ceramics made by local artisans.

1313 Newell Rd. (at Embarcadero Rd.), 650/329-2366, website: www.city.palo-alto.ca.us/artsculture; free parking; admission free;

open Tues., Wed., Fri., and Sat. 10 A.M.–5 P.M., Thurs. 10 A.M.–9 P.M., Sun. 1–5 P.M.

Stanford Health Library

Maintaining health is a vital concern for many Silicon Valley residents, who have a tremendous resource for obtaining free scientifically based medical information at the Stanford Health Library. The library is easily accessible at the Stanford Shopping Center and open to everyone. It contains a large collection of books, medical journals, newspaper clippings, and periodicals devoted to health education. Also available are computer terminals containing a large medical database and health-related videos that can be checked out. The library's foreign language collection provides material in Chinese and Spanish.

2-B Stanford Shopping Center (next to Bloomingdale's at Quarry Rd. and El Camino Real), 650/725-8400 or 800/295-5177, website: www.med.stanford.edu/healthlib; parking in shopping center; admission free; open Mon., Tues., Wed., Fri., and Sat. 10 A.M.–6 P.M., Thurs. 10 A.M.–9 P.M.

Palo Alto Baylands Nature Preserve

This is a superb place for a sunset stroll. Bring your binoculars to observe more than 100 species of birds from the boardwalk and levees on this 120-acre salt marsh. An interpretive center informs visitors on the area's ecology and natural history. Call to find out when guided walks with naturalists are available.

End of Embarcadero Rd. (from U.S. 101 in Palo Alto, drive east to the end of the road), 650/329-2506, website: www.city.palo-alto.ca.us/homepage.html; free parking; admission free; open 8 A.M.–sunset. Interpretive center open Tues.–Wed. 10 A.M.–5 P.M.; Thurs.–Fri. 2–5 P.M., weekends 1–5 P.M.

Palo Alto Junior Museum and Zoo

Although kids of all ages will enjoy this small but charming life science museum, it's an especially good place to take very young children curious about the natural world. Operated by local volunteers, the museum offers simple nature displays. Kids are encouraged to get their hands on the exhibits and learn through playing. The museum explores one subject at a time, and exhibits remain on display for a year. In the past, exhibits have profiled underwater sealife, the growth of Santa Clara Valley trees and forests, and protection of the environment. After visiting the museum, you and your children can wander outside to the small zoo, which holds animals native to Silicon Valley.

1451 Middlefield Rd. (at Embarcadero Rd.), 650/329-2111, website: www.city.palo-alto.ca.us; admission free; open Tues.–Sat. 10 A.M.–5 P.M.; Sun. 1–4 P.M.

Stanford Shopping Center

Located next to Stanford University, this shopping center's gardenlike ambience makes it a leisurely place to stroll and browse through more than 140 specialty shops. It's certainly the poshest Silicon Valley mall. Wander down the European-style street market with its fantastic Parisian mural and discover at its end stores selling fresh produce, meats, breads and pastries, coffee, and other edible goodies.

180 El Camino Real (from I-280, take Sand Hill Rd. east and drive 3.5 miles), 650/617-8585 or 800/772-9332, website: www.stanford-shop.com; major stores: Neiman Marcus, Bloomingdale's, Nordstrom, Macy's; open Mon.–Fri. 10 A.M.–9 P.M., Sat. 10 A.M.–6 P.M., Sun. 11 A.M.–6 P.M.

Palo Alto Players

For nearly seven decades, the Peninsula's oldest continuously performing theater company has staged musicals, comedies, and dramas for the enjoyment of Santa Clara Valley audiences. Past performances have included Edward Albee's *Three Tall Women* and Steve Martin's *Picasso at the Labin Agile*. The season runs from September to July.

Lucie Stern Theatre, 1305 Middlefield Rd. (one block north of Embarcadero Rd.), 650/329-0891, website: www.paplayers.org; individual tickets: $16–24, season tickets (five shows): $65–95.

Milpitas

Calling itself "the gateway to Silicon Valley," Milpitas is the region's boomtown. From a population of 825 when it incorporated on January 26, 1954, the city swelled to more than 65,000 inhabitants at the start of the 21st century, and it continues growing at a rate of almost 1,000 people every year. This population explosion has created some serious urban problems with which the former farm town must now contend. It enjoys a location near the gentle foothills along the Diablo Mountain Range, and its city government has been fairly successful in heading off massive housing development in this pastoral environment. But traffic can often be a serious problem, with backups of cars clogging its freeways and downtown shopping areas during heavy commute hours.

The most northeastern of Silicon Valley communities, Milpitas is bordered on the north by the city of Fremont, on the east by unincorporated foothills, on the south by San Jose's Berryessa district, and on the west by San Jose's N. First St. corridor and Alviso. Milpitas is the blue-collar community of Silicon Valley. The industrial town is home to more Fortune 500 companies than any other city in the Bay Area. A number of its citizens have jobs as engineers and manufacturing workers at the high-tech companies situated in Milpitas's 24 industrial parks. Some of the city's biggest companies include LSI Logic, Lifescan, KLA-Tencor, Lucent, Linear Technology, Solectron, Sun Microsystems, and Adaptec. Milpitas received its major industrial impetus in the early 1950s when it became the home of a massive Ford auto plant. After this manufacturing facility closed, the site remained vacant for years. But in the 1990s, the can-do spirit of Milpitas converted the facility into The Great Mall of the Bay Area, luring hordes of shoppers to the biggest shopping outlet in the region.

Milpitas' 1955 Ford Motors assembly plant has been converted into the 1.5–million square foot Great Mall of the Bay Area, home to almost 200 off–price outlet stores.

Milpitas has the most ethnic diversity in Santa Clara County. An estimated one-third of its population is Asian-American, with Filipinos making up the largest portion of people (about 23 percent) of Asian heritage. The city also has a large Chinese and Vietnamese population, which support a variety of Asian cultural shops and restaurants. Caucasians are the city's largest group at 42 percent of the population, Hispanics make up about 19 percent, and African-Americans are about 5 percent. Most of the city's residents belong to middle-class, hard-working families. Milpitas has the highest number of people per household in the county, with about 3.5 people per home. Compared with other Silicon Valley cities, it contains twice the number of homes. The majority of the city's dwellings are apartment complexes or standard ranch-style houses set in quiet neighborhoods, but since the region's major economic boom, some luxurious custom-built homes in the hills have gone on the market for well over $1 million.

Despite the city's industrial make-up, its inhabitants have access to many outdoor spaces, including 20 public parks. These provide a number of recreational opportunities such as golf, swimming, and tennis. Just east of the city along its foothill boundary is Ed R. Levin County Park, where residents enjoy horseback riding, fishing, and hang gliding. Often, they simply hike to the top of the peaks in this hilly park to get a magnificent view of the sun setting over Silicon Valley.

HISTORY

The land that Milpitas is located on was originally settled by the Ohlone Indians. Occasionally, their burial grounds and various other archaeological sites are still discovered throughout the city. In 1993, an archaeological excavation found an Indian cemetery mound at the Elmwood Rehabilitation Facility. The Spanish settlers originally called the area Penitencia because of a small adobe house where the padres could hear confession. The house was located at what is now Oakland-Milpitas Rd. and Trimble Rd., conveniently placed halfway between Mission Santa Clara and Mission San Jose (in what is now Fremont). In the fertile soil of this part of the valley, the mission's Indian converts grew corn, calling it *milpas* (the Nahuatlia Aztec word for "cornfields"). The Spanish language added its own twist to the name, referring to the location as Milpitas, which means "little cornfields."

During the Mexican rule of California, the Milpitas region was divided into various land grants. Like several other land grants throughout the Santa Clara Valley, an ongoing property dispute over ownership continued for many years. It involved José Maria de Jesus Alviso, the son of Francisco Javier Alviso of the Anza expedition, and Nicolas Berryessa, the son of another early Spanish settler. In 1834, San Jose's Alcalde Pedro Chabolla granted Berryessa the 4,800-acre tract of land, but the following year, Governor José Castro granted the same stretch of land to Alviso, who called it Rancho Milpitas. The legal battle over who was the true owner waged for years, and when tempers flared, houses were sometimes

THE BOOMS AND BUSTS OF ALVISO

Walk the quiet Alviso streets and breathe in the sea-salt aroma of marshland mixed with the scent of a fish-fry at a neighborhood restaurant. Stroll past magnificent Victorian houses and small cottages that almost make you believe you've traveled a century back in time. The tranquil mystique of a fishing village pervades this small town.

Like a Brigadoon, the San Jose neighborhood of Alviso, just west of Milpitas along Hwy. 237, is caught in a docile time frame far from the 21st century. This historic waterfront town is where the Guadalupe River ends its journey, flowing into soggy marshes at the most southern tip of San Francisco Bay. The place has such an easygoing tempo, you'll wonder how it could possibly exist so near Silicon Valley's hustle. Locals who know this well-kept secret of a town come here to restore their weary spirits.

Alviso County Park contains a small marina where you can observe private boats bobbing in the high tide. You can also bike or hike along the levees that stretch out into the marshes, passing by bird-watchers with binoculars to their eyes spying on the multitude of gulls flocking here. Far off in the north by Newark is what looks like a large hill. This is the Cargill Salt Flats, where the mineral is harvested. An Amtrak train passes through the marsh, and if you were to follow its tracks north for a mile or so, you'd find the ghost town of Drawbridge, its buildings slowly sinking into the bay's muck.

If you're in Alviso at dusk, the golds and reds of the sunset create impressionistic illusions on the still flatness of the bay waters. It's an eerie feeling standing in the midst of this vast plain of water and land; you get a sense of the simple paradise the valley must have been before the Spanish came. In the mystical quiet, you'll almost swear you can see the ghosts of Ohlone Indians fishing on their reed rafts among the marshes.

In the mission days, what is now Alviso was called the Embarcadero de Santa Clara. It served as a landing site for the Spanish missionaries to receive supplies and to ship out beaver skins, tallow, and cow hides. In 1838, Ignacio Alviso, a member of the original de Anza settlers, established his Rancho Rincon de los Esteros on the land. Eleven years later, four Americans with burned and fences were cut, allowing cattle to roam beyond their pastures. Finally, in 1855, the U.S. Land Commission confirmed that Alviso was the rightful owner. By that time, much of the land was distributed to reimburse the lawyers who, like today's attorneys, were the only true winners in the property squabble. Mentally insane from the never-ending battle for the land, Berryessa died in 1863.

After gold was discovered in the Sierras, many immigrants lured to California by the rush for wealth started settling in eastern Santa Clara Valley. In this section, a small farming community began to form. The first of these newcomers was an Irish immigrant named Michael Huge, who in 1852 built a house along the dirt road passing through this location. It was the first wood-frame building constructed on what would eventually become a village site. Soon, a blacksmith shop opened as well as two adobe saloons, and in 1857, a hotel was built. On May 31, 1858, a merchant named Frederick Creighton established a small post office in his store here. The Yankee tongue had a difficult time pronouncing Penitencia, so Joseph R. Weller, the assistant postmaster, suggested calling their little community "Milpitas" after Alviso's original ranch. In 1861, the Milpitas Township was formed, and the village was officially established.

"As Milpitas goes . . . "

During the Civil War, debates raged throughout the state about whether to support the Northern or Southern cause. One of these debates in San Jose was presided over by a well-known Unitarian preacher named Reverend Thomas Starr King. During the rally, he happened to see a sign carried by a Milpitas citizen dreams of building a port city here bought the land and named it Alviso after Ignacio. In 1849, the port community became the first incorporated city in California. With San Jose as the new state's capital, people predicted big things for Alviso's future as its bay gateway.

As the main junction between Northern and Southern California in the 1850s, Alviso grew into a bustling town, with Santa Clara Valley farmers shipping out much of their agricultural products to the rest of the world from here. Not just cargo came through the town but passengers coming from or going to San Francisco. Steamboats such as the *Boston* and *Jenny Lind* came up Steamboat Slough to the dock, charging $35 for a one-way fare. The stage coach from Alviso to San Jose charged an extra $5. Peter Burnett, California's first American governor, found the place worthy enough to make his home.

Alviso's fortunes changed with the construction of the San Francisco-to-San Jose Railroad in 1864. Over time, farmers and passengers found train transport faster and cheaper, and Alviso's days as a shipping port waned. Still, people dreamed. In 1891, a speculator named P. H. Wheeler thought he could build a major port at this location on the bay's southern end. He called his proposed city New Chicago. To reflect the original Chicago, he named dirt streets after State, Grand, Wabash, Dearborn, and La Salle Avenues. Wheeler's plan was to build a watch company here and sell tracts of the land as the business prospered. Out of 4,000 lots, he sold 800 in the first week. But production and financial problems with the San Jose Watch Company extinguished his dream. In 1929, the city of San Jose bought the New Chicago land to build a sewer system outflow into the bay. One more halfhearted attempt to make Alviso a great port took place in the 1960s with a proposal to build a major airport on the marshland, but thankfully for the bay's fragile ecology, this idea never caught on. Today, Alviso is listed in the National Register of Historical Places, protecting it from any major development.

From I-880 in Milpitas, take Hwy. 237 west for several miles to the 1st St. exit, then head north. For information, call the Alviso Marina, 408/262-6980.

CITIES OF THE VALLEY

reading: "As Milpitas goes, so goes the State." He drew attention to the slogan, and it quickly became a popular saying throughout California, bringing a sort of fame to the farm town of less than 400 people. In vaudeville's early days, the boast even brought Milpitas notoriety around the United States as comedians repeated the slogan to get a laugh from the audience. One vaudeville comic praised the "wonders" of Milpitas, describing its museums, cathedral, and moldering ruins, prompting a naive Frenchman to journey to the town. He was disappointed to find a sleepy burg containing a small railroad station, a blacksmith shop, and a few saloons.

In the 1870s, the major event in Milpitas was the selection of the Calaveras Valley east of the town as the site for an immense dam. This would create a reservoir to provide water for San Francisco residents. The Spring Valley Water Com- pany bought much of the farmland in this area, but the dam was not completed until 1918. It cost $2.5 million to build and was at that time the largest concrete dam in the world.

In the 1880s, a large number of Portuguese families began to settle on farms in the Milpitas area. Many of the men were whalers from the Azores, and when their sailing vessels landed in San Francisco, the captains encouraged the sailors to jump ship so that they could get back with only a skeleton crew. Many of these sailors brought their families over from Portugal and started farming the rich soil.

Horseless Carriage

The 1890s proved uneventful for the small village. The highlight of this decade occurred in May 1896, when a newfangled contraption called a "horseless carriage" passed along the

Milpitas country road on a historic journey from Oakland to San Jose. A reporter from a San Francisco newspaper wrote: "At Milpitas the whole population turned out to see the novelty. All through the town the party was tendered an ovation, but there was an agreeable feeling of security when the sound of the puffing had died away." Those witnesses never would have dreamed that first automobile was the predecessor of the many that have made Milpitas one of the most car-congested regions of Silicon Valley.

By the start of the new century, Milpitas's population had remained constant at about 500 people. Unlike much of the Santa Clara Valley, which was covered with orchards, the main agricultural products here were vegetables, hay, and wheat. The 20th century remained fairly uneventful for the town during the first five decades. But after World War II, the community's simple lifestyle and warm climate started to attract many veterans who had first passed through the Santa Clara Valley on their way to the Pacific war front. In 1951, Ford Motor Company announced it would transfer its Bay Area automobile assembly plant from Richmond to this quiet agricultural community of about 800. This move changed the town dramatically. With the waves of workers now coming in, the community's population grew astoundingly during the next decade. When the citizens incorporated the city in 1954, it had only 840 residents. By 1970, the population had risen to about 25,000 people. During this period, Santa Clara County opened up its Elmwood Rehabilitation Facility here, named after the elm trees growing on the property.

With the region's new focus on high-tech, Milpitas's industrial growth really started to take off. In 1978, the city opened Oak Creek Business Park, its first high-tech trade development. This venture was incredibly successful and sparked a trend toward high-tech companies coming into Milpitas. There are now 24 industrial parks in the city. But success also brought problems to the area. The city's traffic problems are some of the worst in Silicon Valley, with daily backups along its highways and streets

during the work week. The city has made it a priority to address these transportation problems and other urban dilemmas, and is currently considering an extension of the Tasman Corridor Light Rail line as one possible way to alleviate commuter traffic.

TOUR

A Milpitas tour shows the extent of the city's evolution from a rancho to one of Silicon Valley's most prosperous high-tech manufacturing areas. The place to start is at the Mexican-era José Higuera adobe. To get there from San Jose, take I-680 to the Scott Creek Rd. exit, which is actually located in the southern portion of Alameda County in the city of Fremont. Turn right at Scott Creek Rd. and drive about one block into a residential area. Turn right on Green Valley Rd., and drive a short distance to the Milpitas city limits, where the road turns into Park Victoria Drive. Follow this for about half a mile until you see on your left **Higuera Adobe Park** on the corner of Wessex Place. Turn left here and drive into the cul-de-sac that ends in the parking lot.

The historic adobe from the 1840s exists inside the walls of the more modern building you see here, built in the 1960s. Pepper trees shade the structure, and a row of olive trees planted during the Mexican era run along the park's border. Cattle grazing in hilly pastures next to the adobe park give a sense of what this part of the valley must have looked like during the days of Mexico's rule. The adobe is generally not open to the public, but you can glance through the windows to see the rooms inside. Your visit here should take 10–15 minutes.

Drive back to Park Victoria Dr., turning left at the stop sign and following this street through the eastern neighborhoods for about three-quarters of a mile. At the Jacklin Rd. intersection, turn left; it soon becomes Evans Road. This country road on Milpitas's eastern city limits climbs into the foothills for about a mile, allowing you to enjoy the hilly vistas on your left, with suburbs on your right. Evans Rd. ends at Calaveras Rd., where you will turn left. Follow Calaveras Rd. about one mile to the sign on your left showing the way to **Ed R. Levin County Park,** 408/262-6980. Turn left here and follow the road into the park, passing the **Spring Valley Golf Course** on your right.

Just several minutes from Milpitas's downtown, Ed R. Levin Park is a favorite place for locals to escape Silicon Valley life for a while. The land here was once the home of the Tamien Ohlone tribe. Later it consisted mostly of the Rancho Tularcitos (Little Tule Thickets Ranch), the name referring to the tule reeds growing in the lagoons in the park's Laguna Valley. This 4,395-acre land grant was given to José Higuera in 1821 by Pablo Vicente de Sola, California's last Spanish governor. American pioneer Josiah Evans bought 800 acres of the rancho's land in 1853; Evans Rd. is named after him. The park contains the two-acre historic Laguna Cemetery on the southeast corner along Calaveras Road. It dates from the early 1860s and includes Evans's grave. About 16 miles of trails run through the park, including one leading up to beautiful hilltop vistas overlooking the valley on clear days. Search the peaks and you might make out hang gliders taking off from the slopes. Expect to spend at least one hour exploring the park.

Just after the park's main entrance gate, turn right on *Old* Calaveras Rd. (not to be mistaken with the Calaveras Rd. you came up on), and head west. From the hills along this route, you'll get some spectacular views of Silicon Valley as you follow the steep, windy road down to Milpitas's city limit at Evans Road. Turn left here at the stop sign, and take this road back to Calaveras Rd., this time turning right at the stop sign. As you travel west, Calaveras Rd. will turn into Calaveras Blvd., passing through an older neighborhood of the city. Follow the boulevard under I-680, coming into Milpitas city center. At the corner of S. Milpitas Blvd. stands the **Milpitas Civic Center,** 408/942-2318, a complex of buildings including city hall, a community center, and the library. The Civic Center's garden area features a lagoon pond with a prominent geyser fountain next to a playful mermaid statue. If you wish to find out about local events or need information on Milpitas, stop at the city's **Chamber of Commerce,** 408/262-2613, near this location. To get there, turn right at Milpitas Blvd. and take the next right into Sand Hurst Dr., which leads into the strip mall beside the Civic Center. You'll see the chamber's sign prominently displayed over its office.

Back on Calaveras Blvd., head west through Milpitas's downtown area, which consists of a series of shopping centers with many chain stores. At the stoplight intersection of S. Abel St., turn left, following the street for about a mile. On your right, you'll observe a large, imposing facility bordered by containing walls. This is **Elmwood Rehabilitation Center,** a Santa Clara County prison. (Public tours are not available.) At the stoplight intersection after Elmwood, turn left onto Great Mall Pkwy., following it about a quarter mile and taking the Great Mall Dr. entrance into the immense shopping mall parking lot encircling this consumer mecca.

The Great Mall of the Bay Area, 800/625-5229, describes itself as "the largest off-price outlet center west of the Mississippi." The building was originally constructed as the Ford assembly plant, which began manufacturing in 1955, producing cars such as the Falcon, Mustang, Pinto, and for a very brief time, the Edsel. After the plant's manufacturing years ended in 1983, it remained vacant until the mid-1990s, when a developer converted the 1.5 million-square-foot building into a monstrous shopping mall. The Great Mall houses more than 185 specialty stores, many of which sell apparel and shoes. Major stores include Oshman's Supersports, Marshalls, and a Saks Fifth Avenue outlet. Its four main entrances feature transportation theme motifs, such as railroads, ships, cars, and planes. The mall's public area is a large oblong circuit, which forces shoppers to do a lot of walking to get to stores on the far end. Major renovation of the Mall has now been completed. Depending on your shopping habits, plan to spend at least an hour here.

Leaving The Great Mall, turn left back onto Great Mall Pkwy. and drive a quarter mile south to the Montague Expwy. intersection. Turn right at this intersection, driving along the expressway and passing over I-880 more than a mile away. After this point, turn at the next road to the right, McCarthy Blvd., which is the start of the **Oak Creek Business Park,** the city's oldest industrial center. Driving along this road, you'll pass the facilities of some of Milpitas's largest high-tech companies, including Creative Labs, LSI Logic, Lockheed Martin, and Lucent Technologies. Not that long ago, it was set beside large farm fields, where it was not uncommon to see migrant laborers working near this high-tech site: the contrast between the age-old practice of agriculture and the ultramodern Information Revolution was readily apparent here. But those fields have been recently bulldozed and office buildings are being erected on them.

At Bellew Dr., turn right at the stoplight and drive to the end of this street and into the parking lot of **Milpitas Square.** The **Ranch 99 Market** forms the centerpiece of this shopping center, with a playful fish fountain situated in front of this Asian-oriented grocery store. The market is a fun place to stop and shop for exotic edibles such as frozen frog legs, live fish and lobster, and preserved duck eggs. A Chinese deli here serves food that you can enjoy in a sit-down eating area. Reflecting Milpitas's large Asian community, Milpitas Square contains many traditional Chinese eateries, such as the **Mayflower Restaurant** and **Hot Pot City.** For jewelry shoppers, high-quality merchandise can be purchased from several jade and watch dealers, such as **Jade Galore** and **Chong Hing Jewelers.** The **M.V. Trading Company** sells a unique hodgepodge of Asian items, such as porcelain Buddha figures, housewares, and gifts. Plan to spend about an hour browsing through the shops and enjoying one of the restaurants here.

Head west down Bellew Drive. You'll shortly turn right at the Cypress Drive stoplight. Follow this street one block north to Hwy. 237. Merge onto this highway heading east. A short distance away is the I-680 interchange. The southbound entrance leads to San Jose; the northbound entrance leads to Fremont.

POINTS OF INTEREST

Museum of Garbage

Waste disposal and recycling play such an important part in the Silicon Valley lifestyle that it doesn't seem all that weird to find a small Milpitas museum devoted to the history of garbage collection. The museum's self-guided tour provides a good place for families to see how much waste a vast metropolitan area creates. Its Wall of Garbage visually demonstrates the amount of trash Santa Clara County residents generate in three minutes. Interactive displays give visitors a hands-on way to learn about recycling, including a "Zap the Scrap" game that lets kids shoot a small laser at whatever objects they think are recyclable. The museum is located at the Browning Ferris Industries (BFI) recycling plant behind the booth where people bring cans and bottles for recycling.

Western end of Dixon Landing Rd. off I-880 (watch out for BFI trucks as you enter the dumping grounds), 408/262-1401, website: www.bfi.com; admission free; open Mon.–Fri. 7:30 A.M.–3:30 P.M.

NUMMI

Milpitas's auto manufacturing days are over, but if you want a look at what a modern assembly plant looks like, head to nearby Fremont. The New United Motor Manufacturing, Inc. (NUMMI) plant provides a 90-minute tram tour through the giant factory, showing visitors the complicated steps of putting a car together. It's a fascinating process, especially because the automobile is such a vital component of Silicon Valley culture. Call tour guide Sara Rogers at least three months in advance to make a reservation. Shorts and sandals are prohibited for safety reasons. Up to 48 guests can go on a tour, and they must be 10 years or older.

45500 Fremont Blvd., Fremont (take I-880 to the Fremont Blvd. exit heading west, and turn into the plant on Industrial Dr.), 510/498-5765 or 510/770-4008, website: www.nummi.com; visitor parking is just off main gate 5; admission free; tours Tues.–Fri., 9:30 A.M. and 11:30 A.M.

Ed R. Levin County Park

This 1,544-acre park in the Milpitas foothills was named after a county supervisor who campaigned to buy the land from the state and turn it into a park. Hikers can take a rugged trail to 2,594-foot Monument Peak for a magnificent vista of Silicon Valley or watch hang gliders take off from its slopes. A trail leading into open-space protected land outside the county park will take you farther up to the prominent Mission Peak.

From I-680 or 880 in Milpitas, take the Calaveras Blvd. exit and drive east to park entrance sign and turn left, 408/262-6980, website: claraweb.co.santa-clara.ca.us/parks; park in parking lot; entrance fee is $4; activities: reserved campground, children's playground, golf, biking, horseshoe pits, volleyball, horseback riding, fishing, hang gliding; 16 miles of trails.

Chaparral Ranch

This family-run stable has day camps for kids as well as English and western-style riding lessons. You can also make a reservation for a guided horseback tour of the Diablo Range foothills. Call to find out about various rides and their prices.

3375 Calaveras Rd. (east off I-680), 408/263-3336.

Spring Valley Golf Course

Built in 1956, this is one of Silicon Valley's oldest golf courses, set in a canyon in the Milpitas foothills. Its golf school is considered one of the area's best, with friendly instructors providing expert guidance.

3441 E. Calaveras Rd. (next to Ed R. Levin County Park), 408/262-1722; par 72; fees $22–61.

Mission Soaring Center

Professional instructors provide hang-gliding flight lessons for beginner to advanced levels.

Beginners learn the basics of controlling the hang glider on a virtual-reality simulator, then are taken to bunny slopes to work on their technique. The center also has a retail shop selling hang-gliding equipment.

1116 Wrigley Way, 408/262-1055, website: www.hang-gliding.com; try-out lesson is $140; open Wed.–Sat.; lessons must be reserved.

The Great Mall of the Bay Area

A major renovation of the old Ford Motor Company's huge auto manufacturing plant has created this massive outlet center. Its layout forms a circle—which means a *lot* of walking to get from one side to the other. It has an expansive food court and several family-oriented restaurants. A major remodeling in 2000 has made the mall more user-friendly with a walkway through the center of the mall. New Century movie theaters have also been added as well as a 60,000 square foot skateboard and inline skating park designed by some of the world's top skaters.

940 Great Mall Dr. (from I-880, take Montague Expwy. heading east and turn left at Great Mall Pkwy.), 408/956-2033 or 800/625-5229, website: www.greatmallbayarea.com; open Mon.–Sat. 10 A.M.–9 P.M., Sun. 11 A.M.–8 P.M.; major stores: Marshalls, Media Play, Oshman's Supersports, Old Navy, Burlington Coat Factory.

McCarthy Ranch Marketplace

This larger-than-life shopping center built in a faux western ranch style focuses on nationally known chain stores and restaurants. Among these are Wal-Mart, SportMart, Ross Dress for Less, and Borders Bookstore. If you're into country clothes, the Western Warehouse is a fun place to browse through a large selection of cowboy apparel and gifts.

Ranch Dr. (from I-880, take Hwy. 237 exit heading west and turn right at McCarthy Ranch Blvd.), 408/934-0304; hours vary with each store.

Mountain View

© MARTIN CHEEK

CITIES OF THE VALLEY

Civic efforts have restored interest in charming downtown Mountain View.

Around noontime, the spicy-oily aroma wafting from a multitude of Asian restaurants fills Castro St., Mountain View's downtown district. Drawing office workers for their lunch break, the district's energetic pace picks up with increased pedestrian traffic. At night, downtown Mountain View's restaurants and nightclubs turn it into one of Silicon Valley's most dynamic attractions. This once-neglected part of the city experienced a renaissance in the late 1980s, when $60 million was poured into a major renovation to give the area a more upscale appearance. The construction of a modern civic center and performing arts auditorium added significantly to the facelift. Much of the money for the project came from the surge of high-tech companies that established corporate operations here, creating newfound wealth for the city.

Mountain View is a busy industrial city of about 75,000 residents, expanding to 100,000 people during the day with the incoming workforce. Its territory is bordered on the west by Palo Alto, on the north by the San Francisco Bay and Moffett Field, on the east by Sunnyvale, and on the south by Los Altos. Like other Silicon Valley cities, Mountain View has left its agricultural past and now focuses extensively on high-tech. With more than 4,400 employers based here, the city's largest employer is Silicon Graphics. Netscape Communications, which employs about 2,000 people, also has contributed significantly to Mountain View's prosperity. Other major companies include Sun Microsystems, Hewlett-Packard, Intuit, and high-tech market research group Frost & Sullivan.

Mountain View balances its residential and industrial areas well, but it has a high housing density compared with other Silicon Valley cities. Two-thirds of its residents live in apartments and condominiums, and monthly rents for two- or three-bedroom apartments range from $1,100 to $1,700. An average sales price for a single-family home here is about $530,000. Mountain View has been included on the *San Francisco Chronicle*'s list of "Most Livable Cities in the Bay Area," and its excellent public parks contribute to its enviable quality of life. One of the most popular is a 660-acre open-space preserve called Shoreline Park. Located along bay tidal lands, it attracts visitors who come for golf, windsurfing, bird-watching, and other recreational opportunities. In the park's vicinity is the Shoreline Amphitheatre, an outdoor complex built on a landfill that brings major entertainers to Mountain View.

Adjacent to Mountain View is Moffett Field, a historic airfield used as a base for military operations as well as by the National Aeronautics and Space Administration. NASA's prestigious Ames Research Center is located here, performing state-of-the-art research in astronomy, virtual reality, and aircraft design. With the government's military closure of Moffett Field due to federal budget-cutting, the cities of Mountain

View and Sunnyvale are currently working with NASA to develop an Air & Space Center in Hangar One, a massive structure originally built to house U.S. Navy dirigibles. To be completed some time in the early 21st century, the museum will become the West Coast's premier space museum, housing high-tech vehicles such as a decommissioned Space Shuttle. (Check out the website casc.arc.nasa.gov for the progress on this ambitious project.) Already, Moffett Field has started its transformation into a recreational attraction with its U.S. Space Camp facility, where youngsters can learn what it's like to train as an astronaut.

Mountain View's cultural life centers on the downtown Castro St. area. Annual events held here include an art and wine festival, an Asian New Year parade, and an Affribean festival. It's also the setting for a farmers' market held on Sundays. The stunning Center for the Performing Arts in the Civic Center's plaza is a state-of-the-art auditorium, as well as the home of TheatreWorks, a theatrical company that has received national accolades. Mountain View's focus on developing cultural pursuits includes the Community School of Music & Arts (CSMA), Silicon Valley's largest not-for-profit arts education center. Founded in 1968, it has more than 75 professional musicians and artists on its faculty providing classes for thousands of students, from children to senior citizens.

HISTORY

The Ohlone Indians once lived on the marshland area around what is now Mountain View's Shoreline Park and NASA Ames Research Center. Their community was conveniently located near the bay, where they often fished from reed rafts. After the Spanish settled the area, the Ohlone village got smaller as the Indians joined the mission. They began to spend their time tending sheep on mission land a few miles south of the bay they once had fished on.

During the Mexican control of the region, the mission's grazing land became known as Rancho Pastoría de las Borregas (Ewe Lambs Pasture Ranch), as well as Rancho Refugio (Refuge

Ranch). In 1842, Governor Alvarado granted this massive piece of property to Francisco Estrada. After Estrada's death a short time later, it passed to his father-in-law, Don Mariano Castro. It was later halved into two sections, with the Permanente Creek as the official dividing line. Castro sold the southern portion to Irish-American immigrant Martin Murphy Jr., and this bit of real estate would eventually become the city of Sunnyvale. He held onto the northern section, which would later form much of what is now Mountain View's city limits.

Another portion of land making up today's Mountain View was located along the San Francisco Bay. In 1844, Mexican governor Micheltorena gave 1,697 acres of the original Indian land by the bay to Chief Lope Ynigo, one of the valley's few natives to receive a land grant. Ynigo called it Rancho Posolmi. This land would later be bought by Robert Walkinshaw, who changed the name to Mountain View Ranch. The new owner allowed Ynigo to stay on the ranch until the chief's death in 1864 at the age of 104. The bay land would eventually be used as Portuguese dairies as well as for seed-growing fields.

Fremont House

In 1852, the village of Mountain View took root when American settler James Campbell established a stop for the Butterfield Stage Line that ran between San Francisco and San Jose. This stop was located near what was then the intersection of Alviso Road. Close by stood a popular inn called Fremont House, where travelers could rest during arduous journeys and locals could socialize. The inn became a prominent spot in the area, so much of a landmark, in fact, that the area now consisting of Palo Alto, Los Altos, and Mountain View was officially christened the Fremont Township. A supply store was built across from the Fremont House, and it soon became evident that a village was emerging. One lovely day, the legend goes, the locals were trying to think of a good name for their new community, but all of their suggestions never seemed adequate to describe the area's pristine beauty. Finally, store owner Jacob Shumway looked out from his business, admired the scenic vista of the Santa Cruz Mountains, and suggested that they call the town Mountain View. Few disputed the name that seemed to describe the area perfectly.

One of Mountain View's most important pioneers was Henry Rengstorff, a German who reached San Francisco in the fall of 1850 with only $4 in his pocket. While working on the steamer *Jack Robinson,* which traveled between San Francisco and Alviso, he realized the opportunity for tremendous wealth in the fertile South Bay region. After saving enough money, in 1860 Rengstorff bought many acres of marshland along the Mountain View shoreline. At what is now Shoreline Park, he built wharves and warehouses to accommodate the increase in shipping as Santa Clara Valley's agricultural industry grew. The enterprise became known as Rengstorff's Landing.

Realizing the importance of education for the area's children, Rengstorff established Mountain View's first school, Whisman School. To show that the poor immigrant had "arrived," in 1867 he built himself a magnificent Italianate house and garden on his property about a half mile from his landing. It was the growing village's most attractive home, and it's now Mountain View's most important historic landmark. (To make room for office buildings at Shoreline Business Park, the Santa Clara County Historical Heritage Commission relocated the house to Shoreline Park.)

In 1864, the Central Railroad laid tracks for its San Francisco–San Jose line about a mile northwest of Mountain View's original village area. Seeing a future for the community near the railroad, Crisanto Castro, the son of Don Mariano, laid out new streets next to the area where the present Caltrain station is located. Although the original town still received much commerce and many travelers along El Camino Real, the new Mountain View began to grow as the railroad brought it to life. A business area began to form along Castro St., named in honor of the farsighted Crisanto.

Despite the railroad's competition, Rengstorff's Landing remained a bustling business for the next two decades. In 1890, it was shipping up to four million pounds of freight per month from Santa Clara Valley farmers. The Mountain View area also produced its own agricultural products, including fruit from orchards and wine from the 22 wineries operating near the city. By the turn of the 19th century, the town had a population of about 900 people.

Mountain View's first few decades of the 20th century were relatively uneventful. It incorporated on November 7, 1902, and the city grew slowly, with agriculture still its primary economic focus. In the 1930s, the U.S. government was experimenting with the use of dirigibles for the military. The navy chose the unincorporated land east of Sunnyvale and Mountain View to build a massive hangar to house these lighter-than-air crafts designed to carry military biplane fighters. Originally known as Navy Air Station Sunnyvale, Moffett Field was used as an airship base for only a short time until the program ended with the crash of the **Akron** and the **Macon.** During World War II, the navy used the site as an airstrip to train pilots. The base later became home to NASA Ames Research Center, where many advances in space and aeronautics technology have taken place.

The postwar years saw a dramatic increase in the population of the entire valley, including Mountain View. High-tech business came into the city when in 1955, Nobel Prize–winner William Shockley, co-inventor of the transistor, set up his laboratory and corporate headquarters here near El Camino Real. After a couple of years, eight of his employees left to establish Fairchild Semiconductor, also based in Mountain View. Fairchild was an important company in Silicon Valley's history—many of its engineers went on to start their own semiconductor companies. Among these was Intel, which started with 12 employees in a single room in Mountain View, and later moved to Santa Clara to become the industry's largest chip maker.

With the PC revolution of the 1980s, many high-tech companies wanted to establish bases in Mountain View. The inflow of tax revenue made the city prosperous, and about $60 million of this money was spent in the late 1980s and early 1990s renovating the downtown district along Castro Street. The project included a new civic center as well as the construction of one of the valley's most elegant performing arts centers. In February 1993, President Clinton and Vice President Gore toured the Mountain View headquarters of Silicon Graphics. During this visit, they announced their administration's vigorous policy on supporting the high-tech industry. This choice of locale demonstrated to the world that Silicon Valley was in the enviable position of being the United States' most prominent technology center.

TOUR

This tour of Mountain View follows its historic and high-tech developments. From Hwy. 85, take the El Camino Real exit, heading west along this busy roadway. In the vicinity of Grant Rd., you'll pass through the site of the **original village** of Mountain View. Imagine El Camino Real as it was in the mid-1800s, a stage route along the country road connecting San Francisco and San Jose. The Fremont House once stood in this part of the city as a stop for weary stagecoach travelers. This historic hotel has been replaced by modern motels and fast-food restaurants.

Continue driving down El Camino Real until you reach the stoplight intersection of Castro Street. Turn right here, and enter Mountain View's **downtown business district.** Park on the street or in one of the free public parking lots on either side of Castro Street. Begin your tour of the downtown area at **Pioneer Park,** where the terra-cotta-colored **Civic Center** is located. Pioneer Park was the location of a frontier-era cemetery where many of the city's early citizens were laid to rest. You'll find here some antique farming equipment as well as Silicon Valley's most modern library—its second-story reading room overlooking the park has a cozy fireplace. Among the modern sculptures you'll view in the **Civic Center Plaza** is a fanciful one propelled by breezes that decorates the front of the stunning **Mountain View Center for Performing Arts,** 650/903-6565. In the small building in the park's southern portion, you'll find the office for the **Mountain View Chamber of Commerce,** 580

Castro St., 650/968-8378. Here you can get information such as upcoming community events, as well as pick up a pamphlet describing a walking tour of the downtown's historic buildings. The nearby public library has a small **Mountain View History Room,** 650/903-6335, filled with memorabilia as well as documents telling the city's story. It's open Tues., Thurs., and Sat. 1–5 P.M., Wed. 5–9 P.M.

After Pioneer Park, continue strolling down Castro Street. The downtown area takes on a more colorful atmosphere as you cross California Street. Continuing along the street, as you pass **Colonel Lee's Mongolian Bar-B-Que,** 650/968-0381, take a moment to look through the window to watch the chef preparing meals at the immense grill. Across the street from this restaurant is the **Printers Inc. Bookstore,** 650/961-8500, where a wood cutout of a smiling Ernest Hemingway stands to greet you at the front door. With its small coffee shop inside, the bookstore is a favorite place for Mountain View residents and workers to come and browse. Farther north, you'll pass the **Rio Grande,** with its neon sign showing a cowboy on a bucking horse. Opened in 1999, this nightclub-restaurant was originally a movie theater built in 1926. The new owners spent $4 million renovating it into Silicon Valley's most upscale country-western bar and eatery. The downtown district is also known for its coffee shops, and one of them, called **The Coffee Garden,** 650/967-0103, has put up a street sign alerting pedestrians: "Warning! Last chance for espresso coffee for half a block." The Caltrain stop at the end of Castro St. along Central Expwy. marks the end of the downtown district. There's no depot building here, the site at which the second Mountain View community received its start.

After you finish touring downtown, drive east along California St. five blocks until you reach S. Shoreline Boulevard. Turn right here, following Shoreline Blvd. for about two miles. After crossing over U.S. 101, you'll enter the North Bayshore district of Mountain View, an area much in use for office space and research-and-development facilities. Continue along Shoreline Blvd. through the series of office complexes mak-

THE SEARCH FOR EXTRATERRESTRIAL INTELLIGENCE

In 1577, English adventurer Sir Francis Drake sailed on the *Golden Hind* in search of "Terra Australis Incognita." During his quest for this new world believed to lie in the South Pacific, he voyaged along California's coast quite near to the Silicon Valley region, stopping to repair his ship at what is now Point Reyes.

Four centuries later, another exciting search is taking place in Silicon Valley, led by Drake's namesake, a U.C. Santa Cruz astronomy professor named Frank Drake. But instead of looking for earthbound lands, the Search for Extraterrestrial Intelligence Institute (SETI Institute), website: www.seti.org, is on a quest to find proof of civilizations established on worlds orbiting other stars. As president of this nonprofit organization, headquartered in Mountain View, the modern Drake is heading up the search, which scans the radio bandwidth for any signal that might come from an intelligent nonterrestrial source.

Drake and other astronomers began their quest in 1960 with Project Ozma, the first radio SETI program. (It was named after the queen of Oz in author L. Frank Baum's fantasyland.) NASA was involved with the program until 1993, when Congress cut off government funding due to lack of results. Two years later, the privately financed SETI Institute began Project Phoenix, the most ambitious systematic search ever mounted for extraterrestrial radio signals. Using a 210-foot radio telescope in New South Wales, Australia, the scientific organization's computers monitor signals in the 1,000–3,000 MHz band from about 1,000 sunlike stars within 200 light-years of earth. The computers "listen" to 28 million radio channels simultaneously, trying to find a signature signal that could possibly come from some alien civi-

lization. In the movie *Contact,* Jodie Foster discovered the signal while listening to her headset in her convertible, but the chances of such a random discovery would be truly astronomical. Thus, although it's less dramatic than the Hollywood version, it's more likely that one of the SETI Institute's powerful computers will be the one to make this important discovery.

According to a formula developed by Frank Drake in 1961, there's a strong possibility that there exists some race on another planet that has developed the technology necessary to transmit radio signals. Known as the Drake Equation, this string of variables states that the number of communicative civilizations is equal to the rate of the formation of suitable stars times a fraction of stars with planets times the number of Earth-like worlds per planetary system times a fraction of life developing on those planets times a fraction of intelligence forming in those life forms times a fraction of those civilizations that develop radio technology times the lifetime of that civilization.

Depending on what numbers are used (many of these variables are necessarily just intelligent guesses), there might be well over a million civilizations among the 100 billion stars of the Milky Way Galaxy. And perhaps sometime in the 21st century, the SETI Institute might find one of these civilization-broadcast microwave radio signals sent from somewhere in our galactic neighborhood. Just like the discovery of the New World in the 1500s created a revolution of ideas in the Renaissance, the discovery of this important radio signal will shake up humanity's political, social, and religious institutions. For the first time in human history, we will know without a doubt that intelligent life (other than our own) exists among the stars.

ing up the Shoreline Business Park. The twin-peaked structure on your left resembling a circus tent is the **Shoreline Amphitheatre,** 650/967-4040, where Bill Graham Presents brings top entertainers to perform throughout the year. Built on a landfill in the early 1980s, during its first years as an amphitheater, the garbage decaying here produced methane gas that concert-goers in the grassy areas would ignite with cigarette lighters to produce small explosions. Continue driving another half mile, entering into **Shoreline Park,** 650/903-6392, following the curving road that meanders through San Francisco Bay meadowlands, and park in one of the several lots at the end of the road.

Shoreline Park is Mountain View's best recreational facility. It features a well-tended golf course, eateries, and a large lake with a boathouse, from which windsurfing enthusiasts can rent equipment. The park is also where the house of Mountain View pioneer Henry Rengstorff has been relocated, and it is available for tours as well as conferences. A few locals have suggested the house is haunted by Rengstorff's ghost—visitors and former tenants have reported strange cries at night, doors mysteriously moving, and unearthly drafts that send shivers through the body. After checking out the park's attractions, take a walk along the bayland trail. Looking out toward the north, you'll see the Dumbarton Bridge as well as the white mountains of salt at the Cargill Salt Flats. The bay winds can often get chilly during the afternoon, so bring a sweater or windbreaker if you wish to linger. Expect to spend about an hour here.

After your visit to Shoreline Park, return along Shoreline Blvd. the way you came. Less than half a mile after the park's gatehouse, turn left at Amphitheatre Parkway. The large, modern building on your right is **Silicon Graphics**'s headquarters. Also on your right, you'll see Charleston Park—make sure to catch a glimpse of the comical stainless-steel sculpture of an immense silhouetted figure leaning against a giant podium. Continue through the industrial park area for another half mile or so. Amphitheatre Pkwy. connects with U.S. 101. The northbound entrance leads to San Francisco. The southbound entrance, which leads to San Jose, can be a little tricky to get onto.

POINTS OF INTEREST
NASA Ames Visitor Center
At this small visitor center, space buffs can get a look at NASA's research programs in Silicon Valley. A free two-hour tour of the Ames facilities is available by reservation. It includes the flight simulation area, the world's largest wind tunnel, and a centrifuge to test the force of increased gravity on the human body.

Moffett Field (from U.S. 101 along Mountain View, take Moffett Field exit), 650/604-6274; parking in visitor center lot; admission free; open Mon.–Fri. 8 A.M.–4:30 P.M.

Space Camp
Children dreaming of being the next explorer to set foot on lunar soil will definitely find Space Camp a memorable experience, perhaps their first small step toward cosmic achievement. The program originally started in Huntsville, Alabama, and in the mid-1990s, a modified California version opened at Moffett Field. The camp provides an introduction to the technologies and sciences necessary for celestial voyages. Participants will experience the 1/6th Gravity Chair, which simulates their weight on the moon, and

the historic home of Henry Rengstorff, Mountain View's shipping–port magnate and education booster

CITIES OF THE VALLEY

© MARTIN CHEEK

WHERE THEY AMES FOR THE STARS

Silicon Valley's sacred shrine to the study of space and aircraft is NASA's Ames Research Center in Moffett Field. Situated between Mountain View and the San Francisco Bay, its origins date from December 20, 1939, when it was founded as an aircraft research laboratory by the National Advisory Committee on Aeronautics (NACA). The center was named after Dr. Joseph S. Ames, NACA chairman from 1927 to 1939, and has become one of the world's premier centers for advanced aircraft and spacecraft research and development. In 1958, as the world entered the Space Age, the NACA turned into the National Aeronautics and Space Administration, and Ames has been run by NASA ever since.

More than 1,600 government workers and 2,000 contractor personnel work on the 430 acres at Ames. As NASA's Center of Excellence in Information Systems site, the facility performs cutting-edge research in the fields of supercomputers, networking, artificial intelligence, computer modeling, and virtual reality. Many of its supercomputers—some of the world's fastest—are used for computational analysis in aircraft and spacecraft development. In the field of space research, Ames is the site of NASA's Astrobiology Institute and the Center for Mars Exploration, which studies Mars's ecosystem. Ames is also currently developing proposals and technologies so that humans can, at some point in the 21st century, voyage to the Red Planet (actually, scientists now describe it as "butterscotch" in color).

Ames also is home to three wind tunnels, one of them the world's largest, at 40 by 80 feet. This was used to study a one-third-scale model of the space shuttle (which can be viewed outside Ames's visitor center). It also has several advanced flight simulators to train pilots and astronauts. Also here is the Computer Museum History Center, 650/964-1231, a developing organization that is the California division of Boston's well-known Computer Museum. Currently, this center is open by appointment only, but plans include a public display of its artifact collection of pioneering personal computers and supercomputers, as well as a library where scholars can study software, photographs, and technical specs. Only about 5 percent of the center's massive collection is available for viewing.

A small visitor center located next to the center's largest wind tunnel provides a look at NASA's various research programs. Here, you can view artifacts from the United States' space explorations, including a backup Mercury capsule for Alan Shepard's Freedom 7 flight and a chunk of moon rock from the Apollo 15 mission. A gift shop sells NASA-related items such as flight patches, posters, and T-shirts. Free two-hour tours of the Ames facility, available by reservation, include the flight simulation center, the big wind tunnel, and a centrifuge used to test the force of increased gravity on the human body.

To reach Ames, 650/604-6274, from U.S. 101, take the Moffett Field exit and drive east. Turn left at the stop sign before the main gate, and stop at the small guardhouse (the guard will need to see some form of photo identification). Park in the visitor center lot. Admission is free. Open Mon.–Fri. 8 A.M.–4 P.M.

the Five Degrees of Freedom training chair, which simulates movement in the microgravity of space. Kids learn teamwork in mock Space Shuttle missions, taking on roles as crew members in a Shuttle simulator or as mission control members. For ages 7–11. Moffett Field, 800/637-7223, website: www.spacecamp.com; open all year; tuition is $300–800 depending on program.

Shoreline Park

For water sports or simply taking a relaxing stroll along tidal marshlands, this tranquil park fronting San Francisco Bay is a great place to go for recreation. It's a popular place for bird-watchers because a number of migratory and native birds such as storks, ducks, and gulls find a haven here. **Shoreline Golf Links,** 650/969-2041, was built here in 1982. Designed by Robert Trent Jones Jr., this 18-hole course has numerous bunkers to challenge golfers. Greens fees range from $30 to $42. Casually elegant restaurant **Michaels at Shoreline,** 650/962-1014, overlooks the golf greens. Also in the park, Shoreline Lake is Silicon Valley's most popular spot for windsurfing, and **Spinnaker Sailing** boathouse, 650/965-7474, provides windsurfing lessons and rentals. An adjoining café is a good place to enjoy a meal or hot cup of coffee as you watch the windsurfers or paddleboaters brave the waves.

Of historical interest at Shoreline Park is **Henry Rengstorff House,** 650/903-6988, built by the patriarch of an important Mountain View pioneer family. Overlooking the serene marshlands, this 12-room house is the city's oldest home and considered one of the West Coast's best examples of Victorian Italianate architecture. The house's four parlors showcase four ornate marble fireplaces as well as fine Victorian furnishings. After years of neglect, the house was moved to its present location in the park and restored in 1990. Docent-led tours are free. Open Sun., Tues., and Wed. 11 A.M.–5 P.M. 2600 N. Shoreline Blvd. (take Shoreline Blvd. exit off U.S. 101 in Mountain View and drive north to the end), 650/903-6392; admission free; open daily 8 A.M.–sunset; activities: biking, sailing, golf, bird-watching, hiking.

Farmers' Market

The Mountain View Farmers' Market is held downtown every Sun. 9 A.M.–1 P.M. 100 Castro St. parking lot (corner of Hope St. and W. Evelyn Ave.), 800/806-3276.

TheatreWorks

This nationally recognized theater company performs a variety of stage works, including comedies, dramas, and musicals. It has broken traditional boundaries with its alternative and multicultural casting. Since its founding in 1970 by Artistic Director Robert Kelley, the dynamic company has performed 38 world premieres and 59 regional premieres.

Mountain View Center for Performing Arts (downtown Civic Center at 500 Castro St.), 650/903-6000 or 888/273-3752, website: www.theatreworks.org; also performs at Palo Alto's Lucie Stern Theatre; individual tickets: $20–38; season tickets (eight shows): $144–320.

Sunnyvale

Where Mathilda Ave. crosses the Caltrain tracks, there stands a landmark that serves to remind one of the dramatic changes Sunnyvale underwent in the 20th century. Close to the overpass, a water tower has been painted to look like an immense can of fruit cocktail. The site at one time was a Libby's cannery, one of the busiest enterprises during the time Santa Clara County was known as the Valley of Heart's Delight. The water tower is now surrounded by buildings belonging to Applied Signal Technologies, seeming to emphasize the fact that the former agricultural hub has been engulfed by the high-tech industry.

Sunnyvale's 23.8 square miles are bordered on the west by Mountain View and Los Altos, on the north by Moffett Field and the San Francisco Bay, on the east by Santa Clara, and on the south by Cupertino along Homestead Road. The northern half contains most of the city's high-tech companies, including the headquarters of Advanced Micro Devices and Lockheed Martin Missiles & Space.

As a promotion slogan, turn-of-the-19th-century Sunnyvale marketers gave the community the lofty title "City of Destiny." If they could see what their small town grew to become a hundred years later, they would certainly be amazed to find out where its destiny has led it. From an agricultural town of 1,675 in 1920, it has grown into Silicon Valley's second largest community, home to more than 133,000 people. Established on the development of high-tech industries, the city enjoys a healthy fiscal condition, achieved by planning the budget for a 10-year time frame instead of the usual two-year cycle. In 1995, this successful management brought Sunnyvale national recognition when President Clinton and Vice President Gore singled it out for its efficient government style.

Sunnyvale has a relatively young, family-oriented population, with a median age of 34.5 years, and this is reflected in the active lifestyle of many of its residents. They can often be found enjoying outdoor activities in the city's more than 17 public parks and recreational facilities.

© MARTIN CHEEK

Sunnyvale's historic Murphy Avenue lies at the heart of the city's downtown shopping district.

On the San Francisco Bay marshlands close to the industrial parks in the city's most northern section is Twin Creeks Sports Complex, a major sports facility considered the largest softball park in the world. Next to it lie the serene Sunnyvale Baylands, a nature preserve where citizens can take quiet strolls along marshland walkways. A 10-acre working orchard and interpretative exhibit pavilion called Orchard Heritage Park is now open to the pubic at the Sunnyvale Community Center.

The community's central and southern portion are made up of mature, middle-class neighborhoods and retail businesses in strip malls along El Camino Real and other major thoroughfares. Many of Sunnyvale's residents rent houses or apartments. Although considered high-priced compared with the rest of the United States, Sunnyvale houses are relatively inexpensive for Silicon Valley. The median sales price for a home is $380,477, as opposed to the region's average of $500,000.

At the heart of the city near the Caltrain depot is the picturesque one-block downtown district. This historic portion of S. Murphy St. features a number of colorful boutiques, restaurants, and Irish pubs. Connected to it in an architecturally awkward style is the Town and Country Village Shopping Center as well as the Sunnyvale Town Center Mall. Compared with neighboring Silicon Valley cities, Sunnyvale's cultural scene is not as vibrant (probably due to its young, work-focused population), but it has its share of artistic endeavors. Its Community Center complex at 550 E. Remington Ave. includes a 200-seat auditorium for local theatrical performances such as those performed by the Sunnyvale Community Players. A city-sponsored program focuses on bringing art into public places, with sculptures and paintings displayed at the Civic Center, senior center, and other locations. Among its most popular artworks is one located at the entrance of the city's public library. Called *Out to Lunch,* it's a lifelike bronze sculpture of a young boy engrossed in a book.

HISTORY

The land Sunnyvale now sits upon was originally used by Mission Santa Clara Indian neophytes for grazing sheep. With the Mexican secularization of the valley, the area now south of U.S. 101 was granted by California governor Juan Bautista Alvarado to Francisco Estrada in 1842. The 8,800-acre grant became the Rancho Pastoría de las Borregas, also called Rancho Refugio. A few years later, the property passed into the hands of Mariano Castro, Estrada's father-in-law, who inherited it after his daughter's and son-in-law's deaths.

Among the area's first European-American settlers was Martin Murphy Jr., an Irish immigrant who journeyed overland into California with his father and other family members in 1844. After living on his ranch for several years in the Sacramento area, in 1850, Murphy gave Mariano Castro $12,500 for a large section of the Rancho Pastoría, where he started his own cattle ranch. He called it Bay View due to its expansive overlook of San Francisco Bay's southern waters. With additional land purchases, the property soon expanded to 4,894 acres. By the early 1860s, the Central Railroad built the San Jose to San Francisco railroad through Murphy's property. He gave them the right-of-way permission to construct this important link in exchange for allowing him to put a flag stop not far from his ranch house. This stop quickly became known as Murphy's Station. Murphy later built a $2,000 station depot farther south along the line at what is now the Sunnyvale–Santa Clara border, and this became known as Lawrence Station. It was named after Albert C. Lawrence, who founded a small community there.

The railroads proved an important means for farmers to get their produce to market. With the increased settlement of the valley, orchards and vineyards were soon being planted in the Bay View Ranch region. A New Yorker named Lemuel Perry Collins purchased 320 acres here in 1862, and along with orchards, planted a 160-acre vineyard on the property. Lemuel died in 1879, and his brother, Salvin, took over the business and turned it into one of the region's more profitable enterprises, selling much of the wine he produced at his San Francisco saloon. In 1884, he died and his widow, Angelia, took over the operations, shipping, at the winery's peak, more than 300 gallons a day from the nearby Mountain View docks.

City of Destiny

After Martin Murphy's death in 1884, his large estate was divided among his surviving children and grandchildren. In 1897, one heir, Patrick Murphy, sold 200 acres of his inherited land for $38,000 to real estate developer Walter Everett Crossman. This land was located around what is now the Murphy Ave. downtown district. Crossman, an enterprising real estate promoter who wore stylish fedoras and smoked smelly cigars, saw that a small community was beginning to form around Murphy's Station, so he subdivided the property into lots for residences. To lure San Francisco residents down to the South Bay, he began promoting the property as a pleasant place to live. Initially, he called his embryonic town Encinal (where the oak grows) after the area's Encinal Nursery, and he boasted that it was a place where "five acres will put a man in a comfortable position." But the burgeoning town's name was a major marketing mistake. It created confusion among potential homeowners because there al-

THE GHOST OF MARTIN MURPHY JR.

The story of Martin Murphy Jr. is the kind of saga that could easily be turned into a TV miniseries, but with a surprise ending no script-writing hack (except perhaps one for the *X-Files*) could ever imagine.

Born on November 9, 1807, in the town of Balnamough near Wexford, Ireland, Murphy came with his large family to the United States as a young man. By 1844, as part of the Murphy-Townsend-Stephens party, he was among the first to come overland by wagon across the plains and into California. This party was also the first to open up the Sierra divide by way of the Truckee River (a route now used by skiers along I-80), becoming the main immigrant trail for the Gold Rush as well as serving as the Sierra passage for the transcontinental railroad in the 1860s. Murphy's wife Mary gave birth to a daughter at this point, naming her Elizabeth, the first child of immigrant parents born in California. She almost drowned during a crossing of the Yuba River so they gave her the middle name "Yuba."

In the vicinity of Sutter's Fort, Murphy settled along the Cosumnes River (the nearby town of Murphys is named after his brother John). His ranch was visited by such historical figures as John Frémont, Kit Carson, and William T. Sherman. Murphy became the first to raise grain in the Sacramento Valley and stayed here for about five years, until deciding to join his father in the Santa Clara Valley where there were facilities to educate his children. He bought 5,000 acres of the Rancho Pastoria de las Borregas and named his ranch Bayview because of its proximity to San Francisco Bay. He had a 30-room two-story house precut and milled in Bangor, Maine, and shipped around the Horn. It was put together with pegs and leather straps and became a showcase home of the valley, surrounded by gardens and lawns. For many years, the house was a social destination visited by famous people who came to the area.

The hardworking and intelligent Murphy worked the land, building his fortune to about $5 million (a good sum for an illiterate immigrant who could only sign documents with an "X"). He and his wife were generous to friends and strangers alike, and as a devout Catholic, he remained an honest and trusted businessman all his life. He helped establish the College of Santa Clara (later called Santa Clara University). On July 18, 1881, he and his wife Mary celebrated their golden wedding anniversary, bringing in as many as 10,000 guests and feeding them with barbecue and champagne. It was described as "the most fabulous social event ever held in California." When Murphy died on October 20, 1884, all of California paid tribute to this important pioneer.

As Sunnyvale grew, the Murphy family continued living in the Bayview Ranch house until 1953 when it was given to the city. Sunnyvale neglected this important historic landmark and it weathered severely over the years. On September 28, 1961, bulldozers knocked the frame house into a pile of debris to make room for an ugly concrete community center. The garden area that had surrounded the home was turned into a city park.

Locals claim that Martin Murphy Jr.'s ghost haunts the Silicon Valley, and—of all places—the Sunnyvale Toys "R" Us store. This store was built on the location of Murphy's horse stables where he loved to spend much of his time tending his animals. A friendly ghost reportedly haunts the store and the local legend gained national exposure in an episode of the "That's Incredible!" TV show. The spook moves toys, drops lunch boxes on customers or caresses their hair, turns on lights and faucets, and whispers in people's ears "I hate crowds." One employee claims to have met the ghost in the stock room. It could well be Murphy's spirit, as the California pioneer is said to have an Irish mischievousness in his character.

ready was a community by that name in the East Bay. Crossman realized he needed to come up with a new and catchy name, one that would contrast his community with foggy San Francisco. In 1901 he came up with the pleasant-sounding moniker Sunnyvale. The name stuck, and in his marketing material, Crossman began boasting of Sunnyvale as "The City of Destiny."

Part of Sunnyvale's destiny, in Crossman's farsighted vision, was to be the home of industrial companies. At first, major industry was reluctant to come to this sleepy orchard-farm town. But in 1906, the great earthquake hit the Bay Area, and among the many manufacturing plants demolished by this catastrophe was the Joshua Hendy Iron Works in San Francisco. Crossman promised the company 32 acres of free land if they would relocate to Sunnyvale. The foundry took him up on his generous offer and began construction on the new headquarters near the town's central business district. This proved an important step in Sunnyvale's transformation from a community of orchards to a city of industry. Among other pioneering factories that soon established themselves here were the Jubilee Incubator Company, the Johnson Traction Engine Company, and the Goldy Machine Company. Agriculture still played a vital role in the area, but it entered a new era when Libby, McNeil & Libby's massive canning complex was built near the railroad tracks to ship goods to San Francisco's port.

By 1910, residents were so proud of their growing community that one wrote a four-verse song played to the tune of "My Country 'Tis of Thee." The first verse went:

Sun-ny-vale 'tis of thee/City of Destiny/Of thee we sing;

Home of the Iron Works/Place where nobody shirks/But helps to boost along/Sweet Sunnyvale!

Sunnyvale officially became a city when it incorporated on December 24, 1912. Orchards and industry existed well together for the first few decades of the 20th century, and little Sunnyvale prospered until the Great Depression hit. At this time, the U.S. Navy was looking for a location to base its new program of constructing massive dirigibles for military use. Military leaders believed these ships of the sky could be used as airborne aircraft carriers. The navy had narrowed its choices to San Diego's Camp Kearney and a 1,000-acre tract of undeveloped bayland east of Sunnyvale. A base would bring more than 500 badly needed construction jobs as well as many service jobs to the chosen site, so both San Diego and Santa Clara County offered to provide the land for a token $1.

On December 12, 1930, the U.S. government finally announced its choice: the Bay Area location, calling it Naval Air Station Sunnyvale. On October 5, 1931, construction began on the $2.25 million Hangar One to house these great aircraft carriers, and by the following spring, the gargantuan structure was completed. Two dirigibles, the Akron and the Macon, made Sunnyvale their home base. Unfortunately, just three days before the base's official dedication ceremony, the Akron crashed off the New Jersey coast, and among the dead was Rear Admiral William Moffett, a major promoter of the dirigible program. The base was given the name Moffett Field in his honor. On February 12, 1935, the Macon crashed near Big Sur, killing all but three of its crew. This brought an end to the United States' short-lived dirigible experiment. But the military found other uses for the site. During World War II, the navy used Moffett Field as a training ground for its carrier and bomber squadron pilots, among them actor Jimmy Stewart. The base quickly become an important component of Sunnyvale's economic life and social character.

Lockheed

During the early 1940s, the city of Sunnyvale increasingly moved away from agriculture and toward industrialization as it manufactured equipment for the war effort. One esteemed visitor, Senator Harry S. Truman, visited the Joshua Hendy Iron Works during his 1943 tour of the United States as chairperson of a special committee to probe waste in war production. He seemed pleased with the efficiency of the foundry, which provided massive engines for the Liberty Ships. It's highly likely that during his visit, Truman heard the workers' theme song, which went:

We're the iron men of Hendy/and sing of liberty
And every ship that rides the sea/has a part
of you and me.

We're the iron men of Hendy/all pledge to loyalty
We'll never let a day go by/that won't sock the
Axis in the eye.

In the postwar years, the city encouraged more major companies to create bases in Sunnyvale. Lockheed Corporation established a plant here in 1956 to produce missiles as well as satellite systems, and the city entered the technological era. The plant had a dramatic impact on Sunnyvale's development, drawing in other high-tech businesses. This tremendous growth created a major housing need for all the incoming workers, and during the 1950s and 1960s, many acres of prime orchard land were bulldozed and graded to build subdivisions. Today, with more than 12,000 employees, Lockheed Martin Missiles & Space remains one of Silicon Valley's largest employers.

By the 1980s, if he were still living, Sunnyvale's founding father W. E. Crossman might have considered his dream of turning Sunnyvale into the City of Destiny an outstanding success. The city limits contained more than 650 technology firms, including Amdahl, Advanced Micro Devices, and ESL (Electroservice Laboratories). But serious problems confronted the community as it faced a scarcity of land for housing. The Sunnyvale city council set growth limits on industrial development, and during the 1990s, the community continued to implement this policy by rezoning land from industrial to residential usage.

TOUR

Sunnyvale is a city built on business, so this tour passes through many of the city's industrial sections. Start from U.S. 101, taking the Mathilda Ave. exit, and head north toward the bay. After passing under the Hwy. 237 overpass, you'll see on your left at Moffett Park Dr. a large, pale-blue windowless building surrounded by several immense satellite antennas. Called the **Blue Cube,** this high-security building is located at Onizuka Air Force Base, named in honor of Lt.

Col. Ellison Onizuka, one of seven astronauts killed in the 1986 Space Shuttle Challenger explosion. Inside the Blue Cube are technicians who control military and spy surveillance satellites orbiting the Earth. Continue along Mathilda, following the Light Rail line as you pass on your left the factory-like buildings of **Lockheed Martin Missiles & Space.** Many important space-related projects such as the Hubble Space Telescope and the Space Shuttle were developed in these facilities. After this point, Mathilda Ave. curves and becomes Caribbean Dr., going through a landfill area for about a mile where the city's northern limits border the **San Francisco Bay National Wildlife Refuge.**

On your left, you'll see the **Twin Creeks Sports Complex,** 408/734-0888, Silicon Valley's premier softball facility with 60 acres of lighted fields and facilities. Next to the athletics facility is **Sunnyvale Baylands Park,** 408/730-7708, open until half an hour before sunset. At the stoplight intersection, turn left and drive into the park's entrance. This scenic park is where the San Tomas Aquinas Creek enters the bay, creating a salt marsh that provides a wetland habitat for plants and animals such as the great egret. It has an excellent playground area as well as several pathways to stroll along and take a look at the valley's wildlife. A long boardwalk lets visitors go deep into the marshes to experience the animal life living on the edge of the bay. A T. S. Eliot quote inscribed in the sidewalk at the beginning of the meadow grasslands walk applies not just to natural exploration, but also to Silicon Valley's quest for knowledge. It reads: "We shall not cease from exploration, and the end of all our exploration shall be to arrive where we started and know the place for the first time." Plan to spend about an hour at Sunnyvale Baylands Park.

From the park entrance, turn right at the stoplight intersection and follow Caribbean Dr. back to Crossman Ave., a street named after Sunnyvale's founding father, W. E. Crossman. Turn left here and follow Crossman Ave. through an industrial park area until you reach Fair Oaks Avenue. Turn right at Fair Oaks, which follows the Light Rail line a short distance. You'll cross over U.S. 101 and continue on through a series of

LOCKHEED MARTIN—SHOOTING FOR THE STARS

In 1913, Allan and Malcolm Loughhead, two young men from Los Gatos, received national headlines by flying their self-built hydroplane off of San Francisco Bay. In 1932, during the Great Depression, the brothers founded a small aviation company called Lockheed Aircraft Corp. in Southern California (they had changed their family name by that time). They built it slowly over the decade until the United States entered World War II. Supplying aircraft for the war effort, Lockheed quickly turned itself into one of the nation's largest airplane manufacturers.

In the years following the war, much work was being done by German scientists such as Wernher von Braun and others in the exciting research of rocket development. The Lockheeds realized a potentially huge market in this area, and so in 1954 became among the first companies to commercially step into this new industry. They launched a subsidiary called Lockheed Missiles & Space. Two years later, this company moved north and set up a massive manufacturing site on Sunnyvale's Mathilda Ave. along the Bay. This location was chosen to be near the advanced aviation research being conducted at NASA's Ames Research Center at adjacent Moffett Field. Lockheed Missiles & Space quickly became Silicon Valley's biggest employer, with at one point over 30,000 people working for its Sunnyvale operation. It changed Sunnyvale forever, increasing its population dramatically and altering the farm town by making it a major industrial city in the Bay Area.

From its factory site along Moffett Field, the company has produced more than 750 space vehicles for military, civil government, and commercial uses. It works on projects both as a major contractor as well as a subcontractor. It has a number of firsts to its credit, including the first radio communications from a satellite in 1958, the first remote-sensing intelligence satellites, the first weather pictures from space taken in 1960, the first Television Infrared Observatory Satellite (TIROS-1),

the SatCom-1 satellite that provided commercial communications, and with the Polaris missile, the first submarine launched ICBM.

Among its more grandiose accomplishments is helping to design the Space Shuttle, models of which were tested in the nearby NASA Ames Research wind tunnel. In 1977, Lockheed was contracted to build the Hubble Space Telescope (HST), the world's most famous stargazing tool, which was launched in 1990. Pieced together at the Sunnyvale plant, the HST has allowed astronomers to gaze into realms of heaven never before examined, such as the galactic gas factories where stars are created. Another Lockheed project, the Lunar Prospector, was launched on January 6, 1998, and began mapping the Moon's magnetic field, discovering ice in the north and south poles which might one day be used to establish lunar bases. For the International Space Station, a massive orbiting laboratory that can be seen from Earth, Lockheed was contracted to provide the eight enormous solar arrays, the wing-like structures that generate electricity using the Sun's photons. These arrays cover an area larger than two football fields.

Working with Stanford University, Lockheed is also developing a gravity probe satellite which will test Albert Einstein's General Theory of Relativity by measuring the precession of orbiting gyroscopes moving through the twisting gravitation field of the rotating Earth. Another project that should get significant astronomical attention is the Space Interferometry Mission (SIM) for NASA's Jet Propulsion Laboratory, which is designed to precisely measure the position of stars. Sunnyvale's Lockheed is truly shooting for the stars.

In 1995, Lockheed Corp. and Martin Marietta Corp. merged together to form Lockheed Martin Corporation. The following year, Lockheed Martin bought Loral Corp., a defense electronics firm also based in Silicon Valley. Website: www.lockheed-martin.com.

strip malls and apartment residences. The park on
your left is **Fair Oaks Park,** and here at the traffic light, keep to your right onto Fair Oaks Dr.
(avoid getting onto Wolfe Road). Immediately
after this traffic light, turn to your right onto
Maude Ave., following it through a residential
area. The large building on the left at the corner
of Maude and Sunnyvale Ave. is **Bishop Elementary School;** as you go by, glance at the wall
mural showing various aspects of Sunnyvale's
history, including the Santa Clara Mission days
and Martin Murphy Jr.'s white-painted house.
Follow Sunnyvale Ave. for two blocks to **Murphy
Park** at the corner of California Avenue. Turn
left at this stoplight intersection and drive into the
park's entrance and park in the lot here.

Palms and eucalyptus trees shade this small
city park, which was the home site of Martin
Murphy Jr., the pioneering cattle rancher who
once owned thousands of acres that now make
up Sunnyvale. Until 1953, the Murphy family
lived here continuously, but the original prefabricated house that came around Cape Horn in
1851 is now gone. A plain-looking community
center building contains the **Sunnyvale Historical Museum,** 408/749-0220, where you can
see a collection of relics and photographs telling
the city's story.

From the park entrance turn right and make
a left back onto Sunnyvale Ave. toward a red-
and-white-checkered water tower, site of the
Joshua Hendy Iron Works, now owned by
Northrop Grumman. A small **Iron Man Museum,** 408/735-2020, provides visitors with
details about the historic foundry, at one time
the largest on the West Coast. This museum is
open the second Mon. of each month (except
Dec.) from 11:30 A.M.–12:30 P.M. To get there,
turn left at the stoplight onto Hendy Ave., and
go in the main entrance where the small museum is located.

Back on Sunnyvale Ave., continue on toward
downtown. As you cross the Caltrain tracks into
the downtown area, on your right you'll see the
train depot, located close to the site of **Murphy's Station,** the railroad flag stop from which
the original village of Sunnyvale emerged. After
the railroad tracks, turn right onto Evelyn Ave.,

then turn left onto Frances Ave., where you can
park in one of the free public parking lots on
either side of the street.

On the east side of the parking lot along the
100 block of S. Murphy Ave., you'll come to
Downtown Sunnyvale, a heritage landmark district. The city's first businesses were built in this
one-block area, and once included a firehouse,
post office, plumbing shop, and farmer's hardware store. Now the buildings contain restaurants and small boutique stores. It's a lively place
on weekend nights. One of the eateries on this
block is **The Palace,** 408/739-5179, a converted movie theater with an exotic interior decor.
Check out the mural of two griffins on the
restaurant's tan-colored front. Across the street is
a brewery restaurant called **Stoddard's Brewhouse,** 408/733-7824, with a back-side beer
garden perfect for sunny Sunnyvale days.

In deference to Sunnyvale's Irish origins, Sunnyvale's downtown section also features three
Irish pubs, **Fibbar Magee's, Murphy's Law,** and
Scruffy Murphy's. The Del Monte Building at
the corner was built in 1904 as the Madison &
Bonner Dried Fruit Packing Company, and now
features the **Del Monte Restaurant.** Across the
street from this, **Kiss It Good-Buy Consign-
ments,** 408/730-9300, is a family-operated shop
well worth a visit. It's fun browsing here through
old movie posters, art deco furniture, and high-
quality jewelry. The clothes include vintage fash-
ions from the 1920s to the 1970s. On Sat. from
9 A.M.–1 P.M., a well-attended **farmers' market**
occupies the street, rain or shine.

The downtown district contains two shopping malls. **Town and Country Village,**
408/736-6654, is a series of shops containing
clothing boutiques and travel agencies. The larger **Silicon Valley WAVE,** Walk and Village Entertainment, 408/245-3270, formerly known as
Sunnyvale Town Center Mall, features major department stores JCPenney, and Macy's. Expect to
spend at least an hour visiting the downtown
shops and malls.

From the parking lot, drive south along
Frances Ave., turning left onto Washington Ave.
and making a right at the stoplight onto Sunnyvale Avenue. Follow this along the Sunnyvale

Mall parking lot until you get to Iowa Avenue. Make a right turn here, and on the next street, Murphy Ave., turn left. One block down, at the cross street of Olive Ave., you'll come to the **Sunnyvale Chamber of Commerce,** 408/736-4971, where you can pick up information about the city's businesses and current events.

Follow Murphy Ave. another block to the stoplight intersection, where it curves to the right onto El Camino Real. Immediately on your right, as you get on El Camino Real, you'll see a comedy club called **Rooster T. Feathers,** 408/736-0921. The site, once a bar called Andy Capp's, can be considered the birthplace of the video game industry. This is where Atari founder Nolan Bushnell placed his prototype model of Pong, the world's first video game, to test-market it among the bar's patrons. After the manager called to say the game was no longer functioning, Bushnell thought the experiment was a failure. But the reason it had quit working was that the slot box was so filled with quarters that it couldn't accept any more. Bushnell realized he had a gold mine with this electronic version of Ping-Pong, and a new entertainment industry was born.

Next, turn right at the stoplight at Mathilda Avenue. Immediately on your left you'll see Sunnyvale's Civic Center, where the city hall and public library are located. Continue traveling north on Mathilda for about half a mile, and as you drive on the overpass crossing the railroad tracks, you'll see on your left a large water tower that looks like a giant fruit cocktail can. Once the site of the **Libby's Cannery,** Applied Signal Technologies now operates on the site.

Follow Mathilda Ave. through a series of strip malls and shopping centers. The street eventually meets U.S. 101. The northbound entrance takes you to San Francisco and the southbound entrance takes you to San Jose.

POINTS OF INTEREST

Sunnyvale Historical Museum

This small museum is located in a community center in Sunnyvale's Murphy Park, once the home site of pioneer Martin Murphy Jr. Photographs and objects describe the life of the Irish

In front of the Sunnyvale Public Library, the bronze sculpture, Out to Lunch, offers some inspiration.

Murphy family and their important role in developing Santa Clara Valley's farm heritage.

Murphy Park (at the corner of California and Sunnyvale Aves.), 408/749-0220; free parking; admission free; open Tues. and Thurs. noon–3:30 P.M., Sun. 1–4 P.M. (other days by appointment).

Sunnyvale Center for Innovation, Invention & Ideas (SCI³)

Intellectual rights and patents are a big deal in Silicon Valley. In 1996, Silicon Valley's 3,036 patents put it in first place for the number issued in the United States. If the area were a country, it would rank fourth behind the U.S., Japan, and Germany. To fill the tremendous need for information relating to all these technological innovations, SCI³ provides an excellent resource for researching patents and trademarks. Started in 1994, the center works in conjunction with the United States Patent and Trademark Office to provide up-to-date and complete information. It also offers facilities for seminars and videoconferencing on these subjects.

465 S. Mathilda Ave., Ste. 300 (corner of Olive Ave. across from Silicon Valley WAVE), 408/737-4945, website: www.sci3.com; admis-

© MARTIN CHEEK

sion free; open Tues.–Fri. 9 a.m.–5 p.m., Sat. noon–5 p.m.

Creative Arts Center Gallery

This nonprofit facility run by the city provides a place for local artists to exhibit their works. Many of the paintings and sculptures are done by students in Sunnyvale Parks and Recreation art classes.

550 E. Remington Dr. (at Sunnyvale Community Center), 408/730-7731; admission free; open Tues. and Thurs. 11 A.M.–5 P.M., Wed. and Fri. 1–5 P.M., Sat. 10 A.M.–2 P.M.

Twin Creeks Sports Complex

At 60 acres and with 10 lighted fields, this is billed as the world's largest facility for playing the game of softball. More than 40 weekends a year, games are held at this massive complex next to the San Francisco Bay, drawing 7,000 teams. Built in 1985, the state-of-the-art facility includes a sports bar and a 14,000-square-foot clubhouse, as well as batting cages, basketball and volleyball courts, and horseshoe pits. Many Silicon Valley corporations rent the complex for company events and picnics.

969 Caribbean Dr. (off Hwy. 237), 408/734-0888, website: www.twin-creeks.com; free admission; open Tues.–Thurs. 4:30 P.M. until the park is closed after the last game, Sat.–Sun. one hour before game to closing.

Sunnyvale Baylands Park

Located adjacent to the Twin Creeks along the marshlands of the San Francisco Bay, this joint city-county park is a tranquil place to get away from Silicon Valley's high-energy rush. Its wetlands are home to a number of fowl species, such as long-billed curlews, burrowing owls,

barn swallows, kestrels, black phoebes, and great egrets. A creative playground area lets kids work off some of their energy. A 500-foot-long boardwalk winds over the marshes, affording visitors magnificent views of the bay. From here you can see 3Com's huge Santa Clara headquarters along Hwy. 237.

Caribbean Dr. (from Hwy. 237, take the Caribbean Dr. exit, heading north—park entrance is immediately on the right), 408/730-7709, website: claraweb.co.santa-clara.ca.us/parks; free parking Nov.–Apr., $3 per car the rest of the year; open from 8 A.M. to half an hour after sunset.

Golf Courses

Sunnyvale has two public golf courses, both run by Art Wilson Golf Shops in conjunction with the city. The well-manicured **Sunnyvale Golf Course** is a par 70, 18-hole course with various bunkers, dog legs, and water holes.

605 Macara Ave., 408/738-3666; greens fees are $25 on weekdays, $34 on weekends.

The **Sunken Garden Golf Course** is a nine-hole course ideal for beginners.

1010 S. Wolfe Rd., 408/739-6588; greens fees are $11 on weekdays ($7 for replay), $14 on weekends ($8.50 for replay).

Silicon Valley WAVE (Walk and Village Entertainment)

This tired-looking 1970s mall underwent a major $100 million renovation in 2000. Previously called Sunnyvale Town Center Mall, the new name reflects the image of a family-oriented destination with both retail and entertainment facilities.

2502 Town Center Ln. (off S. Mathilda Ave.), 408/245-3270; major stores: JCPenney, Macy's; open weekdays 10 A.M.–9 P.M., Sat. 10 A.M.–7 P.M., Sun. 7 A.M.–6 P.M.

Santa Clara

Santa Clara Mission, on the grounds of the University of Santa Clara

© MARTIN CHEEK

When tourists, students, and worshipers wander among the roses and adobe walls of Santa Clara Mission's tranquil garden area, few of them probably ponder that they are walking on the historic heart of the valley. The mission played an important role in the Spanish, Mexican, and American settlement of the region; in fact, Santa Clara Valley and the city of Santa Clara are named after this church built in honor of Saint Clare of Assisi, Italy. Father Junípero Serra and the original Franciscan padres would be astounded at the growth of the 19.3-square-mile city that bears the name of the mission they established. Santa Clara has a population of more than 103,000, making it the third most populated city in Silicon Valley. The flat plains that once grew corn and vegetables to feed the converts here are today packed with middle-class neighborhoods and industrial areas supporting more than 500 manufacturing plants.

Santa Clara is bordered on the north, east, and south by San Jose, and on the west by Cupertino and Sunnyvale. "The Mission City," which had its roots in religion, now has a number of shrines dedicated to the digital world. It is home to such world-famous high-tech businesses as 3Com, Intel, National Semiconductor, Ap-

plied Materials, YAHOO!, and Synoptics. Most of these are located in the city's northern half, in industrial parks along thoroughfares such as the Montague and Central Expwys., and Mission College and Scott Boulevards. Set among these industrial parks are other attractions, such as Paramount's Great America theme park, the San Francisco 49ers Training Center, and Mission Community College. The Santa Clara Convention Center draws many visitors to the city for its trade shows. It's conveniently located next to the Light Rail station. The San Jose International Airport adjacent to the city also makes it convenient for travelers heading to the convention center and industrial businesses.

In the city's southern portion, made up of residential neighborhoods, a number of facilities provide a higher quality of life for residents and visitors. Santa Clara has 31 public parks and playgrounds. Among them, Central Park holds the world-famous International Swim Club, where numerous Olympic gold medalists have trained, including Santa Clara High School graduate Mark Spitz, winner of seven gold medals at the 1972 Munich Olympics. The city is also home to Santa Clara University, the West Coast's oldest institution of higher education. Its campus grounds, the most beautiful of Silicon Valley's three major universities, are well worth a visit, as are its mission church and De Saisset Art Museum. Another excellent art museum is the Triton Museum of Art in Santa Clara's Civic Center Park. Among the city's more celebrated statues is *Our Lady of Peace,* located along U.S. 101 at the Great America Pkwy. exit. The colossal 32-foot stainless-steel sculpture of St. Mary was created by sculptor Charles Parks. Due to its location, it's often referred to by locals as "The Cadillac Virgin" or "Our Lady of the Freeway."

HISTORY

On January 12, 1777, Father Junípero Serra founded the Mission Santa Clara de Asis on the banks of the Guadalupe River. The first Euro-

SAN JOSE'S HISTORIC ALAMEDA

Leading from the San Jose Arena to Santa Clara University, the street known as "The Alameda" (Spanish for "the way") provides a romantic glimpse into the history of the valley's early days. Tension had grown between the pueblo of San Jose's civilian residents and the mission's padres. To provide a peace offering, in 1799, Father Magin Catala, "the holy man of Santa Clara," directed about 200 Indians to plant willow tree cuttings taken from the Guadalupe River along a three-mile stretch of road, 40 feet across, between the pueblo and the mission. A ditch was made along the tree bases, irrigating the plants with creek water.

In time, the willows grew to form a cool canopy, a lure to attract pueblo inhabitants to walk the beautiful lane to mass. It also became a popular route for wedding and funeral processions and parades. One Spanish Indian fighter, Juan Prado, rode his horse along The Alameda carrying the head of a native insurgent named Yoscolo stuck on a pole.

The legend of a miracle connected to The Alameda says that during the winter drought of 1823 and 1824, the mission crops faced dangerous conditions from lack of rain. In April, Father Catala prayed for rain and led his Indian neophytes on a candlelight procession down the willow-lined lane. Even though a strong wind was blowing, not a single flame went out, and the padre saw this as a sign that God would answer his prayer. As the procession reached the mission church, drops of water were felt, and soon the clouds released a torrent of rain across the valley. The rain poured down for a week, providing an abundant crop so that the mission did not perish.

During the pioneer days of the mid-19th century, the road was dusty in summer and muddy in winter. Wild cattle roamed along it, and yellow mustard plants grew near the trees, reaching heights of 10 to 12 feet. In 1856, an omnibus line started traveling The Alameda. In 1868, this was replaced by the San Jose and Santa Clara Horse Railroad, which lasted until 1878. In 1886, one entrepreneur attempted to build an underground trolley system (inspired no doubt by the New York subway system), but when he realized how easily the area flooded, he quickly gave up.

Today, paved and heavy with automobile traffic, The Alameda is a modern street with little hint of its original look. Instead of willow trees, office buildings and businesses line the way. Only a single offshoot of one of Father Catala's original trees can be found today—at 1860 The Alameda.

pean settlement of the valley received its start here when Tómas de la Peña and José Murgio placed a cross at this point and said Mass. A small city park now marks this spot at the southeast corner of Central Expwy. and De La Cruz Boulevard. The Franciscan mission was eighth among the 21 that would eventually dot California. Two years later on January 23, 1779, the church and monastery were destroyed when the winter-rain-filled creek flooded. A temporary church was built while the padres found a site safe from the flood zone. At what is now the entrance to Santa Clara University, they built the second mission, which was dedicated on November 19, 1781. A major earthquake in 1812 damaged this mission, and a second quake in 1818 completely devastated the structure. A

third mission was built and dedicated in 1822 at its present site on the university campus. (This third mission stood for more than a century, but was destroyed by fire in 1926. The present mission church is a larger reconstructed version of the second mission.)

The mission settlement continued until 1836, when Mexico's California civil commissioners gained power over its lands and secularized it. By 1839, only 300 Indians still lived at the mission grounds as the Franciscan phase of settling the valley came to an end. In the early 1840s, European and American immigrants started moving into the valley, and the Mexican government grew worried about these newcomers and the U.S. doctrine of Manifest Destiny. During this decade, the crumbling mission adobe buildings served as temporary shelter for the Americans venturing into the valley, many of them later becoming prominent citizens, such as Martin Murphy Sr. With the start of the Mexican-American War on May 13, 1846, tensions increased between the Californios and the incoming Americans. For Northern California, the political strain came to a head on January 2, 1847, when the short Battle of Santa Clara took place near the mission grounds between the American expeditionary forces and the Californios. The Americans won the skirmish, and five days later, a peace treaty was signed by Marine Captain Ward Marston, commander of the U.S. expeditionary forces, and Francisco Sanchez, leader of the Californios.

Santa Clara College

With the increasing flow of Americans coming into the region during the Gold Rush, a small village began to form on the land surrounding the mission. In 1850, pioneer William Campbell parceled the land into lots of 100 square yards, and each citizen received a lot with the condition that a house be built on the land within three months or the property would be revoked. Among the early citizens was Peleg Rush, who shipped to the area 23 prefabricated houses around Cape Horn from Boston. Soon, these homes were occupied by new residents of the village. At this time, the Catholic archbishop in San Francisco instructed the Reverend John Nobili, a Jesuit priest, to make the dilapidated mission into a college for instructing the area's increasing population. Santa Clara College was founded on March 19, 1851, opening its doors to a dozen students. The next year on July 5, the growing town of Santa Clara incorporated, and over the next decade, the city grew with additional homes, churches, stores, and a jail.

One of the city's most thriving industries was the conversion of hides into leather for saddles, shoes, bags, and other products. Since the founding of the mission, cattle hides were turned into goods, but with the founding of the Wampach Tannery in 1848, the seeds of a commercial hide tanning industry took root. In 1866, the tannery was bought by Jacob Eberhard, who re-named it Eberhard Tannery. It was Santa Clara's first successful exporter, sending fine leather goods to the East Coast and Europe until it closed in 1953. Santa Clara's fertile soil also promoted the development of seed farms, the first of which was J. M. Kimberlin & Company, started in 1875. In 1877, Charles Copeland Morse and A. L. Kellogg bought the small R. W. Wilson Seed Company, which eventually grew to become Ferry-Morse, the world's largest producer of seeds. With the city's numerous orchards, fruit canning also became a major industry here.

By 1880, Santa Clara was a community of almost 3,000 people. In that decade, the city's Enterprise Mill & Lumber Company was reorganized into the Pacific Manufacturing Company, which, besides being the region's largest lumber manufacturer, was also a prominent coffin maker. In 1885, the California state legislature established Agnews State Hospital, the state's first hospital devoted to caring for the mentally ill. Facilities were built in the town of Agnews (which, in the 1950s, would be annexed by the city of Santa Clara), and by 1888, the first patients moved in.

The 1890s saw tremendous changes in the city. A $50,000 bond measure was passed, allowing for water pipes to be laid throughout the community. City leaders decided to spend the $3,500 left from this fund on a steam generator and wiring, thus starting an electric utility company. Unusual for Silicon Valley, where other cities get power from PG&E, Pacific Gas and Electric, the Santa Clara city government still maintains its electric utility as well as sewer and water services. The combined cost for these services is the lowest among all Bay Area cities, an important reason so many manufacturing companies have chosen Santa Clara as a business base.

Earthquake

Santa Clara's population at the turn of the 19th century was about 3,650 people, and at this time, the growing city was connected by the Electric Railroad line to other Santa Clara Valley communities. When the 1906 earthquake rocked the region the brick buildings of the Agnews

State Hospital collapsed on patients and staff, killing 112 people. By 1911, the facility was rebuilt and continues today to operate as a state-run mental hospital. A fire devastated the mission in 1926, but reconstruction commenced the next year. On May 13, 1928, the archbishop rededicated the new church, the mission's fourth. In 1940, Santa Clara's population was 6,650, but after World War II, the city expanded beyond its 19th-century boundaries as manufacturers started to set up here. By 1952, the population was 15,178, and by 1960, it hit 58,880.

During the 1960s and 1970s, the northern part of the city saw a tremendous growth in high-tech industry. Among other corporations, Intel and National Semiconductor established their headquarters here; they continue to be two of the city's largest employers. In America's bicentennial year, the city targeted tourism by promoting the construction of Marriott's (now Paramount's) Great America theme park. As the number of business travelers coming into the city continued to increase, construction began in 1986 on the Santa Clara Convention Center, a gathering spot for thousands of conventioneers from around the world. Two years later, the San Francisco 49ers football team moved its headquarters and training facility to a cul-de-sac near the convention center. By 1990, close to 500 manufacturing plants were located in Santa Clara, making products from integrated circuits to minicomputers. Today, the city is one of Silicon Valley's most vibrant high-tech communities.

TOUR

Starting a tour of Santa Clara by heading down **The Alameda** seems entirely appropriate—it was the thoroughfare built by a Franciscan father for the Pueblo de San Jose's inhabitants to reach the Santa Clara Mission. You could travel the whole length of this locally famous street by starting at the San Jose Arena and following it to Santa Clara's southern district. For an abbreviated route, take The Alameda exit along I-880, heading northwest. At the stoplight intersection where El Camino Real meets The Alameda, you'll be in the spot where the Eberhard Tannery

was located. At this intersection, turn right, following El Camino Real to Santa Clara University's main entrance just beyond **Buck Shaw Stadium** at the Railroad Ave. intersection. The **Santa Clara Caltrain station,** the depot for which was built in 1868, is directly opposite the street from this point.

Turn left into the university's main entrance, obtaining a visitor permit. Drive straight down the road until you find the visitor parking area along Palm Drive. The **De Saisset Art Museum,** 408/554-4528, is next to this parking area. Founded in 1955, its changing collection includes African, American, European, and Asian artworks. Basement galleries display artifacts showing the mission's history as well as relics from the area's pre-mission Native American culture. At the museum, pick up a self-guided walking tour of the mission grounds.

The present **Mission Church** is an enlarged replica of the second mission built in 1781. This fourth structure, dedicated in 1928, holds many of the roof's cover tiles from earlier missions. Masses are still said here, and visitors are welcome inside to view the church's serene beauty. The remains of Father Magin de Catala, "the holy man of Santa Clara," are interred in the Crucifix Chapel. He was responsible for constructing The Alameda, which connected the pueblo of San Jose to the mission.

Outside the mission, stroll through its surrounding gardens, which feature religious statues, palm trees, and adobe walls set amid well-kept expanses of lawn. The large **wooden cross** in front of the church dates from the mission's founding in 1777. The **rose garden** beside the mission was an early mission cemetery. The domed building at the garden's southern end is the **Ricard Observatory,** named after Father Jerome Ricard, who was called "the padre of the rains" because of his sunspot theory of weather forecasting. On the lawn near the entrance stands a **granite obelisk** marking where the university's physics professor John Montgomery, "the father of aviation," launched the first heavier-than-air controlled flight of a glider on April 29, 1905.

After exploring the university grounds, return to your car and drive west down Palm Dr., turning right in front of the mission entrance and following the university exit road to Franklin Street. Turn left here, and at the stoplight intersection on Lafayette St., turn left and make an immediate right on Homestead Road. Follow Homestead four blocks to Monroe St. and turn right. You'll pass through **downtown Santa Clara.** The original shopping district here was torn down and renovated in the 1960s, resulting in a dreary complex of small businesses. In 2001, this area underwent another renovation, creating what is called "Franklin Square," which contains boutiques and small restaurants.

Where you see the large globe-shaped water fountain, turn left onto Franklin St., driving to its very end where it meets with Lincoln Street. Spanning about two blocks in length, a tall pink wall runs along this street, with the crowns of palm trees sticking out over the top. Since 1917, this has been the **Carmelite Monastery.** Before that, the land belonged to Judge Hiram Bond, on whom writer Jack London based the opening chapter of his classic novel *The Call of the Wild* (along with the judge's Santa Clara ranch). Turn right on Lincoln St., following it to a monastery entrance gate on your left and turning here to enter the grounds. The ornate church here is designed in Spanish ecclesiastical style, and the olive grove throughout the garden area provides much-welcome shade on summer days. Open to the public Mon.–Sat. 6:30 A.M.–4:30 P.M., Sun. 8 A.M.–5 P.M.

Exit the monastery by turning right onto Benton St., then turning left back onto Lincoln Street. Four blocks later, you'll cross El Camino Real and pass the **Santa Clara Civic Center** on your right. The statue in the midst of the shallow pool at this corner is of **Saint Clare,** for whom the city is named. This is also the site where the peace treaty was signed between the Americans and Californios on January 7, 1847, following the Battle of Santa Clara. Continue to the end of Lincoln St. to the intersection at Warburton Avenue. Directly in front of you is the **Triton Museum of Art,** 408/247-9340, a spacious 22,000-square-foot building with pyramidal skylights. It's well worth a visit to this art gallery, which features many fine examples of contem-

porary works both inside and outside. Looking like a morph of an Apollo rocket and a Franciscan friar, the 85-foot stainless steel sculpture across the street from the museum is called the *Universal Child Statue,* created by former Santa Clara resident Benny Bufano. The bronze equestrian statue just outside the museum's entrance is the *Morgan Horse,* honoring Triton, the horse the museum was named after. The animal belonged to the museum's patron and founder W. Robert Morgan.

Set back in the park behind the museum, you'll find the **Headen-Inman House,** built in the Arts and Crafts architectural style around 1913. The farmhouse was moved here in 1985 and houses the **Santa Clara History Museum,** 408/248-2787. Open only on Sun. from 1–4 P.M., its various rooms contain exhibits of the city's founding pioneers. Farther back into the park is a weather-worn farm home, the historic **Jamison-Brown House,** built in 1866. Its veranda originally was attached to the ranch home of Judge Hiram Bond (located on the Carmelite Monastery grounds) and was later added to this house. A marker here tells that Jack London wrote portions of *The Call of the Wild* on this porch.

Continue driving along Warburton Ave. for two blocks. On your left, at 1850 Warburton, is the **Santa Clara Chamber of Commerce,** 408/244-8244, where you can find out about local festivals and events. Turn right at the stoplight on Scott Blvd., continuing north and entering the city's industrial area as you drive onto the overpass for the Caltrain tracks. After the stoplight intersection at Central Expwy., Scott Blvd. curves west, and soon after you'll come to San Tomas Expressway. Turn right at the stoplight onto this expressway and drive over the U.S. 101 overpass. At the Mission College Blvd. stoplight, turn to your left and drive a short stretch to the headquarters of **Intel,** on your left in the Robert Noyce Building at 2200 Mission College Blvd., 408/765-8080. The last four digits of the company's telephone number—8080—are also the name of the successful Intel chip that helped create the PC revolution. Here you can stop for a visit to the **Intel Museum,** located in the main lobby. This free attraction features a number of hands-on exhibits explaining the history and manufacture of microprocessors. Open Mon.–Fri. 8 A.M.–5 P.M.

After visiting Intel's museum, continue west along Mission College Boulevard. If you were to continue driving straight across the stoplight intersection at Great America Pkwy., you would enter **Mission Community College,** a sister institution to West Valley College in Saratoga. Instead, turn right onto Great America Pkwy., and soon you'll pass on your right the roller coasters and other thrill rides of **Paramount's Great America,** 408/988-1776. This park has been a popular attraction for local families since its 1976 opening. It originally belonged to hotel chain Marriott Corporation but was later bought by the city of Santa Clara, which now leases it to Paramount. The park's rides and shows are suitable for all ages, and you could easily spend the entire day here.

Continue driving north along Great America Pkwy. to Tasman Drive. At the northeast corner of the stoplight intersection here, you'll see the **Santa Clara Convention Center,** 408/748-7000, one of Silicon Valley's two major convention centers (the McEnery Convention Center in downtown San Jose is the other). Turn right onto Tasman Dr., go a short ways until on your left, just after the Convention Center, you'll see the well-kept greens of the **Santa Clara Golf & Tennis Club,** 408/980-9515. On your right at 4949 Centennial Blvd., you'll see the **San Francisco 49ers training facility,** 408/562-4949. The lobby area is open to the public, and visitors can see various team memorabilia, including Super Bowl trophies.

After your short visit here, continue driving east on Tasman Dr., following the Light Rail tracks, as it crosses the overpass above Lafayette Street. At Lick Mill Blvd., turn right, following this street through a quiet residential district built on land once owned by James Lick. An early valley settler, Lick built a four-story flour mill along the Guadalupe River, which parallels the boulevard to your left. The small park on your right is named **Lick Mill Park.** Continue driving southeast, and after Lick Mill Rd. on

your right, you'll see **Agnews Developmental Center,** a state-run hospital for the mentally ill. Turn right at Montague Expwy. and follow this to the U.S. 101 interchange. The northbound entrance heads for San Francisco, the southbound will return you to San Jose.

POINTS OF INTEREST
Intel Museum
Learn how computer chips are manufactured in automated, ultra-clean factories and see the development of the high technology that made Silicon Valley at this corporate museum set in the midst of a Santa Clara industrial park. This self-guided museum contains hands-on exhibits that make it fun for kids to develop their interest in the computer sciences.

2200 Mission College Blvd. (from U.S. 101, take Great America Pkwy. and turn right on Mission College Blvd.), 408/765-0503, website: www.intel.com/intel/intelis/museum; parking in company's lot; admission free; open Mon.–Fri. 9 A.M.–6 P.M., Sat. 10 A.M.–5 P.M.

South Bay Historical Railroad Museum
Railroads played a significant role in building what became Silicon Valley, and it's good to see that the region has a society aiming to preserve the heritage of track and train. The South Bay Historical Railroad Society is a group of train enthusiasts who renovated the historic Santa Clara Depot and made it their group headquarters. The depot contains a small railroad history museum with displays depicting the line that once ran through Santa Clara Valley. HO- and N-scale museum-grade model trains operate on a superb railroad setup.

1005 Railroad Ave. (near Santa Clara University at the Caltrain stop), 408/243-3969; parking in lot; admission free.; open Tues. 6:30–9 P.M., Sat. 9 A.M.–3 P.M.

Triton Museum of Art
Expect to spend about an hour wandering the galleries of this spacious museum displaying a changing exhibition of local contemporary works.

INTEL: "ONLY THE PARANOID SURVIVE"

Over the decades, Fairchild Semiconductor has spun off a number of companies throughout Silicon Valley. But none of them can match the success of Intel, the world's dominant chip company and a darling of Wall Street.

Intel was founded in 1968 by Fairchild cofounders Robert Noyce and Gordon Moore, and Hungarian scientist Andy Grove. These men saw a potentially lucrative business opportunity in the new arena of memory chips. To break into this market by providing affordable computer memory, they set up a small office along Middlefield Rd. in Mountain View. Employing a total of 12 people, Intel earned revenues in its first year of $2,672—a drop in the ocean of billions it would be making by the end of the 20th century.

The young firm first brought out a dynamic RAM chip named simply "1103." In 1971, Intel came out with a second product, which they called a microprocessor. Described as a "microprogrammable computer on a chip," this revolutionary electronic component—not much larger than a postage stamp—now performs as the heart of every PC on the planet, pumping bits of data through the wires of these information machines. Other firsts for Intel in the 1970s included the EPROM (erasable programmable read-only memory), originally used in a Japanese calculator. The company also came out with the first single-board computer.

With the rise of the personal computer, the 1980s were crucial years for Intel. Since then, the company has brought out a series of microprocessors, which grow more powerful with each generation. Founder Gordon Moore came up with a rule well known in Silicon Valley as "Moore's Law." It states that the number of transistors that can be fit on a chip doubles every 18 months. In other words, computer chip technology doubles every year and a half. As one of the principles driving Silicon Valley, it basically means that a consumer who buys the fastest whiz-bang computer available at any given moment owns a relative antique 18 months later.

On constant vigil to protect its multibillion-dollar trade secrets from competitors, Intel has evolved into one of Silicon Valley's most secretive companies. According to Tim Jackson's 1997 book, *Inside Intel*, the chip-maker employs private investigators to keep watch on its employees, one year catching a technician who was pilfering thousands of dollars in gold (used in the fabrication process) while cleaning a centrifuge machine. Much of Intel's corporate image reflects the personality of founder and former CEO Andy Grove, whom Jackson describes as "one of the most extraordinary figures in American business. He is brilliantly intelligent and articulate, driven, obsessive, neat, and disciplined." Grove's personal motto is known throughout the valley: "Only the paranoid survive," which was the title of *his* best-selling book.

Intel is starting to reinvent itself for the 21st century. After having built its business primarily on the booming PC market, it's branching out into other arenas that promise lucrative growth in the new century. This particularly includes the new generation of "information appliances"—digital devices such as cable set-top boxes, handheld computers, and chip-powered telephones.

The newly opened S. H. Cowell wing presents the Austen D. Warburton Collection of American Indian Art and Artifacts. This excellent collection depicts the daily life of tribes from California, the Southwest, and the Pacific Northwest, and includes items from pottery and baskets to baby carriers and musical instruments. Museum founder Robert Morgan donated a bronze sculpture of his horse Triton for the entrance and named the museum after the animal.

1505 Warburton Ave. (next to the Santa Clara Civic Center—take Lincoln St. north from El Camino Real), 408/247-3754, website: www.tritonmuseum.org; parking on street and in lot to the right; admission free; open Tues. 10 A.M.–9 P.M., Wed.–Sun. 10 A.M.–5 P.M.

Santa Clara University and Mission

Founded on March 19, 1851, Santa Clara University is California's oldest institution of higher education as well as the home of the Broncos. It's run by the Jesuits, and in 1985, U.S. education secretary William Bennett brought national attention to its curriculum by describing it as an exemplary model for educators. For visitors, the must-see attraction is the historic Spanish-style mission. The campus's **Louis B. Mayer Theatre,** 408/554-4015, seats about 500 people in an intimate auditorium. The **De Saisset Museum,** 408/554-4528, displays both art and historical exhibits. For visitors interested in the area's Spanish history, the museum features permanent displays of religious and Native American artifacts from the early mission period. The museum was named after Pedro de Saisset, a native of Paris, who arrived in San Jose in 1849 and made his fortune with the Brush Electric Light Company in 1882. The museum is located next to the visitor parking area. Admission is free; open Tues.–Sun. 11 A.M.–4 P.M. **Campus tours,** 408/554-4700, teach visitors about the university's history and traditions. June–Sept., tours run Mon.–Fri. 10:30 A.M.; Oct.–May, they run Mon.–Fri. 10:30 A.M. and 2:30 P.M., Sat. 10 and 11:30 A.M.

500 El Camino Real (at north end of The Alameda), 408/554-4000, parking free to visitors (get pass at entrance gate); website: www.scu.edu.

Harris Lass House

This 1865 farmhouse built in an Italianate style was saved from demolition by Santa Clara's historical society. It now serves as a facility to educate the public on the valley's agrarian life from the early 1900s through the 1930s. Inside, the home showcases a fine collection of antique furniture, such as a fainting couch and an old-fashioned pump organ. Farm equipment is displayed in a barn beside the house. A tour lasts about half an hour.

1889 Market St. (in a quiet residential area just east of Winchester Blvd.), 408/249-7905; admission costs $3 for adults, $2 for seniors over 60, $1 for children 6–12, and free for 5 and younger; guided tours; open Sat.–Sun. noon–4 P.M.

San Francisco 49ers Headquarters and Training Facility

See where the San Francisco 49ers spend grueling hours preparing for gridiron combat. The public is not allowed to view practices and no player autographs are allowed, but you can look at the Super Bowl trophies and other memorabilia in the entrance lobby.

4949 Centennial Blvd. (off Tasman Dr. near the Santa Clara Convention Center), 408/562-4949, website: www.sf49ers.com; admission free; open Mon.–Fri. 8 A.M.–5 P.M.

Paramount's Great America

In the middle of an immense industrial park sits Paramount's Great America, Northern California's largest amusement park. Open Mar.–Sept., the 100-acre theme park features rides and attractions that make for a fun family outing. The park is divided into sections representing various parts of the United States, such as Orleans Place, Yankee Harbor, Yukon Territory, and Hometown Square. If your kids are into thrill rides, Great America is a sure bet, with high-tech roller coasters such as Top Gun and old-fashioned wooden ones such as The Grizzly. The park also has a number of rides and attractions suitable for smaller children, such as Nickelodeon Splat City, a watery attraction designed to cool off kids during hot summer afternoons, and

SANTA CLARA'S FLYING PIONEER

Much of the development for human flight was done in the Santa Clara Valley during the late 19th century by local physics professor John Joseph Montgomery.

Born in Yuba City, Arizona, Montgomery enjoyed tinkering with mechanical and electrical devices as a young boy. In 1874, at the age of 16, he arrived at Santa Clara College (now Santa Clara University) to study physics. After graduating, he began experimenting with the concept of human flight, supporting himself by teaching science classes at his alma mater. Like Leonardo da Vinci, Montgomery studied birds in flight, gathering data by measuring their bodies and wingspans as well as examining their wing curvature. It was this study that helped him discover the principle of the cambered wing, which produces lift and stability for flight. Orville and Wilbur Wright used many of Montgomery's discoveries in building their airplane, and the cambered wing is the basis of all modern aircraft, from the Wright flyer to supersonic military planes.

Montgomery limited his experimentation to glider flights. In 1905, in front of Santa Clara University's small observatory, a hot-air balloon lifted glider test pilot Dan Maloney up to a height of 4,000 feet. The pilot cut the cords from the balloon and piloted the glider to a planned landing site at Poplar and Alviso Sts. in Santa Clara. Although this was two years after Kitty Hawk, the event was historic—the first controlled flight of an aircraft.

More demonstration glider flights thrilled valley locals. The U.S. Army was interested in Montgomery's "aeroplane device" for military operations. At San Jose's Agriculture Park along The Alameda, Montgomery staged one public demonstration on July 18, 1905, advertising with dramatic posters designed by his brother Richard that boasted, "Winged Man Sweeps Skyward. Most Daring Feat Ever Accomplished by Man." Adults paid $.25 and children $.10 to see "aeronaut" Jack Maloney fly the glider. Maloney's balloon carried him high into the blue, but when it came time to cut loose, one of the ropes caught the glider wing, bending the strut. To the horror of the watching crowd, the pilot plummeted to his death. Seeing the dangers of flight, the army refused to sign a contract.

Montgomery didn't let the tragic accident defeat him. He continued developing glider designs and test-piloted his gliders himself from the slopes of the Evergreen district in San Jose, taking at least 50 flights. In October 1911, he took off from what is now known as Montgomery Hill. A gust of wind hit the glider and rolled it violently into the ground. The aircraft pioneer hit his head sharply on one of the glider's bolts, injuring himself so seriously that he died several hours later.

In the Santa Clara University gardens stands a small obelisk marking the spot where Montgomery's first controlled glider flight took off. A quote from Alexander Graham Bell on this monument reads: "All subsequent attempts in aviation must begin with the Montgomery machine."

© MARTIN CHEEK

CITIES OF THE VALLEY

Kidsville, with 18 rides and attractions suitable for ages 2–7. The park also features the world's largest 3-D movie theater, showing eye-popping IMAX films daily. A number of Paramount movie characters such as Star Trek Klingons and Borg wander the park grounds, meeting with guests. The park's Redwood Amphitheater seats 10,000 people and provides a venue where famous musicians frequently perform. Separate admission is required for performances, and concertgoers must also purchase a park pass.

Great America Pkwy. (between U.S. 101 and Hwy. 237), 408/988-1776, website: www.pgathrills.com; parking $6 (the Great America Light Rail stop is located within walking distance of the park entrance); admission for ages 7–59 is $42.99, child admission $32.99, seniors $36.99, individual and family season passes available.

Genealogy Room

Located in the Santa Clara Public Library, this extensive collection of documents pertaining to the area's pioneers is an excellent place to research family and local history. Run by the Santa Clara Historical and Genealogical Society, formed in 1957, members of this group help visitors trace their family roots.

2635 Homestead Rd. (near Kiely Blvd.), 408/984-3087; admission free; open Mon.–Thurs. 9 A.M.–9 P.M., Fri.–Sat. 9 A.M.–6 P.M., Sun. 1–5 P.M.

Santa Clara International Swim Club

Since its opening in 1951, nearly 50 of America's Olympic swimmers have practiced at this world-renowned swimming center, and these Olympians have brought home 33 gold medals. The three exceptional pools are also used by competitive divers and synchronized swimmers. The facility remains open all year for adult residents 18 and over for masters lap swimming.

2625 Patricia Dr. (off Homestead Ave., next to the public library), 408/984-3257, website: www.santaclaraswim.org; masters swimming, $4 per swim plus $15 club registration fee; call for schedule.

Planet Granite

As Silicon Valley's only indoor rock-climbing center, this is a great place to take kids who feel compelled to climb things. With 14,000 square feet of contoured artificial rock-climbing surface towering overhead, it's also an excellent learning facility for adults who want to get into the sport. The center rents climbing equipment and offers special rates for corporate group activities and children's birthday parties.

2901 Mead Ave. (near Bowers Ave.), 408/727-2777, website: www.planetgranite.com; climbing fee: $9–16; open Mon., Wed., and Fri. 11 A.M.–11 P.M., Tues. and Thurs. 6:30–11 P.M., Sat. 10 A.M.–9 P.M., Sun. 10 A.M.–6 P.M.

Valley Fair Shopping Mall

You'll feel like you're walking forever in this two-level mall, Silicon Valley's longest, with more than 170 shops and an immense food court. For kids who are into toys and paraphernalia of animated characters, it contains a Disney and a Warner Brothers store. To alleviate a longtime parking shortage, a large parking garage was recently added. The mall straddles the city border of San Jose.

2855 Stevens Creek Blvd. (at I-280 and I-880), 408/248-4450; open Mon.–Fri. 10 A.M.–9:30 P.M., Sat. 10 A.M.–9 P.M., Sun. 11 A.M.–7 P.M.; major stores: Macy's, Nordstrom.

Santa Clara Chorale

Performing in the serene atmosphere of the Mission Santa Clara since 1963, this singing group has provided Silicon Valley with high-quality inspirational choral music, such as Beethoven's Ninth Symphony. The group, led by musical director Lynn Shurtleff, a member of the Santa Clara University music department, has performed overseas in cities such as Vienna, Prague, and Salzburg.

Mission Santa Clara (on Santa Clara University grounds), 408/554-4700, website: www.scc.org; parking free at visitors' lot; tickets $8–10.

Cupertino

This modern sculptural fountain welcomes visitors to the Flint Center in Cupertino.

Cupertino is the core of Apple Computer country. The famous rainbow apple logo features prominently on many building signs in industrial parks scattered throughout the city. And one of the firm's immense office complexes shadows the intersection of Stevens Creek and De Anza Blvds., the historic heart of the city. But there is much more to Cupertino than a famous computer company named after a piece of fruit.

The more than 52,000 Cupertino residents have benefited greatly from the area's high-tech boom, as evidenced by the number of mansions set in the scenic foothills of the city's western Monta Vista district. The 13-square-mile city is bordered on the east by Santa Clara and San Jose's Westgate district, on the north by Sunnyvale, on the west by unincorporated county land, and on the south by Saratoga and the Stevens Creek County Park. In the last 20 years as the computer boom impacted the region, Cupertino's local government has created a generally successful blend of residential, commercial, and industrial developments. The high-tech economic benefits have contributed much in raising the city's quality of life, such as the construction of a modern civic center and a nicely designed community center at the city's Memorial Park. But the city's quickly growing population also has meant more traffic congestion as well as

a loss of prime agricultural lands to suburban development.

Cupertino is an ethnically diverse community, emphasized by its various annual galas such as the Japanese Cultural Festival and the American Indian Pow Wow and Arts Festival. About one-fifth of its population is Asian, whose influence can be seen in stores and shopping centers, where signs feature Chinese characters as well as English. The city has many high-quality school facilities and a dynamic parks and recreation department, which draw families to move to its middle- and upper-class neighborhoods. Because of the large population of families living here as well as its high percentage of athletically active individuals, the city's parks and recreation department offers more than 200 sports and cultural activities, including after-school music programs. The city's excellent public school system is considered one of the best in the Bay Area. In 1994, Vice President Gore visited Monta Vista High School and praised its computer-education program, calling it a model for the nation. A year later, Cupertino's citizens passed a $71 million bond measure to renovate and improve its elementary schools. Many of the city's schoolchildren score at the top of the nation in math and science, and several local high-tech companies have educational programs for Cupertino's schools.

Cupertino is unusual among Silicon Valley communities because it has no downtown district, often making it difficult for first-time visitors to find a focal point. This lack of an identifiable downtown makes it hard to create a civic image. The community started as a small farming service stop, and during its early stages, never had a strong need to build a downtown area. It incorporated in the mid-1950s to avoid being taken over during San Jose's Annexation Wars land grab. At that time, the city's government decided not to develop a centralized business district. Local residents usually describe Cupertino's identity not in terms of its agricultural past (which has virtually vanished except for a few small pock-

CITIES OF THE VALLEY

ets in public parks), but in the context of its recent evolution into one of Silicon Valley's most modern cities.

HISTORY

Tired from their long trek from San Diego, explorer Juan Bautista de Anza's small band of settlers camped the night of March 25, 1776, near what is today Monta Vista High School. A gentle creek meandered through the oaks near their camp, and de Anza's cartographer, Petrus Font, gave it the name Arroyo de San Guiseppe de Copertino after the patron saint of the Italian city Copertino. Later, the creek would gain its Latinized spelling of "Cupertino." Font wrote in his diary: "This place of San Guiseppe Copertino has good water and much firewood, but nothing suitable for a settlement because it is among the hills very near to the range of cedars which I mentioned yesterday, and lacks level lands."

Among the first white inhabitants to start settling in the region was a cantankerous American named Captain Elisha Stephens, famous for leading the Stephens-Townsend-Murphy overland party of settlers across the Sierras in 1844. In 1848, he settled on four acres near the site of de Anza's encampment and started a vineyard called Blackberry Farm, named after the blackberry patches growing on the land. Stephens's vineyard became the first wine-growing enterprise in this part of the Santa Clara Valley, and he expanded his land on February 8, 1859, with the purchase of 155 acres from Jeremiah Clarke for $855. Other settlers followed his example, including a number of sailing-ship captains who came here to retire on small farms after many years of ocean voyages. Stephens, frustrated by the growing population,

THE STORY OF APPLE

America's bicentennial year marked the anniversary of a political revolution, of course, but it also marked the advent of a revolution in the world of computers. In 1976, two young men—26-year-old Hewlett-Packard employee Steve Wozniak, and 21-year-old Atari employee Steve Jobs—started Apple Computer in Jobs's adoptive parents' garage in Cupertino.

The two had met at the Homebrew Computer Club, which got together the second Wednesday of every month in a conference room at Menlo Park's Stanford Linear Accelerator. Wozniak had shown the club his Apple I computer, which, with innovations such as a printed circuit board, had wowed the other members, including Jobs.

Jobs, who had tremendous marketing skills, was convinced that the company should have a non-threatening name that wouldn't intimidate the general public. They decided on Apple because Jobs was a fruitarian at the time and had worked one summer in an Oregon apple orchard. One Silicon Valley store they approached ordered 50 units of the Apple I, starting the company on its way to becoming a computer giant.

Their more advanced Apple II computer came out in 1980, providing the company with $100 million in revenues. Soon after, a computer was introduced called the Lisa, named for Jobs's young daughter and heavily influenced by his borrowings from Xerox PARC's experimental Alto computer. Although a technical marvel, with its many innovations such as a mouse and easy-to-master software, the powerful Lisa's high price aimed at a high-end market, where it never caught on.

In 1984, Apple's low-end Macintosh provided a saving grace for the company. The easy-to-use Mac was the first commercially available computer to come with a point-and-click mouse, menu-driven icons on the screen, and windows. A famous Orwellian TV ad broadcast during the Super Bowl that year got the word out about this ground-breaking computer. The year also brought Wozniak's departure from the company to enjoy his millions, some of which he spent putting on U.S. rock-and-roll concerts.

Jobs's autocratic management style and quick temper made him difficult to work with, and the next year the board of directors fired him, replacing sold his property to W. T. McClellan and left the area in 1864 with the irate complaint that it had become "too durn civilized." Cupertino Creek was renamed after Stephens, but a cartographer misspelled it on a map as "Stevens Creek." Today the names of Stevens Creek County Park and the well-traveled Stevens Creek Blvd. continue the error. Stephens's Blackberry Farm became a popular resort in the 1870s, and today it's run by the city's parks and recreation department as a golf course and picnic grounds.

West Side Story

In 1882, a U.S. post office was started at San Francisco lawyer John T. Doyle's Las Palmas Winery near what is now McClellan Rd. and Foothill Boulevard. The postmaster called the branch Cupertino after the original name of the creek that flowed near the site. At about the same time,

a village developed around the intersection of Stevens Creek Rd. and Saratoga-Sunnyvale Rd. (now called, respectively, Stevens Creek and De Anza Blvds.). The small community was called West Side for its location on the valley's western foothills, and it serviced nearby farmers with such businesses as a blacksmith shop.

In the 1890s, the *phylloxera* parasite devastated the vineyards in the Stevens Creek area by attacking their tender roots. The destruction of much of the grapevines brought an end to many of the area's wineries, and some farmers turned to horse breeding, a successful enterprise that proved quite profitable in the valley's pre-automobile era. By the turn of the 19th century, this part of Santa Clara Valley was well known for its equestrian business. In 1902, as the area's population steadily increased, a post office was started at the Home Union

him as CEO with John Sculley, a former Pepsi-Cola executive whom Jobs himself had personally recruited at great length. Jobs started a company he called NeXT, which was involved in developing object-oriented software. On Sculley's watch, Apple's market share began to erode as IBM-compatible PCs began to skyrocket in popularity. Microsoft Windows used many of the principles of Apple's graphical user interface, and a nasty legal battle ensued over the theft of the "look-and-feel" of the Mac's GUI.

In the public's perception, Apple was definitely an easier computer to use, but the number of clones of IBM's PC had created a highly competitive market, thus lowering the price (and profit margins). The popularity of the PC and its many clones also meant that the market potential for PC-based software was larger than that for Mac-based applications, so the library of software titles was commensurately larger for the PC clones than for Apple's machine. Also, with IBM's corporate image behind it, big business tended to go with the PC.

In the 1990s, Apple's shaky fortunes gave rise to a high turnover at the top. In 1993, Sculley was

ousted for Michael Spindler. In 1996, with Apple's share of the computing market diminishing steadily, Spindler was replaced for a short time by Gil Amelio. After he was forced to resign, in a move that surprised Silicon Valley, the board asked Steve Jobs to step back in to lead the company again. Jobs is now the permanent CEO.

In 1998, under Jobs's leadership, Apple introduced its iMac computer, marketed not just as an easy-to-set-up way of connecting to the Internet but also an attractive, faintly retro, faintly New Beetle-ish designer computer. The iMac's popularity helped raise the Cupertino firm's stock, proving that Apple is the comeback kid of computer companies.

In 1999, the made-for-TV movie *Pirates of Silicon Valley* wittily—and accurately—depicted the intense competition between Microsoft's Bill Gates (played by Anthony Michael Hall) and Apple's Steve Jobs (played with courageous self-absorption by *ER*'s Noah Wyle). Available on video, the movie is an entertaining behind-the-scenes look at two very complex personalities who were instrumental in shaping the computer industry.

Store, a popular hardware shop located at the West Side village crossroads. There were already too many California towns named West Side, so the locals decided to name their village Cupertino after the original post office at the Las Palmas Winery. By this time, many of the wineries were rebounding from the blight that had destroyed so many vineyards, and once again Cupertino received worldwide attention for the quality of its wines. In prestigious international competitions, many of the community's vineyards competed successfully against the finest French wines.

Turn-of-the-century Cupertino served as the vacation home for Charles and Ella Baldwin, San Francisco socialites who kept their vineyard estate Beaulieu on land now occupied by De Anza Community College. They hired locally renowned architect Willis Polk to build a palatial house on their estate where they could entertain in an aristocratic setting. Polk designed a smaller, modernized version of Louis XIV's Grand Trianon at Versailles for the wealthy couple. Now known as Le Petit Trianon, the architectural jewel stands today on the college grounds and serves as the home of the California History Center. The house's former wine cellar does duty as the college bookstore.

R. Cali & Brothers

A family of Sicilian immigrants named Cali moved to Cupertino around 1900 to work in the vineyards, and among its members was an ambitious young boy named Rosario. By 1928, a number of chicken ranches were operating in the area, and the now grown-up Rosario started his R. Cali & Brothers feed store to sell hay and grain to the local ranchers. The popular business was located at the De Anza Blvd. and Stevens Creek Blvd. crossroads, and it grew into one of the city's major industries, eventually becoming Cupertino's first million-dollar business. One of the feed store's more popular Christmas traditions was to put a Christmas tree on top of the grain silo. When the property was sold to Apple Computer to build a modern office complex in the early 1980s, the deed stipulated that the new owners continue to place a Christmas tree on

top of their building. Apple has maintained this holiday tradition every year.

By 1950, Cupertino was still primarily farms and had less than 500 homes, but the postwar growth of the valley started a trend toward building housing divisions on the city's fertile soil. Led by local rancher Norman Nathanson, the Cupertino–Monta Vista Improvement Association pushed a proposal to incorporate the city and protect it from becoming annexed by San Jose. On September 27, 1955, citizens voted for incorporation.

In the mid-1970s, Cupertino started its swift change from a small agricultural town into a booming high-tech city. Much of Cupertino's modern development was financed by the success of Apple, especially during the computer company's phenomenal growth in the 1980s. But in the 1990s, with Apple's future uncertain, Cupertino wooed other high-tech companies, including Symantec and Tandem. Surprisingly, Apple is now the city's second largest computer employer. After a series of layoffs, it has 3,000 workers here compared with Hewlett-Packard's roster of 3,500. But the rainbow apple icon still predominates the local scenery, and with its late-1990s renaissance, the company that had its birth in Cupertino will remain a vital part of the city in the foreseeable future.

TOUR

Cupertino is not known for being an especially scenic city, but this driving and walking tour can provide you with a glimpse of its urban and rural character as well as a few historical highlights. Start from Hwy. 87, taking the De Anza Blvd. exit heading north. You'll pass through several blocks of the Westgate district of San Jose, entering Cupertino's city limits at Bollinger Road. Continue driving a few more blocks until you reach Silverado Ave. (you'll see a KFC restaurant at the corner here.) Turn right at this intersection, and you'll see on your immediate left the **Cupertino Chamber of Commerce visitor's center,** 20455 Silverado Ave., 408/252-7054. Here you can get information on current community events, lodging, and dining.

From Silverado Ave., turn right at the stop sign back onto De Anza Blvd., driving a quarter mile north to the stoplight at Stevens Creek Boulevard. Make sure you get into the left turn lane. Although there's nothing particularly exciting to see at this intersection, it is considered the historic heart of Cupertino. From this site sprung up the village of West Side, the community out of which Cupertino eventually emerged. The large modern-style buildings beyond the vacant lot on the right are **Apple Computer** offices, constructed where the R. Cali & Brothers feed store once stood. The razing of this granary was seen by locals as the symbol of high-tech's overthrow of the city's agriculture heritage.

Turn left onto Stevens Creek Blvd. and drive west one-half mile to Stelling Road. Turn right at the intersection here and take the first left into the parking lot of the **Robert W. Quinlan Community Center,** 408/777-3120. Inside this beautifully designed, 27,000-square-foot building resembling a Mediterranean villa, you can visit the **Cupertino History Museum,** 408/973-1495, with displays showcasing the community's past. Particularly interesting are the old-fashioned children's toys and the mementos from its family-run wineries. Plan to spend about half an hour at this small museum run by the local historical society. (A small **satellite gallery** at Cupertino's Vallco Fashion Park mall is open Tues. and Sat. noon–3 P.M.).

In the Quinlan Center's back patio area, take a look at the water fountain representing the artesian wells that irrigated the valley's farms in the 19th and early 20th centuries. Beyond the water fountain, the 28-acre **Memorial Park,** 408/777-3120, invites you to take a leisurely stroll. This is Cupertino's primary park, and the city holds a number of festivals here throughout the year, including the Cherry Blossom Festival, the Art in the Park exhibit, and an occasional Shakespeare Festival at the small outdoor amphitheater. For families, the park has a wooden playground resembling a frontier town and fort. The park's large ornamental ponds attract so many pigeons, ducks, gulls, and other feathered friends, you'll be reminded of Alfred Hitchcock's movie *The Birds.* But these fowl are unlikely to attack you—they're tame from years of bread-crumb feedings.

From the Quinlan Center's parking lot, take a right and follow the park exit road, turning right at Stevens Creek Boulevard. Directly across the street is **De Anza Community College,** 408/864-5678, website: www.deanza.fhda.edu. Turn left at Mary Ave. to enter the college grounds. Vending machines require coins or bills for the $2 parking fee. The college has a student population of about 25,000 per quarter. Its mellow Spanish-style architecture, water fountains, and sculpted artwork make it a pleasant place for an afternoon stroll.

Visitor attractions at the De Anza campus include the 2,500-seat **Flint Center,** 408/864-8816, which has brought performers such as Johnny Mathis and the Peking Acrobats to the city. Next to the Flint Center is the small but well-managed **Euphrat Museum of Art,** 408/864-8836, a free gallery displaying various styles of visual art. Also on campus, the **California History Center,** 408/864-8712, houses one of the world's largest collections of California historical documents. Equipment for the campus's **Minolta Planetarium,** 408/864-8814, was donated by the well-known camera company. In the **Advanced Technology Center,** opened in 1994 with a major contribution from Apple co-founder Steve Wozniak, you'll find a small display of Apple Computer artifacts, including a motherboard for the Apple I labeled "Our Founder." Plan to spend at least an hour visiting the various campus attractions.

Get back on Stevens Creek Blvd. and turn left from the college, driving west. Immediately on your right just across the street from De Anza College, you'll see **The Oaks Shopping Center,** a popular gathering spot for students. It has several restaurants such as **Hobee's,** 408/255-6010, which in 1998 made the front page of *The Wall Street Journal* as the spot for an illegal meeting between Apple and Microsoft representatives. The Oaks also has a popular discount movie theater. Next, cross Hwy. 85 and venture into Cupertino's **Monta Vista district,** where the foothills begin. This affluent area of the city provides a pleasant touring opportunity. On your left, the boulevard will pass the tree-bordered northern section of pioneer Elisha Stephens's **Blackberry Farm,** 408/777-3140. The former vineyard is now a 33-acre city-run golf course and picnic grounds. At this point, you're driving into Cupertino's hilly Monta Vista district, where you'll observe million-dollar homes belonging to many of Silicon Valley's high-tech workers.

About a mile past Blackberry Farm, you'll arrive at the Foothill Blvd. intersection. If you were to continue a mile or so down Stevens Creek Blvd., you would soon reach the private property of **Kaiser Permanente Cement Plant.** Instead, turn left at this crossroad, driving south along Foothill Blvd. through a residential area of ranch-style homes. Soon, you'll leave the houses behind as the road makes its winding way through rugged canyon country. On your left, turn into the entrance of **Stevens Creek County Park,** 408/867-3654, an excellent location for recreational outings such as hiking and picnicking. Admission is free. You can spend at least two hours here exploring the hills and meandering canyons carved by Stevens Creek. The park also has a small reservoir with a boat launch for water activities.

From the county park, turn right at Foothill Blvd., returning north for about one mile to McClellan Road. Turn right on McClellan Rd., which winds through a residential area for about a mile. After the hairpin curve, you'll see the 52-acre **Deep Cliff Golf Course,** 408/253-5357, on your right. Across the road from this exquisitely maintained course is **McClellan Ranch Park,** 408/777-3120. This free 18-acre city park was a horse ranch in the 1930s and '40s, and many of the red-painted farm buildings come from that period. The park's barn is the site of California's first successful artificial insemination experiment. You'll also find near the park's entrance the Santa Clara County branch office of the **Audubon Society,** which runs a small gift shop. From the park office, get one of the brochures providing a self-guided tour of the nature trail that meanders along Stevens Creek and takes visitors through an acre or so of organic community garden plots. Plan to spend about 45 minutes here.

Turn left back on McClellan Rd. and follow it through a residential area. On your right you'll see **Monta Vista High School,** the location of de Anza's brief encampment in 1776. Continue driving east, passing over Hwy. 85 and along the southern boundary of De Anza College. At the intersection where McClellan Rd. meets Stelling Rd., you'll see the campus's **environmental study area,** which contains a small botanical garden of regional plants. Continue driving to De Anza Blvd. (you'll arrive near the chamber of commerce office). Turn left at the stoplight here and continue heading north on De Anza Blvd., this time passing through the Stevens Creek Blvd. intersection. Drive less than a mile, and on your right, observe the modern office complex containing **Apple Computer's headquarters.** It's on Infinite Loop Dr., a designation derived from a software programming term. The site is private property, but from the street you can see several fanciful sculptures representing its famous software user-interface icons. Apple is conveniently located next to the I-280 on-ramp. The southbound entrance leads to San Jose, the northbound entrance leads to San Francisco.

POINTS OF INTEREST

Cupertino History Museum

Cupertino's agricultural history is presented in this small community museum run by friendly docents. Furniture, household objects, maps, and photographs help paint a picture of the town's yesteryears, including a look at its fruit orchards and family-run wineries.

Quinlan Community Center, 10185 Stelling Rd. (next to Memorial Park, across the street from De Anza College), 408/973-1495; free parking in lot; admission free; open Wed.–Sat. 10 A.M.–4 P.M.

De Anza Community College

Many of Silicon Valley's high-tech employees make up the student body of this fine community college, a sister institution to Los Altos Hills's Foothill College. More than 150,000 residents take the campus's community education classes to enhance skills in areas such as public speaking

THE VALLEY'S AUDUBON

Although much of its land has now been taken over by suburbs, shopping malls, and industrial park complexes, Silicon Valley still has enough natural terrain—and an amazingly diverse range of habitats—to attract a variety of birdlife. The valley is located along the Pacific Flyway, and on fall and early winter mornings, the area's population can sometimes witness V-shaped groups of wild ducks and geese flying south to warmer climates.

Among the earliest of the area's birders was pioneer Andrew Jackson Grayson. The son of a rich Louisiana plantation owner who, with his wife, Frances, crossed the Sierras in 1846 (just a few days before the unlucky Donner Party), Grayson served for a time as a U.S. officer during the Mexican-American War. He went on to work the goldfields before settling in what's now Marin County. In 1852, after viewing John James Audubon's just-published *Birds of America* folio, which focused on Eastern birds, Grayson was inspired to create a similar work describing the birds of the Pacific region.

He and his wife moved to San Jose and built a home, which they called Bird's Nest Cottage. There, he painted finely detailed illustrations of many bird species found in the Santa Clara Valley. These included roadrunners, finches, and the now-endangered California condor. He corresponded with Spencer Fullerton Baird, a leading 19th-century ornithologist, and sent preserved specimens to Washington, D.C.'s Smithsonian Institution—helping to establish its massive bird collection.

Many of Grayson's bird paintings lay for more than a century in U.C. Berkeley's Bancroft Library until they were finally collected into a book, *Birds of the Pacific Slope,* published in 1982. The quality of the illustrations and the text rivals that of his hero Audubon, and Grayson has been called "the Audubon of the West."

Birding Today

There are a number of excellent places to bird-watch in Silicon Valley.

• The levees in city and county parks on the southern banks of San Francisco Bay afford abundant opportunities to spot a range of waterfowl. Several of these parks offer docent-guided tours that explain the area's birds and wildlife. Try **Don Edwards National Wildlife Refuge** in Alviso, **Sunnyvale Baylands Park,** and Palo Alto's **Baylands Nature Preserve.**

• The **Los Gatos Creek and Coyote Creek Trails** provide an excellent habitat for green and great blue herons, egrets, and red-winged blackbirds.

• **Rancho San Antonio County Park** contains foothill habitats for birds such as California quail, Western tanager, red-tailed hawks, and woodpeckers.

• At **Uvas Canyon County Park,** west of Morgan Hill, you can view band-tailed pigeons, Steller's jays, grosbeaks, phoebes, and thrushes.

• With its wooded terrain and Guadalupe Reservoir, San Jose's **Almaden Quicksilver County Park** is a scenic spot to view birds such as loons, wild turkeys, turkey vultures, golden eagles, and red-breasted sapsuckers.

For more information on the area's bird wildlife, call or visit the Santa Clara Valley Audubon Society, 408/252-3747, headquartered in Cupertino's McClellan Ranch Park at 22221 McClellan Road. The nature shop, stocked with books and gift items, is open Mon.–Thurs. 10 A.M.–6 P.M., Fri. 10 A.M.–5 P.M., and Sat. 10 A.M.–noon.

CITIES OF THE VALLEY

WHO IS DE ANZA?

De Anza Boulevard is a major thoroughfare cutting through the western section of Silicon Valley. And the city of Cupertino has De Anza Community College. Obviously, the name de Anza is significant to the valley's history, but few who live here know why.

Captain Juan Bautista de Anza was born in 1736 at the Presidio of Fronteras (near what is now the city of Douglas, Arizona). He grew up to serve the Spanish Crown as a soldier in New Spain, rising in rank to become Commander of the Presidio at Tubac (about 45 miles from the present city of Tucson).

To help in the colonization of California, the Spanish needed an overland route to take supplies from the Sonora region of Arizona to the Presidio of Monterey along California's coast. In September 1773, de Anza, with the aid of an Indian guide named Sebastian Tarabal, started out to find a route with enough water and pastures for immigrants to travel. By early 1774, de Anza arrived in Monterey, successfully blazing the desired land route.

The Spanish knew that colonial settlement was the only way to keep a firm political hold on their Alta California territory, and they wanted to establish a base in the area of what is now San Francisco to show other nations this vital bay port was occupied. On November 28, 1774, de Anza was charged with the task of finding colonists brave enough to make the treacherous trek through the desert and over the Sierras to San Francisco. The colonists' reward would be title to land in California.

De Anza spent nearly a year rounding up settlers willing to embark on this dangerous venture. At 11 A.M. on October 23, 1775, de Anza led 240 soldiers and settlers, 165 mules, 340 horses, and 302 head of cattle from Tubac on the long march to San Francisco. Only one death occurred during the hard ordeal. Within a day of leaving Tubac, Senora Felix died while giving birth to a boy. After six months of traveling, the colonists arrived in Monterey on March 10, 1776.

After a couple weeks' rest, de Anza, along with Lieutenant Jose Joaquin Moraga and Father Pedro Font, left the group to find a suitable route to San Francisco. The three explorers made their way through a Santa Clara Valley with a level fertile plain, meandering creeks, oaks and other trees, and abundant game animals. They also met gracious Indians who traded fish and other supplies with them.

On March 25, de Anza wrote in his diary: "After traveling a short distance in the plain we turned to the west-northwest, and then began to meet many heathen, who went notifying those ahead, greedy for the glass beads which I gave them. With such company as this we continued for about a league and half, after which they left us. Continuing our route in the same direction for about three leagues and a half, we turned to the west, going close to some small hills to our left and arrived at the arroyo of San Joseph Cupertino, which is useful only for travelers. Here we halted for the night, having come eight leagues in seven and a half hours."

If de Anza could peer ahead 225 years, he would see that the land surrounding his Cupertino campsite "useful only for travelers" would be covered with million-dollar homes and industrial parks filled with computer companies.

and personal finances. De Anza's beautiful grounds contain a number of facilities that make it an interesting stop for a visit. The nonprofit **California History Center,** housed in the stunning Le Petit Trianon mansion, often holds special events such as lecture series. It has a frequently changing exhibit that presents various aspects of the state's colorful past. The **Stocklmeir Library** here is a large resource of books, pamphlets, videotapes, oral history, and research papers. The center is open Mon.–Thurs. 8:30 A.M.–noon and 1–4:30 P.M. or by appointment, 408/864-8712, website: www.deanza.fhda.edu/CalifHistory/CalifHistory.html.

The college also features the **Minolta Planetarium,** which provides a range of astronomy-related shows on its 150-foot dome. Named for the camera company that in 1970 provided the million-dollar optics for its projector, it's the second largest planetarium in Northern California. On Fri. and Sat. nights, it puts on a spectacular laser light show set to music. Tickets cost $4 for adults and $3 for children under 12, 408/864-8814, website: planetarium.fhda.edu/pltwww/ghome.html.

Also at De Anza is the **Flint Center,** an auditorium built in 1971 that was named after Calvin C. Flint, the first chancellor of the Foothill–De Anza Community College District. Performances include Broadway shows and San Jose Symphony concerts. Ticket prices vary. Call the box office at 408/864-8816, Mon.–Fri. 10 A.M.–2 P.M., or visit their website: www.flintcenter.com.

Rain or shine, De Anza College also holds a **flea market** the first Sat. of the month. 21250 Stevens Creek Blvd. (just off Hwy. 85), 408/864-8820, website: www.deanza.fhda.edu; parking $2 (coins or bills accepted at ticket machines).

Rancho San Antonio County Park

This small but much-enjoyed park connects with the Mid-Peninsula Regional Open Space District to create a combined 2,300-acre recreational area in the foothills below Skyline Ridge. The land was part of Rancho San Antonio, granted to Juan Prado Mesa in 1839. **Deer Hollow Farm,** located within the Open Space District, is run by the city of Mountain View. Agricultural educa-

tion programs are often held in this rural setting, which is also popular for family outings.

On I-280 in Cupertino, take Foothill Blvd. exit and head south to Cristo Rey Drive. Turn right and drive one mile to park entrance, 408/867-3654, website: claraweb.co.santa-clara.ca.us/parks. Activities: tennis, biking, horseback riding, non-gas-powered model aircraft, hiking (23 miles of trails).

Stevens Creek County Park

Combined with the Open Space Preserve for a total of 2,137 acres, this park provides a diverse environment of canyons, meadowlands, evergreen and oak forests, and Stevens Creek. A 93-acre reservoir is set in the foothills, and horses can be rented at **Garrod Stables,** 408/867-9527, near the south entrance on Mt. Eden Road.

For the park's northern entrance, in Cupertino take I-280 to Foothill Expwy. exit, heading west three miles. For the park's southern entrance, from Saratoga, take Hwy. 9 north, turn onto Pierce Rd. and travel about two miles to Mt. Eden Road. Turn left and travel 1.5 miles, 408/867-3654, website: claraweb.co.santa-clara.ca.us/parks. Activities: biking, horseshoes, volleyball, horseback riding, nonpower boating, fishing, kayaking, archery. Trails connect with the Mid-Peninsula Regional Open Space District.

Deep Cliff Golf Course

Silicon Valley's best executive course is also one of its most scenic. Set in a verdant foothill canyon, it was a shooting location for MGM's classic 1944 movie *National Velvet.*

10700 Clubhouse Ln. (off McClellan Rd. near McClellan Ranch Park), 408/253-5357; par 60; greens fees $23–30.

Vallco Fashion Park

An acronym of its original owners—high-tech firm Varian Associates and the families Leonard, Lester, Craft, and Orlando—Vallco is Cupertino's only shopping mall. Although its double-story layout can make it confusing to maneuver through, this is one of the best malls in Silicon Valley to take children. It features a skating rink and a large video arcade with many of the latest electronic games. Restaurants include TGI Friday's and El Torito.

10123 N. Wolfe Rd. (one block south of I-280, take Wolfe Rd. exit), 408/255-5660, website: www.shopyourmall.com; major stores: Sears, JCPenney, Macy's; open Mon.–Fri. 10 A.M.–9 P.M., Sat. 10 A.M.–7 P.M., Sun. 11 A.M.–6 P.M.

Cupertino Village Shopping Center

Most of the shops and restaurants in this tranquil courtyard shopping center are Asian, such as its 99 Ranch Market, a specialty grocery store where locals buy Asian ingredients and live seafood. It's also the site of the Duke of Edinburgh, 408/446-3853, Silicon Valley's most authentic British pub, where you can get fish and chips as well as beef Wellington.

Corner of Wolfe and Homestead Rd. (north of I-280 from Wolfe Rd. exit).

Campbell

© MARTIN CHEEK

CITIES OF THE VALLEY

local Campbell institution, Fung Lum Chinese restaurant

Commuters racing home along Hwy. 17 get an afternoon treat as they near the Pruneyard Towers in Campbell. It's the mouth-watering aroma of Andy's BBQ, a well-known Silicon Valley landmark. The scent of barbecuing meat drifts from the popular eatery, in a squat, homely building set right beside the busy highway's overpass. Andy's typifies Campbell's plain but friendly personality. West of the smokehouse is the downtown district, a slice of Americana with its hometown restaurants and shops. Shadowing this area is the Campbell Water Tower, another historic landmark from the valley's agricultural years. It's located on the perimeter of an office building complex that once was the world's largest fruit canning and drying operation. The water tower serves as a reminder of the small-town, rural spirit that not long ago filled the region. It was this spirit, at least in part, that inspired President Teddy Roosevelt to spend a night sleeping in one of the town's orchards in 1903.

Today's community of more than 40,000 people prides itself on preserving its old-fashioned, small-town charm. The city covers an area of about six square miles, surrounded on the west, north, and east by San Jose suburbs and on the south by Los Gatos and Saratoga neighborhoods. Although reminders of its agricultural heyday still dot the town, Campbell has transformed into a modern community of middle-class Silicon Valley residents. California ranch-style homes, apartment complexes, and shopping strips such as the Pruneyard rise out of areas that once sprouted nothing but hay fields and orchards.

The close-knit city hosts a number of community festivals throughout the year. During the holidays, the city lights its Christmas tree during the Carol of Lights festival. In spring, an Easter parade is held downtown. Every May, the town holds a Prune Festival, which draws a large crowd from throughout Silicon Valley. A Scottish festival takes place every summer in commemoration of Campbell's founding family. Perhaps pioneer Benjamin Campbell's spirit haunts the annual Campbell Highland Games and Celtic Gathering, where bagpipes are droned, hammers are thrown, cabers are tossed, and costumed residents perform Ceilidh dances. Helping to enhance the good-ol'-summertime spirit, every Thurs. evening during July and Aug., the Orchard City Green at the Civic Center is the site of a popular free concert series. Residents bring lawn chairs and picnic dinners, and listen to music ranging from big band and jazz to rock and reggae. With the arrival of fall, downtown Campbell draws thousands of locals to its Oktoberfest, which includes live music, arts and crafts, and German food and beer.

While an integral part of Silicon Valley, Campbell residents are fiercely determined to maintain the community's identity and character. They take pride in the city's history and have worked hard on several preservation projects, raising more than $1 million, for example, to relocate and renovate the historic Ainsley House. Campbell is a Silicon Valley community that never forgot its small-town roots—it keeps a well-balanced mixture of historic homes and buildings among the modern electronic and high-tech industries that have set up shop here.

HISTORY

In 1846, William Campbell and his family journeyed west from Missouri for the promise of a new life in the Mexican territory of California. After an arduous six-month trek, they arrived in the Santa Clara Valley in late October. Tension between the American and Mexican governments made the future of the region uncertain. But when the pioneer family saw the valley's fertile soil and temperate climate, Benjamin Campbell, William's 20-year-old son, knew that this would be the place he would call home for the rest of his days.

In 1851, Benjamin purchased 160 acres of land that would later become the city's downtown district. He planted hay and wheat, and the small farm prospered. What is now busy Campbell Ave. was originally the tranquil tree-lined driveway leading from Benjamin Campbell's two-story farmhouse to the country road that later became Winchester Boulevard.

Completion of the transcontinental railroad in 1869 connected Santa Clara Valley farmers with East Coast customers. To take advantage of this lucrative market, the valley's ranchers planted fruit orchards on the fields that had once supported wheat and hay. Railroad lines quickly began to crisscross the valley, shipping produce from the area's abundant orchards and farms to the hungry customers on the East Coast.

Campbell's Station

In January 1877, Benjamin Campbell made a deal with the South Coast Railroad Company that allowed it the right-of-way through his farm for the San Jose-to-Los Gatos line. This railroad link became an important transit route for the Campbell region, thus helping Benjamin's farm to prosper. So indispensable did the railroad become in shaping the valley's economy and culture that Benjamin began to dream of forming a community on his property. In 1886, he sold 1.15 acres of his land for a five-dollar coin so that the railroad could build a depot stop. They named it Campbell's Station after the ambitious farmer. That small, wood-framed building served as the seed for what eventually became the town of Campbell.

On January 3, 1888, Benjamin officially listed his first subdivision for the Campbell Tract at Campbell's Station. By spring, he had started selling subdivision lots to future residents. A small village quickly began to grow around the depot as churches and shops were built, a newspaper was started, and an association was formed to begin construction of a town hall. In a few years, Benjamin had sold so many lots that his dream of creating a thriving village on his property had come true.

The many apricot and prune orchards surrounding the town quickly brought international recognition to Campbell. The proud community named itself "The Orchard City" because of this abundance of fruit trees growing around it. And with the improvement in canning and drying techniques, Campbell's fruit products were soon enjoyed by consumers

MURDER IN THE SILICON VALLEY

In comparison to many metropolitan areas of the United States, Silicon Valley is a relatively safe place to live and visit. But that doesn't mean the region has not had its share of sensational mass murders (and plots that were averted).

In February 2001, Silicon Valley made national news when San Jose police stopped a plot by Al DeGuzman, a 19-year-old student at Cupertino's De Anza Community College, to kill students and teachers at that college. The young man had planned a scenario much like what happened at Columbine High School in Littleton, Colorado. Tipped off by a Longs drugstore clerk who processed DeGuzman's film and saw his arsenal in the photos, San Jose police averted tragedy when they burst into his bedroom and discovered guns and 60 pipe bombs.

February 16, 1988, was a dark day in the valley when Richard Wade Farley stormed into Building M5 of defense contractor ESL loaded with 100 pounds of guns and ammunition. He intended to kill former coworker Laura Black, who had rejected his romantic advances. Farley shot seven people to death. Black survived the attack, and Farley is now on death row.

But one of the most gruesome mass killings that shocked 19th-century America took place in the valley's farm village of Campbell. Colonel R. P. McGlincy, a Civil War veteran, married a widow named Ada Wells, and helped her run the large orchard she had inherited. Ada had a daughter, Hattie, and a son, James, by her first marriage. Despite the protests of her family, 27-year-old Hattie married James Dunham on Valentine's Day 1895. That same year, the McGlincy's moved into a comfortable Victorian home they had recently built on their land. Ada's son James lived with them.

Hattie gave birth to a boy on May 4, 1896, and soon after left her husband due to Dunham's cruel treatment. She and the baby lived in the farmhouse with her mother, stepfather, and brother. On the evening of May 26, 1896, the colonel and James Wells went to San Jose for a meeting of the American Protective Association. While they were gone, Dunham came to the farmhouse, took off his shoes, and crept upstairs. He found Hattie taking care of the baby and tried to persuade his wife to return to

all through the year virtually everywhere in the world.

A staunch Methodist, Benjamin believed in the strict prohibition of alcohol. In order to dissuade a rougher class of people from becoming citizens of his growing settlement, he inserted a rigid clause in the town deeds prohibiting the construction of saloons and the sale of alcohol. Anyone who violated this clause forfeited their property to the Campbells or their heirs. The city's founding father once proclaimed, "If we were to have a lot of saloons crowded in here, I wanted to be excused from it."

Campbell R.F.D.

On July 3, 1885, Campbell gained its first woman postmaster. Louisa Weitzenberg was a handsome woman who managed a well-run post office in the downtown district. During these years, the National Grange, a farmers' association, promoted free delivery of mail to those people residing in rural areas of the United States. The Grange argued that this would save farmers time from traveling into town to pick up mail. Because of the numerous farmers living in the vicinity, Weitzenberg supported this concept of "rural free delivery."

In 1896, U.S. Congress provided $40,000 to test the rural free delivery system in five selected areas throughout the United States. The postmaster general chose Campbell as the site for the first R.F.D. mail service in the West. The initial Campbell rural route was tried on February 1, 1897, with the U.S. Postal Service providing three horse carriages to deliver letters and packages directly to the farmers surrounding the town. The experiment proved to be a huge success, and many other communities him. When she refused, he put a gag over Hattie's mouth and broke her neck with his hands.

Minnie, a maid hired to help tend the baby, heard the commotion upstairs and came up to find Dunham standing over his dead wife's body. Dunham grabbed Minnie, put a gag over her mouth and plowed an axe into Minnie's skull. Realizing that Ada was in the bedroom below, he next raced down the stairs and gave her five axe blows into her skull. After this, he searched the house for photographs of himself, destroying each one that he found (he missed one that would later appear on wanted posters). Then, with two revolvers, he waited for the colonel and James Wells' return.

The two men returned home at 11 P.M. As the colonel stepped into the house, Dunham hit his father-in-law's head with the axe, but only dazed him. Then, still using the axe, he fought with the athletic James. The struggle continued through the downstairs, and in the parlor, Dunham pulled out his revolver and shot James several times in the chest. The young man fell dead in front of the fireplace.

The colonel climbed out of a kitchen window and staggered into the hired help cabin. Dunham came after him with the revolver and shot through the locked cabin door, demanding that McGlincy come out. McGlincy opened the door and Dunham shot him in the heart. Hired hand Robert Briscoe tried to escape out of the cabin through a rear window, but Dunham heard the broken glass and raced around the cabin, shooting the defenseless Briscoe in the head. Another hired hand happened to be in the barn. Hearing the gunshots, he climbed into the loft and hid himself in the hay. Dunham entered the barn and unsuccessfully searched for him. The killer then fled the scene on his horse.

L. C. Ross, a friend of James Wells, was a witness to the crime. He happened to be passing by the house and, hearing the gunshots, hid behind a palm tree. After Dunham escaped, he ran to his father's nearby farm for help. Dunham was never captured. The last he was seen was the next day riding his horse near Smith Creek on Mt. Hamilton Road.

in the Santa Clara Valley began requesting their own R.F.D. services.

At the turn of the 19th century, the question arose in Campbell of whether to incorporate the town. On February 24, 1906, the issue went to the polling booth so residents could vote on the proposal. The result on that election day was a definite no to the idea of incorporation.

Great Depression and War

As it did in much of the United States in the 1930s, the Great Depression hit Campbell hard. The town's farmers were devastated when canneries could only pay $2 a ton for fruit. But in 1941 with the United States' entry into World War II, the demand for canned food increased dramatically as the need arose to feed American soldiers fighting in Europe and the Pacific. Campbell began to prosper again. Women were

extensively employed in the canneries. The war years and bumper crops did much to help revive the town's economy.

After World War II, Campbell's population stood at about 5,000 residents. During these postwar years, the Santa Clara Valley was being transformed from a sleepy agricultural region to a vibrant industrial one. As new residents began pouring into the area, orchard trees were torn down and fields were leveled to construct suburbs and shopping centers. During the 1950s, the city of San Jose began a massive expansion program, devouring unincorporated land throughout the Santa Clara Valley to turn itself into "the Los Angeles of the north." Faced with the danger of being annexed, Campbell residents decided they didn't want their town's identity to become lost as they turned into just another San Jose suburb. Unlike the 1906 election, on March 11, 1952, the town's citizens voted 687 to 637 to incorporate. On March 28, Campbell officially became a city. In the last half century, Campbell's population has increased eightfold, filling out the remaining orchards and fields with suburbs and shopping malls.

TOUR

If Benjamin Campbell were to return to the city that bears his name, he might hardly recognize his community as it begins the third millennium. Only a few historic homes, several historic buildings in the downtown area, the former Hyde Cannery, and the meandering Los Gatos Creek would help him get his navigational bearings. Begin a tour of the city by taking the Hamilton Ave. exit off of Hwy. 17 and heading east. Immediately near the freeway, take a right turn on

Creekside Dr. and follow it along, turning left at the stoplight intersection onto Campisi Way. Follow this street a short distance to the stoplight intersection on Bascom Ave., and turn right at this corner. Immediately on your right at 1815 Bascom Ave., you'll see the exotic facade of the well-known **Fung Lum Restaurant,** 408/377-6955. Its fascinating exterior of statues and waterfalls makes this Chinese eatery a Campbell landmark pleasing to the eye.

At the next stoplight intersection along Bascom, turn right into the **Pruneyard Shopping Center,** 408/371-4700, and follow the side road into the parking area in back. After finding a parking place (a three-hour parking limit is enforced here), enjoy browsing among the many boutique shops and specialty stores. The Pruneyard is Campbell's biggest shopping center, and it's hard to miss with the monolithic black-win-

ROUGH RIDER TEDDY PLANTS A TREE IN CAMPBELL

One of turn-of-the-century Campbell's most memorable days was when Teddy Roosevelt stopped by. In anticipation of the presidential visit, the citizens lavishly decorated local businesses and residences with banners and flags and set up a bandstand from which the big stick advocate could address the crowd.

On the afternoon of May 11, 1903, Roosevelt's carriage traveled down Santa Clara–Los Gatos Rd. (now Winchester Blvd.), and the Rough Rider arrived at the Campbell Ave. intersection. Here, town founder Benjamin Campbell presented him with a new shovel festooned with silk ribbon. Roosevelt used the shovel to ceremoniously enlarge a previously prepared hole, then proceeded to plant a coast redwood tree. Speaking to the crowd, he particularly addressed the town's children, telling them, "I believe in play and I believe in work. I want to see you play hard while you play, and when you work do not play at all." Later that night, as Roosevelt's rail car passed through town, he decided to have it pulled onto a siding in a quiet orchard so he could sleep there that night.

The redwood that Roosevelt planted grew to a height of 70 feet. It was cut down in 1964 when the city of Campbell voted to widen Winchester Boulevard. But it didn't die in vain—the base and roots were replanted in Vasona Park, and seedlings were taken and planted on the grounds of Campbell High School, across the street from where it had stood. This tree still stands, and during the holiday season serves as the city's official Christmas tree—in the Carol of Lights celebrations, local citizens come together to sing carols around it.

And shortly after the original tree was cut down, Lilyann Brannon, a member of the local Garden Club, ventured to the municipal dump to see if she could salvage the historic stump. She found it, and the Garden Club replanted it at Vasona County Park in Los Gatos. It took root and grew once again into a robust tree. In 1975, the club members placed a commemorative plaque beside it. A bench made from the original tree's wood can be viewed at the Campbell Historical Museum.

dowed skyscrapers called the Pruneyard Towers jutting up alongside Hwy. 17. The shopping center comprises 250,000 square feet of retail space and a 110-room hotel. Built in the 1970s, over two decades it became somewhat run-down in appearance. But a major remodeling job in the mid-1990s has made it a high-quality place for commerce. The center's major draw for locals is bookseller **Barnes & Noble**, 408/559-8101. Also popular are **Trader Joe's**, 408/369-7823, a specialty retail store that sells unique, upscale grocery items at reasonable prices, and the **Chabot Gallery**, 408/559-6693, one of Silicon Valley's best commercial galleries for fine art. For dining here, try **Hobee's Restaurant**, 408/369-0575, a local chain many Silicon Valley residents highly praise, or the excellent **Kyoto Palace**, 408/377-6456, a traditional Japanese restaurant that grills food right at customers' tables. Next to an immense beer fermentation tank is the **Rock Bottom Brewery**, 408/377-0707, a lively restaurant that's a good stop for lunch and dinner. Expect to spend at least an hour at the Pruneyard.

Near the **Outback Steakhouse**, 408/371-5384, take the Union Ave. exit out of the Pruneyard and turn right onto E. Campbell Avenue. Drive under the Hwy. 17 overpass and continue on past **Andy's BBQ**, 408/378-2838, to **Campbell Park**, 408/866-2105, on your left at the corner of Gilman Avenue. Turn left at the stoplight intersection on Gilman and drive into the parking lot immediately to your left (occasionally there's a fee for parking). This park underwent an extensive renovation in 1999. It is connected to the **Los Gatos Creek Parkway** that links Campbell with San Jose's Meridian Ave. area as well as Los Gatos's Vasona County Park. The trail leads as far south as Lexington Reservoir, which is several miles away beyond Los Gatos. Campbell Park serves as the start of a scenic par course trail that wanders two miles along the creek. About one mile south, a pedestrian bridge crosses the creek and provides a view of a man-made waterfall cascading from the Campbell percolation ponds. Plan to spend at least 15 minutes in Campbell Park and about an hour if you plan to stroll the complete par course trail.

Exiting the park back onto Gilman, turn right and return to Campbell Ave., turning left here and following this street to where the Southern Pacific railroad tracks cross it. At this point, keep to your right instead of heading straight into downtown Campbell. Following the street, take the first right at Harrison Ave., and enter the public library parking lot at the corner here. This is Campbell's Civic Center, and you'll find here the **Ainsley House**, 408/866-2119, a quaint Tudor-style cottage that at one time belonged to John Ainsley, a prominent citizen who earned his wealth by building the town's canning industry. In the small **Historical Museum** located next to this exquisite house, you can get a close-up look at exhibits showcasing Campbell's colorful agricultural past. Historic photographs, an orientation video, and memorabilia such as cannery equipment offer a glimpse at the city's bygone years. Expect to spend at least an hour touring the house, museum, and attractive flower garden.

From the Ainsley House, stroll through the **Orchard City Green**, crossing Civic Center Dr. and walking one block to the historic **Campbell Downtown** district along E. Campbell Avenue. A stroll through downtown provides further glimpses into the city's past. The **Gaslighter Theatre**, 408/866-1408, website: www.gaslighter.com, is a 1921 city landmark. Old-fashioned vaudeville revues put on by local amateur performers still provide many nights of lively entertainment. The building was originally constructed as the Campbell branch of the Mercantile Trust Company of California. Next to the Gaslighter Theatre is the **Bruni Gallery**, 408/370-4700, website: www.brunijazzart.com, open 1–6 P.M. daily. This interesting art gallery features the works of Bruni Sablan, an accomplished Silicon Valley artist developing a local reputation for painting vivid portraits of jazz masters. Across Campbell Ave. at the corner of Central St. stands a one-story brick building painted an olive color. An unoccupied historic downtown site, the **Farley Building** once housed the Bank of Campbell, the city's first financial business. It operated from 1895 to 1911 and is considered Campbell's oldest commercial building.

Downtown eateries worth visiting include the friendly Irish pub **Katie Bloom's,** 408/379-9687, the **Orchard Valley Coffee Roastery,** 408/374-2115, which provides customers with Internet access, and **Shebele,** 408/378-3131, an Ethiopian restaurant known for its vegetarian dishes. Antique shoppers will find downtown Campbell a great place to browse for deals. A variety of antique stores dot the downtown district, with the majority found in **The Courtyard** at 295–329 Campbell Ave. in the middle of downtown. This cooperative of small shops specializes in items from collectable china and silverware to antique clocks and dolls. The **Campbell History Museum Store,** 408/871-2259, sells memorabilia and gift items related to the city. Visitors looking for good-quality cowboy gear or country gifts should check out **The Silver Buckle,** 408/378-1111, at the corner of 1st St. and Campbell Ave., known throughout Silicon Valley for its western wear. If you're interested in finding out the latest town news, stop by the offices of the *Campbell Express,* 334 E. Campbell Ave., 408/374-9700, for a copy of the community newspaper.

Walk one block south of the downtown district, and you'll come to the two-story **Water Tower Plaza.** It's easy to find—just look for the big water tower looming over the brick buildings that once housed the Hyde Cannery after its construction in 1894. Cannery and drying operations ended in 1971, and the buildings were converted during the 1980s into a complex of small offices. The designers did a nice job of enhancing the red-brick labyrinth architecture with flower gardens and patios, and it's well worth a short stroll through the heart of Campbell's once-thriving canning and drying industry. Most of the businesses now located here are consulting, design, insurance, and other firms, but Water Tower Plaza also features **Khartoum,** 408/379-6340, a bar with a relaxed atmosphere that many locals frequent for its Irish coffees and steam beers. On the east side of the complex, you can get a glimpse of the railroad line that helped create Campbell. The original depot was torn down in the 1950s, but visitors can get a feel for those days from the dilapidated former loading warehouse at 289 Railroad Ave., where Campbell farmers came to ship their produce to market.

After visiting the downtown area, return to your car and drive out of the Civic Center parking lot, turning right at Harrison Ave. and taking another right back onto Civic Center Drive. Continue driving west for five blocks until you come to the Winchester Blvd. intersection, and get in the left turn lane here. On the far right corner, you'll see the **Campbell Community Center,** 408/866-2138. The buildings here once served as the city's high school and provide an excellent example of 1920s Spanish architecture. The community center provides classroom facilities for people interested in studying topics ranging from dance and painting to computer science. It includes a fitness center, running track, weight room, and lap swimming pool, and offers daily aerobics and fitness classes. On-site day care is also available. The redwood tree towering over the center's sign grew from a sprout taken from the original Teddy Roosevelt Tree. It now serves as Campbell's Christmas tree and is decorated during the holiday season. If you wish to visit the **Campbell Chamber of Commerce,** 408/378-1666, from this point, continue driving straight along W. Campbell Ave. for about 1.5 miles. The chamber's office is located at 1628 W. Campbell Ave. in the Kirkwood Shopping Plaza at the corner of San Tomas Aquino Road.

After looking at the Community Center, turn left onto Winchester Blvd. and follow this often busy thoroughfare containing a diverse choice of restaurants. Along this route, you'll find just about any kind of cuisine, from Chinese to Russian to American hot dogs at an old-fashioned A&W Restaurant. Continue driving about one mile, passing by the Plaza Shopping Center on your right and St. Lucy's Church on your left. Drive under the overpass and take the Camden Ave. exit heading east. Drive about a quarter mile to the Hwy. 17 freeway entrance. The southbound entrance heads toward Santa Cruz, the northbound entrance will take you to San Jose.

THE FRUIT TYCOONS—THE VALLEY'S FIRST VISIONARIES

In 1887, an Englishman named John Colpitts Ainsley, owner of a 7.5-acre ranch located where Campbell Ave. and Winchester Blvd. now intersect, began experimenting with the idea of mass-producing canned fruit for commercial distribution. It took several years of trial and testing, but Ainsley refined his methods and developed his machinery to the point that by the turn of the century his notion was a reality, and canned fruit from Campbell became a popular item among the teeming masses on the East Coast.

Ainsley's fortunes grew, and he became a prominent citizen in the growing town, but he was also, as it happens, a compassionate man who cared about the welfare of his workers. He provided them with many benefits that were ahead of their time. For example, he bought land east of the railroad tracks and built residences for the seasonal cannery workers. These houses provided the workers with various conveniences such as stoves and electricity in addition to tables, beds, and chairs.

In 1925, Ainsley began applying some of the wealth he'd made from canning to the construction of a home that is now a local landmark. Reflecting his English heritage, the Ainsley house was built in a Tudor revival style, and a beautiful cottage garden surrounded the structure. The residence was located at the corner of Hamilton and Bascom Avenues. In 1989, Ainsley's granddaughter donated the house to the city of Campbell, and the structure was moved to the Campbell Civic Center. It now serves as a splendid attraction for the Campbell Historical Museum.

The same year Ainsley first began tinkering with his can, two brothers—George and Charles Fleming—bought land west of the Southern Pacific Railroad line and invented an industry of their own. Near what is now Orchard City Dr., they established a grounds and a packing plant and began exploring the possibilities of *drying* fruit to preserve it. In 1890, the Flemings sold the operation to Frank Buxton, who built it into one of the world's most extensively mechanized plants in the fruit-drying industry—once the apricots and prunes reached the processing stage, human hands hardly touched them.

At first, the fruit was stored in low wooden buildings. But these structures failed to stay cool enough during storage, and the fruit got too dry and shrunken. To solve this problem, a brick warehouse was built in 1894. This cooler building saved farmers thousands of dollars in fruit shrinkage loss. Located next to the railroad tracks, it became the largest prune-drying facility in the world—a distinction that helped win Campbell the proud title of Prune Capital of the World. The brick building, called the George E. Hyde Packing House (for a subsequent owner of the company), still stands. Today known as Water Tower Plaza, it has been converted into a complex of offices set in beautifully landscaped grounds.

Like Ainsley, George Hyde was a businessman who was concerned about his workers' well-being. Hyde paid excellent wages and provided a range of farsighted benefits. Because many of his workers were women, for instance, he established one of Santa Clara Valley's first day care centers to tend to their children.

More colorful tales of Campbell's orchard-growing years appear in former mayor Jeanette Watson's *Campbell: The Orchard City.*

POINTS OF INTEREST

Ainsley House and Museum

Campbell fruit-drying pioneer John Ainsley built this charming English cottage near what's now the corner of Bascom and Hamilton. The 286-ton building was moved to the city's Civic Center to become its Orchard City Green centerpiece, located between the library and police station. Inside, the house is exquisitely furnished with 1930s-style decor; outside, it's surrounded by a delightful flower garden best seen in full spring bloom. An informative museum of Campbell history is located in the home's detached garage. The museum provides an afternoon "Tea and Tour," treating visitors to an English tea in the garden after viewing the house. The special tour costs $12.95 per person. The garden area can also be rented for weddings with up to 200 guests.

Campbell Civic Center (at Civic Center Dr. and Central Ave., one block north of downtown), 408/866-2119, website: web.nvcom.com/chm/; free parking; museum admission is free; docentled tours of the house and gardens cost $6 for adults, $4 for seniors 55 and over, $2.50 for ages 7–17, and children under 7 free; open Thurs.–Sun. noon–4 P.M.

Los Gatos Creek Parkway

At Campbell Park, you can enter this well-used paved trail following Los Gatos Creek. The trail is popular with bikers, joggers, and in-line skaters (especially on weekends, when it can get crowded). The nine-mile trail winds its way along urban and natural settings, stretching from the residential area near San Jose's Leigh Ave. to Lexington Reservoir above Los Gatos. An observation tower in Campbell lets visitors view birds living in the wetlands near the Hwy. 17/85 interchange. For fly fishers, the parkway has special practice ponds near the Dell Ave. entrance (take Hacienda Ave. off Winchester Blvd.).

Corner of E. Campbell and Gilman Aves. (this is the Campbell Park entrance, near Andy's BBQ), 408/356-2729, website: claraweb.co. santa-clara.ca.us/parks; the trail can be accessed at various points, including Lexington Reservoir, Vasona Park, and San Jose's Blackford Elementary School near Leigh Ave. and Willow St.; activities: biking, jogging, in-line skating, fishing, birdwatching.

Pruneyard Shopping Center

A pleasant place for browsing, the shopping center was named after the prune drying yards once so pervasive in the Campbell area. More than 50 specialty shops and restaurants can be found here. A good stop for a sweet treat here is Swensen's Ice Cream shop, which provides calorie-laden smile-inducers with an old-fashioned ambience. For entertainment, the Pruneyard has a small nightclub called Boswell's as well as a United Artists movie complex.

Corner of Bascom and Campbell Aves. (look for the dark skyscrapers known as the Pruneyard Towers), 408/371-4700; hours vary among shops and restaurants, but generally 9 A.M.–6 P.M. for specialty stores.

Gaslighter Theatre

For more than 30 years, Campbell's only live theater has provided a charming evening out in its 1920s mercantile building. The main performance is followed by an old-fashioned vaudeville revue, where audiences cheer the dashing hero and hiss the oily villain.

400 E. Campbell Ave. (downtown Campbell), 408/866-1408, website: www.gaslighter.com; performances Fri. 8 P.M. and Sat. 2 and 8 P.M.; tickets $15 for adults, $11 for children 12 and under.

San Jose

The nation's 11th largest city, San Jose is the corporate, financial, and cultural center of Silicon Valley as well as Santa Clara County's government seat. As the United States' No. 1 exporter of high-tech, it is also considered the world's most quickly developing frontier of digital-based commerce. Every year, hundreds of thousands of people from around the globe come to do business with the multibillion-dollar companies based here. A much smaller number but one that's increasing every year is the amount of adventurous vacation travelers who make San Jose their base while exploring Silicon Valley. It's no wonder that this city of one million people can claim the lofty title of "the capital of Silicon Valley."

San Jose covers 174 square miles of land. It borders several Silicon Valley cities such as Saratoga, Los Gatos, Cupertino, and Santa Clara on its western boundaries. Milpitas and the San Francisco Bay flank its north, the unincorporated Diablo Range lies on its eastern edge, and the South Valley city of Morgan Hill borders its southern portion. Due to its aggressive policy of annexing communities during the 1950s and 1960s, it has a number of neighborhoods and districts that seem like small towns in themselves, such as Willow Glen and Alviso. The infamous "Annexation Wars" led to its amoeba-like surrounding of the city of Campbell, a farm town that incorporated to protect itself from being swallowed up by the avaricious San Jose. Creating holes in the fabric of its geography, some of its neighborhoods such as the Burbank district near downtown never were incorporated and are under county jurisdiction.

This sprawling city has much going for it, which has placed it favorably on a number of prestigious lists. The FBI ranks San Jose the No.

CITIES OF THE VALLEY

© MARTIN CHEEK

the San Jose Center for Performing Arts

1 safest city for communities over 400,000, a major turnaround from the 1970s and 1980s. *Money* magazine has ranked the community as No. 2 among best places to live in the United States. *Fortune* magazine has listed it high on its top 10 list of best U.S. cities for business. *Fortune* also has reported: "San Jose/Silicon Valley is one of the nation's economic powerhouses . . . and still far and away the single most important high-technology center in the U.S." *Demographics* magazine ranks San Jose and Silicon Valley No. 1 in terms of spending on leisure activities. And as proof of the city's ethnic viability, *Hispanic Magazine* put San Jose as its No. 1 choice in its list of "Top 10 Cities for Latinos."

San Jose has successfully developed its city-wide cultural diversity. Compared with many major U.S. cities, it experiences a significantly lower incidence of racial problems among its citizens. The many ethnic backgrounds here include African-American, Korean, Japanese, Vietnamese, Mexican, and European nationalities. Its enormous Vietnamese population of more than 80,300, many of whom came here during the late 1970s, makes it the largest population of any U.S. city for this group. Many of the city's ethnic neighborhoods such as Japan-town and the Hispanic Eastside create a kaleidoscopic diversity in the shops, restaurants, and cultural centers found here, as well as at the annual festivals.

San Jose is also a city with a variety of indoor and outdoor activities, many of these (along with its school system) making it an attractive community for families. Its abundance of performing arts groups include a professional opera company, a world-class symphony, and one of the nation's top ballet companies. It also has a treasure trove of amateur and professional drama companies, including the San Jose Repertory Theatre, which in 1998 opened up a spacious downtown auditorium. Other popular San Jose attractions include the Rosicrucian Egyptian Museum, the Children's Discovery Museum, and The Tech, a downtown museum that lets visitors discover through hands-on exhibits the wonders of science and technology. The city's 125 parks and gardens covering more than 3,000 acres of land

also add to the quality of life. These range from Alum Rock Park in the Diablo Range to Kelley Park, with its serene Japanese Friendship Garden. In recent years, San Jose has also developed its sports culture, establishing several professional teams. Its star sports attraction is the National Hockey League's San Jose Sharks, which plays at the state-of-the-art downtown Arena.

Many other U.S. cities that have redeveloped their infrastructures have depended heavily on federal government funding. But with its solid tax base, coming largely from high-tech corporations (particularly in the N. 1st St. "Golden Triangle" area), San Jose has spent more than $1 billion in the last 20 years to transform its one-time derelict downtown area into a showcase business area for the 21st century. Because of its increasing political and financial stature, some have compared modern-day San Jose to the Florence of Renaissance Italy. The city has definitely developed political clout on a national level. And although with its traffic congestion and smog, life isn't always perfect here, the richness of the city's heritage and vibrancy of its people makes San Jose a fascinating place to visit or call home.

HISTORY

San Jose can rightfully lay claim to the title "first city in California." The city was founded because, to continue the Spanish colonization of Alta California, a continuous supply of food was needed for the Santa Clara Mission and presidios at Monterey and Yerba Buena (later called San Francisco). The Spanish government decided the time had come to establish civilian communities in the frontier that would grow crops. Thus, a group of 68 Spaniards led by Lieutenant Don José Moraga set out to find a place to establish such a community. The group was made up of 14 settlers and their families, as well as 15 soldiers needed to defend the new venture. Ten of the men had been among de Anza's original expedition that explored the Santa Clara Valley almost a decade earlier. On November 29, 1777, Moraga founded the Pueblo de San Jose de Guadalupe along the banks of a quiet creek in the valley's heart. Named after Saint Joseph, the pueblo was the first civil settlement of California. It would be followed in 1781 by a pueblo in Los Angeles and in 1797 by the pueblo Branciforte (a settlement near the present-day coastal town of Santa Cruz).

The *pobladores* (citizens) received enough land for a house and two garden plots, 10 pesos a month, horses, cattle, and farm supplies. However, the first choice of location was a poor one for the new settlement. The placid creek flooded during the winter months after heavy rains, the water overflowing the banks, washing away crops, and melting adobe houses back into the mud. The flooding continued to make life so unbearable for the settlers that by 1797, the original site was abandoned and the pueblo moved about two miles to the south. Containing a number of adobe homes scattered on various lots, this *nuevo pueblo* surrounded a large central plaza (an area now called Plaza de César Chávez after the United Farm Workers labor leader).

Tension with the Mission

As the small pueblo grew, tension increased between the settlers and the Franciscan priests at the mission three miles away. The missionaries worried that these civilians given to drink, gambling, and other vices would have an unhealthy influence on their Indian neophytes. Relations between the two groups were strained severely when, simply for entertainment, two pueblo boys drowned an Ohlone child in the creek. Because of their age, the boys were given lashings as punishment. But the event underscored the vast difference between an unruly civilian population and the disciplined religious order. Over time, both the mission and pueblo worked out their difficulties, and as a gesture of peace, the Padre Magin de Catala and 200 Indians planted willow trees forming a road between the mission and pueblo. This road would become known as The Alameda (The Way).

Mexico won independence from Spain in 1822, and the pueblo adjusted to the change of government. Now the Spanish no longer shipped supplies and money, and the citizens had to rely on their own hard work and resources to sur-

vive. The mission lands were secularized and, to encourage further civilian settlement, the Mexican government began granting massive tracts of the valley's land to its soldiers and citizens. Trading ships voyaged into San Francisco Bay, and the people of the pueblo went down to the Embarcadero de Santa Clara (now called Alviso) with cow hides, otter skins, tallow, and wheat. These were exchanged for clothing and furniture, and civilization began to flourish in the frontier town.

Settlers

In the early 1800s, the American, British, and French started venturing into California, many of them settling in the Santa Clara Valley. In 1818, a French sailor named Antonio Sunol was left ashore in San Francisco to convalesce from a recent illness. He journeyed south to the warm valley and became the first foreign settler in San Jose. In time, he became one of its best educated and wealthiest citizens, and helped shape its economic and political structure. Sunol provided land along the Plaza to build the pueblo's first church, named after its patron saint. This site is now occupied by the Saint Joseph Cathedral.

The 1840s were years of increasing political tension in California. Preoccupied with its own problems, the Mexican government had long neglected its northern territory, and the Californios had developed an independent attitude. The tension grew with the increasing immigration of American settlers. The first of these groups to venture overland into California was led by John Bidwell in 1841. That year, San Jose's population was about 300 people, a frontier village with simple houses made of adobe, logs, and earth. At night, coyotes could be heard howling on the outskirts. Three years later, the Stephens-Townsend-Murphy party came overland, many of its members settling in the Santa Clara Valley. Another group of American settlers, the ill-fated Donner Party, tried to cross the Sierras during the winter of 1846 and were caught in a severe blizzard. Many members died from the exposure to the freezing temperatures, and survivors low on food resorted to cannibalism. Among the group was James Frazier Reed, who was able to struggle

JAMES LICK—ACCOMPLISHED AND ECCENTRIC DABBLER

COURTESY OF MARTIN CHEEK

Along the crest of the Diablo Range east of San Jose sit three astronomical observatories. These white domes can be seen from throughout much of Silicon Valley. The Lick Observatory, atop 4,200-foot Mt. Hamilton, is run by the University of California, and for more than a century astronomers have made significant finds among the stars with the telescopes located here. In the late 1990s, using the 120-inch Shane Telescope, Geoffrey Marcy of San Francisco State University and Raul Butler found six "extrasolar planets," large Jupiter-size worlds orbiting distant stars. To make this discovery, they used a special device called a Hamilton spectrograph, which measured with exacting precision the wobble caused by the planet's gravitational pull on the star's orbit.

The observatory is a monument to one of Santa Clara Valley's more colorful pioneers. James Lick was born on August 25, 1796, in Fredericksburg, Pennsylvania, to a German family. By his mid-20s, he had mastered carpentry and the craft of piano-making. His adventurous spirit led him to sail to Buenos Aires, paying for his passage with a piano. His piano-making business proved successful in South America, but the lure of California caused a wobble in *his* orbit, and he arrived in San Francisco in November 1847 with $30,000 in gold and 600 pounds of Peruvian chocolate.

James Lick

There was no demand for his piano-making skills in California, so he ventured into real estate, paying $10,000 for sandy hills in San Francisco as well as purchasing land in the San Jose area. After quickly selling his stock of chocolate, he wrote to a chocolate-making friend back in Peru telling of the large demand here for the sweet treat. His friend followed his advice and sailed to San Francisco, founding the well-known Ghirardelli chocolate company.

When gold was discovered in the foothills of the Sierras, Lick tried his hand at finding some of it, but the drudgery of panning made him give up after one week. However, his real estate investment in rapidly booming San Francisco paid off handsomely—his land was worth more than $2 million by December 1848.

Lick realized that the thousands of gold miners coming to California needed flour, so he began growing wheat in the Santa Clara Valley and built a flour mill on the Guadalupe River near what is now Montague Expwy. (just off Lick Mill Rd.). The mill was only three miles from the port town of Alviso, and Lick's fortunes rose as the mill began producing more than 1,500 barrels of flour a day.

Locals considered Lick cold, crass, and eccentric. The multimillionaire wore clothes that made him look like a bum and often stank from not bathing. One local legend describes how, to test a foreman's ability to take orders, Lick instructed the man to plant fruit trees upside down. The man followed the instructions, and Lick kept him on his staff. Lick also had a son out of wedlock (this child received an inheritance of $500,000).

In 1860, Lick happened to attend a San Jose lecture given by astronomer George Maderia. The lecture stimulated his interest in studying the stars, and Lick soon learned how to work a small telescope. In 1872, his health failing, Lick went to live in a San Francisco hotel he owned, the Lick House. There, he met Joseph Henry, secretary of the Smithsonian Institution. This encounter inspired Lick to establish a similar philanthropic bequest so posterity would never forget his name. His idea was to build the world's largest telescope and place it on a high mountain peak (where viewing would be less impeded by clouds).

The high Sierras were the first choice for the site, but the severe winter conditions there ruled out this option. After several locations were considered, Mt. Hamilton was chosen. Lick contributed $700,000 to buy 1,350 acres of land on the mountaintop and construct the telescope and facilities. Santa Clara County built the winding road to the top of the mountain, at a cost of $73,458. This road allowed mules to haul workers and supplies to the summit. An on-site kiln used a mountain clay deposit to make bricks for construction. In France, the lens for the 36-inch telescope was cast and brought to the United States for polishing.

Lick died on October 1, 1876, at Lick House, never having seen his completed observatory. On January 9, 1887, in a reverent ceremony, his body was placed into the foundation under what was then the world's largest and most powerful refraction telescope as well as the first mountaintop observatory. But that's not the only place that his name lives on in the Bay Area: James Lick High School (home of the Comets) is located at the base of Mt. Hamilton, and James Lick Middle School is located in San Francisco.

The Lick Observatory, 408/274-5061, www.ucolick.org, is open daily 10:30 A.M.–4:30 P.M. Tours of the original 36-inch telescope are given every half hour starting at 1 P.M. on weekdays and 10:30 A.M. on weekends. A limited number of tickets for visitors to look through the telescope are available free by reservation. In summer, the observatory holds occasional "Music of the Spheres" concerts. From U.S. 101 or I-680, take Alum Rock Ave. east to Mt. Hamilton Rd. and follow this up to the summit. The drive takes about an hour, the road is steep and winding, and there are no service facilities along it.

© MARTIN CHEEK

Lick Observatory

across the rugged mountains and seek rescuers. After the ordeal, he and his family settled in San Jose, which at that time had a population of about 800 people. The growing San Jose was one of California's few prominent communities, and by then had a tavern and supply stores.

With its policy of Manifest Destiny, the growing American nation wanted to expand its territory to the Pacific. In the mid-1840s, the U.S. government sent westward the ambitious explorer John C. Frémont on a "survey" mission to discover what riches California contained. On May 13, 1846, the United States declared war on Mexico, and a month later in Sonoma, Frémont declared California independent of Mexico's rule. Called the Bear Flag Revolt, it was a watershed event for both California and San Jose. Mexican general José Castro sought to protect the important pueblo of San Jose from the American invaders, but after U.S. Commander Sloat took the coastal presidio of Monterey, Castro led his men to fight there. Meanwhile, Thomas Fallon, an enterprising Irishman who had traveled with Frémont at one time, ventured with a company of Americans from Santa Cruz, taking the unprotected pueblo of San Jose on July 11. Two days later, he raised the American flag over the *juzgado,* the pueblo's government building. This event signified that San Jose had become a U.S. possession.

First State Capital

With the end of the Mexican-American War in 1848, California officially came into the hands of the United States. The discovery of gold in the Sierras brought even more settlers to the prospering state, many of them eventually establishing homes and farms in Santa Clara Valley and San Jose. Real estate promoters James Frazier Reed and Charles White helped push San Jose as the choice for the new state's center of government, and on December 17, 1849, San Jose became California's first state capital. Reed and White raised $34,000 to buy a two-story adobe structure on the east side of the Plaza to serve as the State House, and Alviso resident Peter Hardeman Burnett became the state's first governor. Known as "the legislature of a thousand drinks"

because of state officials' enjoyment of alcoholic beverages after-hours, they nonetheless accomplished a considerable amount of work, including creating a constitution. They also sent Frémont to Washington, D.C., to represent the new state as one of its two senators. Because it was expected to become California's preeminent city, San Jose's real estate value shot up to $10,000 per acre. But heavy winter rains and the city's isolation drove the legislators to relocate the capital to Benicia in the East Bay. It would relocate again to Vallejo and finally to its present site of Sacramento in the Central Valley. Some San Jose real estate speculators were forced to sell land at a considerable loss of $2,500 per acre.

The population of San Jose in 1850 stood at about 4,000 people. New construction of more than 300 homes took place in the next three years, several of these houses shipped around Cape Horn from New England. In that decade, the region's agricultural industry grew prominently as the Santa Clara Valley fed many of the new settlers coming into Northern California. San Jose began to thrive commercially due to the abundance of wheat, fruits, and vegetables grown in the fields surrounding it. By 1854, a city hall was needed, and a site was found on an empty lot at 35 N. Market Street. Local architect Levi Goodrich constructed a government building that resembled a medieval castle out of a King Arthur legend, complete with turrets.

The Garden City

On January 16, 1864, the San Francisco & San Jose Railroad Company completed its rail line connecting the two cities. An extension line was later built through Niles Canyon leading to Sacramento, connecting San Jose with the transcontinental railroad completed in 1869. This proved a major boon to the town, allowing it to export much of the area's produce to the growing East Coast population, as well as bringing in new immigrants eager to settle here. The railroad allowed for easier freight shipment, and in the next several decades, the region's canning, fruit drying, and winery industries flourished. Throughout the world, San Jose became known as "The Garden City."

Many ethnic groups played important roles in shaping the city during these formative years. Among them were the Germans, who developed a large community here. They formed a *Verein* (social club) in the Germania Hall near St. James Park, and this building became an important gathering spot. The Germans also started an orchestra that eventually grew into the now nationally respected San Jose Symphony. In 1870, German immigrant Adolph Pfister was elected mayor, and in the next three years, he established the city's first public park at Alum Rock as well as its first library. The French also played a role in developing San Jose; among them were Louis and Pierre Pellier, who promoted the fruit industry, bringing cuttings from their native France. Frenchman Pedro de Saisset, the son of one of Napoleon's lieutenants, had become rich in the goldfields and later came to San Jose to invest in real estate. He also established in the city an electric company, and with the introduction of this modern utility, San Jose took its first step toward enjoying the many benefits of electricity.

Many of the Chinese workers who had helped build the western section of the transcontinental railroad stayed in California and brought their families across the Pacific to join them. A high percentage settled in San Jose, and their Chinatown community developed along the eastern flank of the Plaza. These Asian immigrants worked hard in the fields and orchards, helping to build the valley's thriving agricultural industry. However, there was a strong racial prejudice against the Chinese by a number of local people. On May 4, 1887, San Jose's Chinatown settlement burned down from a fire of suspicious origin. It happened one day before a bond measure vote to build a new city hall in that location. The Chinese were relocated to another district of the city, and the former Chinatown area was filled with office buildings and shops. Later that same year, the new city hall, designed by local architect Theodore Lenzen, was constructed in the Plaza. This building also contained the city's jail and a drunk tank located directly underneath the council chamber. Often during civic meetings, prisoners and drunks interrupted the discussion with boisterous singing and banging on

the cell bars. In 1889, the 150-room Hotel Vendome was opened. Built in Queen Anne style, it was one of California's most luxurious lodgings and quickly became a prestigious spot for the city's elite to gather. It also helped promote San Jose's tourist industry as it became a popular place to stay for visitors who came here from throughout the nation. Many of them took the one-day carriage journey up to the peak of Mt. Hamilton to see the new Lick Observatory with its world's largest telescope.

Turn of the 20th Century

In 1901, Lewis E. Hanchett purchased land that was once the Agricultural Park near The Alameda and turned it into an upscale neighborhood. Heir to a Gold Rush fortune, Hanchett had increased his wealth by investing in the San Jose and Santa Clara electric railroads. The turn of the 19th century was an optimistic time for the city, whose population had reached 21,500 people. But the city's confidence was severely shaken on April 18, 1906, when the San Andreas Fault gave way in a massive earthquake. Structures throughout the city collapsed, killing several occupants. Among the city's government buildings, the just-finished Santa Clara Hall of Justice was completely demolished (it would be reconstructed a year later). To protect the city from looting, the National Guard pitched tents in St. James Park, camping there with many of the citizens made homeless by the earthquake. The damage from the temblor was just as severe in San Jose as San Francisco, but because San Jose didn't suffer the devastating days of fire that the northern city experienced, it was spared the greater destruction.

A new San Jose quickly emerged from the ruins, a modern city ready for the 20th century. Later in 1906, the city's first skyscraper was completed at the San Fernando and 1st St. intersection. Built by the city's real estate tycoon T. S. Montgomery, the Garden City Bank and Trust Building rose an astonishing seven stories high, a marvel for a farm town. Even more amazing was the technical miracle that occurred in the building in 1909, when Dr. Charles Herrold broadcast the world's first commercial radio station from the

SAN JOSE'S CHINATOWNS

Many ethnic groups have migrated to San Jose to make it the diverse city that it is today. And in the 19th century, among the most colorful immigrants were the Chinese. Their story is one of struggle and perseverance as they built five Chinatown communities in the city.

Hearing stories of a "Gum San," a Gold Mountain, villagers from the Kwangtung province of China sailed to California in search of their fortune. Although few made it rich in the goldfields, many found that the Santa Clara Valley's fertile soil was a paradise compared to their homeland's exhausted soil that had been plowed for thousands of years. They brought their families across the Pacific and stayed to work on the farms here. In the 1860s, many more would immigrate to California and help dig tunnels during construction of the transcontinental railroad.

In 1870, one-third of San Jose's population was Chinese. It had the second largest Chinese population in America (San Francisco had the most). But racial tension made life difficult for the Chinese in California. Prejudiced whites saw the Chinese cultural differences as a threat to their own lifestyle. For social stability, San Jose's Chinese population of over 1,000 created their own community along the Plaza's eastern border, an area where the Fairmont Hotel now stands. Here, they had their own stores, schools, temples, and theaters.

In January 1870, an accidentally set fire burned down the ramshackle homes and buildings of San Jose's first Chinatown. The city's white firemen did little to stop the blaze. A temporary Chinatown was built along the eastern bank of the Guadalupe River while construction began on rebuilding the first site. By 1872, this new Chinatown showcased modern brick buildings.

A national depression in the 1870s served to generate resentment in whites toward the Chinese. They saw the Asian immigrants taking jobs, and segregation laws were passed to restrict Chinese rights. The tension grew. At the commencement services on May 23, 1878, the oration at the California State Normal School (now San Jose State University) was entitled "The Chinese Must Go."

On May 4, 1887, San Jose's Chinese population suffered another loss of their community when their Chinatown burned down under suspicious circumstances. This happened one day before a public election to build a new city hall in the Plaza. Whites wanted the land to expand the downtown business district, so the Chinese rebuilt their community at San Pedro and Hobson Streets. This was only a temporary Chinatown. In the 1890s, many of San Jose's Chinese moved into a community bounded by 6th, Taylor, 7th, and Jackson Streets. The area was owned by John Heinlen, a German immigrant, and thus this final Chinatown for San Jose became known as "Heinlenville."

Today, San Jose has no Chinatown. The Chinese population is spread throughout the city, and many from this ethnic group work as engineers and managers in Silicon Valley's computer firms. Perhaps, living in their mansions, they have found their Gum San, the Golden Mountain which their ancestors had journeyed to California to find.

5th floor and out through the rooftop antenna. San Jose had another world first that year. One of its Italian sons, Amadeo Peter Giannini, who had been born in his immigrant parents' downtown hotel, had left his hometown to establish the Bank of Italy in San Francisco. The bank had done especially well after the 1906 earthquake, when it lent money to rebuild the city of San Francisco. In 1909, the Bank of Italy revolutionized finance by establishing the world's first bank branch in San Jose. The San Jose branch was also the first to allow women to keep accounts, a rather shocking idea for the post-Victorian mind-set that believed females could not manage money. Later, at a cost of $1 million, the Bank of Italy constructed a 13-story skyscraper in downtown San Jose at 1st and Santa Clara Sts., and with its jutting tower and spire, this building became a prominent landmark. It still forms part of San Jose's skyline. The Bank of Italy changed its name in 1930 and has since grown into one of the world's major financial institutions, the Bank of America.

Political Machine

Despite the development of its modern infrastructure, the city's politicos did a lot of behind-the-scenes deal making during the Great Depression years. From the mid-1920s to 1944, the city's government was controlled by an influential political machine headed by a powerful boss named Charlie Bigley. Hardly ever mentioned now in San Jose's history, Bigley made his legitimate money from taxi, ambulance, and funeral limousine services, but his real wealth came from unlawful gambling rooms and liquor sales during Prohibition. He built his power by calling in favors from the people he had loaned money or obtained jobs. Bigley played puppet master to four of the city's seven council members, often instructing them how to vote from his garage office on Market Plaza near City Hall. Aiding Bigley considerably in his power quest was Clarence Goodwin, the city manager, who got his influential position due to Bigley's city council lackeys. Also adding to his tight hold on the city was his considerable political leverage in controlling the hiring in San Jose's police and fire departments. The turning point in San Jose's city government came in 1944, when local businessmen and lawyers formed a group called The Progress Committee to loosen Bigley's grip on the council. In the hotly contested election of that year, they ousted Bigley's men, thus ending his 20-year reign.

During World War II, a large number of military men passed through San Jose on their way to the Pacific and European fronts. Hundreds of thousands of these servicemen received a warm welcome at a U.S.O. hut on the southern corner of Market Plaza (the hut was torn down in the mid-1970s). Many of these men had found the city so inviting that they returned after the war with their families to make their homes here. The city's population boomed with these new residents, and its area expanded as large housing divisions and shopping centers were hastily constructed. During these postwar years, aerospace and electronics companies started setting up bases in the San Jose area. The city also began to see its surrounding family farms and orchards converted into business parks and manufacturing plants, including one along Monterey Rd. by monolithic General Electric. In 1955, computer giant IBM gave San Jose its big jump into high-tech by buying 190 acres of farmland along Monterey and Cottle Rds. and building a sprawling complex here.

Annexation Wars

In 1950, San Jose was a city of 95,000 people on 17 square miles of land. That year, Anthony "Dutch" Hamann was hired as city manager, and during the 19-year reign of this Santa Clara University alumnus, San Jose would undergo its most massive alteration. The city government and the chamber of commerce saw the immense inflow of new residents and dreamed of transforming the farm town into one of the nation's biggest metropolises. Civic leaders boasted how San Jose would one day rival a certain sprawling city in Southern California. As unpalatable as it sounds today, the city proudly proclaimed it intended to make San Jose "the Los Angeles of the north." But to achieve this goal, the city needed to expand its territory into the surrounding family farms and orchards. San Jose started incorporating the valley's "uninhabited" farmland (legally defined as holding less than five persons per acre). The Annexation Wars had begun.

So ruthless was Hamann's staff in taking over farms, orchards, and communities for the city's expansion that they were derided as San Jose's "Panzer Division," a comparison to Adolf Hitler's soldiers, who ruthlessly took over small European countries. While many farmers put up a fight to save their way of life, others saw the value of their land improve as real estate holdings and sold out. Valley communities such as Saratoga, Milpitas, Campbell, and Los Altos incorporated as cities during the 1950s to avoid becoming just another San Jose suburb. Ultimately, the Annexation Wars resulted in San Jose's city limits stretching into the rural terrain of South Valley and, to the north, reaching the San Francisco Bay at Alviso. Some areas such as the Burbank district refused to incorporate, and so today, resembling a large Swiss cheese, the city surrounds portions run by Santa Clara County's government.

The Annexation Wars caused a dramatic downturn for San Jose. So much of the city's political energy and money had been spent for the purpose of expansion that the quality of life drastically declined. The hardest hit was the downtown area, which became severely blighted, and among the major reasons for its decline was lack of planning by the city government. The most significant sign of its decay came in 1958, when City Hall was relocated from Market Plaza two miles farther north to the Civic Center on 1st St., which happened to be where the first pueblo had started in 1777. Adding to the rapid decline of the downtown's retail business was the construction of the Valley Fair Shopping Mall at Winchester and Stevens Creek Blvds. to the west. This leached away many of downtown's department stores and shops. At midcentury, thriving downtown San Jose had been the valley's most prestigious gathering spot. Two decades later, it was a derelict wasteland.

By 1970, San Jose, with its more than 400,000 people on 136 square miles of land, was the United States' fastest growing city. Its

BOB RACE

A.P. "Dutch" Hamann

mayor, Norman Mineta, became the nation's first Japanese-American mayor of a major city. Dutch Hamann's dream of turning San Jose into a huge city had come true, but at an equally huge cost. The pleasant Garden City had vanished, replaced by a Los Angeles–like sprawl covered in urban smog. With San Jose's downtown consisting of weedy vacant lots, empty stores, prostitutes, and drug dealers, it had become an ugly example of urban decay. Citizens believed that things just couldn't get any worse. Then the shame was compounded by embarrassment when Dionne Warwick released her rendition of Burt Bacharach's cheesy ditty "Do You Know the Way to San Jose?"

During the 1970s, there were attempts at redevelopment, but they never worked out as hoped. Among the more ambitious projects was the construction of several office buildings at Park Center Plaza designed to attract banks and financial institutions. And Mayor Janet Gray Hayes, the United States' first woman mayor of a major city, mistakenly thought that an extensive cement water fountain along the Paseo de San Antonio would lure the good times back. The expensive Center for the Performing Arts was

SAN JOSE'S WILD-WEST PAST

Running somewhat counter to its current repu-tation as one of the safest major cities in the United States, San Jose has a long history of crime—and punishment. During Mexican rule, bandits roamed the area terrorizing local citizens. The governor of California empowered San Jose's alcalde, or mayor, to make and enforce the laws and to judge any violators (who were held in the *juzgado,* a combination of jail and city hall located at the northern end of the plaza). One American settler, perhaps naively accustomed to the consti-tutional separation of powers, compared the al-calde to "the Grand Autocrat of the Russians." Unlike the Russian autocrat, however, his life was not one of ease: the sum total compensation he received was the honor of the position—no salary; he was required to wear black clothing to declare his official status; and he was not allowed to leave the city limits without the governor's permission.

Among San Jose's many outlaws of the 19th century, the most notorious was the sinister-look-ing José Tiburcio Vasquez. The son of one of Mor-aga's original pueblo settlers, Vasquez pillaged and murdered throughout California. After killing three men in Tres Pinos, a small village in San Benito County south of Santa Clara Valley, he was captured and brought to San Jose to stand trial. On January 5, 1875, he was found guilty. While he was in prison, a Catholic priest visited him for confession, but Vasquez was unrepentant. He cursed the priest and vowed that if God did ac-tually send him to the fires of eternal damnation, he would return and burn down the local St. Joseph's Church. Vasquez was hanged on March 19. The next month, St. Joseph's Church did, in fact, burn to the ground.

In the early days of the Great Depression, a kid-napping and its aftermath put San Jose on news-paper front pages across the nation. Hart Department Store downtown had been started in 1866 by Leopold Hart and was run by descen-dants of the well-liked family. On the chilly evening of November 9, 1933, Brooke Hart—son of owner Alexander Hart—was closing the store when he was kidnapped by Thomas Thurmond and John Holmes. The two kidnappers hadn't thought out their plan well, however, and the scheme quickly began to go awry—as soon as they realized that Brooke could easily identify them. They drove up the Peninsula to the San Mateo Bridge, tied up their victim with wire, then threw him over the railing. Hart plunged to his death in the Bay, and Thurmond and Holmes returned to San Jose to calmly call Hart's parents and make arrangements for the ransom.

On November 15, police traced a ransom call to the Sabette Brothers Garage, on S. Market Street. As he left the building, authorities apprehended Thur-mond; they arrested his partner a short time later. On November 26, two duck hunters discovered Hart's decomposing body. Later that day, an angry crowd began to gather in St. James Park, outside the jail behind the courthouse. As the crowd began turning into a violent mob, the nervous sheriff or-dered his deputies to barricade the jail. But citi-zens grabbed pieces of pipe from the construction site of a new post office next to the courthouse and stormed the jail. The sheriff shot tear gas into the ad-vancing throng, but that only served to infuriate the mob, leading to a two-hour battle between po-lice and citizens—which transpired as Thurmond and Holmes huddled in their cells.

The mob reached Thurmond first. He passed out, but they stripped him naked, slung a rope from one of the park's trees, and hanged him. Holmes battled hard for his life, but eventually he, too, swung from a second rope on the same tree. The crowd then attempted to burn the bod-ies but soon gave up and dispersed. Limbs and leaves were taken from the hanging tree as sou-venirs. The tree was so badly damaged that park gardeners cut it down a few days later. Despite photographs and eyewitnesses, no one was ever arrested for the lynching.

also constructed at this time, its costs increasing when a design flaw caused the roof to completely collapse one day. But these costly projects failed to revive San Jose.

Redevelopment

Just like in the Spanish colonization days when the pueblo of San Jose was forced to relocate away from the flooding creek, in the last quarter of the 20th century, the modern city of San Jose was forced to remake itself in order to successfully survive as a city. In 1983, the man who would revive San Jose stepped into office. Newly elected Mayor Thomas McEnery came up with an ambitious proposal to give the downtown's infrastructure a major facelift. This proposal was based on a report drawn up by the Downtown Working Review Committee, a group McEnery had started. To head the Redevelopment Agency, McEnery hired Frank Taylor, an up-and-coming architect who had successfully helped redevelop Cincinnati, Ohio.

Among the redevelopment projects that met with various levels of success were the new Arena sports stadium (now called the Compaq Center), the luxurious Fairmont Hotel, the Tech Museum, the Children's Discovery Museum, the massive McEnery Convention Center, and the Light Rail mass transit system linking San Jose's downtown with the Almaden Valley, Santa Clara, Mountain View, and other Silicon Valley communities. The redevelopment also had its failures, among the most notable the poorly designed Pavilion, which was intended to bring upscale boutique shops downtown. The site has recently undergone extensive remodeling to turn the former shops into offices.

More than $1 billion has been spent on the redevelopment program, the largest chunk of this coming from the tax bases of high-tech firms situated in the industrial parks of the N. 1st St. area. By the mid-1990s, businesses were starting to return downtown, including software developer Adobe, which relocated its headquarters here in two towering buildings along Almaden Boulevard. By the start of the 21st century, work was proceeding on bringing City Hall back to the downtown area, with a proposed $320 mil-

lion edifice just north of San Jose State University. San Jose still is undergoing its redevelopment and shaping its identity, but with the new millennium, it has elevated its worldwide reputation as one of the most successful of major American cities.

SAN JOSE NEIGHBORHOODS AND DISTRICTS

San Jose can easily seem like a massive urban sprawl with no discernible pattern, but a closer look shows it's a city sectioned off into neighborhoods and districts that reflect its growth and history. Many of these segments, such as Willow Glen and Alviso, started off as small towns later gobbled up by San Jose during the Annexation Wars of the 1950s and 1960s. These sections have merged together as the city's population expanded, so it's often impossible to see distinct boundaries between them. In many cases, the divisions are formed by natural terrain such as hills and creeks or by man-made constructions such as freeways and roads. Because there often is no official designation, locals sometimes enjoy debating where one district ends and the next begins. The multifaceted character of all these diverse neighborhoods has made San Jose a dynamic mosaic of people and places, cultural values and economic lifestyles.

Almaden Valley

This district is named after the New Almaden quicksilver mines located in a canyon at its southern tip. It starts along Hwy. 85, following the Almaden Expwy. south to around McKean Road. The Santa Teresa Hills are on the valley's eastern flank, and the Santa Cruz Mountain foothills rise to the west. Magnificent homes built on these hills overlook Silicon Valley. **Almaden Lake,** corner of Coleman Rd. and Almaden Expwy., 408/277-5130, once a quarry owned by 19th-century entrepreneur Levi Goodrich, provided the sandstone blocks used to build the Quadrangle at Stanford University. Other sites of interest include the **Almaden Plaza Shopping Center,** 408/264-3766, the historic **Almaden Quicksilver County Park,** 408/268-8220, and

SAN JOSE'S MEXICAN HERITAGE PLAZA

San Jose's Latino roots run deep. Mexico's influence on the city goes back to 1777, the year of the pueblo's founding as California's first civilian settlement. And modern San Jose culture is very much flavored by its colorful Mexican heritage. The city's large Mexican community has contributed much to the city in the realms of art, music, theater, dance, cuisine, and architecture. In 1998, the city elected Ron Gonzales its first Latino mayor. And *Hispanic* magazine has declared San Jose the top U.S. city for Latinos to live in.

This doesn't mean that life has always been a fiesta for the Latino culture in San Jose. As far back as the Mexican-American War of the mid-1840s, the struggle with the white culture has persisted in one form or another. After the discovery of gold and the massive influx of Americans and Europeans into California, the Latinos in the Santa Clara Valley lost much of their land in legal struggles. They also faced the prejudice that comes with conflicting cultures. The struggle continues today, with racial discrimination often coming to the surface in ugly incidents which make the news.

Many San Jose residents take pride in the fact that César Chávez, one of the Latino culture's greatest heroes for social justice, got his start in this city. As a young man in 1952, Chávez moved his family to San Jose, where he worked in a lumber mill. The family made a home in the East San Jose barrio called Sal Si Puedes (Spanish for "get out if you can"). Marking a turning point in his life, Chávez met Father Donald McDonnell, a Catholic priest who worked with farmworkers. McDonnell helped spark in the young Chávez an interest in the church's doctrines of social justice.

Chávez became an organizer for Saul Alinsky's Community Service Organization, a group established to inform migrant workers of their legal rights. In 1962, at the age of 35, Chávez devoted himself to the task of organizing the farmworkers into a union. Half a year later in Fresno, the National Farm Workers Union (later called the United Farm Workers) held its first meeting. This marked the true advent of "La Causa." The movement expanded over the next few years, and by 1965, because grape growers wouldn't acknowledge the union's demands, the workers went on strike. Grapes rotted on the vines, and stores that sold grapes were boycotted. Among the first of these was a Safeway supermarket in East San Jose on the corner of Alum Rock Ave. and S. King Rd., not far from where the Chávez family had once lived.

The Safeway is now gone, but in its place stands a kind of monument—the Mexican Heritage Plaza, opened in September 1999. The plaza, a joint project of the nonprofit Mexican Heritage Corp. and San Jose's Redevelopment Agency, is a $34 million complex built to showcase the city's multicultural heritage. Expected to attract over 100,000 people a year, visitors can stroll through a traditional garden plaza with Hispanic art accenting irrigation canals and pools of floating reeds. They can also view works of art in a large gallery. A 500-seat theater hosts performances by groups such as the resident dance troupe Los Lupeños de San Jose, as well as Teatro Vision. A 3,500-square-foot museum displays exhibits from the Smithsonian Institution that pertain to the Latino culture. Appropriately enough, its first exhibition portrayed the struggles of César Chávez in establishing the United Farm Workers.

1700 Alum Rock Ave. (at S. King Rd.), plaza open Mon.–Fri. noon–9 P.M., Sun. 10 A.M.–5 P.M.; gallery open Tues.–Fri. 10 A.M.–6 P.M., Sat. 10 A.M.–4 P.M. Admission and parking are free. For more information, call 800/642-8482; website: www.mhcviva.org.

the quiet **Almaden Golf and Country Club,** 408/268-4653.

Alum Rock

This district gets its name from **Alum Rock Park,** 408/259-5477, the city's oldest public park, set here in its foothills and established by General Henry Morris Naglee. At the turn of the 19th century, the park featured a resort famous for its hot mineral springs. The park derived its name from an immense rock there that contained a large amount of alum sulfates. The district extends east from I-680, following Alum Rock Ave. (which once was a trolley line route leading up to the park), bordered on the north by Berryessa Rd. and on the south by Story Road. Near Alum Rock Park is the **San Jose Country Club,** 408/928-3420.

Alviso

Located at the point where N. 1st St. comes to an end at San Francisco Bay's southern tip, the community of Alviso was originally called the Embarcadero de Santa Clara. The Spanish missionaries used it as a landing site to receive supplies and ship out beaver skins, tallow, and cow hides. In 1838, Ignacio Alviso, a member of the original de Anza settlers, established his Rancho Rincon de Los Esteros on the land, and the village that sprang up here was named after him. It's now a quiet neighborhood of low-income homes, with a somewhat independent spirit that sets it apart from San Jose's suburban sprawl. It's an excellent place to take a late afternoon stroll along the marshland levees at **Alviso County Park,** 408/262-6980, afterward enjoying a dinner at one of the local family-run restaurants.

Berryessa/North San Jose

Named after the Berreyesa family (the spelling was later changed), which settled here, this district is located in San Jose's northeastern corner adjacent to Milpitas. Roughly, its borders are the Western Pacific railroad tracks in the west, Berryessa Rd. in the south, and Landess Ave. at the Milpitas city limits. It's a mixture of industrial areas and middle-class homes. Attractions to see here include the massive **San Jose Flea Market,** 408/453-1110, on Berryessa Road. The Penitencia Creek, which flows through this district, was given its name because the Franciscan padres had a small adobe house in the area where they often gave penitence.

Blossom Valley

The enchanting name of this neighborhood comes from the hundreds of orchard acres that once spread throughout this small valley area. The springtime blossoms created a fragrant white-flowered panorama that many Silicon Valley residents still remember. The orchards are now gone, replaced with middle-class neighborhoods. The area roughly borders Blossom Hill Rd. north of the Santa Teresa district and south of the Edenvale district.

Burbank District

An unincorporated area just west of downtown San Jose, this county-governed district was named after Luther Burbank, the father of American horticulture (a public school in the area was also named after him). Because of the X-rated entertainment along the district's Bascom Ave. strip, including a porn-flick house called **The Burbank Theater,** 408/295-7238, and the notorious **Pink Poodle nightclub,** 408/292-3685, a favorite for risqué bachelor parties, the Burbank district has gained a reputation as one of the seediest sections of Silicon Valley.

Cambrian Park

Named after the Cambrian region of Britain's Wales, this suburban district in San Jose's southern region is bordered on the southwest by Campbell and Los Gatos, on the north by Camden and Hillsdale Aves., and on the south by the Almaden Valley along Coleman Road. It's an area developed during the 1950s and 1960s with ranch-style tract homes.

Central San Jose

This diamond-shaped district is bordered by U.S. 101 on the east, I-280 on the north, Hwy. 87 on the west, and Capitol Expwy. on the south. It includes a strip of industrial businesses such as auto junkyards and seedy motels along Mon-

DOWNTOWN REDEVELOPMENT—
THE SAGA CONTINUES

Take a stroll through downtown San Jose and you'll see that more than 20 years after Mayor Tom McEnery's redevelopment program began, major changes are still being made that are transforming the city's heart and soul.

One of the most significant projects planned is to bring back the civic center to the downtown area. San Jose's city hall once stood in the historic Plaza, but in the 1950s, a new civic center was built in the Hedding St. district two miles north of downtown. This move helped hasten the decline of the downtown region. However, in June 1999, the city council approved a projected $320 million plan to build a modern city hall and parking garage along E. Santa Clara St. near San Jose State University.

Groundbreaking for the project is scheduled for spring 2002, and it won't be completed until 2006. The new building was designed by architect Richard Meier of Los Angeles and it has already been the source of much controversy. At 320 feet, the city government tower will be far higher than any building in San Jose. Because it's also close to San Jose International Airport's flight path, it exceeds the Federal Aviation Agency's safety rules. Many shops and businesses located at the site will have to be evicted, and owners have complained they have not been fairly compensated for their losses. And residents in the neighborhood have criticized the plan, saying it will increase traffic, take parking spaces, and damage the quality of life in the district.

Another significant project planned by San Jose's Redevelopment Agency is the redesign of 1.6 million square feet of five blocks just north of the Plaza. In 2000, the Palladium Company was chosen as the preliminary master developer to create synergy in this underused area of downtown. Plans call for redevelopment to include more high-density housing, retail shops, and entertainment and office spaces. Streetscape improvements are also planned to provide better connection for this part of downtown with the underutilized St. James Park. This area contains many historic buildings, so great care must be taken to preserve its architectural heritage.

One redevelopment project in the South of First Area (the SoFA district) is the renovation of the historic Fox California Theater to its 1927 grandeur. The theater will be converted into a permanent home for Opera San José as well as a film house. This ambitious project will also include a new two-story building (built on a vacant lot next to the theater) which will include a café and outdoor courtyard. A vacant lot on Market St. will include a three-story building for use in theatrical support facilities.

terey Road. Attractions here include the **Santa Clara County Fairgrounds,** 408/494-3247, **San Jose State's Spartan Stadium,** 408/924-1000, and **Municipal Stadium,** where the San Jose Giants minor league baseball team plays. Across the street from Municipal Stadium is **Kelley Park,** 408/297-0778, where you can visit the **Japanese Friendship Garden, Happy Hollow Park and Zoo,** and the **San Jose Historical Museum,** which has become the city's preservation orphanage for historic homes. **San Juan Bautista Hills** is an unincorporated area in this district's southern tip. The large tower you see on the ridgeline here is the Santa Clara County Communication Center, the broadcasting station that sends out calls to the sheriff, fire department, and other county services.

Civic Center

The neighborhood bordering the Civic Center along N. 1st and Hedding Sts. is a mixture of grand Victorians and middle-income apartment complexes. Here you'll find San Jose's unimaginative **City Hall,** and next door, the monolithic building that looks like a large plate of rusting iron is the **Santa Clara County Building.** Close by is the County Jail and the National Guard Armory. Half a mile north just off Hwy. 87 (the

CONTROVERSIAL COYOTE VALLEY

Between Morgan Hill and the Santa Teresa hills of San Jose lays Coyote Valley, the last great expanse of undeveloped land in Silicon Valley. Portions of this area have hardly changed since the Spanish explorer de Anza came through here and observed great oaks growing in grassy meadows. But in recent years, this peaceful region has become a battleground as Internet powerhouse Cisco Systems plans to build a 6.6 million-square-foot corporate headquarters here.

With the blessing of San Jose mayor Ron Gonzales and other city council members, Cisco has initiated procedures to build its $1.3 billion complex for 20,000 workers in Coyote Valley. It is called the Coyote Valley Research Park Project, and the impact on Silicon Valley (particularly the South Valley region) will be huge. To house workers, 70,000 homes are to be built in Coyote Valley. Gridlock along U.S. 101 will increase. And a greenbelt for Silicon Valley will lose much of its rural ambience.

Adding to the heated debate is a proposed plan by Calpine Corp. to build a power plant along Coyote Valley's Metcalf Road. This would provide over 600,000 Bay Area homes with energy. Cisco doesn't like the idea of a power plant next door to its headquarters, and residents in the Santa Teresa area worry about health risks and decline in property values.

An estimated $47 million in city and state money will go to pay for roads, water, and sewer lines for the Coyote Valley development. Cisco is expected to put in more than $122 million for roads, freeway interchanges, and flood control. Cisco is not the first computer company to propose building in Coyote Valley. In 1982, Apple and Tandem bought land here in the hopes of building major facilities. Both projects were later junked. And once Cisco moves into Coyote Valley, other corporations are sure to follow. Chip-maker Xilinx Inc. bought 100 acres of farmland in the region. And the Sobrato Development Company owns large chunks of land across the street from the proposed Cisco campus with hopes of renting it out to corporations.

Success of the proposed complex hinges on whether or not Cisco can realistically sustain its amazing growth through the next 10 years. The rapid fall of tech companies (particularly the dotcom firms) in 2000 and 2001 has had a negative impact on Cisco's stock. The company shocked Silicon Valley when it announced it would lay off thousands of workers. The economic turnaround at Cisco has pushed pack the projected completion of the Coyote Valley campus from 2005 to 2010. For now, Coyote Valley is in a wait-and-see period, but no doubt sometime in the coming decades, this rural strip of Silicon Valley will face the arrival of bulldozers and concrete trucks.

Guadalupe Pkwy.) is the **San Jose International Airport,** east of the Santa Clara city limit line.

Coyote Valley

Just south of the Santa Teresa district along Monterey Rd. and U.S. 101 is rural Coyote Valley, named after the howling animals that roamed here during pioneer days. The area stretches south from Metcalf Rd. to the edge of Morgan Hill. In 1999, Internet router company Cisco Systems proposed building a large manufacturing site in this valley, thus opening up the South Valley area to industrial development. The only community in the area is the small village of **Coyote** along

Monterey Road. The county's **Motorcycle Park,** 408/226-5223, is located nearby.

Eastside

This district has a reputation for being one of the rougher areas of San Jose, but through neighborhood watch programs, the residents have worked hard to turn around the prevalence of crime and drug use. A small city called East San Jose incorporated here in 1906, but five years later was annexed by Greater San Jose. Today, the area is bordered on the east by U.S. 101, stretching to the foothills between the Alum Rock and Evergreen districts. It features a number of apartment houses and strip malls, and contains a large population of Silicon Valley's Hispanic and Vietnamese residents. The district includes **Alexian Brothers Hospital, Eastridge Shopping Mall,** 408/238-3600, on Tully Rd., and **Reid-Hillview Municipal Airport,** 408/929-2256, just off Capital Expressway. Among its attractions are **Lake Cunningham Regional Park,** 408/238-8028, the farm heritage **Emma Prusch Park,** 408/926-5555, and **Overfelt Botanical Gardens,** 408/251-3323.

Edenvale

The gardenlike orchard land in the valley along Monterey Rd. reminded early visitors of the paradise in the book of Genesis, so they christened the area Edenvale. It's bordered by Capitol Expwy. on the north, U.S. 101 on the east, Snell Ave. on the west, and Blossom Valley along Blossom Hill Rd. on the south. A Western-themed amusement park called Frontier Village was once set in this area alongside Monterey Hwy., and childhood visits to this long-gone attraction are among the favorite memories of many Silicon Valley residents. Sites to visit here include the beautiful **Hayes Mansion and Convention Center,** 408/226-3200, and **Hellyer County Park,** 408/225-0225, where the **Coyote Creek trail** starts.

Evergreen/Silver Creek

These affluent sister districts are located in the Diablo Range in east San Jose. The northern portion was named Evergreen after the always verdant oaks growing here, and it's the more developed of the two districts. In this district are the **Mirassou Winery,** 408/274-4000, on Aborn Rd., and **Evergreen Community College,** 408/274-6700. It's also where aviator John Joseph Montgomery died after his glider crashed in an area just north of the college (the small **Montgomery Park** here commemorates his achievements). In the valley to the south of Evergreen, Silver Creek Valley is a community of large estates in a gated country club setting. It was named after a quicksilver mine that started in the 1860s in this area but never produced much mercury. The two districts are bordered by U.S. 101 on the west, Capitol Expwy. and Quimby Rd. on the north, and Silver Creek Valley Rd. on the south.

Fruitdale

This triangle-shaped area just south of the Burbank district is named for the prune and other fruit orchards once growing here. The trees are now gone, replaced by middle-class homes, apartment complexes, and strip malls. The area is bordered along the north by I-280, on the west by Hwy. 17, and on the southwest by Los Gatos Creek. The Southwest Expwy. that borders the Southern Pacific railroad tracks cuts through the Fruitdale district and is often used by Silicon Valley locals as a shortcut to get to Campbell from downtown San Jose. Located in this district is **San Jose City College,** 408/298-2181, where decathlon gold medal–winner Bruce Jenner trained for the 1976 Montreal Olympics (an annual Bruce Jenner Classic sporting event is held here). Nearby is **Santa Clara Valley Medical Center.**

Japantown

San Jose's Japanese heritage comes alive among these few blocks near the Civic Center between Taylor and Empire Sts. and N. 4th and N. 6th Streets. Shops sell interesting Asian gifts, and traditional Japanese restaurants offer a cultural feast for the eye as well as the palate. In the Issei Memorial Building, the small **Japanese-American Museum,** 408/294-3138, provides a look at the valley's Japanese history through photographs and artifacts.

Naglee Park

The oldest neighborhood in San Jose was named after 19th-century Brigadier General Henry Morris Naglee, who owned a 140-acre estate here (his home is at 14th and E. San Fernando Sts.). The area is just east of San Jose State University, bordered by 10th St. on the west, I-280 on the south, Coyote Creek on the east, and Santa Clara St. on the north. Although small, the neighborhood contains a large number of architectural gems, including many stately Victorian homes. The **Northside Theatre,** 408/288-7820, per-

THE INCENDIARY LOVE LETTERS OF GENERAL NAGLEE

In one section of San Jose's St. James Park stands a frieze depicting a distinguished-looking military officer with a thick mustache and mutton-chop sideburns. The honoree of this monument is General Henry Morris Naglee, a colorful figure from the city's past whose name lives on in a neighborhood and an avenue east of downtown.

Naglee was born in Philadelphia and graduated from West Point at the top of his class in 1835. The U.S. Army sent him to California in 1846, during the Mexican-American War. After resigning from the military, he stayed in the new state, buying land in Santa Clara, Sacramento, and San Joaquin Counties. On January 8, 1849, he and a partner, Richard Harcourt Sinton, established California's first bank in San Francisco, but the enterprise failed the next year after a national financial panic.

In 1858, at a Christmas party, he met a young woman named Mary Schell and became romantically involved with her, leading her to believe he would marry her. But the Civil War started in 1860, and Naglee returned East to serve as a brigadier general in the Union Army. During the four years he was away, Naglee kept up an intimate correspondence with Schell, demonstrating the depth of his devotion with flowery prose and an overabundance of exclamation points. "I love you, dear Baby! And oh, how intensely!" he wrote to her. "One only equal to the intensity of my love would be my misery, and pain and suffering, if my love was for one moment forgotten. . . . Who has been to you always, from the first moment you first knew him, as faithful, as watchful, as truly devoted to you, as your own Harry." In his letters to Schell, Naglee also unleashed a little intemperate criticism of his superior officers, including Generals Hooker and Peck, whom he claimed stole credit for many of his ideas.

After the war ended, in 1865, Naglee returned to San Jose. But his first meeting with Schell was a frigid one, and he dismissed her from his life. Hurt by his sudden rejection and the public disgrace, she considered taking Naglee to court. Instead, she wreaked a more cunning revenge. She took the war hero's correspondences to a San Francisco publisher, who in 1867 published the book *The Love Life of Brigadier General Henry M. Naglee, Consisting of a Correspondence on Love, War and Politics.* The sensational volume was a best-seller on both coasts, embarrassing Naglee with his impassioned prose as well as his heated comments on his fellow officers.

But Naglee managed to outlive that short-lived Victorian scandal. He became famous for producing a popular and esteemed brandy, clear in color but so strong that a sip is said to have brought tears to the drinker's eyes. In 1876, at the Centennial Exposition in Philadelphia, his *Naglia* brandy earned a special award as "the only American brandy on exhibit that approached the fine French spirits of brandy."

To learn about more misadventures of San Jose's General Naglee, pick up a copy of Jack Douglas's highly enjoyable book *Historical Footnotes of Santa Clara Valley.*

forms dramas in a small auditorium next to William Street Park.

Rose Garden and Shasta-Hanchett Districts

This exquisitely kept neighborhood is just west of downtown San Jose. It was named after a world-famous **municipal rose garden**, 408/277-2757, located in a small park at Dana and Naglee Streets. The Rose Garden neighborhood is bordered by **The Alameda** on the east, I-880 on the northwest, and the Burbank district on the south. Besides viewing the many handsome Queen Anne and Tudor-style homes here, be sure to stop at the **Rosicrucian Egyptian Museum**, 408/947-3636, the West Coast's largest collection of artifacts from that ancient land. The museum charges admission, but the beautiful gardens surrounding the building, a scaled-down replica of the temple at Luxor, are free to the public. The southern portion of the Rose Garden district is sometimes called the Shasta-Hanchett district, after a turn-of-the-19th-century developer. Here, at the Race St. intersection, where The Alameda curves to the right, there once stood a toll gate run by the Turnpike Road Company. Race St. was named after the horse racetrack at Agricultural Park (a Victorian version of a county fairgrounds) that stood from 1859 to 1901 in this section of San Jose. The property was bought from General Henry Naglee in 1859 for $6,000 to build this favorite attraction, and among the performances once given here was Buffalo Bill's Wild West Show.

Santa Teresa

This area was named for the Rancho Santa Teresa, owned by Joaquin Bernal, who lived here beginning in 1826 (Bernal Rd. was named after him). In 1834, he petitioned for a small land grant of one league, but Mexico's California governor Figueroa gave him twice that amount. Bernal named the ranch after hearing an Ohlone legend of a female spirit who dressed in flowing black robes and created springs in the area that cured an Indian village from a devastating disease. To the Catholic Bernal, the story sounded simi-

lar to that of Santa Teresa de Avila, the patron saint of healing, so he named the springs and his ranch after the religious figure. In the 1960s, the area was developed into middle-income neighborhoods. Today, the Santa Teresa district is bordered by Blossom Hill Rd. on the north, Santa Teresa Blvd. on the west, and Monterey Rd. on the east. Hilly **Santa Teresa County Park**, 408/225-0225, is along its southern boundary. Climb to the top of Coyote Peak here, and you'll get a spectacular view of Silicon Valley and South Valley, seeing where **IBM** established its corporate complex along Hwy. 85.

Westgate

Set in a cubbyhole of west San Jose, Silicon Valley residents often refer to this district as the Westgate area after the **Westgate Shopping Center**, 408/379-9350, located here. The district is bordered by Santa Clara on the north, Cupertino and Saratoga on the south, and Campbell on the southeast. It is made up of middle- and upper-class homes as well as a number of strip malls along Saratoga Avenue.

Willow Glen

Named after the willow trees that grew along the Guadalupe River here, this area is located just southwest of downtown San Jose. It's bordered by Los Gatos Creek and the city of Campbell on the west, Hwy. 87 on the east, and Hillsdale and Camden Aves. on the south. The area was part of the Rancho San Juan Bautista land grant given to José Agustin Narvaez by Governor Micheltorena in 1844. Once a community that was later annexed to San Jose, it has a delightfully engaging **downtown** area along Lincoln Ave., where you can find a number of eateries, coffeehouses, and boutiques. This street is particularly well known for being one of Silicon Valley's best antique shopping areas. At Christmastime, Willow Glen attracts sightseers with its old-fashioned holiday atmosphere, its charming homes decorated with lights and ornaments. Many of the district's more splendid homes were built in the 1930s and feature well-kept, spacious gardens.

SAN JOSE'S LITERARY PAST (AND PRESENT)

San Jose has never been considered a literary hotbed—as on many other topics, it just tends to maintain a lower profile than other, better-publicized locations. Surprisingly, the city actually can lay claim to brushes with quite an impressive roster of authors.

Mark Twain got his start as a lecturer right here in San Jose, the first step in establishing what would become an immortal reputation as one of history's greatest raconteurs and public speakers. Though Samuel Clemens had yet to establish himself as an author, he had already adopted his famous pseudonym and made something of a name for himself with the story of Calaveras County's jumping frog. In *Pen and Inklings,* Ralph Rambo relates how the financially strapped Twain returned to San Francisco from his adventures in and around the Hawaiian (then the Sandwich) Islands in 1866 and decided to see if he could make some quick cash giving humorous lectures—sort of the Victorian version of stand-up comedy.

Twain didn't want to perform these lectures in San Francisco, afraid that if they failed he'd embarrass himself in front of friends. But he had met a colorful character in the goldfields named Stewart, and the two men had become friends. Frank Stewart, who was known locally as "the Earthquake Man" for his claimed ability to predict temblors, owned a saloon on San Jose's Fountain Alley, and he invited Twain to make the short journey south for his trial run in the lecture business. So Twain wound up giving his first public lectures in San Jose. The hilarious talks were a huge hit, and the rest, as they say, is history. (In later years, when he'd returned to the East Coast, Twain wrote a satirical article poking cruel fun at Stewart. Stung, Stewart wrote an angry letter to Twain, who promptly replied with a long apology and a promise to help promote a book of Stewart's poetry. The friendship was mended.)

On April 3, 1882, another literary giant came to San Jose—also on a lecture tour. In his *Historical Footnotes of Santa Clara Valley,* Jack Douglas tells the story of Oscar Wilde giving a talk on interior decorating at downtown's California Theatre. Known for his witty one-liners, Wilde that night failed to inspire much reaction from the San Joseans who attended the dull talk. They seemed more interested in his strange personal appearance than what he had to say about aestheticism. The *Mercury* newspaper reporter described the scene this way: "[B]efore the audience stood a most grotesque boyish-looking young man, whose dress may have been modeled after that of dead and gone aesthetes of some forgotten age, but which was, nevertheless, the most atrociously ugly suit of wearing apparel that could well be devised by man. A suit of dark velvet, with somber suggestiveness of having been buried for a century or more . . . the coat was rounded and short, the vest exposed a liberal area of shirtfront and knee breeches met a pair of thin black stockings, through which showed another pair of white ones."

Bret Harte, famous for his short western stories as well as serving as the first editor of *Overland Monthly* magazine, occasionally came to San Jose to give lectures. Local legend has it that while he was here, he heard a bittersweet story set in the Santa Cruz Mountains logging town of Roaring Camp (not far from today's Felton). Harte kept the town's name but changed the location to the more exciting gold country for his famous short story "The Luck of Roaring Camp."

Literary giant Jack London knew San Jose well, coming here frequently to visit friends. He often even *bicycled* the 40 miles from Oakland to spend time with his girlfriend Mabel Applegarth, an intelligent young woman with blue eyes and golden hair. London was a fervent so-

BOB RACE

Mark Twain

cialist and spent much of his time lecturing on the social injustices of capitalism. While in San Jose, he helped establish a Labor Temple on N. 2nd St., near St. James Park and across the street from Trinity Episcopal Church. The site is now a small parking lot, but a historical marker tells of its past. At this Labor Temple, London wrote portions of *The Call of the Wild* and *The Sea Wolf.* In *The Call of the Wild,* Buck, the canine hero, is born on Judge Bond's estate in Santa Clara. Legend has it that London was inspired to write the story after actually kidnapping a dog and placing the animal on a train at the College Park depot on Stockton Avenue.

Not as well known a name today, San Jose poet Edwin Markham was a literary meteor in the first half of the 20th century. His homage to President Lincoln, "Lincoln, the Man of the People," is inscribed onto the walls of the Lincoln Memorial. Markham came to San Jose in 1872 to study to be a teacher at San Jose Normal School (now San Jose State University) and was a member of the first graduating class. For 20 years, he lived in a small cottage with his mother at 432 S. 8th St., a couple of blocks from the school. It was here that he wrote his most famous poem, "The Man with the Hoe." Inspired by a Millet painting and dealing with the issue of labor, the poem created a literary sensation. Markham was friends with Senator Phelan, a patron of the arts who often invited artists and authors to his Villa Montalvo manor in Saratoga. To honor his friend, Phelan established the Edwin Markham Poetry Society, helped declare the 8th St. cottage a literary shrine, and in his will, endowed the Markham literary award. Today, the dilapidated cottage sits on the grounds of the San Jose Historical Museum in Kelley Park and is currently undergoing renovation. A dormitory at San Jose State University is also named in honor of the poet.

Visit the alleyway on the south side of the Fairmont Hotel, and you'll observe a table and chair monument dedicated to Mexican-American activist Ernesto Galarza. A migrant worker during his childhood, this nationally acclaimed author lived during the 1950s in the city's Willow Glen district. His books, such as *Strangers in Our Fields, Spiders in the House,* and *Merchants of Labor,* are considered classics of labor history. Galarza's writings helped significantly to change many of the United States' migrant labor laws.

More recently, former mayor Thomas McEnery wrote a novel about colorful rogue Thomas Fallon (one of his many predecessors in the mayor's post) and former police chief Joseph McNamara has written several crime novels set in Silicon Valley (specifically in the well-disguised "Silicon City"), San Francisco, and other Bay Area locations. And rock-and-roll musician (and classic-rock DJ of San Jose's KFOX 98.5 FM morning drive-time show) Greg Kihn has written several offbeat horror novels including *Mojo Hand, Horror Show, Big Rock Beat,* and *Shade of Pale.* Occasionally, Kihn can also be found in Silicon Valley bookstores signing his novels.

CITIES OF THE VALLEY

TOUR

San Jose is a large, expansive city, and a complete exploration of its entire geography would be a massive undertaking. This tour covers only the downtown area. It involves a good deal of walking, so consider wearing comfortable shoes.

From I-280 on the edge of the downtown area, take the 7th St. exit, driving north along this street through a residential area of stately Victorian houses. Rooms in many of these dwellings are rented to San Jose State University students (your author, for example, lived in one near the corner of 9th and William Sts.). This neighborhood is the **Reed Street district,** named for James Frazier Reed, a pioneer who bought land here, speculating on San Jose's growth in becoming California's first state capital. Several streets in this area are named after Reed family members, including Virginia, Margaret, and William.

Turn left at the stoplight intersection at Reed St. and drive six blocks to the stop sign at 1st Street. Turn right onto 1st St., noticing the corner city park on your left. Called **Parque de los Pobladores** (Park of the Citizens), it's dedicated to the small group of Spanish settlers who established San Jose in the late 1700s. You are now entering the South of First Area, often referred to as the **SoFA district.** This part of downtown San Jose is known for its art galleries, small theaters, coffeehouses, restaurants, and nightclubs. The place is usually buzzing with activity on weekend nights, particularly with San Jose State University students so nearby. The best place to park your car here is in the 2nd St. parking lot next to the **Camera One Cinema,** 408/998-3005. To get there, go down 1st St. to San Carlos St., turn right at this intersection, go one block to 2nd St. and turn right here. The lot's entrance is halfway down the block on your right and charges $5. From the parking lot, stroll down 1st St., taking a moment to look at the grandiose architecture of the now-closed **Fox Theater** across the street from Camera One. Plans call for this landmark movie theater to eventually be renovated as the permanent home of Opera San José.

At the corner of San Carlos St., you'll see **Original Joe's Restaurant,** 408/292-7030, or O.J.'s, as some locals call it. Opened on May 24, 1956, the Italian eatery is a San Jose institution known for its comical waiters and ample portions. Famous people such as President George Bush and country singer Willie Nelson have chowed down here.

Walk west along San Carlos St., and at the corner of Market St., you'll come to the entrance of the **Hyatt Sainte Claire Hotel,** 408/885-1234, designed in a tasteful Spanish-Italian Renaissance Revival style. Listed on the National Register of Historic Places, the hotel was built by developer T. S. Montgomery on land once occupied by the Eagle Brewery. It opened on October 16, 1926, and was immediately nicknamed the Million-Dollar Hotel. Take a moment to enter the hotel and view its luxurious lobby lounge.

After the hotel, cross Market St. and head toward the immense **McEnery Convention Center.** The lot on the southwest corner, empty much of the year, is turned into a popular outdoor skating rink during the holiday season. Completed in 1989 at a cost of $147 million, the convention center was named after Mayor Thomas McEnery, a key figure in the downtown's redevelopment. The abstract tile facade was designed by Danish artist Lin Utzon, and conventioneers like to hang out at the playful fountains in the front plaza during their breaks from trade shows. Just inside the center near the front entrance, you'll find an information booth run by the San Jose/Silicon Valley **visitors bureau,** 408/977-0900, website: www.sanjose.org. Here you can obtain current information on the area's attractions and events. Return outside and take a look at the building across San Carlos Street. This is San Jose's **Civic Auditorium** and **Montgomery Theatre,** built during the Depression on land donated by T. S. Montgomery.

Return to the Market and San Carlos Sts. intersection and cross San Carlos, going over the Light Rail tracks here. In spring and summer, the San Jose Historical Museum operates antique trolleys, which make a fun way to tour the downtown area. Cross Market St. heading east, entering the southern end of the **Plaza de César Chávez,** San Jose's preeminent plaza around which the pueblo grew in the late 1790s. In the 1990s, it was renamed after the famous farmworker labor leader who lived for a time in the city's Eastside district. This park is the location of several popular music festivals during the summer. In December, it's the site of the city's Christmas in the Park display of automated holiday scenes. The ominous-looking statue at the southern corner is of the plumed serpent **Quetzalcoatl,** a mythological god worshiped by the Aztecs and Toltecs. It was placed here to honor Santa Clara County's Hispanic culture, although the artwork has received unfavorable critiques by locals who complain it looks more like an enormous dog dropped a pile in the plaza.

Stroll down through the plaza's center pathway. The garish mango-colored building with the azure tiles on your left is the **Tech Museum,** 408/279-7150, opened in fall 1998 at a cost of more than $100 million. Its exhibits showcase many of the technologies developed in Silicon Valley. The austere mass of buildings just north of The Tech is **Park Center Plaza.** This complex was built in the early 1970s to attract banks and financial companies to San Jose. Architectural critics have complained that the cold fortress layout of these skyscrapers keeps this area cut off from the more human-scaled plaza.

Continue walking down the path. San Jose sometimes refers to itself as "the heart of Silicon Valley," and Plaza de César Chávez is the city's historic heart. And at the center of this parklike plaza is a simple yet delightful **fountain,** where water columns playfully shoot upward. This popular downtown attraction is a pleasant place for families and tourists to come and cool off on hot days. Stop for a moment at this spot, and ponder that this fountain sits at the very center of the heart of Silicon Valley. Just north of this point, in the shade of oak trees, stands a marker noting the location of **California's first state capitol building.** In a cramped adobe building on this spot, the state's first legislature met for about two years starting in December 1849. The politicians, however, decided to relocate to Benicia after major winter storms in 1851 dropped 32

inches of rain on the valley and made life unbearably muddy.

Cross Market St. at the pedestrian crossing to the towering **Fairmont Hotel,** 408/998-1900. A historical sign here marks the location of San Jose's long-gone **Chinatown.** Many of the Chinese immigrants who came to California to build the western section of the transcontinental railroad later moved to this area of San Jose. They served as an important labor source for the valley's agricultural industry. On May 4, 1887, a fire started under mysterious circumstances, reducing Chinatown to smoldering ashes and forcing its inhabitants to relocate to other parts of the valley. The fire made way for the Victorian development of San Jose's business district.

Pass through the valet parking entrance into the Fairmont, and take a short stroll through the posh lounge area of this luxury hotel. The Fairmont quickly became a Silicon Valley landmark when it opened in October 1987. Presidents and celebrities often stay in the hotel's spacious suites. Follow the signs to the hotel's **Fountain Restaurant** (a personal downtown favorite), and take the exit at the end of the corridor here into the small plaza known as **Corona of Palms.** Walk into the ring of palm trees here and take a look at the immense bronze plaque set into the ground. It depicts the California state seal, and along the cement area bordering it are inscribed quotes explaining San Jose's role as the first state capital.

The skyscraper to the southeast of the plaza was once known as Fairmont Plaza Tower, but it's now the **Knight-Ridder Building** after the publisher of the *San Jose Mercury News,* which set up offices here. San Francisco–based TV station KRON Channel 4 also has its Silicon Valley bureau at this location. During the early part of the 20th century, the site was the location of San Jose's first skyscraper, the Garden City Bank and Trust Building. This seven-story building housed the world's first broadcasting station when, starting in 1909, Dr. Charles Herrold began regular broadcasts of his radio station FN. The station provided music and news to San Jose's residents, and radio technology was so new that Herrold and his assistants had to build receivers in their spare time so listeners could pick up the signal. In 1949, the station changed its call letters to KCBS and relocated to San Francisco, where it still broadcasts news and talk shows.

Adjacent to the north side of the Corona of Palms stands the **San Jose Museum of Art,** 408/294-2787, the city's finest public gallery. It's a successful architectural merging of San Jose's old and new spirits. The Romanesque-style sandstone western portion of the museum was originally built as the city's post office, and its first clock tower collapsed during the 1906 earthquake. The modern-style east wing was added in the 1990s and contains spacious rooms specially designed to house the museum's often-changing exhibitions.

From here, walk to the northern end of the Plaza de César Chávez. At the corner of San Fernando St., you'll see the magnificent **Saint Joseph's Cathedral,** 408/283-8100, with its paired towers and Renaissance-style domes. This site is where the pueblo's first adobe church was built, founded in 1803 and named after the city's patron saint. Saint Joseph's is California's oldest parish. The cornerstone of the present building, the site's third church, was laid on March 19, 1876, after a fire destroyed the second wooden structure. Occasionally referred to with deepest affection as Holy Joe's, the cathedral suffered earthquake damage and weathering over the years. After undergoing a major $20 million renovation, the basilica was rededicated October 28, 1990, in a reverent ceremony. If services are not being conducted, feel free to step through the colossal portico doors and enjoy the brilliant religious artistry of the interior. Expect to spend about 20 minutes here.

After visiting the cathedral, continue walking north down Market St. for one block. On the other side of the street in front of Keegan's Kafe is a historic marker showing where San Jose's *juzgado* (the Mexican government's city hall) once stood. It was at this site where Thomas Fallon raised the American flag on July 14, 1847, symbolically taking the city for the United States. Take a glance to your left down Post St. and at the corner a short distance away you'll see **Waves Smokehouse & Saloon,** 408/885-9283. Built

around 1873, it's the city's oldest saloon and a onetime brothel. If you believe in hauntings, you'll find it interesting to learn of two ghosts said to occupy this historic San Jose landmark. A woman purportedly haunts the 2nd-floor restaurant, sometimes whispering the names of diners in their ears. The story goes that she was a fervent Catholic and never dared venture into "the light" for fear she'd be punished for having once had an abortion. An Irish ghost named Blackie is rumored to roam the 1st floor, sometimes tapping patrons on the back. The bartender will tell you Blackie haunts the tavern, suffering from overwhelming guilt about a murder he committed.

Continue walking down Market another block to Santa Clara Street. Turn right and follow Santa Clara one block east to 1st Street. The magnificent 1920s-style tower at this corner is the **Bank of America Building.** It's Silicon Valley's oldest skyscraper, and still *the* graceful lady of the skyline. For a time after it was built, a light at the top provided weather forecasts. A green light predicted sunny weather while a red light predicted rain. Turn left onto 1st St. and cross Santa Clara Street. Across from the Bank of America Building at the intersection's northeast corner is the **Valley Transportation Authority customer service office,** 408/321-2300. Here you can get information on Silicon Valley's public transportation as well as buy weekly or monthly VTA passes.

Continue north down 1st St. for one block, arriving at **St. James Park,** an area of significant historical importance to San Jose. Surveyed in 1848 by Chester S. Lyman, a Yale University professor who came to California for his health, this property was developed into a parklike city square during the 1850s. After the 1906 earthquake, the National Guard camped in the park to protect property from looters, and many of the homeless also pitched tents here after the destruction of their houses. The park is also the notorious site of California's last lynching. This took place in 1933, when the son of the owner of Hart's Department Store was kidnapped, his body found in the bay, and the two men responsible were dragged out of the courthouse jail by a mob and strung up in a tree. Also, two major labor rallies occurred here in 1931 and 1933. Nowadays, many of San Jose's homeless people stay in St. James Park during the day.

The neo-Federal-designed building at the park's southwest corner once served as **San Jose's Main Post Office** (it's now the downtown branch). The building was built in 1933 as a W.P.A. project. If it's open, walk inside and take in the Gothic-like interior. Next to the post office stands the **Santa Clara County Courthouse.** Designed by local architect Levi Goodrich, it was built in 1867 in a failed attempt to lure the state capital back to San Jose with a magnificent building. The courthouse originally was topped by a large dome, which collapsed during a 1931 fire. The building suffered severe damage in the 1989 earthquake but has since been renovated.

Across the Light Rail tracks from the courthouse is a statue honoring **U.S. president William McKinley,** who stood here on May 13, 1901, while giving a speech. Carved on the pedestal is a quote from that address that's just as relevant now as it was 100 years ago: "The Constitution is a sacred instrument; and a sacred trust is given to us to see to it that its preservation in all its virtue and its vigor is passed on to the generations yet to come." Just south of the statue is another park monument, an ugly cement sculpture marked with graffiti. It was built in honor of **Senator Robert Kennedy,** who spoke at this spot shortly before his assassination in Los Angeles during the 1968 presidential election.

Continue walking through St. James Park to its northern boundary along St. James Street. At the corner of St. James and 2nd Sts., behind a cyclone fence, there stands a building with four Ionic columns at the entrance that looks much like an ancient Greek temple. This splendid ruin is the **First Church of Christ Scientist Building,** designed in 1905 by renowned San Francisco architect Willis Polk. The classic structure has stayed abandoned for many years due to an uncertainty by the city's government on what to do with it and how to finance its resurrection as a public facility. Plans have been suggested to turn it into a public art gallery or a performance hall where local groups can put on productions.

Cross the 2nd St. intersection, and at 65 St. James St., you'll find yourself in front of the **Sainte Claire Club,** built in 1893. This former men's club was established by James Phelan, a former mayor of San Francisco and a prominent patron of the arts for Santa Clara Valley (he also built a stately mansion called Villa Montalvo in Saratoga). At the Sainte Claire Club, San Jose's political power brokers used to meet to do their behind-the-scenes dealings. Further down St. James St. at the corner of 3rd St. is the **Scottish Rite Temple,** built in 1924–25. Note the somber Egyptian sphinxes standing guard at the entrance. It's now Capital Club Athletics, a gym for executives who work in the area. The building doubled as the museum in the 1998 movie *Mad City* starring John Travolta and Dustin Hoffman. Next door is the **First Unitarian Church,** a Richardson Romanesque–style building that sheltered injured citizens after the 1906 earthquake. Also that year, it became the site of San Jose's first day nursery. Step inside for a look at the chapel's labyrinth, open to the public weekdays 11:30 A.M.–1 P.M. for lunch-hour meditations.

Continue across St. James Park back to its southern boundary at St. John Street. Here, at the corner of 2nd St., is a small monument honoring **General Henry Morris Naglee,** an important city benefactor and one of the more colorful personas of 19th-century San Jose. Cross St. John St. at the corner of 2nd St., where you'll find the **Trinity Episcopal Church.** Built in 1862, it is the city's oldest surviving church structure. Across the street from the church in what is now a small parking lot is where San Jose's **Labor Temple** once stood. Author Jack London wrote the last part of his best-selling story *The Call of the Wild* here, as well as portions of *The Sea Wolf.* The building was demolished in the 1950s.

Continue strolling south down 2nd St., crossing Santa Clara St. and walking through a retail area. Half a block later, you'll see on your left the now-closed **Jose Theatre,** the city's oldest surviving auditorium, which in its early history showcased vaudeville acts along with silent movies. Escape artist Harry Houdini, as well as movie comedians Fatty Arbuckle and Charlie Chaplin, once performed here. Sadly, the future of this landmark building is in jeopardy because a developer wants to raze it and build apartment buildings. Continue walking to the end of the block, crossing San Fernando Street. On your right, you'll see a major Redevelopment Agency project called **The Pavilion,** an unsuccessful attempt to bring upscale retail boutiques to downtown. When that failed, an immense nightclub called San Jose Live! filled the entire second story, but it attracted too many gang members and so was eventually closed. Most of the shops have remained empty, and the building's owners are considering leasing spaces for offices.

Farther along 2nd St. at the Paseo de San Antonio, you'll see on your left a blue sheet-metal structure that looks like a huge garden shed. This is the new home of the **San Jose Repertory Theatre,** 408/291-2266. The Rep is the city's most prestigious dramatic company. On your right at the corner of San Carlos St. stands the modern **Federal Building,** which houses U.S. government offices. At the eastern entrance is an emotionally moving **memorial to Japanese-American citizens** forcibly interned during World War II, ironically at a time when the United States fought to preserve democracy abroad. It depicts images of daily life in many of the internment camps throughout the western region. An inscription describes Franklin D. Roosevelt's infamous Executive Order No. 9066, which provided the legal basis for this discrimination against U.S. citizens by their own government. More than 3,000 Japanese-Americans from the Santa Clara Valley were interned in these camps, many of them losing their property and livelihoods.

Cross the San Carlos St. intersection and return to your car if you have parked at the 2nd St. parking lot. Go around the block, back onto 1st St., and turn left at the light onto San Carlos St., following it west for two blocks. At the northwest corner of San Carlos St. and Almaden Blvd., you'll see the **San Jose Center for the Performing Arts.** You might think it looks like a second cousin to New York's Guggenheim Museum—that's because it was designed by architects from Frank Lloyd Wright's Taliesin Associates. Turn right at the palm-tree-centered Almaden Blvd.,

and one block on your left you'll see the domineering **Adobe Towers,** headquarters of the well-known software company. At the end of Almaden Blvd. stands the historic **De Anza Hotel,** named after the famous Spanish explorer. It was built in 1931 and served as a social center for the city until the 1950s, when its prestige began to falter with the downtown. In danger of being razed, it was preserved as a historic site and completely renovated to its original glory in 1990.

Turn left at the stoplight and continue on along Santa Clara St., crossing under the Hwy. 87 overpass. The natural setting to your right is the **Guadalupe River Park,** which is evolving to eventually become San Jose's version of New York's Central Park. It stretches several miles along the Guadalupe River from the Children's Discovery Museum at I-280 to the Civic Center at Hedding Street. A park **visitor's center,** 408/277-2757, is located just west of the Hwy. 87 overpass. The immense stadium you see on your right is the **San Jose Arena.** This is where the Sharks, San Jose's hockey team, play their home games. It also holds concerts and performances throughout the year.

Turn left at the Montgomery St. stoplight intersection, and follow this south for about a quarter mile. Cross over the San Carlos St. intersection where Montgomery turns into Bird Avenue. Two blocks later, you'll come to the I-280 interchange. The right entrance lane heads north to San Francisco, the left entrance lane takes you south back to downtown San Jose.

POINTS OF INTEREST

The Tech

Originally called "The Garage," in honor of the several valley companies that began in local garages, the Tech Museum of Innovation (affectionately known as "The Tech") is *the* Silicon Valley destination for young science enthusiasts. The original Tech was located across the street from San Jose's Martin Luther King, Jr., Library, but the wonder-filled science and technology museum moved in October 1998 to a newly constructed location along the Plaza de César Chávez. The futuristic-looking structure

OWEN'S FOLLY

San Francisco has the Golden Gate Bridge. Los Angeles has the Hollywood sign. New York City has the Statue of Liberty. But the closest Silicon Valley has to an iconic symbol is Hoover Tower at Stanford University—not exactly widely recognized throughout the world.

At one time, however, the valley did have such an icon which, for its time, was considered a wonder of the modern world. At the dawning of the electric age, downtown San Jose's light tower brought the 19th century farm town international fame for its great technological advances.

The tower was the brainchild of J. J. Owen, editor of the *San Jose Mercury* newspaper. He reasoned that if a tower was built high enough and lit with electric lightbulbs, it would illuminate the entire city, thus making the streets safe after sundown. The *Mercury* began a campaign among its subscribers to raise the $4,000 needed to build the unusual edifice. Soon, at the intersection of Market and Santa Clara Sts., construction workers began assembling the iron pipes and wiring for the 237-foot tower.

On December 13, 1881, it was lit for the first time, a wondrous sight of 24,000 candlepower luminescence seen throughout the valley and surrounding hills. One highly questionable story tells of a Morgan Hill chicken rancher who threatened to sue the city of San Jose because his hens refused to lay eggs, so confused were they of whether or not it was night because of the tower's beam.

Unfortunately, the tower never fulfilled its goal of illuminating the city. Its light could never penetrate the various buildings surrounding it, so many dark corners still remained. The construction quickly became known as "Owen's Folly." But in a sense, its light went much farther than the editor had expected. With its spreading celebrity, the marvel served to illuminate San Jose and Santa Clara Valley to the world. In fact, letters addressed to "City with the light tower" easily found their way to San Jose.

San Jose's tower of power gained such international fame that it reportedly inspired a certain Monsieur Eiffel in Paris to consider building one for that city. Some historians say he even sent his assistants to San Jose to inspect the light tower. And indeed, sharing the same elegant tapering, the light tower and the Eiffel Tower built nine years later do seem like engineering brethren.

The electric light tower stood almost 34 years, a proud symbol of the city. But over those decades, the pipes began to rust. A severe storm in February 1915 damaged the tower. On December 3 of that year, it collapsed completely. No one was hurt, but San Jose had lost its landmark icon.

A half-sized replica of the tower now stands at San Jose's History Park located at Kelley Park just south of downtown. Some locals have talked about rebuilding the tower again at its original location, possibly using laser lights to symbolize Silicon Valley as the high-tech capital. This proposal will very unlikely ever come about, and Silicon Valley will continue looking for its one great icon in some other landmark.

CITIES OF THE VALLEY

THE STRANGEST HOUSE IN THE WORLD

Next to a complex of San Jose movie theaters looms a Queen Anne–style structure that has gained global renown as possibly the strangest house in the world. One of Silicon Valley's most popular tourist attractions, it is, of course, the Winchester Mystery House. Well over two million people have toured the weird dreamscape of its halls, stairways, and 160 rooms, questing through the labyrinthine structure for the puzzling story behind it.

© MARTIN CHEEK

the world-famous Winchester Mystery House

The legend of the house starts in New Haven, Connecticut, in 1857. That was the year Oliver Winchester started the New Haven Arms Company, which produced a rifle that became hugely popular during the Civil War. It gained fame not as the New Haven Repeater but rather as the Winchester Repeating Rifle. The weapon, which was also used to kill many Native Americans during the settling of the West, made Winchester a huge fortune. After his death, his son William took over the business, and the family's fortune increased even more. William was married to Sarah Pardee Winchester, a beautiful woman who stood only four feet and ten inches tall. The couple had a daughter, but the child died in infancy, causing Sarah considerable grief.

William died in 1881 after a bout of tuberculosis, and legend has it that Sarah visited a Boston psychic, who convinced her that the deaths of her loved ones were the revenge of the ghosts of the thousands of people killed by Winchester rifles. The psychic reportedly told her to move West and, to appease the spirits, continuously build a house 24 hours a day, seven days a week. The psychic said Sarah would remain alive as long as she continued building.

Sarah moved to Santa Clara Valley and in June 1886 paid farmer J. H. Hamm $12,570 in gold coins for a 43-acre tract of land. Located west of San Jose on Santa Cruz–Santa Clara Rd. (now Winchester Blvd.), the eight-bedroom farmhouse on the property was a modest structure. But it underwent a dramatic transformation thanks to Sarah's inheritance of $20 million as well as an income of $1,000 a day from gun royalties. Local carpenters and field hands were hired to begin working on additions to the farmhouse, following architectural designs Sarah sketched. Work continued nonstop for years, and the house grew amazingly, receiving such innovative features as stairways that lead to the ceiling, doors that open into brick walls, and ornate stained-glass skylights placed in the floor. Sarah is said to have often communed with the spirit world in a special "seance room" in the house. Considering the number 13 exceptionally lucky, she incorporated it into the design of many of its furnishings—such as 13 candles in the chandeliers.

Carpenters never complained about the never-ending project—Sarah paid them well and treated them kindly. Some locals who knew her say that it was the eccentric woman's architectural tastes, not spiritual forebodings, that led her to construct her "hobby house." At its peak, the house covered more than six acres of land. In 1906, the San Andreas Fault gave way, and a large section of the house collapsed in the San Francisco earthquake, trapping Sarah in her bedroom. After being rescued, she instructed her workers to clear the rubble and continue with the construction. The sounds of hammers and saws continued 24 hours a day, seven days a week until Sarah's death in 1922, at the age of 85. The total cost of the house was $5.5 million.

For some years after her death, the place lay dormant, decaying, and earning a reputation for being haunted. Bought and tidied up by the Winchester Mystery House Association, the bizarre home quickly became a popular San Jose tourist site—and still draws a large number of visitors. It's unlikely you'll find yourself encountering any ghosts during the guided tour, but you will observe a fine collection of Sarah's Tiffany glass and gilt Victorian furniture, including a pipe organ. Outside, you can wander in the Victorian garden or visit a small gun museum.

525 S. Winchester Blvd. (from Hwy. 17 or I-280, take Stevens Creek Blvd. exit and drive west; turn left at Winchester Blvd. and drive south two blocks; located next to the Century Theater complex), 408/247-2101, website: www.winchestermysteryhouse.com. The 65-minute guided tour costs $13.95 for adults 13–64, $10.95 for seniors over 65, $7.95 for children 6–12, free for children under 6. Special tours are given on Halloween and any Friday the 13th, and a behind-the-scenes tour takes visitors to areas not generally open to the public.

CITIES OF THE VALLEY

was designed by renowned Mexican architect Ricardo Legorreta. Fast becoming a Silicon Valley icon, the bright mango-colored museum with the azure tiled dome contains about 250 hands-on exhibits on three levels covering 112,000 square feet.

Visitors—youngsters and adults alike—can appraise and exercise their technology skills in four galleries (though you should expect a wait for the more popular exhibits). The Innovation Gallery showcases technologies used throughout Silicon Valley, including a $10 million "clean room" that simulates how the element silicon, found in sand, is transformed into thin crystalline wafers, the basis for computer chips. With another exhibit in this section, visitors at computer workstations design and ride a virtual roller coaster. The Life Tech Gallery highlights advanced tools such as genetic testing and DNA fingerprinting. Popular with kids is the virtual simulator used to train the U.S. bobsled team for the Olympics. In the Exploration Gallery, visitors see the technologies allowing researchers to study the depths of the ocean or the edge of the universe. One exhibit here simulating a Martian base camp lets the visitor maneuver a remote-controlled Martian rover. The Communication Gallery, in the lower level, presents an updated look at many of the technologies now creating the information age. These include a section explaining the Internet as well as a digital studio in which visitors can capture video of themselves acting in front of a blue screen and later edit and manipulate their performance on a workstation, choosing assorted backgrounds including a lunar landscape. The unique Center of the Edge section displays cutting-edge tech-related exhibits, changing every four to six months.

The Tech also features a 295-seat IMAX dome theater which shows one-hour documentary films that surround the viewer in a visually mind-blowing experience. A complete Tech tour can easily last five hours, but hungry visitors can take advantage of the Cafe Primavera on the entrance level (or a public lounge if you've brought your own food). A gift shop in the entrance lobby is stocked with science books and toys and does not require an admission ticket.

Downtown San Jose at Park Ave. and Market St., 408/795-6100, website: www.thetech.org. Open Tues.–Sun., 10 A.M.–5 P.M., some Thurs., 10 A.M.–8 P.M.; admission: ages 13–64, $8.95 for exhibits, $12 for IMAX, $19.95 for both; ages 3–12, $6.95 for exhibits, $10 for IMAX, $14.95 for both; ages 65 and older, $7.95 for exhibits, $11 for IMAX, and $17.95 for both; under 3 free. A yearlong pass is also available.

Rosicrucian Egyptian Museum

In San Jose's Rose Garden district, this museum boasts the West Coast's largest collection of Egyptian and Babylonian artifacts. The mummy gallery mesmerizes with wrapped-up remains of priests, cats, and birds, as well as other animals the ancient Egyptians considered sacred. It's an incredible but true story that one mummy—an ancient priest—was discovered in a sarcophagus sold by the department store Neiman-Marcus. Kids will love the tour of a full-sized, walk-in replica of an ancient tomb. The museum was built in 1966 as a reproduction of the Karnak Temple at Thebes in Upper Egypt. It's surrounded by well-kept grounds resembling a pharaoh's pleasure garden. A planetarium next door offers daily shows about the cosmos.

Corner of Park and Naglee Aves., 408/947-3636, website: www.rosicrucian.org; admission: adults $7, seniors and students $5, ages 6–15 $3.50, under 6 free; open daily 10 A.M.–5 P.M.; free parking on street.

San Jose Historical Museum

Hands down, this is Silicon Valley's best history museum. The 25-acre villagelike complex showcases various old homes saved for preservation as well as reconstructed buildings highlighting San Jose's past. The museum includes a scaled-down model of the original San Jose Light Tower; the O'Brien's Old-Fashioned Ice Cream & Candy Parlor, where visitors can purchase sweets; and a printing shop, where volunteers demonstrate typesetting skills. An antique trolley shop repairs mass transit vehicles from yesteryear and includes one of the world's first electric cars, a turn-of-

the-19th-century carriage powered by batteries. Visitors can take trolley rides around the park's Main Street. Expect at least a three-hour visit to take it all in.

1600 Senter Rd. in Kelley Park (across the street from Municipal Stadium), 408/287-2290, website: www.serve.com/sjhistory; parking $4 on weekends; admission: adults $6, seniors $5, youths 6–17 $4, and children 5 and under free. Open Tues.–Sun. noon–5 P.M.

Ira F. Brilliant Center for Beethoven Studies and Museum

West magazine calls this "the Valhalla for Beethoven fanatics in the Western Hemisphere." It's North America's only research archive devoted to the German musical genius who composed such chart-bustin' hits as "Moonlight Sonata" and "Für Elise." This fascinating center contains kitsch memorabilia as well as first and early editions of his music. Frequently scheduled lectures and events celebrate Beethoven's life and works. Run by noted Beethoven scholar William Meredith, the collection got its start by Ira F. Brilliant, a Phoenix-based land developer.

San Jose State University, Modular A, Room 100 (on 9th Street Mall near corner of San Fernando St.), 408/924-4590, website: www.sjsu.edu/depts/beethoven; parking $3 in university lots; admission free; open Mon.–Fri. 1–5 P.M. or by appointment.

Children's Discovery Museum

The whimsical pyramid angles and lavender color of this museum has made it stand out in downtown San Jose since it opened in 1990. Located in Discovery Meadow conveniently close to its own Light Rail stop, the 52,000-square-foot museum is the largest children's museum on the West Coast. It features interactive exhibits that teach about science, high technology, the humanities, and the arts. The Streets of San Jose exhibit helps children learn about the various aspects of modern city life, such as the electric power grid and traffic control. Other exhibits look at the ebb and flow of modern-day currency as well as the global communications infrastructure. The series of locks, canals, and waterwheels in the pop-

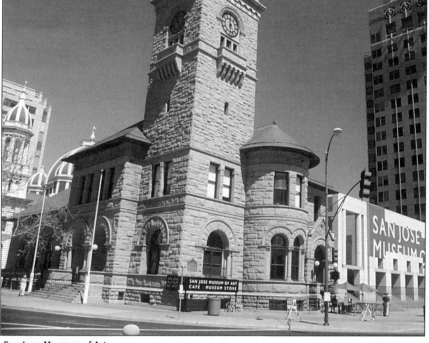

© MARTIN CHEEK

San Jose Museum of Art

CITIES OF THE VALLEY

ular Waterworks exhibit shows youngsters how water is distributed throughout a community. ZOOMzone, based on a PBS children's series, gives children a chance to test their analytical abilities with mind-teasing activities. They can even step into a bygone era of San Jose by trying on period attire.

180 Woz Way (at the eastern end of Auzerais St.), 408/298-5437, website: www.cdm.org; parking $2 in the lot across from the museum, but on weekends, it's free in the building at the corner of San Carlos St. and Woz Way; open Tues.–Sat. 10 A.M.–5 P.M., Sun. noon–5 P.M.; admission: adults $6, seniors $5, children 2–18 $4, under 2 free.

Japanese-American Museum

Located in San Jose's Japantown, this small historical museum features photographs and artifacts of the Japanese-Americans who immigrated to the Santa Clara Valley in the last century.

535 N. 5th St. (between Jackson and Empire Sts.), 408/294-3138, website:www.jarcm.org; free parking on street; admission free; open Tues.–Fri. 11 A.M.–3 P.M. and Sun. 11 A.M.–2 P.M.

San Jose Museum of Art

A mixture of the old and new, this gracefully designed art museum sits in the northeast corner of Plaza de César Chávez. A portion of it built as a federal post office in 1892 now serves as a café. A modern addition built in the 1990s more than doubled its length and provides space for a frequently changing collection of contemporary paintings, sculptures, drawings, and photographs. Occasional special events include jazz and classical concerts. The museum also has an art school, where budding child artists can learn to draw, paint, and create.

© MARTIN CHEEK

San Jose State University's Tower Hall

110 S. Market St. (at the corner of San Fernando St.), 408/294-2787, website: www.sjmusart.org; Tues., Wed., Fri.–Sun. 10 A.M.–5 P.M., Thurs. 10 A.M.–8 P.M.; admission: adults $7, seniors (over 62) and children 7–17 $4, under 5 and members free (free for everyone first Thurs. of the month, free for seniors first Tues. of the month, and half price Thurs. evenings 5–8 P.M.).

San Jose State University

Novelist Amy Tan, comedians Tom and Dick Smothers, and poet Edwin Markham all graduated from this superb public university set on the eastern edge of downtown. Originally founded in San Francisco in 1857 by George Washington Minns as a "normal school" (a school to train teachers), it moved to its present downtown location in 1870. A century later in 1972, it became San Jose State University (SJSU). More than 26,000 undergraduate and graduate students attend each semester, many of them working in high-tech fields. Among SJSU's more renowned schools are its journalism, English, aviation, engineering, social sciences, and art departments.

If you're touring the downtown, the campus is well worth strolling through, particularly the western section with its beautiful ivy-covered Tower Hall and fountain-sprayed lawn. The Walquist Library building in this area was torn down in spring 2000 and they are now building a new library.

In the mid-1990s, San Carlos St. was closed and, after a $3.2 million renovation, turned into a verdant walkway called Paseo de San Carlos, which better connects the campus with downtown. Also worth visiting is SJSU's highly esteemed art department galleries in the institutional Art Building, which (no joke) was constructed from a standardized design used for California state prison cell blocks. Seating 6,500 people, SJSU's **Event Center Arena,** 408/924-6333, has become a prestigious site for college sporting events, big-name concerts, and famous guest speakers such as the Dalai Lama, who spoke here the week after he won the Nobel Peace Prize.

One Washington Square (between 4th and 10th Sts.), 408/924-1000, website: www.sjsu.edu; parking $3 in university garages.

California Room

On the 3rd floor of San Jose's Martin Luther King, Jr., Main Library, you'll find this immense collection of materials pertaining to California history and emphasizing San Jose's past. Yearbooks from San Jose's various high schools are kept here, as well as local maps and city directories from 1870 to 1979. The library's 2nd floor also contains a small exhibit chronicling the Civil Rights struggle.

180 W. San Carlos St., downtown San Jose, 408/277-4867; open Mon. and Thurs. 2–5 P.M., Tues.–Wed. 3–9 P.M., Fri. 10 A.M.–1 P.M., Sat. 1–6 P.M.

GALLERIES
Quilts and Textiles

A changing exhibition of beautiful American quilts from the 19th and 20th centuries can be viewed in this small downtown museum near SJSU. Besides quilts, the museum displays textile works such as cloth dolls, and a gift shop provides patterns and other items for quilters.

110 Paseo de San Antonio (in the pedestrian walkway between the Repertory Theatre and SJSU), 408/971-0323, website: www.sjquiltmuseum.org; public lot parking; general admission $4, seniors and students $3, children under 12 free; open Tues., Wed., Fri., and Sun. 10 A.M.–5 P.M., Thurs. 10 A.M.–8 P.M.

CITIES OF THE VALLEY

Bay Area Glass Institute

Visitors can watch artisans working next to the intense heat of a furnace blowing unique glass creations at this gallery in downtown San Jose. An ever-changing array of exquisite glass-sculptured works can be found here. Holiday events include a glass pumpkin patch of about 3,000 glass pumpkins at the Palo Alto Center for Art. Resident designers Mariko Takada and Jonathan Tepperman also give classes, limited to only two students at a time.

202 N. 25th St. (corner of St. James St.), 408/993-2244, website: www.bagi.org; parking on street; admission free; call for tour times.

Machu Picchu Gallery and Museum of the Americas

Displaying folk art and pre-Columbian artifacts from Mexico and Central and South America since 1974, this one-room gallery in the back of a Peruvian restaurant is a hidden downtown treasure. Here, you'll find a delightful assortment of handmade toys, musical instruments, ceramics, handwoven alpaca textiles, and other objects. Visitors are encouraged to touch many of the exhibits—founder Olga Enciso-Smith considers this a "living museum." The gallery also sells various ethnic crafts, books, and music. Come on musical nights or during poetry readings and enjoy a Peruvian meal while soaking up the rich atmosphere.

87 San Fernando St. (in the Inca Gardens Restaurant near 3rd St.), 408/280-1860 or 408/977-0816; admission free; open Mon. 11:30 A.M.–3 P.M., Tues.–Fri. 11:30 A.M.–3 P.M.; Sat. 1–9 P.M., Sun. 1–8 P.M.

San Jose Institute of Contemporary Art

This nonprofit visual arts gallery in the SoFA district showcases works by Silicon Valley's contemporary artists. New exhibits open about every six weeks, and the openings are well attended by local art lovers. The Valentine auction is a popular fundraiser held during the month of February, when local artists create works around the Valentine's Day theme. The institute also promotes budding young Jackson Pollocks with

its youth art classes, and many of their works are displayed in the gallery. A gift shop provides a quality selection of items, such as artistic jewelry and paperweights.

451 S. 1st St., downtown San Jose (between San Salvador and William Sts.), 408/283-8155; parking in public lots; admission free; open Tues.–Sat. noon–5 P.M.

MACLA/Center for Latino Arts

Brilliantly colored paintings and vibrant sculptures are what you'll find in this well-lit gallery showcasing Hispanic artists. Besides art, the center also puts on a literary program featuring poetry and performances from members of the Latino community. A gift shop called La Tiendita sells various items, including books, T-shirts, and collectibles focusing on Latino arts.

510 S. 1st St. (corner of E. William St., across from the Parque de Pobladores), 408/998-2783; public parking in lots; admission free; open Wed.–Sat. noon–7 P.M.

WORKS/San Jose

Calling itself "an alternative exhibition space," this large gallery near St. James Park pushes the envelope when it comes to experimental visual and performance arts. Founded in 1977, it displays exhibits in various media forms such as film, video, dance, music, and computer and electronic arts. It also presents more traditional photographic, sculpture, painting, and installation works. The gallery also has studios where visitors can watch artists create.

30 N. 3rd St. (between Santa Clara and St. John Sts.), 408/295-8378, website: www.workssanjose.org; public parking on street; admission free except for performance art nights, which usually run $8 for general, $5 for members; open Tues.–Sat. noon–4 P.M., Thurs. noon–7 P.M.

HISTORIC SITES

Peralta Adobe and Thomas Fallon House

The last remaining structure from San Jose's original pueblo, the Peralta Adobe was built in

THE MINES THAT HELPED SAVE THE UNION

The sleepy village of New Almaden lies in a narrow canyon between the Pueblo Hills and the Santa Cruz Mountains 11 miles south of downtown San Jose. Registered as a historic landmark district on the National Register of Historic Places, the small town, its streets lined with cottages, is part of Almaden Quicksilver County Park. Its significant role in California history arises from an abundance of a crimson-colored ore called cinnabar, found in the hills around the town. The ore is made up of sulfur and mercury, which is sometimes called "quicksilver" because it acts like "living" silver.

More than 135 years of mining history pervades Almaden Quicksilver County Park. It contains the first mines in California—established 27 months before gold was discovered at Sutter's Mill along the American River farther north—and the first and richest mercury mine in North America. With more than $70 million in quicksilver taken from these hills, New Almaden was the site of California's richest single mine. The quicksilver taken here played a vital role in the Gold Rush and, later, the Civil War.

The Ohlone Indians knew of the cinnabar, which they collected, ground into a fine powder, and used to paint the mission walls as well as their bodies. But mercury is a toxic metal, and many of these natives suffered painful damage to their health from long-term exposure to the element.

In 1846, Captain Andres Castillero of the Mexican Army saw the crimson rock at the Santa Clara Mission and, having been educated at the College of Mines in Mexico City, realized the importance of the mineral. He obtained control of the area and planned to petition for a $100,000 award the Mexican government granted for significant mineral finds in California. But with the outbreak of the Mexican-American War, Castillero had to shift his focus to military matters. He sold his rights to the mine to Barron, Forbes Company, an English textile firm based in Tepic, Mexico.

Alexander Forbes came to the area to set up operations, naming the site Nuevo Almaden, after the famous Almaden mines in La Mancha, Spain, which had produced vast amounts of mercury since the days of ancient Rome. Almaden comes from the Arabic word for mine, *al maden*.

The mines of New Almaden drove the California Gold Rush. Mercury acts much like a magnet in attracting gold, so the establishment of the mines immediately prior to the advent of the Gold Rush was a lucky event. Without New Almaden, the gold seekers might never have collected the vast amounts of the precious metal that they did. In 1850, inspired by this sudden great need for mercury, Henry Wagner Halleck, a captain in the Army Corps of Engineers, hired on to mechanize the mine and manage its workers. (Halleck would later serve as Abraham Lincoln's chief of staff.)

The mines also played a significant role in helping the Union win the Civil War. Without New Almaden's mercury, California and Nevada would never have been able to supply enough gold and silver to the Union forces to help finance the war. Quicksilver was also used in the production of Union Army matériel such as blasting caps.

So important were the lucrative New Almaden facilities to the war effort that foolish New York speculators prompted Lincoln to seize the mines for the United States away from its English owners. In July 1863, Lincoln's agent Leonard Swett and a district marshal came down from San Francisco to New Almaden with a writ of ejection. Greeted at the gate by Superintendent Sherman Day and a gang of miners carrying shotguns and pistols, the two federal agents swiftly left without seizing the property. Violence was avoided when, on August 26, 1863, Barron, Forbes

Company sold the property—for $1.75 million—to American owners, who named the new operation New Almaden Quicksilver Company. If the federal government had used force to seize the land, the incident could have easily tipped California and Nevada to the Confederate cause, perhaps changing the outcome of the Civil War.

In 1870, James B. Randol, an authoritarian boss, began what would become a 20-year rule of New Almaden. He controlled the company town rigidly, laying down strict rules for the miners. Two smaller communities sprang up in the hills near

© MARTIN CHEEK

Casa Grande, in New Almaden

the mine entrances. Spanishtown was made up of Mexican laborers called *tanteros,* who hauled ore up the shafts in burlap bags. They made from 20 to 30 trips up a day, carrying as much as 200 pounds a load. Englishtown, which had actually begun in the 1860s, was home to a colony of Cornish men and their families, former workers in Britain's tin mines who had come to New Almaden during an economic depression in England.

The hard work and inhalation of mercury and sulfur fumes caused many of the mine's workers severe health problems. By 1912, the market for mercury had all but died, and the mines closed after the company went bankrupt.

The bustling mercury mining industry lives on only in memory. More than 100 miles of tunnels—some as deep as 2,500 feet—catacomb the hills in Almaden Quicksilver County Park. For safety reasons, these are closed to the public. Roads once used to transport cinnabar to the reduction works still traverse the park, and hikers and joggers often follow these winding trails through oak woodlands, chaparral, and placid grassland. The Mine Hill Trail provides a good overlook of Guadalupe Reservoir.

Also in the park, you'll see a three-story, 27-room Italianate house. This is Casa Grande, which the company built for its manager, Halleck, in appreciation for the mines' prosperity. The house now serves, in part, as an informative local history museum, and a small theater in the building also packs in audiences as the home of the New Almaden Opry House, a local melodrama company.

There are three access points to Almaden Quicksilver County Park. The McAbee entrance is at the north end. Turn south off Camden Ave. on McAbee Rd. and follow the road to its end at a small dairy. For the Mockingbird Hill entrance, take the Almaden Expwy. exit from Hwy. 85 and drive south to Almaden Road. About half a mile down Almaden Rd., turn right on Mockingbird Hill Ln. and drive to the parking area. For the Hacienda entrance, continue along Almaden Rd. through the small town of New Almaden, and park in the unpaved lot on the right side of the road.

Parking and admission are free. Open 8 A.M.–sunset; available activities include horseshoes, horseback riding, catch-and-release fishing, and hiking on 29 miles of trails. New Almaden Historical Museum is open Fri.–Sun. 10 A.M.–4 P.M., admission free. For more information, call 408/268-8220, or visit website claraweb.co.santa-clara.ca.us/parks.

HIS HISTORIC, ROGUISH HONOR
THOMAS FALLON

On the northern edge of downtown San Jose's San Pedro Square, at 175 St. John St., stands a graceful Italianate home. The house once belonged to Thomas Fallon, the region's most controversial historic figure. Pictures of him depict a devilishly good-looking man with thick, curly dark hair, a mustache, and the 19th-century equivalent of a goatee.

The dynamic Fallon continues to elicit a mixture of reactions in Silicon Valley. For years, an $820,000 equestrian statue of him has sat boxed up in an Oakland warehouse, the city's politicians too afraid to display it publicly. They feared offending the city's Hispanic population by honoring Fallon—whose treatment of the city's Mexican inhabitants during the Mexican-American conflict in the late 1840s wasn't exactly politically correct.

Fallon was born in Ireland in 1825 and sent as a boy to a town on Canada's eastern seaboard. There, he started an apprenticeship in the trade of saddle making. At the age of 18, the quest for adventure took him to Texas. In 1844, he met explorer John C. Frémont and marched with him to the Pacific, arriving in the spring at what is now Santa Cruz. He settled here to begin a business making ornate Mexican saddles.

In June 1846, the high-strung Fallon heard about the Bear Flag Revolt and, awarding himself the title of captain, raised a troop of 22 volunteers to join the American revolution for control of California. He and his men crossed the Santa Cruz Mountains and entered San Jose on July 11 to find it virtually unprotected. Encountering little resistance from the city's inhabitants, he took the pueblo *juzgado,* the Mexican government house on the plaza's northern end. Commander Sloat, commander-in-chief of the U.S. Navy in San Francisco Bay, sent Fallon an American flag, which he raised on the *juzgado*'s 25-foot pole, an aggressive signal that the Americans had taken control of Mexico's San Jose territory. Although Fallon was lauded in his time as a man of "courage and distinction," he somehow managed to avoid any real confrontation with Mexico's soldiers.

In 1848, the socially ambitious Fallon married Carmelita Lodge, the beautiful daughter of one of the region's largest landowners. That year, he made a small fortune in the goldfields, then returned to make his home in Santa Cruz. He built a large frame house that served as a store and hotel. But he got restless and moved his family back to Texas for two years. After three of his children died there, he returned to California and began to buy land around San Jose, growing wealthy from real estate ventures. Off San Pedro Square, he built his 15-room home, which, with its surrounding formal gardens, was one of the town's finest houses. In 1859, he served a term as mayor of the city.

Fallon was notorious for having an eye for women. One day, his wife

Mayor Thomas Fallon House

came home to find him in a compromising position with Annie, their Irish servant. Carmelita picked up the fireplace poker and began to beat the pair with it. The next day, she took the children to San Francisco and filed for divorce. Fallon married again but, after a second divorce, left San Jose for good, moving to San Francisco. He died there in 1885 at the age of 60.

After his departure, the house remained vacant for several years. It became a kindergarten for a short time and a boardinghouse in 1894. In the 20th century, the house began slowly decaying. The cellar became an Italian restaurant and bar that proved popular with San Jose State University students in the 1980s. In the 1990s, the house underwent a major renovation, restoring it to the splendor of its past. It is run now by the San Jose Historical Museum, and docents regularly provide tours, telling tales about the intriguing man who once lived in it.

1797 and is the centerpiece of a small historic park depicting daily life during California's early Spanish and Mexican period. Across the street from the adobe is the renovated Thomas Fallon House and gardens, a finely crafted 1855 building filled with Victorian treasures. The building was originally the home of Thomas Fallon, a San Jose mayor who has gone down in local history as one of its most colorful figures (another San Jose mayor, Thomas McEnery, even wrote a historical novel about Fallon). A historical museum in the basement traces the area's past, and a diverse gift shop in a side building sells local books and souvenirs.

184 W. St. John St. (off downtown's San Pedro Square on the corner of San Pedro St.), 408/993-8182, website: www.serve.com/sjhistory; parking on street and in nearby city lots; admission: adults $6, seniors $5, youths $4, children under 6 free; open Tues.–Sun. noon–5 P.M. (last tour starts at 3:30 P.M.).

Hayes Mansion

Built in 1905 by the wealthy Hayes family, one-time owners of the *San Jose Mercury News,* this 60-room Mediterranean-style mansion covering 41,000 square feet is an elegant Edenvale home designed by noted architect George Page. Among its many distinguished guests, Teddy Roosevelt, William McKinley, and Herbert Hoover visited the socially prominent family. In the 1950s, when the Hayes family no longer owned it, the man-

sion decayed to the point where it had an ivy-grown haunted house look. But in 1994, the historic landmark was restored and now serves as the Hayes Conference Center, a superb meeting facility for Silicon Valley businesses.

200 Edenvale Ave. (off Monterey Rd.), 408/226-3200, website: www.hayesconference-center.com; free parking; admission free; open 24 hours a day.

St. Joseph Cathedral

The awe-inspiring Italian-style dome of St. Joseph Cathedral makes it a downtown jewel. To replace the previous church that burned down, this magnificent basilica was built in 1876, designed by architect Bryan J. Clinch. In the early 1990s, it underwent a $20 million restoration after years of earthquakes, storms, and inadequate attempts at remodeling had taken their toll. The first church was established here in 1803, making it San Jose's oldest site of Christian worship and California's oldest parish. Whatever religious beliefs a visitor might hold, he or she is warmly welcome to come inside the historic cathedral and see the stunning religious artwork inside. Its majestic dome rises 70 feet over the elegant center altar. Paintings and sculptures of religious figures fill every nook and crevice. The Cathedral Performance series raises money for parish projects with concerts and dance recitals. A gift shop is located next to the cathedral.

Corner of S. Market and San Fernando Sts. (across from the San Jose Art Museum), 408/283-8100, website: www.stjosephcathedral.org; parking on street or in city lot; admission free; tours by appointment; open weekdays 7 A.M.–5 P.M., weekends 8 A.M.–8 P.M.

Oak Hill Memorial Park

Established in 1839, California's oldest secular cemetery is the final resting place for many of the valley's pioneers. Its who's-who list includes such historic figures as "Mountain Charley" McKiernan, winegrower Paul Masson, the Reed family (Donner Party survivors), and Dr. John Townsend, who, as a member of the Murphy-Townsend-Stevens Party, was the first graduate doctor to reach California. Ask at the front office for a map pointing out the grave sites of various celebrated pioneers among the well-tended grounds.

300 Curtner Ave. (corner of Monterey Rd.), 408/297-2447; open daily 8 A.M.–dusk.

PARKS AND GARDENS

Most of these county and city parks are open from 8 A.M. to sunset. City gardens generally are open from 10 A.M.–sunset. Several of the more popular parks charge weekend parking fees of about $4–5, but most are free.

Don Edwards San Francisco Bay National Wildlife Refuge

A series of trails meander among the tidal marshes of this refuge, where a wide variety of birds make their seasonal homes. The entire refuge encompasses a large area, stretching as far north as Union City. Its Environmental Education Center in Alviso contains a small museum with a number of kid-oriented, hands-on exhibits. Volunteers provide walks along levees on weekends, educating visitors on marshland ecology and the center's butterfly garden.

Off Grand Blvd. (from I-880 or U.S. 101, take Hwy. 237 toward Alviso; turn north on Zanker Rd., continue two miles to Grand Blvd., turn right at this dirt road, and follow it to the visitor's center), 408/262-5513; the cen-

ter is open weekends 10 A.M.–5 P.M. and weekdays by appointment; activities: hiking, bird-watching, biking.

Joseph D. Grant County Park

The winding road leading to Lick Observatory on Mt. Hamilton passes through a secluded valley deep in the Diablo Range. Halls Valley is the location of Grant Park, at 9,522 acres one of the largest of Santa Clara County's parks. It was named after Joseph D. Grant, the owner of a cattle ranch who deeded much of the land for preservation. Grant's invited guests on the property included Herbert Hoover, who spent a month here after losing to FDR. The park includes pristine oak woodland, a lake, small ponds, and grasslands. It has also served as a preserve for tule elk. The best season to visit the park is spring, when the wildflowers burst with color.

Off Mt. Hamilton Rd. (from U.S. 101 or I-680, take Alum Rock Ave. exit and drive east; turn right on Mt. Hamilton Rd. and drive up the steep road for eight miles), 408/274-6121, website: claraweb.co.santa-clara.ca.us/parks; activities: camping, amphitheater, horseback riding, biking, fishing, observatory, hiking (40 miles of trails).

Hellyer County Park and Coyote Creek Parkway

The 223-acre Hellyer County Park marks the beginning of the Coyote Creek Parkway, a long trail meandering through the foothills of the Diablo Range foothills and ending at Anderson Lake in Morgan Hill. For speed-racing bikers, Hellyer Park contains an Olympic-sized velodrome built as a training facility for U.S. athletes competing in the 1962 Pan American Games. The park's popular Cottonwood Lake is stocked with rainbow trout. The Coyote Creek Parkway is a relaxing, relatively flat trail roughly paralleling U.S. 101. It passes through marshlands bordering the creek, where waterfowl such as great blue heron live. Near the southern end of the parkway is an asphalt runway area for radio-controlled model airplanes.

Off Hellyer Ave. (from U.S. 101 in south San Jose, take Hellyer Ave. west to Hellyer Park; access

SAN JOSE'S LOVELY ANSWER TO CENTRAL PARK

It's still in development, but there's a lot to see and do at the new 400-acre Guadalupe River Park and Gardens, located in downtown San Jose, under the flight path of San Jose International Airport. Paved bike and walking paths meander through the $338 million park, which stretches three miles along the Guadalupe River. Situated between I-280 and I-880, this is Silicon Valley's answer to Central Park.

Start at Arena Green on the corner of Autumn St. and The Alameda, across from the San Jose Arena. The "Five Skaters" columns stand beside a small, cement "ice rink," symbolizing the ice hockey and figure skating tradition steadily developing in San Jose. Another highlight here is the old-fashioned carousel with its menagerie of 38 animals, including five representing indigenous inhabitants of the river. At the nearby visitor center, you can obtain information about the park wildlife and activities. During the spring, park rangers provide interpretive walks.

South of Arena Green is Discovery Meadow, where you can stroll near the lavender architectural fantasy of the Children's Discovery Museum. Various sculptures given as gifts by San Jose's sister cities dot the riverscape here, including, near the Center for the Performing Arts, the statue of a "monkey boy" relating a Japanese children's story. Near this statue stand poles holding white flags that fly in honor of veterans of war. Off Julian St. and still being developed is the River Street Historic District. This collection of historic Italian homes of early-20th-century architecture will eventually house restaurants, art galleries, and specialty stores.

At the northern end of the park near the Taylor St. entrance is the Columbus Park sports field and a series of small gardens that make excellent places for sunny-day visits. Called Coleman Loop because of its proximity to Coleman Ave., this area once held 600 homes that the city of San Jose removed due to airport noise. The land lay vacant until the early 1990s, when work began on this area of the park. Low-maintenance, drought-tolerant California native plants grow in the Rock Garden, their colors vividly displayed during the spring months. Nearby is the Heritage Rose Garden, the city's second public rose garden, which more than 750 volunteer gardeners planted in 1995. Its 4,000 different varieties, blooming from mid-April through fall, makes it one of the world's foremost rose gardens.

When you long for a change from roses, you can stroll over to the nearby Courtyard Garden. Here grows an abundance of annual and perennial flowers, including evening primrose, basket-of-gold, and California poppies. To get a glimpse of what the region might have been like when it was still considered the Valley of Heart's Delight, stroll over to the 3.3-acre Historic Orchard, with its more than 60 varieties of fruit trees reminding visitors of the once abundant crops that spread their blossoming branches across the valley. Here, you can wander in the shade of Moorpark apricots, Bing cherries, Mission figs, and Italian and French prunes.

In downtown San Jose, the park parallels Hwy. 87 north of I-280. Take San Carlos St. for Discovery Meadow, Santa Clara St. for Arena Green, and Taylor St. for Columbus Park and the gardens. Open 8 A.M. to a half hour after sunset. The visitor center, 408/277-5904, is open daily 11 A.M.–5 P.M.

CITIES OF THE VALLEY

Coyote Creek Parkway at the U.S. 101 exits on Blossom Hill Rd. and Bernal Rd. about a quarter mile from the highway), 408/225-0225, website: claraweb.co.santa-clara.ca.us/parks; activities: horseshoes, volleyball, fishing, playground, amphitheater, biking, hiking (15 miles of trails).

Calero County Park

The highlight of this 2,421-acre park is the large Calero Reservoir, which draws visitors for sailing, power boating, water-skiing, personal watercraft riding, and fishing. Hikers and horseback riders also enjoy the trails that wind through the oak woodland and grasslands of the Santa Cruz Mountain foothills. Bird-watchers come to Calero to spot predatory birds, including golden eagles, osprey, red-tailed hawks, and black-shouldered kites. The county plans to renovate the historic Bailey Fellows House, an Italianate Victorian at the south end of the reservoir, into a visitor center and museum.

Off McKean Rd. (on Hwy. 85 in south San Jose, take Almaden Expwy. exit, drive south and turn right on Harry Rd.; turn left on McKean Rd. and drive three miles), 408/268-3883, website: claraweb.co.santa-clara.ca.us/parks; activities: catch-and-release fishing, boating, horseback riding, hiking (12 miles of trails).

Alum Rock Park

From 1890 to the 1960s, Alum Rock Park was popular with visitors who came for its world-famous spa of 27 hot mineral springs. The springs still exist, the rotten egg stench of sulfur lingering around them. But the festive spa atmosphere is gone, replaced by a more sedate setting of oak-shaded nature trails through canyons and lookout points. In spring, California poppies and other wildflowers add a dash of gold to this 720-acre park. The nearby Alum Rock Stables, 408/251-8800, hires out horses to ride on the park's trails.

16235 Alum Rock Ave. (from U.S. 101 or I-680, take Alum Rock Ave. exit and drive east up the foothills to park entrance), 408/259-5477; parking fee; activities: Youth Science Institute, biking, horseback riding, playground, hiking (13 miles of trails).

Almaden Lake Park

Almaden Lake was created from the remains of a rock quarry. Run by the city of San Jose, the 65-acre park is especially popular with families during the hot summer months. A large sandy beach borders a lifeguarded swim area.

6445 Coleman Ave. (from Hwy. 85 in south San Jose, take Almaden Expwy. to Coleman Ave.), 408/277-2757; activities: nonpowered boats under 16 feet, paddle boats, volleyball, horseshoes, fishing, windsurfing, swimming, hiking (3.9-mile Los Alamitos Creek Trail leads to Santa Teresa County Park).

Santa Teresa County Park

From March through June, wildflowers create a kaleidoscope of color at this 1,688-acre park set in the Santa Teresa Hills bordering San Jose's Almaden Valley. In summer and fall, the dry grass turns the rolling hills bronze. A good view of Silicon Valley as well as South Valley can be taken in from Coyote Peak's 1,155-foot elevation. Visitors might chance to encounter coyotes, bobcats, and black-tailed deer. The park's land was once part of the Rancho de Santa Teresa owned by Joaquin Bernal, an important Mexican-era settler of the valley.

Off Bernal Rd. (from U.S. 101 or Hwy. 85 in south San Jose, take the Bernal Rd. exit and drive west to park entrance), 408/225-0225, website: claraweb.co.santa-clara.ca.us/parks; activities: archery range, volleyball, biking, horseback riding, golfing, hiking (14 miles of trails).

Lake Cunningham Regional Park

Water fun is the main attraction at this popular 200-acre park in San Jose's Eastside district. You can rent a paddleboat, canoe, or sailboat to journey out on the 50-acre lake. The park is a haven for birds, including snowy white egrets and white pelicans. Also at Lake Cunningham is Raging Waters, a water theme park with slides and pools to cool off in during hot summer days.

2305 S. White Rd. (from U.S. 101, take Tully Rd. exit, drive east, and turn left on S. White Rd.), 408/277-4319; parking fee charged; activities: nonpowered boats, wind-

THE LEGEND OF SANTA TERESA

Follow a winding trail through the chaparral of Santa Teresa County Park and, if you know where to look, you'll eventually discover a cool grotto where a natural spring flows out of a rock. About 800 gallons per hour flow out of the site, filling a small pond. The spring has flowed for centuries. This is an enchanted place of healing, or so goes the story told by the Ohlone Indians.

Long before the white people entered the valley, an Indian tribe lived peacefully in this location of rolling hills and shrubland. But a plague hit the village and many of its people died from the sickness. The ancient medicine and rituals did not cure the sick, and the villagers continued to grow weak and die.

The tribal chief called the remaining members together and met at a rock one night under a full moon. There was much discussion and debate about what to do, but no one could come up with a solution to end the plague. Finally, the chief stood up with his bow and put an arrow with eagle feathers on the quiver. He said a prayer asking the gods for help, and shot the arrow up toward the stars.

Soon after, the vision took place. All the tribe saw floating near the rock a beautiful woman clothed in a black, flowing robe. She was lit by a mysterious light. The frightened Ohlones bowed down before the woman, but she told them to rise. Out of her robe, she pulled out a silver cross and touched the rock with it. A thunderbolt filled the air and the rock split. From the crevice poured clear water and formed a small pond. The woman told the tribe to drink and bathe in the water and they would be cured. Then she vanished just as mysteriously as she had appeared. When the Indians took their sick to the pond and drank from its waters, they discovered the sickness quickly left their bodies. The water indeed healed them.

When Joaquin Bernal received the land grant here, he heard the Ohlone's story of the mysterious woman and the healing water. To the faithful Catholic, the story sounded similar to one attributed to St. Teresa, and so he named his property Santa Teresa in honor of the legend. In the grotto, he set up a statue of the Madonna to pay homage to the legend. Some Silicon Valley locals still say that, if you look closely at the rock, you can make out the image of a woman in a black robe with her arms stretched out as if in worship. People still venture to the natural spring, perhaps hoping for a cure, or just to enjoy the serenity of the site.

CITIES OF THE VALLEY

surfing, fishing, horseshoes, volleyball, playground, one-mile par course.

Motorcycle County Park

This unique 442-acre recreational area along Coyote Valley is the Santa Clara County park system's only off-road vehicle site. It provides 15 miles of dirt trails for beginning, intermediate, and expert motorcycle and ATV riders. It also has motocross and quarter midget tracks. Daily fees are $5 per off-highway vehicle.

Off Metcalf Rd. (from U.S. 101 or Hwy. 85 in south San Jose, take Bernal Rd. exit, then take Monterey Hwy. south to Metcalf Rd.; turn left and drive up Metcalf Rd. 2.5 miles to park entrance), 408/226-5223, website: claraweb.co.santa-clara.ca.us/parks; activities: motorcycles, ATVs.

Emma Prusch Farm

Some of Santa Clara Valley's farming heritage can still be discovered at parks throughout the area. The Emma Prusch Farm close to downtown San Jose is one of them. Situated where I-680, I-280 and U.S. 101 intersect, this 47-acre park was deeded to the city under the stipulation it would always be run as a farm. Here, you'll see an original 19th-century farmhouse, step into the "third largest barn in California," and wander among cows, sheep, pigs, and other farm critters. Kids can play by the farm's pond and get to know the resident chickens, peacocks, geese, and ducks. Large vegetable gardens invite leisurely strolling; one garden features plants from international locations such as Africa, Asia, and Central America. There's also a fruit orchard showcasing 100 varieties of rare fruit from all over the world.

647 S. King Rd. (from U.S. 101, take Story Rd. exit east to King Rd. and turn left), 408/926-5555.

Overfelt Botanical Gardens

This serene 33-acre garden is a favorite afternoon retreat for Eastside San Jose residents and visitors. It's a perfect place for a walk beside babbling brooks or for contemplation by peaceful fishponds. The garden's eastern side contains the Chinese Cultural Garden, which features several gifts from the People's Republic of China, including a 30-foot bronze and marble statue of Confucius overlooking a reflecting pool and an ornamental Friendship Gate.

2145 McKee Rd. (from I-880, take McKee Rd. east to Education Park Dr.), 408/251-3323.

San Jose Municipal Rose Garden

This 5.5-acre park is a small gem for rose lovers and gives the Rose Garden district its name. Since its dedication on April 7, 1931, the garden has attracted thousands of visitors every year, who come to see the blooms between Apr. and November. More than 4,000 rosebushes grow in the park, showing off the beauty of 189 shrub varieties.

Dana Ave. (from I-880, take Bascom Ave. exit and head south to Naglee Ave.; turn left and drive to Dana Ave.), 408/277-2757.

Japanese Friendship Garden

As you watch the red and gold koi swim lazily in the ponds surrounded by ornate sculptures and footbridges, this happy garden will make you think you're in the Land of the Rising Sun. Located in San Jose's Kelley Park, the Japanese Friendship Garden was a gift from the people of Okayama, Japan, and follows the design of that sister city's Korakuen Park. The halcyon garden with its winding paths and water fountains is a favorite spot of Silicon Valley photographers.

1300 Senter Rd. (at Kelley Park, across the street from Municipal Stadium), 408/277-5254.

Happy Hollow

This family-oriented playground and zoo is suitable for kids under 12. Youngsters can monkey around in a tree house, explore a riverboat replica, and enjoy various rides with fairy-tale themes. But it's the petting zoo that families really come here for. It contains more than 150 animals, including such barnyard creatures as goats, chickens, and ducks. Other creatures that can be safely observed include lemurs, a pygmy hippo, and a jaguar. A walk through the aviary allows kids to observe feathered friends closely. During the Christmas season, the park holds a special feeding of the animals called Feast for the Beasts. A locally renowned puppet show is presented at the park's theater several times a day. Expect to spend at least two hours at the park.

1300 Senter Rd. in Kelley Park (across from Municipal Stadium), 408/252-3488; general admission $4.50 for ages 2 and up.

ACTIVITIES

Golf Courses

San Jose Municipal Golf Course is a well-maintained, 18-hole course with a flat layout that's ideal for beginning golfers trying to develop their skills.

1560 Oakland Rd. (off Brokow Rd.), 408/441-4653; par 72; greens fees $26–35.

Santa Teresa Golf Course is set in the south San Jose foothills near IBM's research center. Built in 1963, this course was designed by George Santana. It can get a little muddy after rainstorms but is a popular Silicon Valley public course.

260 Bernal Rd. (near Santa Teresa County Park), 408/225-2650; par 71; greens fees $26–41.

San Jose State University Aquatic Center

The general public as well as students come to this immense pool next to SJSU's Event Center for lap and recreational swimming as well as diving in the deep end. It's occasionally closed to the public for water polo games and swim meets.

SJSU campus, 8th St. (between San Salvador and San Carlos Sts.), 408/924-6341, website: www.union.sjsu.edu/Aquatic_Center;   open

Mon.–Fri. 7 A.M.–8 P.M., weekends 1–5 P.M.; admission $2–4 (free to SJSU students with I.D.)

Ice Centre of San Jose

Young fans of the San Jose Sharks NHL team can watch their favorite athletes practice here—the team often trains at this large facility near San Jose's Municipal Stadium. The center has three rinks, one always open for public skating. Weekday nights the rinks can sometimes get crowded, but generally there's plenty of room for graceful figure eights. The center offers figure skating and ice hockey lessons, along with a sports shop selling skating apparel and hockey supplies for budding Wayne Gretzkys. The Pacific Hockey League, 408/293-2087, whose participants include Sun Microsystems CEO Scott McNealy, often practices and plays games here.

1500 S. 10th St. (at Alma Ave.), 408/279-6000, website: www.icecentresj.com; admission: kids under 12 $5, 13 and older $6, skate rentals $3; call for session times.

Bamboola

Designed for children up to the age of 12, Bamboola is an entertainment and learning center where families can enjoy "play to learn" activities in a secure environment. Children can explore a three-story soft playground, a pretend village, a giant maze, and a rock-climbing area with caves and tunnels. They can also dress up in fancy costumes, paint their faces, and dig for "dinosaur fossils" in a giant interactive sandbox. Clowns entertain with puppets, songs, games, and balloon art. During the summer months when school is out, this place can quickly fill up with children.

5401 Camden Ave. (about half a mile south from Hwy. 85 on the right), 408/448-4386, website: www.bamboola.com; open Tues. 10 A.M.–5 P.M., Wed.–Sat. 10 A.M.–9 P.M., Sun. 10 A.M.–6 P.M.; admission: adults and kids under 1 year are free; ages 1–2 $4.95; ages 2–12 $9.95.

Raging Waters

This is Silicon Valley's only water theme park. The 14-acre site is home to more than 30 water attractions, including swimming and diving pools, twisting-turning waterslides, a Polynesian lagoon, and a children's play area. There's even a large sandy beach for catching some rays.

Lake Cunningham Regional Park (off Capitol Expwy. at Tully Rd.), 408/270-8000; general admission: $24.95 (or $19.99 after 3 P.M.), under 48 inches tall $19.99 (or $15.99 after 3 P.M.), over age 55 $15, under age 2 free; parking fee $2; open daily 10 A.M.–7 P.M. mid-June through Labor Day; Sat.–Sun. 10 A.M.–6 P.M. day after Labor Day to mid-September.

SHOPPING

Malls

San Jose has three major indoor malls, where you can find shops from specialized boutiques to nationally recognized department stores. In the Eastside, the two-story **Eastridge Shopping Center** is the city's largest mall, with a Sears, JCPenney, and Macy's as its anchors. Its Eastridge Ice Arena, 408/238-0440, is a good rink for children.

Corner of Tully Rd. and Capital Expwy. (near Reid-Hillview Municipal Airport), 408/238-3600; open Mon.–Fri. 10 A.M.–9 P.M., Sat. 10 A.M.–8 P.M., Sun. 11 A.M.–6 P.M.

In south San Jose, **Oakridge Mall** features stores such as Macy's and Sears. It's also the site of movie complex Oakridge 6 AMC Theater, 408/227-6660, and the Oakridge Lanes bowling alley, 408/578-8500.

Corner of Blossom Hill and Santa Teresa Blvd. (just off Hwy. 85), 408/578-2910; open Mon.–Sat. 10 A.M.–9 P.M., Sun. 11 A.M.–6 P.M.

Westgate Mall is an excellent stop for ski and outdoor enthusiasts, with the exceptionally well-stocked Any Mountain store (look for the mountain facade outside).

1600 Saratoga Ave. (on the San Jose side of Saratoga's northeast corner), 408/379-9350; open Mon.–Fri. 10 A.M.–9 P.M., Sat. 10 A.M.–7 P.M., Sun. 11 A.M.–6 P.M.

San Jose Flea Market

Crowning itself "the world's largest flea market," with more than 2,000 sellers and eight miles of alleys, it's definitely a contender for that title since its opening in 1960. With its carnival-like ambience, this is a great place to spend a day browsing for collectibles and antiques as well as that odd item you didn't think you needed until you set eyes on it. Besides other people's used goods, it also includes shops with new discount merchandise. Its shaded Produce Row is a quarter-mile-long series of vendors selling fruits and vegetables from around the world. A carousel provides rides for the kids. Special annual events include an Oktoberfest and a Salsa Festival, where people can taste homemade salsa.

1590 Berryessa Rd. (from I-680, take Berryessa exit and drive west about one mile to parking lot), 408/453-1110, website: www.sjfm.com; open Wed.–Sun. dawn to dusk; admission free; weekday parking $1, weekend parking $5.

Farmers' Markets
In the Cambrian Park district, a small farmers' market, 800/806-3276, is held every Sun. 10 A.M.–2 P.M. at the Princeton Plaza Mall parking lot at Kooser Rd. and Meridian Avenue. In Japantown near the Civic Center, a farmers' market, 408/298-4303, is held every Sun. 8:30 A.M.–noon on Jackson St. between 7th and 8th Streets.

ENTERTAINMENT
San Jose's entertainment scene is Silicon Valley's liveliest. Theater, dance, symphonic concerts, sports, and movies provide something for every taste. The city's downtown area has several major venues that play host throughout the year to concerts, dramatic performances, and sporting events. The **Montgomery Theatre,** 408/277-3900, seats 537 people and is located next to Civic Auditorium at W. San Carlos and S. Market Sts. (near Plaza de César Chávez). The **San Jose Center for the Performing Arts,** 408/277-5277, is located at the corner of W. San Carlos St. and Almaden Blvd. (near Discovery Meadow). The **San Jose Arena,** 408/287-9200, is located at Santa Clara and Autumn Sts. (between Hwy. 87 and Caltrain tracks). The **SJSU Event Center,** 408/924-6360, is located on the campus at S. 7th and San Carlos Streets.

© MARTIN CHEEK

the striking San Jose Repertory Theatre

San Jose Repertory Theatre
Established in 1980, "The Rep" has become Silicon Valley's most prestigious professional theater company. In 1998, it moved into its new downtown San Jose theater, a controversial blue sheet-metal construction some locals have compared to a large barn. But regardless of the building's architecture, the group performs both comic and dramatic productions to sell-out crowds. It occasionally does world premieres, such as Holly Near's *Fire in the Rain . . . Singer in the Storm.* Six plays are performed in a season lasting Sept.–June.

101 Paseo de San Antonio (between 2nd and 3rd Sts.), 408/291-2266, website: www.sjrep.com; parking in nearby public lots; individual tickets $17–37, season tickets also available.

San Jose Children's Musical Theater
Local youngsters from ages 6 to 20 get a chance to shine in the spotlight through this unique nonprofit group, which focuses on helping children and young adults discover theatrical magic.

Whatever their ethnic, social, or economic group, every child who auditions is cast. Actress Teri Hatcher is among its alumni who have gone on to careers in show business. Besides children-oriented shows such as *The King and I* and *The Wizard of Oz,* the young performers also are often cast in more adult-themed musicals such as *A Chorus Line.*

Montgomery Theatre (also in Santa Clara's Louis B. Mayer Theatre), 408/288-5437, website: www.sjcmt.com; parking in public lots; individual tickets $6–15, season tickets (six shows) also available.

Lyric Theatre

If you're in the mood to be "the very model of a modern major general," the Lyric Theatre is your ticket. Operated by the Gilbert and Sullivan Society of San Jose, this group of more than 150 volunteers is known for putting on fun, disarming theater performances by the masters of English light opera. In recent years, the theater has also branched out in its repertoire of comic operas, offering works by Offenbach such as *Orpheus in the Underworld,* as well as English translations of Strauss's *Die Fledermaus* and Donizetti's *Il Camponello.* After each performance, the cast comes out into the lobby to chat with audience members.

Montgomery Theatre, 408/735-7292, website: www.lyrictheatre.org; individual tickets $20, seniors and students $16.

American Musical Theatre

Established in 1934, this dynamic Silicon Valley–based theater company brings four hit Broadway musicals to San Jose every season, running Oct.–May. Its high-quality talent and fantastic show sets have made it Northern California's largest subscription professional theater company. Past performances have included *Big River* and *La Cage Aux Folles.* It also occasionally performs West Coast musical premieres, such as *Hot Mikado.*

San Jose Center for the Performing Arts, 408/453-7108, website: www.amtsj.org; individual tickets $40–60, season tickets (four shows) also available.

San Jose Stage Company

Performing in its own intimate 200-seat theater, this midsized professional company in the middle of San Jose's SoFA district produces five contemporary and classical plays in its Oct.–July season. Every alternate season, a summer musical is added. The company's philosophy is to provide a mixture of classics with new works exploring contemporary themes. It also performs West Coast premieres. Past performances included the stunning *Defying Gravity* by Bay Area playwright Jane Anderson, whose drama explores the human impact of the Space Shuttle Challenger accident.

The Stage, 490 S. 1st St. (at William St.), 408/283-7142, website: www.sanjose-stage.com; parking in public lots; individual tickets $16–30, season subscription (five plays) also available.

City Lights Theater Company

Besides lively plays such as *Rosencrantz and Guildenstern are Dead* and *Hair,* Silicon Valley's well-respected alternative theater company tries to stay on the cutting edge with its daring choices of adult-themed plays. Past performances have delved into the realms of nudity, lesbianism, and—perhaps reflecting the Donner Party's connection to San Jose—cannibalism. City Lights puts on five dramatic shows a year as well as occasional musicals.

529 S. 2nd St. (the pink and purple building between Reed and William Sts.), 408/295-4200, website: www.cltc.org; parking on street; individual tickets $15–20, season tickets (five or three shows) also available.

Teatro Vision

Highlighting Latino-Chicano actors, playwrights, and directors, this company performs its three shows a year in the English language. Past plays have included *The House on Mango Street.*

Mexican Heritage Plaza Theater, 1700 Alum Rock Ave., 408/272-9926, website: www.teatrovision.org; individual tickets $8–17 ($25 for galas).

Northside Theatre Company

Performing in its own community center theater in a neighborhood just east of downtown,

OPERA SAN JOSÉ

Opera San José aims to take the stuffiness out of opera and make it a form of entertainment everyone can enjoy. Started by Irene Dalis, a San Jose–born diva, the professional company has been enchanting Silicon Valley audiences since 1981.

Dalis's singing talents brought her major international opera stardom. She sang as a principal artist in New York's Metropolitan Opera for 20 consecutive seasons. When she retired from the Met in 1977, she returned to Silicon Valley and started an opera workshop at San Jose State University. That workshop evolved into what is now Opera San José. Singers give more than 200 performances a year, 44 of them full performances of four productions (the rest are educational and community performances—the company boasts one of the largest educational outreach programs in California, designed to take opera into schools).

Past productions have included such classical works as Mozart's *The Magic Flute* and Rossini's *Il Turco in Italia*. Showing a cutting edge of its own, the company has also performed an operatic version

of John Steinbeck's novel *Of Mice and Men* composed by Carlisle Floyd. Bringing opera to the masses, its artists regularly perform in such venues as the San Jose Art Museum and in outdoor park settings such as the Plaza de César Chávez.

The company is unique in America in that it's the only one with a "resident ensemble" program. Instead of simply being chosen for one opera show, performers are interviewed and hired to work on a series of productions for at least one season. This policy helps create a dynamic chemistry in performances. Opera San José was also among the first in the nation to include supertitles over the stage to translate the lyrics, thus opening the opera story to a wider audience. And with the eventual renovation of the Fox Theatre in downtown's SoFA district, Opera San José will get a new home.

Montgomery Theatre (corner of San Carlos and Market Sts.), 408/437-4450, website: www.operasj.org; season runs Sept.–May; individual tickets $40–54, season tickets (four productions) also available.

---

this company showcases some of Silicon Valley's best emerging drama talent. A favorite yearly Silicon Valley tradition during the holidays is the theater company's haunting version of Charles Dickens's *A Christmas Carol*.

848 E. William St. (across the bridge from William St. Park), 408/288-7820, website: www.northsidetheatre.com; parking free; individual tickets $8–10, season tickets (five plays) $42–52.

Melodramas

The "locally world-famous" **Big Lil's Barbary Coast Dinner Theater** offers audiences old-fashioned melodramas where the squeaky clean hero is guaranteed to always outwit the villain with the pencil-thin mustache. The theater is decorated with hand-painted murals of San Francisco's Barbary Coast, as well as crystal chandeliers. The show includes ragtime piano songs,

dances, and tawdry vaudeville skits. Audience participation is always encouraged.

157 W. San Fernando St. (between Almaden Blvd. and Market St.), 408/295-7469; street parking free after 6 P.M., garage across from theater; Fri. and Sat. dinner starts at 7 P.M., performance at 8 P.M.

Los Lupeños de San Jose

Since 1969, this San Jose–based nonprofit company has locally performed graceful Mexican regional and religious dance wearing traditional costumes. The dancers are accompanied by singing musicians playing violins, guitars, and *jaranas*. The group also has a dance and cultural school where children from age 5 and adults learn the fancy footwork of Mexican dance forms.

Various venues throughout Silicon Valley, studios at 42 Race St. (where The Alameda curves), 408/292-0443; ticket prices vary.

THE WEST'S OLDEST SYMPHONY

The San Jose Symphony is the oldest orchestra west of the Mississippi—and one of the nation's best. It boasts roots among the valley's German population and dates back to the formation of the San Jose Germania Verein (a social club) in 1865. The Verein's musically inclined members often gave informal concerts at which they performed classical works. Later, the group purchased Professor Frank Loui King's Conservatory of Music, on N. 2nd St., one block north of St. James Park, giving the musicians a hall seating 500 in which to perform. (King had come to San Jose to head the music department at the city's University of the Pacific). Renamed Germania Hall, this building still stands—though today it serves as a German restaurant.

Classical music concerts were an important part of the cultural life of this region, and the local group of amateur musicians developed a wide esteem. A famous photograph of the members, taken around 1892, shows all the members sitting together wearing formal suits. But the photo is much more remarkable than it seems at first. Only one tuxedo was available, so the various members were photographed separately (including one sick member, whose image the photographer captured by going to his house), each changing into the tuxedo

in turn, and—long before the days of Adobe PhotoShop—seamlessly montaged together.

The symphony barely survived the early days of the Great Depression, but by the end of the 1930s, it had 76 members and was conducted by William Van den Borg. In the 1950s, it started to achieve semiprofessional status when Stanford University music professor Sandor Salgo conducted. It became a fully professional orchestra in the mid-1960s and has since earned world renown.

Today, led by conductor Leonid Grin (a protégé of Leonard Bernstein), this lively symphony orchestra puts on a number of well-received concerts throughout its season. It has four different concert series. Familiar Classics offers well-known favorites; Family Concerts are priced for families to enjoy and often include guest appearances by such celebrities as Garfield the Cat and the San Jose Sharks' mascot, S. J. Sharkie; the Signature Series draws star guest performers; and SuperPops plays familiar crowd pleasers.

San Jose Center for the Performing Arts (also at Cupertino's Flint Center, on the campus of De Anza College), 408/288-2828, website: www.sanjosesymphony.org; individual tickets (depending on the concert series) $6–55, season tickets also available.

CITIES OF THE VALLEY

Ballet San Jose Silicon Valley

Silicon Valley dance aficionados flock to this well-respected company. It was formerly the San Jose–Cleveland Ballet until financial difficulties broke apart that two-city union. Dennis Nahat, its talented artistic director, has created several original ballets, including *Marilyn & Company,* about the legendary film star, and *Blue Suede Shoes,* a popular show set to Elvis Presley recordings. The four-show season runs Oct.–May.

San Jose Center for the Performing Arts, 408/288-2800 or 800/895-4708, website: www.balletsanjose.com; individual tickets $15–60, subscription tickets $50–280.

The San Jose Chamber Music Society

This community-based society formed in 1986 puts on eight concerts during the year, bringing chamber music performers from throughout the world. They perform works by 14th- to 20th-century composers, with a wide stylistic diversity ranging from baroque and Beethoven to modern chamber music. The concerts are presented in the intimate Le Petit Trianon, a historic performing hall in downtown San Jose that seats about 350 people.

Le Petit Trianon, 72 N. 5th St. (downtown near Santa Clara St.), 408/286-5111, website: www.acoates.com/sjcms; parking free on street and in Methodist Church parking lot; individual tickets $10–25, season tickets (six concerts) $53–131.

San Jose Symphonic Choir

Started in 1924 and now performing as the Bay Area's oldest choral organization, this talented group of singers is made up of local residents who have performed in Europe, New York City's Carnegie Hall, and downtown San Jose's St. Joseph Cathedral. Led by Leroy Kromm since the mid-1980s, the group provides awe-inspiring choir music at three concerts a year. Concerts are generally held in Nov., Mar., and May, as well as a Sing-it-Yourself Messiah during the holiday season.

Westminster Presbyterian Church, 100 Shasta Ave. (corner of The Alameda), 408/879-9709, website: www.sanjosesymphonicchoir.org; individual tickets $15–18.

San Jose Wind Symphony

Established in 1958 by Darrell Johnston, who still conducts, this ensemble is composed of Bay Area professional and amateur musicians who play strictly wind, brass, and percussion instruments. In 1998, they won the John Philip Sousa Foundation's prestigious Sudler Silver Scroll Award, one of the highest honors for a community concert band. Their lively repertoire, including Strauss marches, has long made them a favorite with Silicon Valley residents.

Various locations throughout Silicon Valley, 408/927-7597, website: www.sjws.org; ticket prices vary according to venue.

Cinema

Filmgoing is a favorite after-hours activity for many of San Jose's residents, and the movie industry often uses the city's various cinemas to test-market their latest epics. Among the films that received excellent responses from their first test screenings here were *Star Wars* and *E.T.* San Jose has a movie house to suit almost every taste, and it also has Silicon Valley's only drive-in theater.

Sometimes referred to as "the training bra" cinemas because of their curving dome shape, the **Century Theaters** play first-run movies on giant screens with Dolby digital sound systems so good, you'd swear the *Jurassic Park* dinosaurs were stomping down the aisles.

Century 21, 22, and 23, Winchester Blvd. (next to the Winchester Mystery House), 408/984-5610; $5–8.75.

Century Capitol 16, Capitol Expwy. and Snell Ave., 408/972-9276; ticket prices $5–8.75.

Get absorbed in the super-realistic audio and visual experience of the one-hour documentaries shown in the 299-seat domed **Hackworth IMAX Theater** with more than 14,000 watts of digital sound. Past shows have taken viewers to the top of Mt. Everest and to the depths of the ocean.

201 Market St. (inside the Tech Museum of Innovation at the corner of Park and Market Sts.), 408/294-8324, website: www.thetech.org; tickets $7–9 (prepurchase recommended).

If you prefer *My Dinner with Andre* over *Lethal Weapon 4,* **Camera One** and **Camera Three** are your kind of theaters. Located near each other in downtown San Jose, these art-house venues show foreign and independent films in intimate surroundings. Camera Three has a European-style cinema café where you can chat with film fans over lattes. Each Feb., San Jose's film festival Cinequest is held at these two theaters.

Camera One, 266 S. 1st St. (in SoFA district), 408/998-3300; Camera Three, 288 S. 2nd St. (corner of San Carlos St.); validated parking in the 2nd St. parking garage; tickets $5–8.25.

For a nostalgic trip, the **Capitol Drive-In,** Silicon Valley's last drive-in, offers immense screens to see Hollywood's epics from the front seat of your car. The Capitol Flea Market, 408/225-5800, is held at the drive-in movie complex Thurs., Sat., and Sun. 6 A.M.–5:30 P.M., Fri. 7 A.M.–5:30 P.M.

Capitol Expwy. and Snell Ave., 408/226-2251; free parking with admission; tickets $3.75–6.

SPORTS

Due to the highly competitive nature of the place, sports are a big deal in Silicon Valley. Die-hard fans have long trekked up to San Francisco to watch professional athletes such as the

49ers or Oakland Raiders football teams, the San Francisco Giants or Oakland A's baseball teams, and the Golden State Warriors basketball team. For a long while, the South Bay never did achieve the professional sports status it so much desired, although there were several attempts, such as the 1970s San Jose Earthquakes soccer team. But that situation has rapidly changed as San Jose has become home to various sports teams bringing it national athletic recognition. The turnaround started with the San Jose Sharks (which originally played in South San Francisco's Cow Palace until the downtown Arena was built). Women's sports still need to find a niche here; unfortunately, the San Jose Lasers, a women's professional basketball team, folded its franchise when the American Basketball League couldn't compete with the marketing muscle of the NBA.

San Jose Sharks

Playing in the National Hockey League, the Sharks are Silicon Valley's premier professional team, always providing fans with hard-hitting ice action. During NHL playoffs, locals often call San Jose "Teal Town" in reference to the team's Pacific teal, black, and gray colors. S. J. Sharkie, the ever-smiling great white shark, is the team's cool mascot, who often makes his dramatic entrance by repelling down a rope from the Arena rafters (except for one time in 1999, when he got stuck halfway down due to his uniform catching).

San Jose Compaq Center (home games), 408/287-7070, website: www.sj-sharks.com; season: Sept.–Apr.; tickets $18–87.

The Earthquakes

The world's most popular sport gets played in San Jose by this Western Conference division team of Major League Soccer. For four years, the team was known as the Clash, but in October 1999 it changed its name. The mascot, an orange scorpion named José Clash (whom some fans admit bore a stronger resemblance to a lobster) was also slated to change, but the new one was undetermined as of this writing. The Earthquakes have team colors of blue, silver, and yellow.

Spartan Stadium (home games), E. Alma Ave. and 7th St., 408/985-4625 (or 408/260-6339 for Spanish-language information), website: www.sjearthquakes.com; 16-game season runs Mar.–Sept.; tickets $10–40.

The Rhinos

Started in 1994, San Jose's professional Roller Hockey League team won the world championship in 1995. In this fast-paced, high-scoring sport, athletes race on in-line skates around the rink. The team mascot is the comical Rocky the Rhino.

Compaq Center (home games), 800/207-4466, website: www.rhinos.com; season: June–Aug.; tickets $10–16.

Sabercats

High scoring and fast action make arena football just as exciting for many of its fans as the NFL version of the sport. San Jose's arena football team has been gaining momentum since it played its first home game in May 1995. Its cheerleaders are known as the Saber Kittens.

San Jose Compaq Center (home games), 408/573-5577, website: www.sanjosesabercats.com; season: Apr.–Aug.; tickets $5–49.

San Jose Giants

An air of enchantment fills the warm evening as you watch San Jose's minor league baseball team play under the arc lights of Municipal Stadium. Fans fill the bleachers of "The Muni," a 1942 W.P.A. project that serves as the pastoral home for the Class A California League team. The smoke of Turkey Mike's Barbeque mixes with the perfume of fresh-cut grass. With a mustard-and-relish smeared polish dog in hand, you watch intently the uniformed players standing in their field of dreams. No millionaire ballplayers complaining they're not getting enough salary, these young guys simply love Abner Doubleday's blessed game. A Giants hitter comes up to bat. Smack! The ball arcs over the fence advertisement for Bob Lewis Volkswagen. In the stands, baseball fanatic "Crazy George," a balding clown of a man, screams and shouts and violently shakes his tambourine like a madman. Since 1988, the San Jose Giants, a farm team for its San Francisco namesake, have won more games than any other minor league team.

Home games are played at Municipal Stadium (Senter Rd. at E. Alma Ave., across from Kelley Park), 408/297-1435, website: www.sjgiants.com; season: Apr.–Sept.; tickets: box seats $9, general admission $7, youths 4–10 and seniors over 65 $4, children under 4 free.

Bay Area CyberRays

Established in 2001, this is Silicon Valley's entry into the Women's United Soccer Association (WUSA). One of the team's founding members is Olympic player Brandi Chastain. The team's song is called "It's Our Time!"

Spartan Stadium (home games), E. Alma Ave. and 7th St., 408/535-0980, website: www.BayAreaCyberRays.com; season: Apr.–Aug.; tickets: $12–22.

Los Altos and Los Altos Hills

It can often be a confusing concept for Silicon Valley newcomers, but despite their common name and heritage, Los Altos and Los Altos Hills are distinctly separate communities with their own respective local governments. Located in the western foothill region of the valley, the two cities are geographically situated next to each other, with I-280 serving as a rough boundary line. But their unique characteristics provide quite a contrast. Los Altos is located in the valley's flatland, and with its shopping districts and light industry has developed more of an urban feel compared

the History House Museum in Los Altos

with its neighbor community to the west. Los Altos Hills is definitely rural and is, as its name implies, set in the foothills. With no industry and its numerous million-dollar homes set on vast lots, Los Altos Hills also has the tonier reputation of the two communities.

Los Altos is a seven-square-mile city of about 30,000 inhabitants bordered by Palo Alto on the north, Mountain View on the east, Cupertino on the south, and Los Altos Hills on the west. Its pleasant downtown district contains a number of retail shops and restaurants in a setting that resembles a friendly, small Midwestern town. It's the site of a number of annual art and wine festivals and community events, such as the Mayfest and Fall Festival. Residents are also active in community theater, with such groups as the Los Altos Youth Theatre, the Los Altos Methodist Players, and the Bus Barn Stage Company producing plays throughout the year. The city also maintains nine parks for residents to enjoy, and various public artworks decorate these outdoor settings. Los Altos actively participates with its sister cities throughout the world, including Bendigo, Australia; Syktyvkar, Russia, the capital of the Komi Republic; and Shih Lin, a district of 310,000 people within Taipei City in Taiwan.

Next-door neighbor Los Altos Hills is an affluent community of about 9,000 people. Much of it is surrounded by Mid-Peninsula Open Space District land. There is no multifamily housing such as apartment complexes here, and homeowners live on plots that, according to local zoning regulations, must be at least one acre in size. This gives the town an open-space lifestyle. The community has no downtown area, shopping district, or industry. Its only major business is Foothill Community College, which serves a campus body of about 15,000 students. This hillside college next to I-280 opened in 1957 and has won a number of architectural awards for its beautiful design. Los Altos Hills residents depend on volunteer efforts for many of their local services. There's a high level of involvement among its residents, who participate in activities such as emergency preparedness or publishing the community newsletter. Lacing the town's foothills are a number of paths where vehicles are not allowed, and these are popular with pedestrians, bicyclists, and horseback riders. Among its recreational opportunities is Hidden Villa, a working farm with miles of trails traversing woodland canyons in the Santa Cruz Mountains. Los Altos Hills is committed to protecting its open space in order to maintain its rural atmosphere.

© MARTIN CHEEK

CITIES OF THE VALLEY

HISTORY

The Ohlone Indians first settled in the Los Altos area, and to get a better look at their life and times, archaeologists have studied a small village and burial ground site on what later became the El Retiro Jesuit Retreat off El Monte Road. The land where Los Altos and Los Altos Hills now are located originally was two Mexican land grants. The first, given to Don Juan Prado Mesa on March 24, 1839, was called Rancho San Antonio. Mesa built an adobe home on this site, which is still standing. The second land grant was given to José Gorgonio and José Ramon, two Indian neophytes from the Mission Santa Clara, on June 30, 1840. Consisting of 4,400 acres, their Rancho Purissima Concepción occupied land that is now Los Altos Hills. In 1854, this rancho was sold to Dona Juana Briones de Miranda, who built an adobe home here that can still be seen on Old Trace Road.

Americans lured by the Gold Rush started to settle into the Santa Clara Valley during the 1850s, and the original massive land grants were parceled off and sold as smaller ranches. Among the buyers was Martin Murphy Jr., an Irish immigrant who had come to the Santa Clara Valley in 1848 and become a prominent landowner with several large ranches throughout the region. From Juana Briones, he purchased 2,800 acres of the Rancho Purissima Concepción, and the land was given as a wedding present to his daughter Elizabeth Yuba when she married William Taaffe, a New York merchant. Born in the Sierras during the first overland wagon crossing in 1844, Elizabeth was the first immigrant child born in California. Her descendants still live on part of the former ranch.

Wheat Fields

During the 1860s, fields of wheat flourished in the Los Altos area, becoming a major crop here. At harvest time, the farmers took their wheat and grain to the port at what is now Mountain View's Shoreline Park and shipped it to San Francisco and the goldfields. Among the farmers was a family with the last name of Bubb, which played an important role in giving the Hearst

newspaper empire its start. John Bubb met George Hearst in the minefields and gave him grubstake money, which Hearst used to gain mining expertise. Later, Hearst purchased a silver mine interest near Virginia City, Nevada, striking it rich after hitting a vein of the Comstock lode. George's son, William Randolph Hearst, later used his family's wealth to build a newspaper chain and construct his famous San Simeon castle. (He also served as the model for the despot in Orson Welles's classic film *Citizen Kane*.) Bubb Rd., which stretches into Cupertino, gets its name from this Los Altos farm family.

In 1888, a petite woman named Sarah L. Winchester bought land here and built a home for herself and her sister, Isabelle Merriman. This house was much more ordinary in appearance than the elephantine house she was building on her property near San Jose. Winchester grew hay on her Los Altos fields. In the 1890s, Los Altos area farmers switched from growing wheat to various fruit trees. Their orchards included prunes, apricots, peaches, and other crops, which created sweeping vistas of blossoms during the spring. At the turn of the 19th century, the area remained rural, but summer residences were being built for San Francisco people, who wanted retreat homes in the pleasant country setting. Attracted to its rustic beauty, Stanford professors also started to build houses along the foothills here.

Paul Shoup

In the early 1900s, with railroad lines expanding throughout the Santa Clara Valley, a small farming community started to develop in this part of the valley. The town's father was Paul Shoup (pronounced like "out"), an ambitious man who started out as the district freight and passenger agent in San Jose for the Southern Pacific Railroad and later became the president of the company. He decided to build a commuter town in this scenic location with a rail stop linking the cities of Palo Alto and Los Gatos. The original intention was to christen the place Banks and Braes, but this ghastly name was quickly changed to the more awe-inspiring Los Altos (The Heights). Sarah Winchester refused to provide

WALLACE STEGNER—DEAN OF WESTERN WRITERS

For all its emphasis on technology and industry, Silicon Valley also has played a historic role in the preservation of California wilderness. John Muir knew the area well when it was called the Valley of Heart's Delight, and several of his essays praise its natural beauty. Photographer Andrew Hill captured much of its outdoor splendor in his prints and also led in the establishment of nearby Big Basin State Park—laying the groundwork for California's splendid state park system. Russ Varian, cofounder of Varian Associates, played a key role in creating Castle Rock State Park in the Santa Cruz Mountains. But one of the most famous conservationists of the region is writer and environmentalist Wallace Stegner, who made his home in Los Altos Hills. Through his books and essays, Stegner helped develop the public's consciousness in appreciating the spiritual wonder and historic impact of the Western landscape.

Born on February 18, 1909, in Lake Mills, Iowa, Stegner enjoyed a 60-year writing and teaching career in which he produced 30 books, including *Angle of Repose,* a Pulitzer Prize–winning novel published in 1972 (much of the novel's early sections are set at the New Almaden Mines). After teaching for several years at the University of Utah, the University of Wisconsin, and Harvard University, Stegner came to Stanford in 1945. The next year, he founded that university's highly respected Creative Writing Program, where he taught until 1971. Stegner's students included Raymond Carver, Larry McMurtry, Ken Kesey, Thomas McGuane, Wendell Barry, Edward Abbey, and Robert Haas, the poet laureate of the United States (who teaches at San Jose State University).

In the 1950s, Stegner became active in the conservation movement when he battled against building a dam on Green River at Utah's Dinosaur National Monument. In 1960, his *Coda: Wilderness Letter* helped promote a national sense of responsibility for preserving America's natural heritage. In that famous letter, he wrote: "Without any remaining wilderness we are committed wholly, without chance for even momentary reflection and rest, to a headlong drive into our technological termite-life, the Brave New World of a completely man-controlled environment. We need wilderness preserved—as much of it as is still left, and as many kinds—because it was the challenge against which our character as a people was formed." Out of Stegner's passionate plea came the 1964 National Wilderness Preservation System, a federal program that protects America's wild lands. During John F. Kennedy's administration, Stegner also served as an assistant to Secretary of the Interior Stewart Udall.

In 1992, he was awarded the National Medal for the Arts, but, distressed by the politics controlling the National Endowment for the Arts, he turned down the honor.

On April 13, 1993, in Santa Fe, New Mexico, Stegner died from injuries sustained in a car accident. Called "the dean of Western writers," he left a legacy in literature, teaching, and the defense of the Western environment that will long have a tremendous impact on Silicon Valley as well as the United States as a whole.

right-of-way for the tracks to come through her land, so the Peninsular Electric Railroad purchased 100 acres of Winchester's property, the area in and around what is now Los Altos's downtown district. Soon after, with his flair for marketing real estate, Shoup formed the Los Altos Land Company and began to promote the area for residences.

In 1907, railroad tracks were laid through the town along what later became Foothill Expressway. A depot station consisting of two boxcars was placed on what is now Loyola Corners at the southern end of Miramonte Avenue. That same year, the streets were laid out, and sidewalks and curbs were built. The next year, the Los Altos Land Company held a massive barbecue picnic under an oak tree in the middle of Main St. for prospective buyers transported by train from San Francisco. The real estate agents promoted their dawning community as "the most beautiful town in California," and steadily, people began to buy plots of land. In 1909, water and electricity were provided and a dozen homes built. By 1911, 50 homes had been constructed, and a small community began to emerge, adding the necessities of civilization such as banks, stores, a church, and a newspaper.

By the 1920s, Los Altos's population was still relatively small, with the few scattered dwellings set next to bucolic fields of grass and wildflowers. During the 1930s, when the Great Depression was at its worst, little real estate was sold in the town. To drum up publicity and encourage some movement of residents into the community, a unique marketing scheme was developed. Los Altos property lots were given away as raffle prizes on "dish nights" at San Francisco movie theaters. Audience members could choose between a set of dishes or a parcel of land. Most opted for the dishes in order to avoid paying property taxes.

In the years following World War II, the Santa Clara Valley had its major population boom as returning veterans moved here. In the 1950s, San Jose's Annexation Wars grew intense. Los Altos's residents realized they needed to take some steps to control their community's destiny, so they voted to incorporate. The town officially became a city on December 1, 1952.

During the last five decades, Los Altos has grown with Silicon Valley's expanding population, but overall the community has kept much of its small-town atmosphere.

The Los Altos Hills Story

The history of Los Altos Hills is perhaps not as eventful as that of its neighboring city, but it has had its dramatic moments. During the mid-1800s, the lumber industry operated in the area. And lumbermen hauling timber down from the mountains on wagons often used what is now Hidden Villa Ranch as a rest stop.

Among the early settlers here was a gentleman named George Washington Moody, who immigrated from Missouri to California in 1847. In the early 1860s, he heard that the Western Pacific Railroad planned to build a coastal branch line from the San Francisco and San Jose Railroad that would extend across the mountains through the vicinity of what's now Los Altos Hills. In anticipation of this proposed railroad route, Moody bought 240 acres of foothill land here in April 1865. The railroad was never constructed, and so for a time, Moody operated a stage line from Mountain View to the coastal resort town of Pescadero.

As Los Altos Hills settled into becoming an agricultural paradise, ranchers made their homes here and life continued quite peacefully for many decades. In 1923, Frank and Josephine Duveneck bought a beautiful piece of rural property along Moody Rd. and called it Hidden Villa Ranch. The Duvenecks, early environmentalists of the Santa Clara Valley, founded the Loma Prieta Chapter of the Sierra Club. In the 1970s, their ranch was converted into an open space preserve for public use. Today, it's a hidden treasure for Silicon Valley residents who want a retreat in a pastoral foothill setting.

The community's quiet lifestyle quickly changed with Santa Clara Valley's population explosion after World War II. In the 1950s, the 500 or so families residing in Los Altos Hills saw the annexations occurring throughout the county. Like the neighboring community of Los Altos, they decided they would have to incorporate their rural territory before it was taken over by a larger community such as Santa Clara or San Jose.

The residents did not want to incorporate as a city but realized it was a necessity to prevent the zoning of their hilly land for major housing development. They formed a homeowners association called the Los Altos Hills Incorporation Committee, among whose members was author and Stanford literature professor Wallace Stegner, a strong advocate for protecting the environment. The group's aim was to keep their hillside community a quiet and rural residential area with no business or major industry other than Foothill Community College.

The city of Los Altos Hills officially came into existence with its incorporation on January 27, 1956. At this time, the local government established a minimum lot size of one acre, thus letting the community preserve much of its open space and wooded areas. Today, affluent Los Altos Hills is the home of many of Silicon Valley's top engineers and business executives. It remains a community of single-family residences.

TOUR

This driving-walking tour will give you a glimpse of the two communities' historical landmarks as well as Los Altos's charming downtown shopping district. To begin your tour, take the El Monte Ave. exit off I-280, and drive east about one mile until you reach University Avenue. Turn left here, and immediately at Edgewood Ln., turn right and drive down this short one-way street. Toward the middle of this street at 762 Edgewood Ln. is Sarah Winchester's *other* house. This attractive two-story frame house demurely hiding behind a spreading oak tree is a much plainer building than the sprawling 160-acre mansion Winchester built in San Jose. Built in the 1860s, the Winchester-Merriman house is considered Los Altos's oldest home. (It's still a residence, so please respect the occupants' privacy.) In 1888, Winchester bought the home for Isabelle Merriman, her younger sister, and additions were built onto it. Isabelle's husband, Louis, tended a vineyard on the land, and Isabelle turned the house into a refuge for homeless children.

After viewing the outside of this home, continue to the end of Edgewood Ln. and turn left on Orange Avenue. As you follow this quiet residential street, you'll drive past 461 Orange Ave. on your right. This historic building is the **Foothill Congregational Church,** designed by Coxhead and Coxhead and built about 1917. Drive down to where Orange Ave. meets Lincoln St. and turn left here, following it a short distance back to University Avenue. In the small building under the parklike shade of redwood trees here on your right, the **Los Altos Chamber of Commerce,** 650/948-1455, keeps an office at 321 University Avenue. Chamber members can provide you with information on Los Altos community events as well as a brochure with a walking tour of the historic buildings in the downtown area.

From University Ave., turn right at Main St. and cross the stoplight intersection at Foothill Expressway. You're now entering **Los Altos's downtown** area, and here you can park on the street or at one of the public lots behind the stores. Take a stroll through this picturesque area, which has retained its quaint hometown style with turn-of-the-19th-century storefronts and American flags fluttering along the sidewalks. Another charming touch is the cement bench draped with a painted copy of the *Los Altos Town Crier,* the community newspaper. The building at 316 Main St. (now occupied by a gift shop) was originally **Eschenbruecher's Hardware Store,** built about 1908. It was Los Altos's first commercial business, and William Eschenbruecher also served as the town's first postmaster.

Here in the downtown district, you'll find a number of restaurants and specialty shops among which to browse. Good places to stop include **Gallery 9,** 143 Main St., 650/941-7969, an art shop specializing in masterfully done watercolor etchings. It's open Tues.–Sat. 11:30 A.M.–5:30 P.M. In the colonial-style brick building across the street from this gallery is **Marjolaine French Pastries,** 650/949-2226, Los Altos's best place to enjoy freshly baked gourmet treats. Next door, pick up a 50-cent copy of the **Los Altos Town Crier,** 650/948-9000, and read the local news as you enjoy one of the pastry shop's creations.

HIDDEN VILLA

Hidden Villa is a working farm park located amidst high-dollar Los Altos Hills real estate along a winding Santa Cruz Mountains canyon. The unspoiled natural setting makes it a true hidden treasure of Silicon Valley.

Every year, visitors come to Hidden Villa to walk its oak-canopied trails and wander along Adobe Creek. Enormously popular with families, this 1,600-acre organic farm and wilderness preserve makes an excellent place to bring kids to teach them how to tend to nature's fragile balance.

Hidden Villa was once the home of Frank and Josephine Duveneck, who bought the property in 1923. For a number of years, it served as a working farm. The well-liked couple, founders of the Loma Prieta chapter of the Sierra Club, were seriously involved in open space preservation. They donated their farm as a public site where the region's residents could come and learn about the human connection with the environment. Josephine once said, "Becoming aware of the relationships of all living things to other living things is the key to knowing ourselves."

During the summer, Hidden Villa hosts camps for children between the ages of 9 and 18. Activities are designed to teach tolerance and respect for multicultural diversity. The farm also offers a number of community programs, such as educational workshops, theatrical performances, and forums on issues dealing with the environment. A community garden on the land provides Los Altos Hills residents with a place to grow fresh vegetables. The farm is also the site of the United States' oldest hostel, which provides accommodations for visitors of all ages.

26870 Moody Rd., Los Altos Hills (take Moody Rd. exit along I-280 and drive east; the preserve will be on your left), 650/949-8660; $5 parking fee; admission free; open Tues.–Sun. 9 A.M.–dusk.

At the V-intersection where Main St. adjoins State St., there's a small **plaza** where you'll see the town clock dedicated to Denny Spangler, a former mayor. The nearby bronze bust of the smiling fellow wearing a bow tie represents Walter Singer, a town benefactor. From here, amble up State St., which is quieter than Main St. but holds several interesting specialty shops. Among them, at 239 State St., you'll find **Tiedown English and Western Saddlery,** 650/948-1719, which sells a variety of goods for horse lovers, such as books, gifts, riding gear, and clothes. Stop and admire the collection of plastic horse figurines in the window here. If you're into fly-fishing, check out **Midge Fly Shop,** 271 State St., 650/941-8871, a most excellent place to pick up some lures.

After finishing your downtown visit, return to your car and drive east on Main St., taking a sharp right at the stoplight intersection onto S. San Antonio Road. Immediately on your left is the entrance to the **Los Altos Civic Center,** which contains the community's city hall, police station, and public library. The two-story redwood shingle building next to the library is the **History House Museum,** 650/948-9427. A visit will last from 45 minutes to an hour. Here, you can view memorabilia from the community's farm-based past. The house was built by J. Gilbert Smith, who owned an orchard in the vicinity. Its 1930s furnishings represent what one of the area's farm homes might have looked like during that decade. Beside the farmhouse is a lovely garden and a small plot of apricot trees that become a fragrant canopy of white blossoms during the spring.

After your visit to History House, return to San Antonio Rd., driving east back to the stoplight intersection and turning left here onto Edith Road. Follow Edith Rd., crossing over the Foothill Expwy. intersection. Soon after this point, you'll enter the more rural terrain of **Los Altos Hills.** At the stop sign at the end of Edith Rd., turn right on Fremont Rd., following this up into the foothills. On your left, you'll pass **Bullis-Purissima School,** and about three-quarters of a mile after this, you'll come to the stop sign intersection where the **Los Altos Hills**

town hall is located. From here, follow a series of curvy roads bringing you into the heart of Los Altos Hills. In these rolling hills, many of Silicon Valley's corporate executives live in stately mansions near picturesque barns and tank houses that dot the landscape.

At the intersection, turn left onto Concepcion Rd. and drive about half a mile. Turn right at Viscaino Rd., and follow this steep and twisting road through the foothills until you reach the summit. Continue downhill, taking a left at Roble Ladera Rd. and following this past the **Fremont Hills Country Club,** 650/948-8261, on your right. You'll see its well-maintained tennis courts and a riding stable at this point. Shortly after this, Roble Ladera Rd. ends at a stop sign at Purissima Road. Turn left here and follow Purissima Rd. to its end at the stop sign on Robleda Road. Turn right here and drive under the I-280 overpass. At the end of Robleda Rd., turn left at the stop sign intersection onto Elena Road. Follow Elena Rd. to where it meets Moody Rd., and then turn right at the intersection here, following this curvy road leading through a canyon of the Santa Cruz Mountains for about 1.5 miles. Moody Rd. was originally used to transport lumber during the valley's timber industry days. It was named after George Washington Moody, who came to California from Missouri in 1847.

On your left at 26870 Moody Rd., you'll come to **Hidden Villa,** 650/949-8660, Los Altos Hills's most scenic open preserve, covering more than 1,600 acres. Here you'll find several historic buildings, including a gable-roofed home that, in the late 1840s, was brought by ship around Cape Horn. Hidden Villa operates an educational farm to teach visitors about agrarian life, and it holds special public events throughout the year. It's open every day except Mon. 9 A.M.–dusk, and there's a $5 parking fee. Expect to spend at least an hour here.

Return down the canyon along Moody Rd. to where it turns into S. El Monte Road. At the stop sign intersection here, continue straight into the entrance of **Foothill Community College,** 650/949-7777. Park here in one of the lots, where you can buy $2 parking permits (quarters only) from the automatic machines. Foothill's buildings and grounds have been described by the *San Francisco Chronicle* as "the most beautiful community college ever built." Los Altos Hills pioneers Elizabeth and William Taaffe had their home on what's now the campus property. Among its more interesting attractions are the **Japanese Cultural Center** and the **Bamboo Garden,** which contains an enchanting Japanese shrine. The campus also has several historic buildings, including the 1904 **Henry Dana home,** now the Faculty Club. Another historic estate on the grounds, built in 1901 for shipbuilder Willard Griffin, includes a **carriage house,** now serving as the Los Altos Hills fire station. Expect to spend about an hour exploring the campus.

After your visit to Foothill College, return to S. El Monte Rd., heading east. Close to the campus, this road meets up with I-280. The northbound entrance leads toward San Francisco, the southbound entrance toward San Jose.

POINTS OF INTEREST

History House Museum

J. Gilbert Smith was the original owner of this redwood-shingled farmhouse, which features a wonderfully rustic surrounding porch. Set in the Los Altos Civic Center next to the city library, today the two-story structure serves as a historical museum, holding many of the community's artifacts and archives documenting Los Altos's past. Inside, visitors can see furnishings from the 1930s. Outside, in the quaint country garden, they can view a tank house and agricultural implements, such as the original Wizard walnut huller invented by William E. Formway in Los Altos. Smith was a successful apricot farmer, and a large orchard still stands near the home, and a sulfur shed display demonstrates how the apricots were dried.

51 S. San Antonio Rd. (in the Los Altos Civic Center near downtown), 650/948-9427, website: www.losaltoshistory.org; free parking; admission free for 18 and under, $3 for adults; open Thurs.–Sun. noon–4 P.M.

Foothill Community College

A sister college to Cupertino's De Anza Com-

THE VALLEY'S EXPANDING GREENBELT

The people of Silicon Valley value the region's environmental riches and abhor the prospect that development might turn the area into another sprawling Los Angeles. In 1972, they voted for an initiative creating a public agency dedicated to buying up land to form a greenbelt around the San Francisco Bay. The Mid-Peninsula Regional Open Space District is funded by a portion of residents' property taxes—1.7 cents per $100 of assessed property value.

Since its founding, the district has acquired more than 41,000 acres of foothills and baylands, preserving Silicon Valley ecological environments as diverse as mountain redwoods, chaparral, salt marshes, oak woodlands, meadows and grasslands, and ponds and creeks. Nature lovers can visit the district's 23 preserves free of charge between dawn and half an hour after sunset. More than 200 miles of hiking trails—many of them open to bikes and horses—cross the varied terrain. One of the district's goals is to acquire land to extend the Bay Area Ridge Trail so that it will eventually loop along the ridge tops surrounding San Francisco Bay. Much of the land in the preserves is left undeveloped with few facilities. Many of the preserves connect with county parks.

The Sierra Azul Preserve contains rugged terrain connected to Almaden Quicksilver County Park. It contains more than 15 miles of hiking trails, which provide overlook views of the valley as well as Monterey Bay.

The Fremont Older Preserve connects with Stevens Creek County Park and contains woodlands, chaparral, and hayfields. In late spring, docents lead tours of Woodhills, the historic 1914 home of crusading San Francisco newspaper editor Fremont Older.

Connected by Hidden Villa Ranch, the Rancho San Antonio and Monte Bello Preserves are set in the foothills south of Los Altos. Combined, they contain 38 miles of trails. Families and school groups can get a glimpse of agricultural life at Deer Hollow Farm, a working homestead and education center in the Rancho San Antonio Preserve.

The district's headquarters, 650/691-1200, www.openspace.org, is located in Los Altos. If you're interested in exploring some of the preserves, call for a map of locations.

munity College, Foothill was founded in 1958 and among its alumni is Wayne Wang, director of *The Joy Luck Club*. It has a student body of about 15,000 people. Visit the Japanese Cultural Center with its well-designed Bamboo Garden featuring more than 50 varieties of the long, spindly stalks as well as a traditional *Azumaya* (meditation pavilion). The garden is sponsored by the Northern California Chapter of the American Bamboo Society. Also at Foothill is a small observatory run by the Peninsula Astronomical Society, often open to the public for nighttime viewing. Call 650/949-7334 for public schedules. The community college is the home of radio station KFJC, 89.7 FM, which began transmitting out of a plumbing closet on October 20, 1959. It broadcasts news, talk shows, and music.

12345 El Monte Rd. (just west of I-280); parking $2 (permit machines only take quarters),

650/949-7777, website: www.foothill.fhda.edu; open daily 7 A.M.–10 P.M.

Draeger's Epicures

London has Harrod's food shop; Silicon Valley has Draeger's. Opened in 1925, this locally famous food emporium provides the ultimate adventure in shopping for culinary items. Browse through rare vintage wines, a wide selection of imported and domestic cheeses, homemade sausages, smoked meats from the store's own smokehouse, and exquisitely baked breads, pies, and cakes. A beautiful selection of plants and flowers are also available. One *New York Times* food columnist was so enraptured by the Draeger's experience that she spent five hours exploring the store. The Menlo Park Draeger's, 650/688-0677, at 1010 University Ave. has a bistro and provides cooking classes.

342 1st St. (just south of Main St.), 650/948-4425; free parking in store lot; open daily 7 A.M.–10 P.M.

Bus Barn Stage Company

This community group of actors puts on six plays a year in the intimate 100-seat Bus Barn Theatre. Performances often receive high local praise, and past shows include Shakespeare's *Taming of the Shrew.*

Bus Barn Theatre, 97 Hillview Ave. (next to Hillview Community Center five blocks south of San Antonio Rd.), 650/941-0551; tickets $15–18, season tickets also available.

Saratoga

Saratoga's charming 19th-century village on Big Basin Way has become a popular escape for Silicon Valley residents and tourists. This designated downtown historical area set in the foothills is well known for its restaurants, many of them the finest in Silicon Valley. But it also has a number of specialty shops, antique stores, and art galleries worth browsing through on sunny afternoons. Weekends, many mountain bikers make their start from the village before facing Hwy. 9's treacherous grade to reach the summit of the Santa Cruz Mountains. In the hills and canyons surrounding the village are large, luxurious estates and small, family-run vineyards with extraordinary views of the valley. These have created in Saratoga a more genteel atmosphere.

With a population of just over 30,000 in its 12 square miles, the city has transformed over the years from a lumber village, to an agricultural town, to the elegant bedroom community it is today. Saratoga is bordered on the east by Monte Sereno, Los Gatos, and Campbell; on the north by San Jose's Westgate district and Cupertino; and on the west and south by unincorporated land covered with towering redwood forests. The city has no zoned land for manufacturing.

Saratogans take pride in retaining the small-town character of their community, and many of them participate in various cultural activities, such as the Saratoga Drama Group and the West Valley Masterworks Chorale. Among the city's popular annual events is the Strawberry Festival, held during spring at West Valley College. At the same location, the annual Rotary Club Art Show takes place, attracting more than 25,000 visitors from throughout the region. Big Basin Way is closed off for an evening in late Sept. during the Celebrate Saratoga! festival sponsored by the local chamber of commerce. This event always draws a large crowd eager to sample the food and wine and listen to music on various stages set throughout the village. Saratoga's scenic Pierce Road district is the site of the Historic Mountain Winery concert series. This famous venue attracts top-name performers to the intimate setting of Paul Masson's former winery, cooled by refreshing evening breezes. Saratoga also has Hollywood connections: sisters Olivia de Havilland and Joan Fontaine grew up here, tak-

the Saratoga Historical Museum

ing their first steps into the acting world by performing in local theater productions. And, during his teenage years, movie mogul Steven Spielberg's family moved to the city from Phoenix. He graduated from Saratoga High School before heading to Los Angeles to begin directing megahits.

Living amid the redwood-covered hillsides of the Santa Cruz Mountains, Saratoga's residents enjoy their natural surroundings. Among the city's parks is the calming Hakone Gardens, a 15-acre park containing formal Japanese gardens, including a 17th-century-style Zen garden. Villa Montalvo, once belonging to James Phelan, is a grand 1912 Mediterranean estate providing awe-inspiring views of Silicon Valley. With its 143 acres of meandering creeks and oak trees, Saratoga's naturally landscaped West Valley College makes it one of the most beautiful community college campuses in Silicon Valley. The city also offers a number of recreational opportunities, such as camping at Saratoga Springs Resort and golf, swimming, and tennis at the Saratoga Country Club. Another popular leisure activity is horseback riding in the mountains from Garrod Farms Riding Stables, one of the city's oldest ranches still operated by its original family.

Although many of Saratoga's residents are wealthy, the town tries to keep ostentation to a minimum. Most of the homes are California ranch style or turn-of-the-19th-century farmhouses. However, in 1984, one resident built a 10,000-square-foot re-creation of Windsor Castle, which received some disapproving frowns from locals displeased with the building's showiness.

HISTORY

Although archaeologists have never found any evidence of long-term Indian settlement here, artifacts have been discovered showing that the Ohlone often camped in the Saratoga area when they crossed the Santa Cruz Mountains on their travels to the Pacific Ocean. Explorer Juan Bautista de Anza was the first European to trek through this part of the valley on March 25, 1776.

It wasn't until 1841 that real settlement of the area began. That year, Governor Alvarado gave a Mexican land grant to José Noriega and his father-in-law José Fernandez. In 1844, the two men transferred ownership of the property to Manuel Alviso, who was more active in developing the property. Alviso named the area Rancho Quito.

In late 1847, William Campbell (the father of Benjamin Campbell, the pioneer who founded the city of Campbell) foresaw that in the coming years, more Americans would be moving into the Santa Clara Valley. He realized that they'd want to live in wood-frame houses like the ones back East instead of the adobe mud homes that the Spanish and Mexicans built. With so many redwood trees covering the mountains, he saw a business opportunity in constructing a sawmill that could supply lumber to these new immigrants. His sons David and Benjamin helped him start building the mill beside the Arroyo Quito (later renamed Campbell Creek and finally Saratoga Creek). The work stopped after gold was found in the Sierras and his sons went off for a time to seek their fortune. But after they returned to the job, the mill was completed in the fall of 1848. It was the valley's second lumber mill, following one built in the Los Gatos area. It stood where the Saratoga Springs campground is now located about two miles west of Saratoga's Village. The mill did well, selling lumber to the incoming Americans at $3,000 per 1,000 board feet and an additional $100 per 1,000 board feet for transportation costs. As it prospered, a small lumber camp began to form at the mouth of the canyon leading up to the mill. This soon became known as Campbell's Gap.

McCartysville

An Irish immigrant named Martin McCarty saw that Campbell's Gap was in an excellent location for a town to grow with the burgeoning lumber industry. The ambitious McCarty, who had once served as a wagonmaster for General Winfield Scott, had come to California in search of gold. On March 1, 1850, he leased the sawmill from William Campbell and filed a claim for 230 acres of land where the little settlement at the

VILLA MONTALVO: A HOME WHERE THE ART IS

Villa Montalvo arboretum

In the early 1900s, James Duval Phelan was "the foremost citizen of California." The son of an Irish immigrant who made his fortune in the Gold Rush by selling supplies to the miners and starting up banks, Phelan served three terms as mayor of San Francisco and was a U.S. senator from 1915 to 1921. After the 1906 earthquake, his influence helped considerably in the rebuilding of San Francisco. But he also had an impact in San Jose, building the St. Claire Club, along St. James Park, as well as the Victory Theatre, an opera house built in 1899 to honor Admiral Dewey's conquest of the Spanish fleet in Manila. But his greatest architectural benefaction was the spectacular Florentine-style estate Villa Montalvo, which overlooks the valley from Saratoga's foothills.

In 1911, Phelan bought 160 acres a mile from Saratoga Village and hired William Curlett to design a 19-room home, which began construction in 1912. The splendid grounds were planned by John McLaren, who also designed the landscape of San Francisco's Golden Gate Park.

The villa was surrounded by sweeping lawns, pergolas, vineyards, fruit trees, statues, and a 3,000-year-old Egyptian obelisk. The estate was the most luxurious home in the valley. Phelan named it Villa Montalvo after Ordeñez de Montalvo, the 16th-century Spanish author who wrote *Las Sergas de Esplandian* (The Adventures of Esplandian), a fantasy novel in which an island called California is visited and ruled by a beautiful black Amazon warrior-queen named Califia. The early Spaniards had believed California to be an island and named it for the one in the story.

Many famous guests visited Villa Montalvo, including presidents, royalty, and authors such as Jack London. Novelist Gertrude Atherton, a special guest of the bachelor Phelan, had her own room on the estate. During a tour of Europe, Phelan discovered a 16th-century carved wooden door in Granada, Spain, which had on it the faces of historical figures, including King Ferdinand, Queen Isabella, and Christopher Columbus. He bought the door and installed it as the front entrance to his Saratoga estate, where it still hangs. Phelan also made his estate available as a home for talented writers and artists. He is widely considered the Santa Clara Valley's greatest patron of the arts. He died on August 7, 1930, and was given, according to newspaper accounts, "the largest and most imposing funeral ever seen in San Francisco."

Villa Montalvo is now operated by the Montalvo Association, which, in keeping with Phelan's will, provides residences for working artists. The grounds are open to visitors, who come to roam the serene, beautiful gardens and nature trails as well as watch performances in the outdoor amphitheater behind the house.

15400 Montalvo Rd. (just off Los Gatos–Saratoga Rd.; look for the stone griffins guarding the entrance gate), 408/961-5800, website: www.villamontalvo.org; free parking; admission to the grounds is free; open during winter daily 8 A.M.–5 P.M., during summer daily 8 A.M.–7 P.M.

CITIES OF THE VALLEY

base of the mountains stood. At a cost of $12,000, he then built a toll road from the mill to this growing settlement, placing a toll gate at 3rd St. and Lumber St. (now Big Basin Way). He charged $3 for a two-horse team and $6 for a four-horse team to pass along this route.

The farsighted McCarty also laid out plots and streets. As the village grew, other businesses such as a flour mill and paper mill were established. In 1854, the fraternal order of the Old Sons of Temperance Hall built a schoolhouse made of hand-hewn redwood shakes, and this also served as a community center and a place of religious worship. The village was initially called Toll Gate, but later McCarty changed the name to McCartysville. During this decade, several mineral springs were discovered about a mile above the village, and chemists testing these waters discovered that the mineral content was similar to that of the Congress Springs resort in Saratoga, New York.

With the area's booming mill business (and because some of the more prejudiced residents didn't want to live in a town named after an Irishman), on December 22, 1863, the name McCartysville was abandoned for Bank Mills. But this new name wouldn't last long. In August 1864, the local mineral springs, named Congress Springs after the resort in New York, was purchased for $2,000 by Darius Ogden Mills and Alvinza Hayward, two San Francisco tycoons. They began to bottle the water and successfully sell it throughout the West Coast. They also built a 14-room hotel here called Congress Hall (resembling a hotel of the same name in Congress Springs, New York) as well as guest cottages. On June 16, 1866, they opened their 720-acre resort with a grand ball and fanfare celebration.

During the tempestuous early 1860s, Saratoga was home to a number of Southern sympathizers. To undermine their influence, supporters of the Union cause held a patriotic town picnic on October 5, 1864. At that event, a vote was taken to change the community's name once again. Because of Mills and Hayward's plans to turn the local Congress Springs into a spa resort, the residents decided to use the elegant name

Saratoga after the town in upstate New York so well known for its own springs. Many of the town's residents probably would have reconsidered their vote if they had realized the new designation was an Iroquois Indian derivative of "Se-rach-to-que," a term that meant "floating scum upon the water." Despite this unpleasant definition, on March 13, 1865, Saratoga became the town's longest lasting name.

By the 1880s, the town's lumber industry was in decline. Many of the hillsides in the mountains surrounding Saratoga were left barren from the heavy cutting of the redwoods. Hearing about the rich soil and sunny climate, a number of European vintners came to the area and established several small wineries here. Among these was a Frenchman named Paul Masson, who brought grape cuttings from his homeland and started a winery in the fertile hills along Pierce Road. Masson's winery would become one of the world's most prestigious. So exemplary was the Saratoga area for growing grapes that the region's string of wineries soon became known as the *Chaine d'Or* (French for "chain of gold").

During the late 19th century, the town of Saratoga further developed its popular Congress Springs resort, and thousands of Victorian vacationers enjoyed camping among the mountain redwoods. So renowned did the resort become that San Francisco's wealthy elite took the 3.5-hour train and carriage journey here to enjoy its hot and cold mineral baths reputed to cure many diseases and afflictions. By 1881, the Congress Hall hotel's business had grown so much that it expanded with a 63-room annex. Unfortunately, the hotel and annex burned down on June 5, 1903, in a fire started by a defective chimney flue.

Blossom Festival

By the turn of the 19th century, an interurban train connected Saratoga with the networks of tracks crisscrossing the valley. This made it easy for people to reach the community, thus increasing its popularity as a tourist destination. The Saratoga Improvement Association published a 76-page booklet to promote the town's resort attractions. The publication, called *Sarato-*

ga Sunshine, gave the town the billing of "the Crown of the Valley, the Pasadena of the North." Among the most popular of the community's spring attractions was the Saratoga Blossom Festival, an event conceived as a thanksgiving celebration when rains came after a two-year drought that had devastated the region. The Reverend Edwin Sydney Williams, known as "Everlasting Sunshine," came up with the idea, and the first blossom festival was held on March 20, 1900. It proved a huge success as thousands of visitors came from throughout the Bay Area to enjoy the town's hospitality during the spring blooming of the local orchards. The festival became an annual event, bringing the small town worldwide fame. It lasted 42 years until the advent of World War II.

For the first half of the 20th century, Saratoga stayed a small agricultural-based community. But after World War II and the inundation of newcomers to the region, the town's population began to boom. To prevent its annexation by San Jose, it incorporated as a city on October 22, 1956. Saratoga has kept its small-town character by preventing industry from taking root in the town.

TOUR

Saratoga's mountainous setting provides visitors an especially scenic drive through the city's rural and developed districts. Much of this excursion includes pastoral foothill country sprinkled with stunning estates set among small vineyards or towering redwood forests. Begin your tour by taking the De Anza Blvd. exit at Hwy. 85, and drive south along Sunnyvale-Saratoga Road. At first, you'll be in Cupertino's city limits, but keep driving toward the mountains, and after a mile or so, you'll pass through Saratoga's northern city limits at Prospect Road. After traveling through a gauntlet of strip malls, turn right at Pierce Rd. (you'll see a sign for Stevens Creek County Park by this road).

Pierce Rd. weaves its way through foothill canyons of the Santa Cruz Mountains, passing among plots of land with million-dollar homes shaded by expansive oak trees. Many of these es-

tates are owned by Silicon Valley corporate executives and electronics industry workers. The Pierce Road district features several excellent wineries, including the **Cooper-Garrod Vineyards** off Mt. Eden Rd. and the **Clos La Chance Winery** along Saratoga Heights Drive. On your right, you'll pass the historic **Mountain Winery,** 408/741-0763, formerly owned by pioneer vintner Paul Masson. It no longer produces wine but is still popular for its celebrated concert series featuring jazz, country, classical, and rock-and-roll singers. The Saratoga area wineries are often closed during weekdays but are open for public tasting hours during weekends.

A quarter mile after the Mountain Winery, Pierce Rd. ends at the intersection along Hwy. 9 (also called Congress Springs Rd. along this point). Turn left at the stop sign, driving along the winding road for about a mile until you come to the entrance of **Hakone Japanese Gardens,** 408/741-4994. You'll see the sign on the right side of the road. The driveway into the garden requires a sharp right turn and a climb up a steep hill to the parking lot just around the bend. Plan on spending an hour roaming through this traditional Japanese ornamental garden set near Saratoga Creek.

After your visit to Hakone, return to Hwy. 9 and turn right, following the road around the curve as it turns into Big Basin Way, where **Saratoga Village** is located. This appealing section of the city has an upscale country-town ambience. Designated a California Historical Site in 1950, many of its businesses and surrounding residential neighborhoods were built during Saratoga's early development years. The white Georgian farmhouse on your left at 14605 Big Basin Way is known as the **Erwin T. King House,** originally owned by a New Yorker who started the Saratoga Paper Mill in 1868. (The house currently is a private residence.) King's mill burned to the ground in a fire in April 1883, and soon after he died from a heart attack. His home later served as a boardinghouse with a "questionable reputation" and as a stage stop hotel called the Oriental House. If you're a Civil War history buff, turn right at 6th St. and drive to its very end at Oak St., where you'll find on a hillside the historic **Madronia Cemetery.** Established in 1854, it contains the remains of many of Saratoga's pioneers as well as the grave of Mary Brown, the wife of abolitionist John Brown, famous for his raid of Harpers Ferry.

Saratoga Village has street parking as well as public lots on side streets. The village gets particularly busy on weekends, when tourists come to browse among its galleries, boutiques, and antique stores. It's also well known for its selection of restaurants offering some of Silicon Valley's finest cuisine. Among them you'll find **Vienna Woods,** 408/867-2410, an excellent European restaurant and deli located in the **Plaza Del Roble shopping center** off Big Basin Way. It serves breakfast all day long as well as various delicatessen meals, such as hot bratwurst sandwiches. On warm days, the patio provides a relaxing place to eat under the shade of an oak tree. **Bella Saratoga,** 408/741-5115, is a fun place to eat lunch or dinner in a more upscale setting. Describing itself as "a romantic ristorante," its outdoor patio dining area in front lets diners soak in the village's atmosphere. Saratogans often stop at the **Blue Rock Shoot,** 408/867-3437, for breakfast bagels and coffee. On many sunny mornings, you can find them reading their newspapers on the roughhewn front porch.

For art lovers, the village has two galleries located at 14531 Big Basin Way. **Aegis Gallery of Fine Art,** 408/867-0171, showcases local artists giving poetry readings, dramatic interpretations, and chamber music the third Thurs. evening of the month. **Gallery Saratoga Co-op** next door exhibits the work of a different artist each month. Both galleries are open every day but Monday.

After exploring the village, get back in your car and drive east to the end of Big Basin Way. Here, take the right turnoff at Saratoga–Los Gatos Rd., and one block later, pull into the parking lot of the **Saratoga Historical Museum,** 408/867-4311. Its displays and photographs chronicle the city's early milling and agricultural industry. The small museum is located in a former drugstore built at the turn of the 19th century. Museum guides give walking tours of the area once a month from Apr. to Nov., relating the stories behind 22 of the city's historical buildings.

The **Saratoga Chamber of Commerce,** 408/867-0753, is next to the museum in a wood-frame building built around 1865 called the McWilliams House. A cabinet on the porch here provides visitors with local business brochures and events calendars. Just around the corner is **Saratoga's first library,** now a nonprofit used bookstore providing funds for the city's library system.

After visiting Saratoga's museum block, get back onto Saratoga–Los Gatos Rd. by turning right at the exit, driving southeast for about one mile until you see the sign on the right side of the road for **Villa Montalvo,** 408/961-5800. The griffins perched on this estate's entrance columns represent the mythical creatures mentioned in a 14th-century romantic novel about the "isle of California" written by Ordoñez de Montalvo, after whom the estate was named. Drive about one mile up the hill along Montalvo Rd., passing well-tended mansions, and park in the parking lot area. Villa Montalvo was the country home of turn-of-the-19th-century San Francisco mayor James Duval Phelan, called "the foremost citizen of California." Art exhibits are often shown at this large Mediterranean-style mansion. The formal gardens contain a number of Victorian-era statues, including sphinxes and other legendary creatures. Finely carved Spanish figureheads grace the panels on an oak door at the side porch entrance. A steep stone stairway behind the villa leads to a nature trail wandering through the park and providing an overlook of Silicon Valley. Plan to spend at least one leisurely hour at Villa Montalvo.

Drive back to Saratoga–Los Gatos Rd. and turn right. About a mile down the tree-lined highway, turn left at the stoplight intersection onto Fruitvale Avenue. The road passes through a residential area for about half a mile. On your right, you'll see Saratoga's **West Valley College,** 408/867-2200, a sprawling campus placed in a glenlike setting of creeks and oak trees. After passing through the intersection at Allendale Ave., you'll see Saratoga's **Civic Center** on your left. The small Queen Anne–style house here surrounded by a country garden is the **Warner Hutton Home,** built in 1896. It is a good example of the farm homes existing in Saratoga at the turn of the 19th century. After having been moved to this location to escape demolition during Hwy. 85's construction, the house now serves as a small community center. A heritage orchard of several acres sits beside the house, serving as a reminder of the blossoms that once covered the valley.

At the corner where the Saratoga Public Library stands, turn right onto Saratoga Avenue. Drive about a quarter mile to Hwy. 85. The right-lane entrance goes southbound to San Jose. The left lane going under the overpass leads to the northbound entrance heading toward San Francisco.

POINTS OF INTEREST

Saratoga Historical Museum

In 1976, a turn-of-the-century drugstore was converted into this hometown museum located in a small park close to Saratoga Village. The museum showcases furniture, household objects, and antique photographs that bring the city's lumber and agricultural history to life. In a shed behind the museum is a small collection of rusting farm equipment.

20450 Saratoga–Los Gatos Rd. (next to the Saratoga Chamber of Commerce), 408/867-4311; free parking; admission free; open Fri.–Sun. 1–4 P.M. (call first to see if a docent is there).

Castle Rock State Park

While writing *The Grapes of Wrath* and *Of Mice and Men,* author John Steinbeck often journeyed from his Los Gatos home to this sylvan park on the 3,200-foot crest of the Santa Cruz Mountains. Here, he found inspiration in its magnificent vistas of oaks, pine forests, canyons, springs, and waterfalls. The 4,800-acre park has more than 35 miles of trails meandering among coast redwoods, madrona, and Douglas firs. From one wooden lookout platform, you can peer down at rock-climbers as they scale the sheer granite walls next to a waterfall. The actual Castle Rock, a short hike from the parking lot, is a fortresslike natural formation of weird caves that kids love scampering through. Trails connect the 3,025-

acre park to Sanborn-Skyline County Park and Big Basin State Park.

Off Skyline Blvd. (from Saratoga Village, drive the winding, steep Hwy. 9 to the intersection at Hwy. 35, a.k.a. Skyline Blvd.; turn left, drive two miles south), 408/867-2952; parking $5, or free along road outside entrance; activities: hiking, rock-climbing, 25 primitive walk-in camping sites.

Sanborn-Skyline County Park

Towering redwoods and coastal fogs provide a breathtaking backdrop for this 3,600-acre park in the Santa Cruz Mountains. Geology buffs can actually see the San Andreas Fault, which cuts diagonally through the park, creating its steep and rugged terrain. Hiking trails were originally mule trails used to bring supplies to lumber camps. Higher into the mountains, Sanborn Park connects with Castle Rock State Park.

Off Sanborn Rd. (from Saratoga Village, drive two miles west on Hwy. 9; turn left on Sanborn Rd. and drive one mile), 408/867-9959; website: claraweb.co.santa-clara.ca.us/parks; activities: Youth Science Institute, theater, American youth hostel, RV and walk-in campground, horseshoes, volleyball, horseback riding, hiking (more than 15 miles of trails).

Saratoga Springs

This pleasant private mountain campground near Sanborn-Skyline County Park is at the location of William Campbell's lumber mill, which helped give Saratoga its start. Facilities for both tent and RV camping include hot showers, water and electric hookups, swimming pool, playground, and laundry. Hiking trails meander around the creek.

Along Hwy. 9 (two winding miles up from Saratoga Village along Hwy. 9 near Sanborn Rd.), 408/867-9999; website: www.saratoga-springs.com; open year-round; fees $25 for tent site, $30 for RV site; reservations highly recommended.

Hakone Japanese Gardens

San Francisco art patrons Oliver and Isabel Stine were inspired to build this lovely garden after viewing Japanese botanical displays at the 1915 Panama Pacific Exhibition. Isabel traveled to Japan and visited the Fuji-Hakone National Park for ideas in building her own version. In 1918, she hired landscape gardener Naoharu Aihara to develop a Hakone Garden on the Stine's 16-acre retreat in the Saratoga hills. Here, you can wander among the placid beauty of reflecting ponds and walk across moss-carpeted stepping stones in the tea gardens. Or you can simply contemplate the universe as you gaze at the raked gravel of the Zen garden. The Cultural Exchange Center, a reproduction of a 19th-century Kyoto tea merchant's house and shop, was prefabricated in Japan using traditional tools and shipped to Saratoga.

21000 Big Basin Way (drive about half a mile north along Hwy. 9 from Saratoga Village; look for sign on left and drive up the steep driveway), 408/741-4994; parking $5; admission free; open Mon.–Fri. 10 A.M.–5 P.M., weekends 11 A.M.–5 P.M.; formal tea ceremony first Thurs. of the month from 1–4 P.M.

Farm Produce

Organic produce and local crafts are sold at the **Saratoga Farmers' Market,** held every Sat. 9 A.M.–1 P.M. at the Saratoga High School parking lot (on Saratoga-Sunnyvale Rd. and Herriman Ave.), 800/806-3276.

Navakovich Orchards is a family-run fruit stand located at 14251 Fruitvale Ave. (across from the West Valley College baseball field), 408/867-3131. Open Mon.–Fri. 9 A.M.–5 P.M.

Saratoga Drama Group

Since 1963, talented Silicon Valley residents have received their chance to step into the limelight with this community-based theatrical company. Performing throughout the year, the group's past shows have included *Brigadoon* and a community theater premiere of Rodgers and Hammerstein's *State Fair.*

Saratoga Civic Theater, 13777 Fruitvale Ave. (across from West Valley College), 408/264-3110; free parking; individual tickets $13–18, season tickets (three shows) $27–45.

Los Gatos

One of Los Gatos's old-fashioned charms is that it insists on being called a "town." Longtime residents easily get annoyed with any visitor who refers to it as a "city." The town of about 30,000 people is set in the Santa Cruz Mountain foothills, providing it with great views of the South Bay. A large number of showcase Victorian homes set on hillside lots lend many of the city's neighborhoods a certain turn-of-the-19th-century charm. Its well-kept middle- and upper-class houses as well as its lack of heavy industry have made the colorful town one of Silicon Valley's most desirable communities to live in.

Los Gatos is bisected by Hwy. 17, a busy mountain freeway crossing over to the coastal city of Santa Cruz. The town is bordered on the west by Monte Sereno and Saratoga, on the north by Campbell, and on the east by San Jose's Cambrian Park district. On the south, it is bordered by unincorporated county land covered with redwoods. It offers several parks where locals can go for outdoor activities, including the immensely popular Vasona Lake County Park.

© MARTIN CHEEK

Los Gatos' idyllic Oak Meadow Park

The Los Gatos Creek Parkway (popular with bike riders) and nearby Lexington Reservoir also make it an ideal place for water-sports lovers. The local farmers' market is held Sun. mornings in Plaza Park, in the heart of its historic downtown district. Throughout the year, residents hold several community festivals and events, including a well-attended holiday parade during the Christmas season.

Famous Los Gatos residents have included Olympic figure skater Peggy Fleming and violinist virtuoso Yehudi Menuhin. Today, Los Gatos is home to many of Silicon Valley's wealthiest computer industry workers. Several high-tech start-up companies also find the town attractive enough for their base of operations. Despite the encroachment of Silicon Valley's fast-paced lifestyle, Los Gatos tries to retain its small-town atmosphere. The upscale shops and restaurants in its renovated downtown district make a visit to the town well worth the effort.

HISTORY

Los Gatos was named after a Mexican land grant called Rancho Rinconada de los Gatos (Corner of the Cats Ranch). Stories vary on how this name came about. The most believable tale is that in 1839, José Maria Hernandez, his brother James, and brother-in-law Sebastian Fabian Peralta were exploring the region of what is now Vasona Park for land to establish a homestead. They found an open field perfect for a farm, but no apparent water source. Suddenly, a demonic shriek rose from the chaparral bushes. The unearthly sound came from two wildcats fighting. Realizing that cats always stay near water sources, the men made a brief search and soon located what is now called Los Gatos Creek. On July 23, 1839, California governor Alvarado granted José and Sebastian 6,631 acres of the land grant.

Another more dramatic story explaining the rancho's name tells the tragic tale of an Indian shepherd named Pedro Vasques who kept his grazing flock near what is now downtown Los Gatos's Main St. bridge. Pedro's wife and new-born lived in a small hut near here. During a heavy winter storm, the rain turned the placid creek into a flooding torrent, and the shepherd drowned while attempting to cross it to reach his flocks. His wife left to get help at the Santa Clara Mission, but the storm's fury was too much and she returned to the hut. There, she found that while she had been away, her tiny baby had been killed and carried off to be eaten by the area's wildcats. Overcome with grief, the mother threw herself into the creek, drowning herself. Whatever the true origin, the wildcats that gave the town its name still prowl the foothill region around Los Gatos.

Forbes Mill

By the late 1840s, the mountains' redwood trees became an important source of lumber for the growing Santa Clara Valley. Julian Hanks and Isaac Branham started a mill on November 29, 1847, on Los Gatos Creek in an area now covered by Lexington Reservoir. The mill cut timber that was sold at a lumberyard on what is now E. Main St. and College Ave., thus becoming the area's first commercial business. Three years later, a Scottish man named James Alexander Forbes came to the area and bought 100 acres near the creek to start a wheat mill. Forbes saw a lucrative flour business developing with California's Gold Rush population boom. He had lived in California since 1831, serving as a manager at the Mission Santa Clara. He had also invested heavily in the New Almaden Quicksilver Mine, losing a fortune over a property dispute in this enterprise. Forbes began construction work on his $100,000 four-story mill, building it of hard graywacke stone, and the structure was completed in August 1854. But the machinery from New York did not reach the site until April 1855. This caused Forbes to lose a considerable sum of money because he was not able to mill that year's large wheat harvest. Having invested so heavily in his Santa Rosa Brand Flour Mill that he faced a huge debt, Forbes declared bankruptcy on December 10, 1856. The mill passed through the hands of several owners, eventually taken over by W. H. Rogers and Company, which made it a prosperous enterprise.

The tiny settlement around Forbes Mill was called Forbestown for a time, but as the settle-

THE HOLY CITY OF HILLTOP HUSTLER "FATHER" RIKER

During the first half of the 20th century, one regular visitor to Los Gatos's businesses and homes was the self-anointed "Father" William Riker, the eccentric leader of a cult called The Perfect Christian Divine Way. A few miles from Los Gatos, the charlatan Riker started his mountaintop "Holy City," which, during the 1920s, made him more than $100,000 a year in the holy pursuits of selling gasoline and food to tourists. Many older Los Gatos residents still recall a billboard placed near Riker's scenic utopia that advised travelers to "see me if you are contemplating marriage, suicide, or crime."

Riker was a third-grade dropout from Oakdale, California, who worked for a time as a necktie salesman in San Francisco. He started a palm-reading and mind-reading act that proved much more lucrative and gave him the idea to start up his own religion. By 1914, calling himself "The Comforter," he started his small cult of believers based on his idea of a white supremacist path to salvation. In 1919, he bought 200 ridgetop acres in the Santa Cruz Mountains and started a commune there, preaching to travelers who stopped to patronize his enterprises, which included a garage, hotel, general store, restaurant, and barber shop. Tourists heading from the Santa Clara Valley to the resort town of Santa Cruz went through Holy City and saw the various placards and miniature church "peep shows" Riker had set up. (These displays often created a comical effect—one memorable diorama presented a series of life-size Santa Claus statues standing next to a statue of a voluptuous woman.)

During the 1920s, Riker also set up a small radio station to broadcast music and his religious rambling. With the call letters KFQU (be careful how you say it), it was closed in December 1931 when the Federal Radio Commission took the broadcasting license away on the grounds that "the station was not operated in the public interest and had frequently deviated from its assigned frequency."

The 1930s were the high-water mark in Holy City's growth—as many as 200 people hit by the Great Depression joined the cult in order to have a place to stay and be taken care of.

With aspirations to political office, Riker unsuccessfully ran for governor of California in 1938, 1942, 1946, and 1950. His bigoted platform targeting Asian- and African-Americans with such statements as, "The White Man can take care of any and all kinds of business in our own, White Man's California State Home, and no longer will the White Man tolerate your undermining and polluting tactics."

With the opening of Hwy. 17 in the late 1930s and the outbreak of World War II, Holy City began its rapid decline. By 1948, it had become a virtual ghost town of about 20 believers. On December 3, 1969, Riker died, at the age of 96, in Agnews State Hospital, a facility for the mentally ill in Santa Clara. Over the years, much of Holy City has crumbled to dust or burned down. However, the sign for its "Holy City Zoo" was taken to San Francisco, where a well-known comedy club borrowed the evocative name.

ment grew, the name was changed to Los Gatos after the original rancho. By the fall of 1858, a toll road was completed from Los Gatos to another toll road built by settler "Mountain Charley" McKiernan. This provided a route to Santa Cruz that roughly follows what is now Hwy. 17. By 1867, the road had become so heavily used that a wagon came by every 15 minutes on busy days. A tollhouse was built at what is now 142 S. Santa Cruz Ave., charging tolls from $.50 to $1. This historic building still stands near the Toll House Hotel. In 1868, an Irishman named John Lyndon came to the area and bought 100 acres along with a hotel called the Ten Mile House, located in what is now the town's plaza and post office area. Renamed the Lyndon Hotel, it grew into an important social point for the growing community.

One of the mountain road's toll keepers was called D. B. Moody, and a small canyon nearby was named Moody Gulch in his honor. Here in 1873, settler R. C. McPherson discovered an oil field that extended throughout this portion of the mountains. Drilling was done for many years, and although quantities were small, Moody Gulch oil was sold in San Jose until 1922, when the operation closed down.

Orchards

With the rise of the region's orchard industry, Los Gatos grew into a farm-based community. Because of its magnificent location between the mountains and the Santa Clara Valley, it was soon called "the Gem of the Foothills." On March 20, 1878, construction was finished on a narrow gauge railroad leading from San Jose to Los Gatos. This helped spur the town's economic growth even more with a depot station near what is now the town's plaza. Another train stop was near a prune orchard belonging to Albert August Vollmer, who had come to the area from Michigan in 1887. Vollmer named the flag stop Vasona Junction after a pet pony he had owned as a boy. The area around the stop later became known as Vasona Lake County Park. On August 10, 1887, with a population of 1,645 people, the town had grown large enough for its residents to decide to incorporate the community.

From the 1880s through the early part of the 20th century, orchards served as Los Gatos's primary industry. Much of the fruit grown here was processed at the Los Gatos Canning Company, one of the town's larger employers. Among the citizens who moved here in 1883 was almond grower John Bean, who enjoyed tinkering with machinery. After a scale disease infested the fruit trees in the Los Gatos region, John developed a powerful double-action force sprayer to combat the blight with pesticides. He called his invention the Bean Spray Pump. Out of this humble beginning, the well-known agriculture machine company called Food Machinery Corporation was established, moving its manufacturing site to Santa Clara's Julian St. in 1910. During World War II, the company switched to making military weapons such as tanks used during World War II in the Pacific. Now known as FMC, its Silicon Valley operations continue to produce tanks, such as the Bradley Fighting Vehicle.

On May 26, 1898, the old Lyndon Hotel burned down; it was replaced by a much-improved version in 1901. The new luxury hotel and the town's idyllic beauty soon made Los Gatos a popular travel destination. In 1922, Los Gatos's most well known landmark was installed. The poet Charles Erskin Scott Wood and his wife, poetess Sara Bard Fields, built a home in "Poet's Canyon," an area in the town's western foothills. Many artists and writers, including Carl Sandburg, often came for visits to their beautiful hideaway home. To watch over the canyon's entrance, the couple commissioned sculptor Robert Paine to create two identical cat statues. Made of cement, the imperturbable creatures stand eight feet tall and are 10 feet in circumference. Today, the cats are affectionately known by locals as Leo and Leona. They serve as the official logo for Los Gatos's town government as well as for its chamber of commerce (408/354-9300), and still can be seen at their original location of 17525 Santa Cruz Highway. Near these cement cats is another Los Gatos landmark named after the statues. Called The Cats Restaurant, it's one of the last remaining true roadhouse taverns left in the United States. The restaurant originally served as a stage stop

JOHN STEINBECK IN THE VALLEY OF SILICON

Adjacent to Los Gatos's northwestern boundary along Hwy. 9 is the community of Monte Sereno. At 3,600 residents and just over one square mile, it's Silicon Valley's smallest incorporated city. It has no chamber of commerce or industry, but serves as an affluent bedroom community for Silicon Valley. The median price of a home here has reached almost $1 million. The city was incorporated in 1956 to prevent its annexation by Los Gatos. It has no major claim to fame other than the fact it was for several years the home of Nobel Prize–winning author John Steinbeck.

The Salinas-born author had a strong connection to the Silicon Valley region. He attended Stanford University for several years, though he left without a degree. His first wife, Carol Henning, was born in San Jose, growing up in a Naglee Park home near what is now San Jose State University. People who knew her described the vivacious woman as a witty, down-to-earth tomboy. Carol was working as an advertising assistant for the *San Francisco Chronicle* when, during the summer of 1928, she and her sister Idell visited a fish hatchery in Tahoe City. There, she met one of the workers, a spirited young man named John Steinbeck.

The romance between the struggling author and the confident young woman bloomed. Shortly before marrying her in 1930, John wrote a friend: "I'd like you to know Carol. She doesn't write or dance or play the piano and she has very little of any soul at all. But horses like her and dogs and little boys and boot blacks and laborers. But people with souls don't like her much."

BOB RACE

along the toll road leading through the Santa Cruz Mountains, and in the Roaring Twenties, it did duty as a speakeasy and bordello. Today, it's a popular hangout for Silicon Valley residents, albeit much tamer than in its wilder days.

TOUR

Los Gatos is located in the southwestern portion of Silicon Valley. To get there from San Jose, drive south along Hwy. 17 and take the Lark Ave. exit. At the stoplight, turn left and drive east, crossing back over the highway. At the next stoplight intersection, turn right onto Los Gatos Blvd., passing through a section of town inhabited by auto dealerships and strip malls.

Turn right at the Blossom Hill Rd. stoplight intersection (where the Super Crown bookstore is located) and continue driving for about half a

mile until you cross over Hwy. 17. After this point, pass the entrance to **Vasona Lake County Park,** 408/356-2729, on your right, and a short distance later, turn to your right into **Oak Meadow Park,** 408/395-7433. A pleasant place to explore some of Los Gatos's natural beauty, this small park has been a favorite among local kids and families for many years. On weekends as well as summer weekdays, visitors enjoy taking short rides on the **Billy Jones Wildcat Railroad.** Its small-scale locomotive pulls open cars through the park's oak groves and grass fields. A classic carousel sits next to the train's depot. Rides for both attractions are $1.

Oak Meadow Park is connected by trails to Vasona Lake County Park, a tranquil place for a stroll around its small reservoir. Someplace along where Los Gatos Creek meanders through the park's boundaries, original inhabitants José Maria

Earlier, while Steinbeck had been living and writing in the Monterey Bay village of Carmel, he had met another young man who was working on a controversial theory of universal themes in myths. Joseph Campbell's book *The Hero with a Thousand Faces* would later have a strong influence on filmmaker George Lucas's *Star Wars* films, but his influence on Steinbeck is also undeniable. It can clearly be seen in Steinbeck's early novel *To a God Unknown* as well as in later novels such as *East of Eden*. But it was Carol who provided her husband with the much-needed encouragement to labor on and develop that mythic theme in his literature.

In 1934, Carol and John built a redwood cottage at 16250 Greenwood Ln. in Monte Sereno, calling their new home "Arroyo Del Ajo." Working on the front patio and in the guest house living room at this location, Steinbeck created two of his most critically acclaimed novels, *Of Mice and Men* (which he handwrote and Carol typed) and the Pulitzer Prize–winning *Grapes of Wrath,* which Steinbeck dedicated "To Carol who willed this book." (As it happens, she also proposed the titles for these two great works of literature.) The two divorced in 1943, and Steinbeck never quite achieved the same depth in his writing as he had during the period of his first marriage.

The Monte Sereno house where the Steinbecks lived is considered a historic site but continues to be a private residence. Additions to the home were made in 1967, but the brickwork, walks, gate, and fence are original to the Steinbecks. Occasionally, when the owner wants to do renovation work such as replace a wall or tear out cement steps that John Steinbeck built, he gets into heated disputes with the local historic board.

The author's Silicon Valley presence can probably best be felt anyway at San Jose State University, which has a small Steinbeck Center containing letters and memorabilia, including a portable typewriter he once owned. The recently opened National Steinbeck Center in downtown Salinas, an hour's drive south from Silicon Valley, provides an excellent overview of the California writer's life and literary genius in its exhibits.

CITIES OF THE VALLEY

Hernandez and Sebastian Fabian Peralta built their adobe home on their Mexican land grant. Plan to spend 45 minutes to an hour exploring these two parks.

From Oak Meadow Park, turn right on Blossom Hill Road. Crossing University Ave., glance to your right and you'll see the site of a Silicon Valley morality tale. In 1983, Eagle Computer, one of the first IBM PC clone makers, went public, earning its founder Dennis Barnhart millions of dollars in stock. During the celebration party, Barnhart became inebriated, then climbed into his Ferrari and raced down University Avenue. Here, among the eucalyptus trees, he crashed the sports car into an embankment, ending his life and thus becoming a Silicon Valley lesson on the fleeting nature of success.

From University Ave., drive one block to the stoplight at the end of Blossom Hill Road. Turn left here onto N. Santa Cruz Ave., following the street for less than a mile. After crossing Hwy. 9 (called Los Gatos–Saratoga Rd. at this point), you'll enter Los Gatos's charming downtown area.

The seasoned charm of **downtown Los Gatos** makes it a favorite destination for Silicon Valley residents. It's a lively place for people-watching. Below the picturesque backdrop of the Santa Cruz Mountains, its streets buzz with activity during the day as shoppers visit its expensive boutiques, art galleries, and restaurants. The action continues on weekend nights as patrons are drawn to its upscale bars and coffeehouses. The downtown's downside is that its free parking lots fill up quickly (especially during the holiday season), and shoppers often must drive around the blocks searching for those elusive parking spaces. Plans are in the works for two new parking garages. Watch out for the restricted parking zones in the residential areas bordering downtown—parking patrols will place tickets on cars not belonging here.

After finding a parking place, spend a couple of hours strolling through the downtown, browsing through its interesting shops. One called **Purrsnickety,** 408/395-2287, keeps true to the town's cat theme by selling feline-oriented gifts. Pippi and Noodle, two rescued kitties, roam the store as mascots. A connected shop to Purrsnickety is called **Bow Wowzer,** where you can find canine-oriented gifts. Despite the downtown's yuppie atmosphere, Harley-Davidson bikers in black leather often wander into **The Black Watch,** 408/354-2200, a long-established bar serving the best kamikazes in Silicon Valley. Set back in its garden away from the busy street is a stately Victorian containing the **Chart House Restaurant,** 408/354-1737. This classic eatery serves steak, seafood, and prime rib. If you're into kitchen gadgets and unusual gift items, stop at **Domus,** 408/354-6630, a shop filled to the brim with unusual gizmos.

At the top of N. Santa Cruz Ave. sits the town's **plaza park,** the heart of Los Gatos. It's a pleasant spot to sit on a bench under its small grove of trees or relax by its rock mound water fountain. In a glass case here, you'll find a small exhibit describing the history behind the mechanism for one of the town's original fire bells from 1899. Around the corner from the plaza on W. Main St. are several popular eateries, including the **Los Gatos Coffee Roasting Company,** 408/354-3263, a favorite gathering spot for weekend bicyclists during their rides along the nearby Los Gatos Creek Trail. So crowded does the place sometimes get that customers often must sit on its outside benches to enjoy its excellent java. Across the street is the **Opera House,** 408/354-1469, a historical 1906 landmark that no longer features classical music productions but instead contains a number of boutiques and antique shops.

From the Opera House, follow Main St. to the stoplight intersection at University Ave.,

crossing here and turning left, and then walking a block. On your right, you'll pass the historic **St. Lukes Episcopalian Church** built in 1902; take a moment to step into its tranquil patio gardens. Next to the church and recessed from the street is a 35,000-square-foot shopping mall. This is known as **Old Town** because it's the location from which the village of Los Gatos originally grew. The present building first served as an elementary school constructed in 1923, but later it was turned into a collection of shops and restaurants. In the late 1990s, it underwent a major renovation. Among its significant changes is the **Borders Bookstore,** in a building that once served as the town's civic theater. Worth visiting at Old Town is the **Oakville Grocery,** a posh gourmet shop selling breads, wines, cheeses, and desserts. If you're hungry, you can buy some snacks here and sit in an alcove with a view of the foothills. Next to this shop is **The Indian Store,** 408/354-9988, which sells finely crafted Native American art and jewelry.

After visiting the various shops here, follow a concrete stairway under the California Cafe sign leading down through the center of Old Town. Continue on through the arching wooden gateway, an entry to the Los Gatos Creek Trail. Directly in front of you is a footbridge that crosses over Hwy. 17. As you follow this over the busy freeway, take a look at various panels of artwork painted on its sides. These demonstrate the creative talents of the town's schoolchildren. At the bridge's opposite end, the sidewalk veers to the right, coming to the historic site of **Forbes Mill.** The original mill section stood four stories high and was demolished to make way for Hwy. 17 in the late 1940s. The two-story stone building standing here now is a later annex, which now serves as the **Forbes Mill History Museum,** 408/395-7375. Inside this local museum, you'll see pictures and mementos providing an enlightening glimpse into Los Gatos's past. (Note: if you wish to drive to the museum, take W. Main St. to Church St., turning left here and following this small thoroughfare down the hill to the museum's parking lot.)

After returning to your car, drive from the downtown parking lot to University Ave., turn-

MOUNTAIN CHARLEY

In downtown Los Gatos, locals often hang out in a popular bar called Mountain Charley's. As it happens, there actually was a real "Mountain Charley," a feisty pioneer of the Santa Cruz Mountains who, the legend goes, intimidated the native California grizzly bears so much that the massive animals never disputed his right of way.

The exact year of his birth is uncertain, but Charley McKiernan was born in Ireland around 1825. As a quartermaster for the British Army, he was stationed in Australia and New Zealand. When gold was discovered in California and with his term of service up, he worked his way on a ship to San Francisco and eventually found himself toiling in the mines, making $20 a day (at a time when $20 a year was a decent wage in Ireland). He saved his money and used his savings to start up a pack-train company carrying supplies in the Trinity area of the Sierras. But Indians attacked him and took all his money and possessions. He went back to work in the goldfields and, when he had saved up enough again, came to the Santa Clara Valley to homestead.

In 1850, much of the valley was already settled, so Charley went in search of land in the mountains. He stopped at a pond where the native Indians often camped, a spot the Spanish called Laguna del Sargento. Here, he cut down redwood trees and built himself a frame house—the first in the mountains. He started a ranch raising sheep and longhorn cattle, often killing mountain lions and grizzlies that attacked his herds. The local Indians were the ones who nicknamed the rugged maverick "Mountain Charley."

Grizzlies are extinct in California, and the only place in Silicon Valley you're likely to see one is flying on the state flag. The last grizzly in the state was killed in November 1886, near Ben Lomond. But during Charley's time, the area abounded with the animals, their size often 800 to 1,200 pounds in mass. It took a brave man and a hail of bullets to bring the creatures down. On May 8, 1854, Charley and a friend named John Taylor were out hunting deer with Taylor's two dogs when they happened to confront in their path a she-grizzly guarding two cubs. Charley plunged his gun muzzle into the bear's chest and fired, and Taylor fired into the grizzly's head, but this only enraged the animal. With her strong paws, she seized Charley, her jaws crunching into the front of his skull, and then tossed his body aside as if it were a rag doll. Taylor's dogs attacked the cubs, and their cries brought the mother to their rescue. Taylor, thinking Charley certainly dead, made his escape to the ridge.

When he returned, he found the blood-soaked Charley still conscious but temporarily paralyzed from the waist down. A gaping hole in his skull showed where the bear's jaws had come down. Taylor attended to the wounds as best he could and brought the mountain man to two doctors in San Jose named Bell and Ingersoll. The medical men fashioned a plate from two silver Mexican half dollars and, without anesthesia, used it to close the gap in Charley's skull. (This rather astonishing surgery won the patient a change of nickname—to "Silver Skull Charley.") Charley suffered from headaches for two years, until he went to a doctor in Redwood City who took off the original plate—which had by that time corroded badly. Underneath, he found a mass of hair growing. (When word of this got out, Charley received yet another sobriquet: "Hair-Brained Charley.") A new plate was fashioned, but, disfigured, Charley always kept his hat cocked at a tilt to hide the injury.

Charley also built toll roads through the mountains using a horse-drawn scraper. Some of these back-country roads are still in use. A one-lane road he built that winds through the redwoods is still named after him, and a historic marker on the site shows where his cabin stood. He died on January 18, 1892, having lived life by his creed: "Right wrongs nobody."

ing right and heading to W. Main Street. Turn left at the stoplight intersection and cross the Main St. bridge over Hwy. 17. Immediately after this, turn right on College Ave. and continue following this curvy road up through wooded hilly terrain. At the top of this road, turn right at Prospect Ave., passing through an ornate iron gate with gilded grapes. Shortly on your left, you'll pass the entrance to the **Mirassou Champagne Cellars,** 408/395-3790, which is open for wine-tasting Wed.–Sun. afternoons.

Continue along where the road curves until you reach the historic **Sacred Heart Novitiate.** You can park at the small parking lot here and enjoy a breathtaking view of Silicon Valley. The novitiate once served as a college to prepare Catholic novices for their lives in the priesthood. Besides providing religious instruction, it was also the site of a foothill vineyard growing wine grapes for sacramental and commercial use. The Jesuits bought the original 39-acre parcel of land here on March 18, 1886, from Harvey Wilcox for $15,000 to establish the novitiate. Among its theology students in the 1960s was a peculiar fellow named Jerry Brown. He later became a controversial governor of California nicknamed "Governor Moonbeam" due to his unorthodox style of liberal government. (In 1998, he was elected mayor of Oakland.) On January 5, 1986, a century after its founding, the novitiate was closed. The land was subsequently purchased by the Mid-Peninsula Open Space District for $3.7 million, and the palatial buildings still remain as a Los Gatos landmark. (The site is private property so please be courteous during your visit.)

After you're through visiting here, go back down to the novitiate entrance gate, continuing straight ahead down Prospect Ave. and curving to the right where it turns into Reservoir Road. Turn left at the stop sign, and immediately after this, turn right onto College Ave., following it to E. Main Street. Turn right on Main St., passing by a complex of modern brick buildings on your right. This is Los Gatos's **Civic Center,** the location of the town's government departments including the library and police station. Continue driving, passing quaint-looking **Los Gatos High School** on your left. Among its graduates are the famous actress sisters Joan Fontaine and Olivia de Havilland. After the high school where the road curves north, Main St. turns into Los Gatos Boulevard. Here you'll pass among a number of finely crafted Victorian homes that are among the town's architectural jewels. At the Los Gatos–Saratoga Rd. stoplight intersection, turn left. After passing the Los Gatos Lodge, you'll come to the freeway entrances for Hwy. 17. The northbound entrance heads to San Jose, the southbound entrance leads over the mountains to the city of Santa Cruz along the coast.

POINTS OF INTEREST

Forbes Mill History Museum
Along the tree-shaded Los Gatos Creek Trail, this two-story stone structure once served as an annex to Alexander Forbes's wheat mill. It's now a picturesque museum devoted to the history of Los Gatos. Besides historic photos and artifacts of the town's pioneering days, it provides a changing array of local memorabilia. Among past exhibits was an excellent collection of Ohlone artifacts containing tools, beads, pendants, and ritual objects.

75 Church St. (near Los Gatos High School off Main St. or, for visitors who don't mind a short walk, across the Hwy. 17 footbridge from Old Town Shopping Center), 408/395-7375; free parking; admission free; open Wed.–Sun. noon–4 P.M.

Los Gatos Art and Natural History Museum
This small museum located in a residential area of Los Gatos combines local artistic talent with natural history exhibits. Silicon Valley artists display their works in well-lit, intimate galleries. Children love the small nature museum that contains hands-on touch tables full of shells, rocks, and pinecones from the nearby Santa Cruz Mountains. Various stuffed animals such as an American bald eagle provide a close-up look at many of the wild creatures that inhabit the area.

Corner of W. Main St. and Tait Ave. (three blocks west of downtown Los Gatos), 408/354-

AMBROSE BIERCE—THE VALLEY'S CYNIC

In the early years of the 1900s, the writer Ambrose Bierce was famous throughout the United States for his cynical prose and poetry. The Civil War veteran knew Mark Twain in San Francisco and, like Twain, wrote biting satire about the human condition. Working for William Randolph Hearst's chain of newspapers, Bierce contributed a weekly opinion piece and is considered the first newspaper columnist.

Probably Bierce's most famous work was his "Devil's Dictionary" which contained brutally barbed definitions for words and phrases. In 1989, Gregory Peck played the role of Ambrose Bierce in director Luis Puenzo's film *Old Gringo*. Also starring Jane Fonda and Jimmy Smits, the movie told the story of the author's last days in Mexico when, in 1915, he was reportedly executed by firing squad for his role in the Mexican Revolution. Bierce mysteriously disappeared at this time, and so legend has grown around the circumstances of his vanishing.

Bierce's connection to Silicon Valley is the fact that he lived for several years in the hills near Los Gatos. A small village called Wright's Station once existed at the mouth of the Los Gatos canyon near what is now Lexington Reservoir, and Bierce made his home near this community.

In his *History of Santa Clara County*, Eugene T. Sawyer tells a humorous anecdote of Bierce's encounter with a bike shop clerk. The satirist frequently rode a bicycle into San Jose and, on one trip, the wheel broke. He took it into a bike shop on Santa Clara St. and the repairer asked, "What name, please?"

"My name is Ambrose Bierce," the satirist said with a haughty tone.

"All right, Mr. Pierce, come back in an hour and your wheel will be ready for you."

The famous writer glared. "Bierce is my name."

"I get you, Steve," the repairer said. "I won't forget."

The proud Bierce left the shop, miffed that there was one man in California who was not aware of his great celebrity. An hour later, he returned for his repaired bike and found a tag attached to it with the name "Ambers Peerce." The young clerk was about to receive a verbal lashing from a master of the art, but Bierce realized his fury would be wasted on this nitwit. The author paid the bill and walked out of the shop with his bike.

2646; free parking on street; admission free; open Wed.–Sun. noon–4 P.M.

Lexington Reservoir

Just south of Los Gatos, this lake is one of Silicon Valley's more popular water recreation spots. In 1952, Lexington Dam was constructed, and as the waters rose, the reservoir flooded two small towns. Alma was simply a stagecoach stop, lumber mill site, and train stop. But the village of Lexington, named after a town in Missouri, had been a booming community for the timber trade, much of its lumber used to prop up the shafts in San Jose's New Almaden Quicksilver Mines. Now a scenic site for Silicon Valley fishing, the 475-acre man-made lake also draws sailboaters, windsurfers, and members of a local rowing club. The 960-acre park is connected to the Los Gatos Creek Parkway and is a favorite destination for weekend bikers seeking a hearty workout.

From Los Gatos, drive south on Hwy. 17 to the Bear Creek Rd. exit; go across the overpass and reenter Hwy. 17 north, taking the Alma Bridge Rd. exit), 408/353-6291, website: claraweb.co.santa-clara.ca.us/parks; admission free; open 8 A.M. to half an hour before sunset; activities: fishing, nonmotorized boating ($3 per day for boat launch).

Vasona Lake County Park

This placid 151-acre park offers activities from picnics and boating to biking and in-line skating along the trail skirting a small man-made reservoir. The lake is the home of tame ducks and geese, so bring pieces of bread if you want to feed these feathered creatures. Kids with poles can also enjoy a lazy afternoon of fishing. Canoes and paddleboats are available for rent during summer months. The park is adjacent to Los Gatos Creek Parkway, popular with bicyclists and skaters.

Off Blossom Hill Rd. (on Hwy. 17 in Los Gatos, take Lark Ave. exit and travel east; turn right on Los Gatos Blvd., then right on Blossom Hill Rd. to park entrance—walk-in entrances are on University Ave. and Garden Hill Dr.), 408/356-2729, website: claraweb.co.santa-clara.ca.us/parks; parking $5; admission free; open 8 A.M.–sunset; activities: children's playground, fishing, boating, Youth Science Institute, biking, horseshoes, volleyball.

Oak Meadow Park

Located adjacent to Vasona Lake County Park is the town of Los Gatos's small Oak Meadow Park. Kids relish the 10-minute train ride on the small-scale Billy Jones Wildcat Railroad that winds through the park. A well-loved institution in the town, the small railroad was built by Jones, a retired railroad engineer who discovered an old train engine in a junkyard and restored it to its original condition. He installed some track in his backyard, and for years enjoyed taking Los Gatos children on rides. After he died, his will gave the train and tracks to the town of Los Gatos, which set it up at the park in 1970 and built an old-fashioned train station to scale. Next to the station is a classic carousel that, like the train, was saved from the scrap heap and restored to its original grandeur. The park also features a playground with swings, a jungle gym, and an old Air Force fighter jet kids can climb on.

Off Blossom Hill Rd. (just west of Hwy. 17), 408/395-7433; parking $3 for non–residents; admission free; rides on carousel and train $1 each, children 2 and under ride free; open daily 8 A.M.–sunset.

South Valley

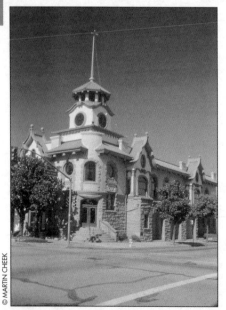

© MARTIN CHEEK

Gilroy's stately 1905 Old City Hall

Travel south from San Jose, and Silicon Valley changes from an urban jungle into a rural landscape of family farms and livestock grazing on rolling hills. This is South Valley, where many technology workers live in the communities of Gilroy, Morgan Hill, and San Martin. From these towns, it's a short commute to the heart of Silicon Valley. Here, the pace of life tends to be slower compared with the frantic hustle in the county's northern sections. Land is cheaper so homes are more affordable, and that's why the last two decades have seen a dramatic population boom in this area.

More than 40,000 people make Gilroy their home. The city still retains some of its agricultural roots but is quickly losing them as the local government tries to balance the protection of open spaces with the lucrative benefits of new construction. Much of the region's fertile ground is fast succumbing to suburbs for Silicon Valley commuters. Middle-class families are the primary buyers of these homes. Residents have a strong volunteer spirit, demonstrated annually by the more than 4,000 volunteers who help out with the Garlic Festival at Christmas Hill Park.

Gilroy also has a small base of manufacturers but hasn't yet developed a real high-tech presence, although several small Internet companies have sprouted in the area. Its major retail development is the Gilroy Outlets, along U.S. 101 off Leavesley Road. The outlets draw customers to Gilroy, away from other parts of the Bay Area. The city also has a substantial wine industry, the quality of its vineyards rivaling that of Napa. Silicon Valley wine connoisseurs journey down here on weekends to taste vintages at the various wineries located along Hecker Pass, a scenic mountain road leading to Watsonville. Set nearby in the foothills southwest of the city is the verdant campus of Gavilan Community College. Many of its students come from Gilroy, Morgan Hill, and San Benito County.

Between Morgan Hill and Gilroy along Monterey Rd. is the small, unincorporated town of San Martin. With a population of less than 2,000, it's the site of South County Municipal Airport as well as home to Wings of History, a remarkable antique airplane museum.

Morgan Hill, a city of about 33,000 people north of San Martin, has its share of South Valley attractions, including several excellent wineries along south Uvas Canyon. But mushrooms give this old ranch town its worldwide fame. The city is home to several mushroom-growing sites, such as Royal Oaks Mushrooms, where the edible fungus sprouts in cool, dark, dank buildings. An annual Mushroom Festival brings local crowds here to sample foods made with the product. Silicon Valley residents also visit its several large parks, such as Anderson Reservoir and Uvas Reservoir County Parks, both popular for water sports, and the immense Henry W. Coe State Park in the Diablo Range. Chitactac Adams County Park, a culturally enlightening park honoring the Ohlone Indians, can be found several miles west of Morgan Hill's historic downtown. And adding to the area's recreational facilities was the opening in summer 1999 of the massive Coyote Creek Golf Course, just north of Morgan Hill off U.S. 101.

Although the communities in South Valley retain much of their small-town atmosphere and the agricultural industry still plays a key economic role here, urban growth is steadily creeping in. One by one, farm fields and orchards are being leveled and graded to create housing divisions and strip malls, a repeat of what happened in the San Jose region after World War II. The signs are clear, with Internet hardware giant Cisco Systems announcing early in 1999 its plans to build a massive corporate campus in Coyote Valley, the northern section of South Valley. Sometime in the 21st century, the rural climate of this beautiful area in Santa Clara County's southern half will disappear completely. Silicon Valley's fast-paced culture will have completely invaded it, replacing farms and ranches with industrial parks for high-tech firms. Enjoy its rural ambience while you can.

MORGAN HILL HISTORY

Standing along Monterey Rd. north of Morgan Hill's downtown is a Queen Anne Victorian house that sets the scene of a bittersweet love story. The story starts in 1844, when Martin Murphy Sr. and his large Irish family were among the first pioneers to travel over the Sierras into California. Murphy purchased 9,000 acres of a Mexican land grant known as the Rancho Ojo de Agua de la Coche (Pig's Spring Ranch), and his youngest son Daniel helped him manage this vast tract. In 1851, Daniel married Maria Fisher, daughter of George William Fisher and heiress to her father's 19,000-acre Rancho Laguna Seca. In time, Daniel purchased property in California, Nevada, Arizona, and Mexico, owning more than one million acres, making him one of the richest land barons in the West.

Daniel and Maria had one daughter, a spirited girl named Diana, who was considered just as radiant as the Roman goddess of the moon she was named after. In 1880, when she was 20, she met a dashing 32-year-old bank clerk in San Francisco. The blue-eyed Hiram Morgan Hill stood six feet tall and moonlighted as a Bullocks clothes model. His charm and social prestige quickly won Diana over, and the two fell deeply in love. Daniel Murphy, however, didn't want Diana to marry Morgan, believing the young man's socializing ways would not make him a decent husband. But headstrong Diana secretly eloped with Morgan in San Francisco. Two months later, Daniel caught a severe case of pneumonia while herding cattle in a snowstorm at his Elko, Nevada, ranch. On his deathbed, he made Diana promise never to marry Morgan Hill. He soon died, never finding out that his daughter had already wed the man he so disapproved of.

MANSIONS, MUSHROOMS, AND MARILYN MONROE

It's all but irresistible to describe Morgan Hill as having truly mushroomed in the last two decades as it has been transformed from a farm community into a bedroom suburb of Silicon Valley. About 60 percent of its residents commute to San Jose and other northern county cities for their jobs. But the city still retains much of its agricultural economy, with several excellent wineries and a flower-farm industry that provides spectacular carpets of blossoms along the roads in spring.

In recent years, though, mushrooms have become a major product of the area's farms, earning Morgan Hill its title of "Mushroom Capital of the World." Each summer, the local Mushroom Mardi Gras attracts people from throughout the region. Anderson Reservoir, a large recreational area east of town, also draws in Silicon Valley residents who enjoy water sports.

In recent years, custom mansions have been built in the canyons and hills around Morgan Hill for Silicon Valley's corporate executives. Marilyn Monroe fans will find interesting the fact that, for his alibi, Robert F. Kennedy told police he was vacationing on a friend's ranch in Morgan Hill on the day the screen goddess died.

Morgan Hill's chamber of commerce is located at 25 W. 1st St. (just off Monterey St. in the downtown area), 408/779-9444.

Diana inherited her father's immense estate. In 1884, the Hills built a beautiful home for themselves on the property her father had first purchased. The six-room Queen Anne house featured crystal chandeliers, Minton-tiled fireplaces, and 10-foot gilt mirrors. The front porch looked out at an unusual conical foothill peak called El Toro. In honor of this breathtaking mountain view, they called their beautifully furnished home Villa Mira Monte. In time, the Hills had their only child, a beautiful girl named Daniella after Daniel Murphy. The proud parents spoiled the girl with lavish gifts from their European trips. But the Hills' marriage was severely strained, some say from the guilt Diana felt of lying to her father while he lay dying.

Near Villa Mira Monte, the railroad line extended down into the valley's southern region. Train operators began calling out the flag stop near this landmark house as "Morgan Hill's Ranch," soon shortening it to Morgan Hill. As settlers moved into the area, a small village called Morgan Hill began to grow around the stop.

Over time, Morgan and Diana's passionate love turned cold, and they finally separated. She spent her time as a socialite between homes in Washington, D.C., and San Francisco, and he moved away from the town that bears his name to run a ranch near Elko, Nevada. Daniella grew up to marry on December 6, 1911, a French baron named Hardoun de Reinach-Werth, a man rumored to have a severe drinking problem. During their European honeymoon, Daniella received word that her father had suffered a major stroke. This grave news caused a further rift in the already bad relationship with her new husband, causing the young woman to suffer a mental collapse. In the St. Pancras sanitorium in London, she committed suicide by throwing herself out of a second-story window and fracturing her skull. Perhaps from grief over his beloved daughter's tragic death, Morgan died the next year, a lonely man in his last days. Ironically, he was buried in the Santa Clara Mission cemetery next to his father-in-law, Daniel Murphy, the man who had so despised him.

The train stop of Morgan Hill had grown into a town of 250 by 1896, incorporating as a city in 1906 when it reached the legal population requirement of 500 people. Today, the city has more than 30,000 residents. Villa Mira Monte, the house standing beside Monterey Rd., served for several years as an antique shop and is now run as a museum by the Morgan Hill Historical Society. Visitors can see the home's original front door, prominently displaying a floral design in Tiffany stained glass intertwining around the initials *M.H.* for the man who once made it his home.

GILROY HISTORY

In 1813, 18-year-old John Cameron, a sailor from Inverness, Scotland, and his friend "Deaf Jimmy" jumped off the British ship *Isaac Todd* in Monterey Bay. (Another version of the story says that they were left at the port to recuperate from scurvy.) Concerned that he'd be tracked down by the Royal Navy, John assumed his mother's maiden name of Gilroy. The two hiked over the Gabilan Mountains to Mission San Juan Bautista, where they stayed for several months, then eventually made their way into the southern part of Santa Clara Valley. Here, the young men reached a Spanish settlement of several adobe houses called Pleasant Valley.

In Pleasant Valley, John met a beautiful and winsome Spanish woman named Maria Clara Ortega. She was the daughter of Lieutenant José Francisco Ortega, who, as the scout in Portolá's exploration party in 1769, was the first European to view the Santa Clara Valley. By this time, the Ortegas owned the land grant of Rancho San Ysidro in the southern section of the valley. Clara fell madly in love with the rugged John Gilroy and married him on Easter 1821. He settled in this South Valley region to work as a soapmaker and millwright, thus becoming California's first permanent English-speaking resident.

By 1850, the adobe settlement became an important link in the crossroads of El Camino Real and Pacheco Pass Rd., which led to the San Joaquin Valley. As commerce came through, a small village developed around what is now Lewis Street. It consisted of five stores, a hotel, and a horse stable. As pioneers came to this area, they liked its warm climate and built their homes here. John had become an important member of the community, and the town was officially called Gilroy in his honor. He had a weakness, however, for gambling and drinking, and as his debts rose, more and more of his wife's land and possessions were sold to pay them off. By the end of his life, he lived in poverty, but he saw the town bearing his name incorporated as a city before he died in July 1869.

Among Gilroy's more esteemed residents was Fanny Stevenson, wife of writer Robert Louis Stevenson, who created such classics as *Treasure Island* and *Dr. Jekyll and Mr. Hyde.* Five years after her husband's death in Samoa in December 1894, Fanny visited the Redwood Retreat Inn in the foothills west of the city and was truly enchanted by the area's tranquil ambience. In June 1900, the 60-year-old woman bought 120 acres of land and camped with her maid here in a tent, planning to build a mountain home on the location. With the help of San Francisco architect Willis Polk, she constructed a quaint cottage resembling an English lodge. She christened it "Vanumanutagi," which means "Vale of Singing Birds" in Samoan.

Fanny invited her friend Frank Norris—author of such classics as *The Octopus, The Pit,* and *McTeague*—and his wife, Jeannette, to visit her new home. She convinced them to buy the ranch next to hers, and Frank called it "Quien Sabe," the Spanish term for "Who knows?" The Norrises built a log cabin on the property, but Frank died soon after it was finished at the age of 32. Near this location, Fanny created a stone memorial topped with an iron cross for her author friend. Its plaque reads: "Frank Norris, 1870–1902. Simpleness and gentleness and honor and clean mirth." Vanumanutagi and the Norris cabin still stand in the area of Redwood Retreat Road.

The land in the Gilroy region is one of the world's most fertile, and agriculture has long served as Gilroy's main industry. Among the major crops grown here in the 19th century was tobacco. The local cigar factory was run by a J. D. Culp, who presented an exhibit of his Gilroy-grown product at the Panama Pacific Exposition in 1915 and received a silver medal for its high

GILROY'S BENEFICENT LAND BARON— HENRY MILLER

Most people associate the name Henry Miller with the writer of such novels as *The Tropic of Capricorn*. But Gilroy was the home of another Henry Miller, a 19th-century German immigrant who arrived in California during the Gold Rush with $6 in his pocket and half a century later had accumulated a fortune of $50 million and owned more land than any single man in history.

Born Heinrich Alfred Kreiser in the Brackenheim hills of Germany, he immigrated to New York and became a butcher boy, selling meat door to door. In 1850, at the age of 23, he journeyed through the Isthmus of Panama to San Francisco, using the ticket of a shoe salesman named Henry Miller. The ticket was nontransferable, so he boarded the ship as Henry Miller. (Eight years later, he legalized the name.) When he reached California, instead of heading to the goldfields, he realized a good living could be made butchering the wild longhorn cattle roaming through the hills. He supplied the miners with meat and saved his money as he built his business. In 1852, he purchased 300 oxen from Livingston and Kincaid—the first American cattle to arrive in San Francisco.

American cattle meat was preferred over the tougher California longhorn, and Miller rode the boom as the price rose from $2 to as much as $40 per head. To expand his business, he decided to buy a ranch near the town of Los Banos in the San Joaquin Valley. Miller traveled the El Camino Real through the Santa Clara Valley, seeing the fertile region for the first time, and passing by Rancho Las Animas. Crossing over the Indian trail through Pacheco Pass, Miller bought the Los Banos ranch, and began building his empire. Not only did he sell the meat from his cattle—he also sold the hides and tallow. As his fortune grew, he bought the Rancho Las Animas near Gilroy, establishing his headquarters at a site he called Bloomfield Ranch, near the overpass where today's Hwy. 25 meets U.S. 101.

In 1858, Miller began a partnership with Charles Lux, another German immigrant whom he had met in San Francisco. Among the partnership's enterprises was the manufacture of a soap made from cattle fat, the Lux soap brand. While Lux managed the paperwork, Miller ran the ranches and expanded his land holdings. Land was cheap—a few cents per acre—and Henry continued buying more and more of it throughout California as well as in Nevada and Oregon. He eventually owned 1.5 million acres and controlled an additional 14.5 million acres—an area larger than Belgium.

Unlike the stereotypical land baron, Miller (who was said to resemble General U. S. Grant in his later years) remained frugal, living simply but providing generously for his friends and workers. Near the summit of Hecker Pass, on what is now Mt. Madonna County Park, he built a large mansion overlooking Gilroy. This estate included a separate 3,600-square-foot ballroom for entertaining, as well as tents for the many guests who attended his famous barbecues to which everyone was invited.

One local legend holds that Miller had an encounter with a bandit while riding to the nearby mission town of San Juan Bautista. The bandit took all his money, but, to have cash to buy food on the trip, Miller asked for a "loan" of $20. The surprised thief gave back $20 of Miller's own money. Two years later, while Clarence Fagalde—one of his workers—was driving him in a carriage, Miller happened to see the outlaw who had robbed him. The land baron shouted, "Fagalde, stop! I owe that man some money."

On October 4, 1917, Miller died at the age of 89, in the Menlo Park home of his daughter, Nellie Nickel. He wanted to be buried in a mausoleum on his beloved Mt. Madonna estate, but Nellie chose to cremate his body. Among his other benefactors, he left $300,000 to build the Las Animas Hospital in Gilroy.

quality. Tobacco no longer is commercially grown in the South Valley area, and the town's claim to worldwide fame is now that pungent bulb garlic. Every mid-July, the city puts on its famous Garlic Festival at Christmas Hill Park, which attracts visitors from all around the world.

TOUR

Travelers in a hurry to reach southern destinations from San Jose usually take U.S. 101, catching a glimpse of South Valley's agricultural vistas and the city outskirts of Morgan Hill and Gilroy. But for those seeking to immerse themselves in the slower-paced environment of this part of Silicon Valley, a second thoroughfare is the better choice. A drive down Monterey Hwy. (Hwy. 82, or Monterey Rd. as it's also called) is the best way to tour the South Valley region because it lets travelers roam through the hearts of the various communities along this historic road.

To get to Monterey Hwy. in south San Jose, take the Bernal Rd. exit off Hwy. 85 and follow this in a southern direction. Keep to the far right lane on Bernal, and take the Monterey Rd. exit heading south, turning left at the stoplight intersection onto Monterey Highway. As you drive south, San Jose suburbs quickly metamorphose into rolling hills dotted with cattle and horses grazing behind barbed-wire ranch fences. On your left, the road follows briefly the bike trail of the **Coyote Creek Parkway,** 408/225-0225, where the recreation lake is open for public fishing and water-skiing.

About 1.5 miles farther is the tiny community of **Coyote,** the gateway to South Valley. Still within San Jose's jurisdiction, its chief enterprises include a tattoo shop, a live bait shop, and the rustic **Coyote Inn,** 408/463-0970, a historic roadside tavern once known as the 12-Mile House stage hotel. The **Coyote Grange Hall** on the left was built in 1892 as a social meeting hall for farmers. Beyond the thick trees just east of the village at **Coyote Ranch** stands a two-story frame house built in 1873, with a porch that goes halfway around the Victorian structure. It was originally owned by a former Bostonian sea captain named George William Fisher. In 1846,

Captain John C. Frémont wintered at Fisher's Rancho Laguna Seca. He stayed until the middle of Feb., preparing for the United States takeover of California from Mexico by purchasing horses and refitting his "exploration" party.

After passing through Coyote, the road stays ruler straight for seven miles, cutting through a picturesque area of farm fields, rustic barns, and old cherry orchards. Fruit stands selling local produce once dotted the length of Monterey Hwy., but most have long closed for business, their vacant buildings disintegrating from the ravages of weather. Monterey Hwy. approximately follows the route of **El Camino Real,** a dirt trail the Franciscan padres took between missions during the Spanish era. During the pioneer days of California's early statehood, the road became the main route for stage lines between San Jose and Monterey. Inns along the route were called 12-Mile House (in the hamlet of Coyote) or 21-Mile House (in Morgan Hill) as a mark of distance from San Jose. In the 19th century, the Southern Pacific Railroad built its extension from San Jose paralleling the road, and the track is still used by Caltrain to its final stop at the Gilroy station. Monterey Hwy. was once considered part of U.S. 101 until the new 101 to the east was opened in the late 1970s. Before that time, so many fatal accidents occurred on this heavily commuted stretch of road that it was known as "Blood Alley." While the new highway was being built, an ugly concrete divider was constructed in the middle of Monterey Hwy., and it still remains, even though it's now a much more placid drive.

Eventually, San Jose's southern boundary butts up against the Morgan Hill city limit, and at the city's unattractive northern district, referred to as the Madrone district, Monterey Hwy. passes through a gauntlet of seedy hotels, bars, and RV storage sites. Soon, the highway passes under the Southern Pacific Railroad crossing, and after Wright Ave., you'll see a single-story Queen Anne–style home on your left sitting on a spacious plot of land. Called **Villa Mira Monte,** 408/779-5755, the house was built by Hiram Morgan Hill and his bride, Diana. The home's porch was designed to provide a stunning view of the unusual mountain to the west resembling a small volcano. Many people mistakenly believe that this 1,423-foot-high landmark is "Morgan Hill," and that the city was named after it. However, its official name is **El Toro.** The Spanish originally called it Oreja del Oso (Bear's Ear), and early American inhabitants referred to it as Murphy's Peak in honor of Martin Murphy Sr., who owned an immense ranch where Morgan Hill now exists. Bret Harte, author and editor of the

GILROY HOT SPRINGS

Visitors to Gilroy often inquire at the local tourist center about the Gilroy Hot Springs. They have seen the historic marker sign along U.S. 101 and wonder what this attraction is all about.

The hot springs are located in the Diablo Mountains 12 miles northeast of the city. They were discovered by a Mexican sheepherder in 1845. In 1879, a resort was built here by rancher George Roop so that people could partake of the hot sulfur water pouring out of natural springs. Guests would take the train to Gilroy and waiting horse-drawn stagecoaches would transport them from the depot through pristine farm and ranch land. They would arrive to stay at a three-story, 32-room hotel or at the 19 cabins built around the springs.

The resort at one time was one of the most popular in California, guests journeying here to soak in the concrete-lined pool into which piped hot water cascaded. Many came here with the belief that the mineral water would help ease their arthritis and other ailments. Other recreational activities included fishing, hunting, horseback riding, and hiking along the resort's various nature trails.

The resort operated until the 1950s. It was closed when interest in hot water natural spring resorts diminished. In 1980, Gilroy Hot Spring's historic hotel burned in a fire. In the early 1990s, a Japanese company considered reopening the Gilroy Hot Springs as a resort and conference center, but nothing ever became of that plan.

Overland Monthly, is credited with thinking up the mountain's current name. The story goes that Harte visited Murphy one day, and the two men rode their horses up the mountain's slope to get a view from the top. They stopped to observe two bulls fighting, and the animals suddenly turned and started chasing them. When Harte later related the story in his famous magazine, he gave the mountain the name El Toro (The Bull).

Monterey Hwy. comes into **Morgan Hill's historic downtown** area, which is the city's heart. In the early 1990s, this business district underwent a $3 million renovation by the city to attract customers with its architectural charm. Much of this money was spent building a long flower bed through the center of the street and putting in old-fashioned light posts. Stereo speakers attached to these posts play country music to entertain pedestrians. Creating a Norman Rockwell atmosphere, farmers wearing overalls often can be seen walking past fancy gift boutiques. Parking is abundant in side-street lots, and the downtown holds several street fairs and festivals throughout the year, including a downtown farmers' market and a Friday night music series. Downtown Morgan Hill makes for a pleasant stroll with its various restaurants, bookshops, art galleries, and sporting goods stores. The large marquee jutting out in the downtown's center tops the **Granada Theater,** 408/779-2992, a local community attraction when Hollywood blockbusters come to town.

Continue traveling down Monterey Hwy., and on the right just south of downtown, you'll see the **United Methodist Church,** on the corner of 4th Street. This quaint American Gothic building with stained glass and a bell in its steeple was built in 1893. It's historically important as the city's first place of worship, as well as its first schoolhouse.

Keep traveling south along Monterey Hwy. as it passes through a series of bland shopping centers on Morgan Hill's southern end. At the intersection of Tennant Ave., a historical plaque marks the site where **21-Mile House** once stood. This stage-stop hotel was operated by William Tennant, one of the area's first settlers, who also served as a postmaster and blacksmith. About half a mile after this point, you'll pass Morgan Hill's city limits and return to farmland scenery. A couple of miles along the highway on the right stands the prominent landmark redwood barn of **Uesugi Farms,** 408/842-1294, attracting Silicon Valley visitors from May to July with its fresh strawberries. In October, thousands of Silicon Valley families visit its famous Pumpkin Patch. Open 10 A.M.–4 P.M., inside the barn you'll find dried flowers for sale as well as antiques and crafts on consignment.

Continue following the rural road until you reach the unincorporated town of **San Martin.** This blink-and-you'll-miss-it community of over 2,000 people features South Valley's only public airport as well as the excellent **Wings of History: California Antique Aircraft Museum,** 408/683-2290. A tragic accident gives this small community its origin. On April 11, 1853, the 61-ton side-wheel steamboat *Jenny Lind* left the port of Alviso on its regular run to San Francisco. Among its passengers planning to attend to business on the trip was Bernard Murphy, the third son of Martin Murphy Sr. Just a little after noon the passengers were enjoying their lunch as the boat passed through the area just north of what's now Dumbarton Bridge. Without warning, the boiler exploded. Flames and scalding clouds of steam engulfed the ship as passengers burned or were severely maimed. Among the 34 dead was Bernard. His grieving father built a small chapel near what's now New Ave. and San Martin Avenue. Murphy named the church after his patron saint, San Martin, and on All Souls' Day, 1853, dedicated it and buried Bernard's body here. The chapel burned to the ground on April 2, 1877, and the small village took its name.

Continue down Monterey Hwy., and after four miles, you'll pass a large wooden sign welcoming you to "the Garlic Capital of the World." Many people know about Gilroy and its claim to the aromatic bulb. Fewer folks probably realize that at one time it was the home of blues singer Johnny Lee Hooker. After passing Gilroy's city limits, Monterey Hwy. goes through a weedy industrial part of town that

Villa Mira Monte in Morgan Hill

includes its share of automobile lots, one of the city's major draws. Local Silicon Valley TV and radio ads try to tempt car shoppers down here with banal slogans like: "Drive a little and save a lot in the friendly town of Gilroy!" After 1st St., **Gilroy's downtown district** begins, a section of the city with a crazy zigzag of flower planters that motorists must weave through. Stop at the **Gilroy Visitors Bureau,** 7780 Monterey St., 408/842-6436, to pick up information on events and local attractions.

The downtown area often looks like a ghost town—business here suffered a major hit in the early 1990s after the Gilroy Outlets and Wal-Mart opened off U.S. 101 on Leavesley Road. Despite its economic downturn, Gilroy's downtown is worth a stop to browse among its specialty shops and more than 15 antique stores. It also has a good selection of family-run restaurants, especially Mexican eateries. Free parking is ample on the street and side lots, and the lot off 5th St. displays a wonderfully detailed giant wall mural celebrating Gilroy's garlic heritage. The shop next to this lot is the **Garlic Festival Store,** 408/842-7081, which provides every type of garlic product or gift imaginable, including boxes filled with a dozen "stinking roses." There's an old-fashioned charm to the downtown area, a quirky character that makes it fun for a short visit. Especially eye-catching is the life-size **fiberglass horse and cowboy** rearing up on a corner store overhang.

On the corner of Monterey and 6th Sts. stands Gilroy's **Old City Hall,** a stately 1905 structure built of sandstone in baroque style with overtones of mission revival. With its stalwart town clock face, it's the graceful lady from Gilroy's yesteryears.

After the Old City Hall building, downtown Gilroy quickly turns shabby. Men in cowboy hats loiter in front of seedy bars. Across the street, a Caltrain locomotive ambles along the track to stop at the end of the line by the **Gilroy depot.** This historic building was renovated in 1998 because of its asbestos hazard. After this point, Monterey Hwy. passes through another industrial section of town highlighted by a mattress outlet center and more car dealerships. A short distance from here at the end of Monterey Hwy. is U.S. 101. The northbound entrance will take you back to San Jose, the southbound entrance heads to the Monterey Bay region.

POINTS OF INTEREST
Gilroy Historical Museum
Set in the converted Andrew Carnegie Library built in 1910, this quaint town museum presents Gilroy's early days with memorabilia showcasing the Ohlone Indians, land baron Henry Miller, and the once-flourishing Gilroy Hot Springs resort. One humorous exhibit tells of Edward Rohr (1866–1945), who with his brother Joseph operated a saloon at the corner of Monterey and Old Gilroy Streets. Because of Sabbath anti-liquor laws, the enterprising Rohr continued making money by opening his establishment on Sun. for church services.

195 5th St. (west of downtown Gilroy on the corner of Church St.), 408/848-0470; admission free; open Mon., Tues., Thurs., and Fri. 10 A.M.–5 P.M., first Sat. of each month 10 A.M.–2 P.M.

BREATHTAKING GOLDSMITH GARDENS

Right near the mouth of Gilroy's scenic Hecker Pass is a floral Eden that makes a perfect spot for a picture or a picnic on a pleasant spring or summer day. The spectacular test gardens of Goldsmith Seed Company lay right along the road, astonishing visitors with vast fields of the brilliant colors of blooming marigolds, zinnias, snapdragons, carnations, and pansies.

The family-run company was founded in 1962 by plant breeder Glenn Goldsmith. It has become one of the world's largest wholesale growers of hybrid flower seeds (it does not sell seeds directly to the public) and has won more than 30 international awards for its hybrid annuals, including such varieties as "Inca" African marigolds, "Peter Pan" zinnias, and "Fantasy" milliflora petunias—the world's first miniature petunia. The Gilroy site is used only for seed testing; actual seed production is done at Goldsmith facilities in Guatemala and Kenya.

Free guided hour-long tours are available Mon. and Wed. mornings, and visitors are allowed to wander among the flowers and hothouses. A minimum of 10 and a maximum of 45 people are needed for a tour. The facility also includes a shaded picnic area (wine is allowed all day on weekends and after 5 P.M. on weekdays) in a two-acre public garden and courtyard next to the office; a viewing platform located here provides a high point for picture taking of the flower fields.

2280 Hecker Pass Rd. (take Hwy. 152 1.5 miles west of Gilroy); parking in lot; admission free; open daily during daylight. Call public information director Keith Muraoka to reserve a tour; 408/847-7333; website: www.goldsmithseeds.com.

Wings of History: California Antique Aircraft Museum

This hidden treasure of aircraft exhibits makes a great excuse to visit the South Valley town of San Martin. The museum is run by friendly volunteers who gladly show visitors their astounding collection of antique flying machines, including a replica of the Wright Flier and the actual glider that Charles and Anne Morrow Lindbergh learned to glide in. (Volunteer Jack Bowlus is the son of Hawley Bowlus, who helped design Lindbergh's *Spirit of St. Louis* in San Diego.) The collection of 30 airplanes includes a 1916 Nieuport XI, which flew in World War I; a replica of the De Havilland Comet, which won the England to Australia race in 1934; and a hybrid automobile-helicopter called a "Car Copter." The museum has an extensive aircraft library and a shop where visitors can watch wooden propellers being carefully crafted.

12777 Murphy Ave., San Martin (just west of U.S. 101 across from South County Airport), 408/683-2290; admission free (suggested donation $5); open Tues. and Thurs. 10 A.M.–3 P.M., weekends 11 A.M.–4 P.M.

Villa Mira Monte

Set in an expansive garden away from the road in Morgan Hill's northern section stands a six-room summer cottage that once belonged to the man for whom the town was named. Railroad passengers on the newly laid Southern Pacific tracks passing the house often asked to be let off at "Morgan Hill's," and the village eventually received this name. The Morgan Hill Historical Society now runs the home as a museum and meeting facility.

17860 N. Monterey Rd., Morgan Hill (just north of downtown), 408/779-5755; parking on street; admission free (call to see if a historical volunteer is on-site to show museum).

Uvas Canyon County Park

A pleasant winding drive takes you through the eastern foothills of the Santa Cruz Mountains to this 1,200-acre park set in a secluded niche of the county near Morgan Hill. Spanish settlers named the canyon after the wild grapes that grew here. The park is famous for its many waterfalls that run vigorously after heavy winter rains.

Off Croy Rd. (from San Jose, take Almaden Expwy. to McKean Rd., which turns into Uvas Rd.; turn right on Croy Rd. and drive 4.4 miles to park entrance), 408/779-9232, website: claraweb.co.santa-clara.ca.us/parks; activities: campground, horseshoes, fishing and nonpowered boating at Uvas Reservoir 10 miles south along Uvas Rd., hiking (seven miles of trails).

Anderson Reservoir County Park

Water sports are definitely the main attraction at the county's largest reservoir. The seven-mile-long, 1,250-acre lake attracts both powered and nonpowered boaters. The 2,365-acre park is connected to Coyote Creek Parkway, popular with in-line skaters, bikers, joggers, and equestrians.

Off Cochrane Rd. or Dunne Ave. (on U.S. 101 in Morgan Hill, take either Cochrane Rd. or Dunne Ave. exit and drive east), 408/779-3634, website: claraweb.co.santa-clara.ca.us/parks; activities: boating, fishing, horseback riding on Coyote Creek Parkway, hiking (15 miles, including a one-mile self-guided nature trail).

Mt. Madonna County Park

If you seek tranquillity among the redwoods, this park is a great place to go. The 3,219-acre park overlooks the Santa Clara Valley as well as the Monterey Bay to the west. The land, originally part of Rancho Las Animas, was bought in 1859 by Henry Miller, a land and cattle baron who built a magnificent $250,000 home on it in 1901. Visitors can stroll an easy nature trail to the mansion's ruins. In 1932, newspaper publisher William Randolph Hearst donated a pair of white fallow deer to the county, and their descendants can be viewed in a pen at the park.

Off Pole Line Rd. (10 miles west of Gilroy at the summit of Hwy. 152), 408/842-2341, website: claraweb.co.santa-clara.ca.us/parks; activities: RV and tent campground, amphitheater, deer pen, archery range, fishing, horseback riding, hiking (20 miles of trails).

Henry W. Coe State Park

At 80,000 acres, this is the largest state park in

BONFANTE GARDENS

Bonfante Gardens is a horticultural-themed amusement park fast becoming a tourist draw for the South Valley community of Gilroy. The park is the creation of Michael Bonfante who took over his father's seven Nob Hill Foods supermarkets, eventually building it into a chain of 27 stores. He sold the business in 1997 and used much of the money to build a $100 million park on his 600-acre nursery ranch along scenic Hecker Pass. The park opened in May 2001.

The focus of the 28-acre garden park is on plantlife. More than 10,000 trees of various species grow in the park, and over half a million flowers and shrubs accent these. There are five dedicated gardens, including a 60-foot-high Monarch Palace greenhouse which showcases tropical and sub-tropical plants. The Rainbow Garden shows annual colors, the Pinnacles gives guests an understanding of edible landscaping, and the Camellia Garden is devoted to shade trees.

A whimsical highlight of the park are the "Circus Trees," 25 convoluted trees placed throughout the grounds at key junctions. These strange trees were the creation of a Scotts Valley man named Axel Erlandson who grafted and twisted the branches to form bizarre shapes. For example, one odd tree is shaped like a zig-zagging lightning bolt. The trees were made internationally famous in the 1940s when they appeared in the column *Ripley's Believe It or Not!*

The park is classified as a nonprofit community charity, and revenue will be used to preserve and beautify local parks in the South Valley area. Future plans also include the prospect of working with Bay Area universities to develop accredited horticulture classes. Noncredit enrichment classes might also be offered.

Unlike the thrill-oriented Paramount's Great America in nearby Santa Clara, Bonfante Gardens is more serene in its entertainment. Rides are targeted at families with children under 12. They include a Ferris Wheel, a monorail, a steam-train railroad, two merry-go-rounds including a restored 1927 Illions Supreme Carousel, and a South County "backroads" miniature car ride. The park's rock maze changes daily. The Garlic Twirl is a ride much like Disneyland's famous teacup attraction except—this being home of the Garlic Festival—using garlic cloves. Two roller coasters are in the park. A gentle one called the Diamond Back is designed for kiddies. And the New Almaden Quicksilver Express Mine Coaster contains more adventurous thrills as it makes a wild run through 500 trees and mercury mining buildings. A peaceful boat ride on a small river allows guests to glide through a variety of gardens.

Other attractions in the park include stage shows, and shopping outlets for collectibles and apparel. Food venues include the usual pizza, pasta, barbecue and taqueria. One stand called Castroville Corners provides local cuisine including deep-fried artichoke hearts, mushrooms, and calamari.

3050 Hecker Pass Hwy. (two miles west of Gilroy along Hwy. 152), 408/842-2121, open Wed.–Sun. 11 A.M.–10 P.M.; website: www.bonfantegardens.com; parking $7; admission for children 3–12, $19.85, adults, $28.95, seniors 65 and over, $25.95.

Home of the Circus Trees!

Northern California. A rugged, undeveloped wilderness in the Diablo Range, the ranchlike park shows visitors how the entire region looked when the Spanish first ventured here. The park was donated by Henry W. Coe Jr., who worked the Pine Ridge Ranch here from 1900 to 1953. Visitors can observe many of the original ranch buildings near the western entrance. A small museum open on weekends interprets California ranch life in the late 1880s and provides information on the park's plant and animal habitats.

Off E. Dunne Ave. (from U.S. 101 in Morgan Hill, take the E. Dunne Ave. exit and drive east), 408/779-2728; $2 parking fee; activities: hiking, mountain biking, backpacking, horseback riding, camping, fishing.

Coyote Lake

This placid 796-acre lake park set in the Mt. Hamilton watershed is a habitat for predatory birds, including great horned owls and golden eagles. Osprey and bald eagles have also been seen here. Its 635-acre reservoir fed by Coyote Creek is popular for boating and fishing.

Off Coyote Reservoir Rd. (from U.S. 101 in Gilroy, take the Leavesley Rd. exit and drive east 1.75 miles to New Ave.; turn left and drive north for a bit, then turn right on Roop Rd. and make a left at Coyote Reservoir Rd.), 408/842-7800, website: claraweb.co.santa-clara.ca.us/parks; activities: boating, fishing, camping, horseback riding, hiking (six miles of trails).

Chitactac Adams County Park

This four-acre park provides a glimpse into the lives of the Ohlone Indians, who once inhabited the region. An easy-to-walk trail around the archaeological site highlights the culture of the valley's original inhabitants before and after the arrival of the Spanish. Ohlone buildings and petroglyphs are displayed as well as exhibits on native food processing and village social structure.

Off Watsonville Rd. (from U.S. 101 in Morgan Hill, take Tennant Ave. exit and head west; turn left on Monterey Hwy. and drive half a mile

south to Watsonville Rd.; turn right and travel about 5.5 miles), 408/842-2341, website: claraweb.co.santa-clara.ca.us/parks.

Outlets at Gilroy

Considered one of the country's top outlet centers, this series of more than 150 factory-outlet stores lets shoppers buy direct from the manufacturer. But compared to sales at regular retail stores, it's hard to see any considerable savings with this "factory-to-you" style of commerce. Still, tour buses bring eager shoppers from all over to hunt for bargains at outlets such as Brooks Brothers, Bugle Boy, Eddie Bauer, Ann Taylor, Waterford/Wedgwood, and London Fog.

Off Leavesley Rd. (east of U.S. 101), 408/842-3729; parking in lot; open Mon.–Sat. 10 A.M.–8 P.M., Sun. 10 A.M.–6 P.M.

Garlic World

If during your visit to Gilroy, you still can't get enough garlic, here's the place to go to satisfy your addiction. It's all here, a cornucopia of products dealing with the king of seasonings. Choose from garlic braids, wreaths, gift baskets, sauces, dressings, and olives, as well as cookbooks, T-shirts, and souvenirs. Nongarlic products include locally produced gourmet foods, pastas, and wines. Farm-fresh produce is also sold here, including cherries, peaches, corn, tomatoes, and—surprise!—garlic. Call for a free catalog to be mailed to you.

4800 Monterey Hwy., Gilroy (alongside U.S. 101 a mile south of the city), 408/847-2251 or 800/537-6122; open daily 9 A.M.–7 P.M.

South Valley Civic Theatre

This nonprofit theater group has showcased local dramatic talents in the South Valley area for over 30 years. It puts on six shows a year including musicals, dramas, and children's plays. It performs at various venues such as Gilroy High School and Live Oak High School in Morgan Hill.

408/842-7469; individual tickets: $8–12, season tickets (six shows) also available.

Accommodations

As an international business mecca, Silicon Valley experiences heavy demand for lodging out-of-towners on business trips or attending trade shows. Many hotels and motels (along with a smattering of B&Bs) have sprung up in the region to fill the need, but rooms fill up fast. San Jose is the definite winner in the hotel sweepstakes, with its downtown and airport areas providing a wealth of large, comfortable hotel chains. Its Fairmont Hotel has become an established downtown landmark, where movers and shakers such as the president, movie stars, and corporate executives stay. Los Gatos and Saratoga have several nice family-run hotels catering to vacationers as well as business travelers. In the South Valley communities of Gilroy, Morgan Hill, and San Martin, you'll find

several comfortable inns and bed and breakfasts perfect if you decide to take a wine-tasting tour in that region. Many accommodations throughout Silicon Valley are within easy walking distance of interesting sightseeing locations, and several in San Jose and Santa Clara are close to Light Rail or Caltrain stations.

Weekdays are notorious for hotels being filled up with visitors attending trade shows and conferences, so make sure you book a room as early as possible during this time. On the other hand, on most weekends, hotels are clamoring to fill rooms. You can find some exceptional $89 bargain packages for weekend stays, and these lower rates often include meals and tickets to museums and performances. Several motels and hotels

Fairmont Hotel, San Jose

offer discounts for members of auto clubs such as AAA or senior citizen groups such as AARP. They also provide special corporate and group rates. Also, you can get special discounts of up to 65 percent if you book through the Hotel Reservations Network, 800/666-4874. Motels and hotels in Silicon Valley accept most major credit cards. Unless noted below, places do not allow pets. Things do change, and price ranges listed here are meant as a general guideline in selecting accommodations. Enjoy your stay.

CAMPBELL
Campbell Inn
Located a short walk from Campbell's historic downtown, this two-story hotel is set along Los Gatos Creek, providing guests with a scenic biking or running trail (10-speed touring bikes are available for guest use). Outdoor trees are lit with white Christmas lights, giving the hotel a festive feel year-round. The scrumptious European-style buffet breakfast is served in a comfortable breakfast room that changes into a lounge after 11 A.M.

Details: 95 rooms; robes, cable TV, refrigerator; some rooms: whirlpool; swimming pool, tennis court, video library; business services; free breakfast. Rates: $99–275.

675 E. Campbell Ave. (near Hwy. 17), 408/374-4300 or 800/582-4449, fax 408/379-0695, website: www.campbell-inn.com.

The Carlyle
Previously known as Executive Inn Suites, this three-story hotel with the nondescript exterior is set in an unattractive industrial district (on busy Camden Ave., with a Midas Muffler shop directly across the street). But don't let the location dissuade you. Inside you'll discover an elegant hotel decorated with tasteful wallpaper, brass chandeliers, and a life-size Victorian nymph statue gracing the lobby desk. The staff is friendly, the service is excellent, and the rooms are well kept. There's also plenty of parking in the underground garage.

Details: 38 rooms (free room upgrades); coffeemaker and refrigerator; some rooms: whirlpool;

some efficiencies available; Carrow's Restaurant across the street; free breakfast (extensive European selection). Rates: $125–145.

1300 Camden Ave. (take Camden Ave. exit off Hwy. 17), 408/559-3600 or 800/888-3611, fax 408/371-5721, website: www.executive-inns-suites.com.

The Pruneyard Inn
Set conveniently near the Los Gatos Creek trail, this three-story hotel pampers guests with spacious, comfortable rooms. Even though it's set in the Pruneyard Shopping Center (which provides guests with a large number of dining and shopping opportunities), it retains a more sophisticated atmosphere than its location might suggest.

Details: 172 rooms; cable TV, modem, voice mail, coffeemaker, hair dryer; some rooms: efficiencies, whirlpool, steam shower, fireplace; video library; house passes to Bamboola children's center; business services; fax, printer; free newspaper, airport transport, and breakfast. Rates: $99–275.

1995 S. Bascom Ave. (in the Pruneyard Shopping Center), 408/559-4300 or 800/559-4344, fax 408/559-9919, website: www.pruneyardinn.com.

CUPERTINO
The Cupertino Courtyard
Targeted at business travelers, this clean and well-kept hotel in the Cupertino Village shopping area has a hospitable staff that has earned it recognition as a "Gold Hotel" from Marriott.

Details: 147 rooms; coffeemaker, free movies; some rooms: refrigerator, microwave; pool, whirlpool, exercise room; guest laundry. Rates: $89–194.

10605 N. Wolfe Rd. (just off I-280), 408/252-9100 or 800/321-2211, fax 408/252-0632, website: www.marriott.com.

Cupertino Inn
Conveniently located near high-tech companies (including Apple's headquarters across I-280), this four-story hotel targets business travelers with its casual surroundings. Its centerpiece is a

sheltered garden area where guests can take a plunge in a large pool or relax in a spa. The courteous service is small-town friendly.

Details: 125 rooms; coffeemaker, fully stocked minibar, hair dryer, robes, free movies; some rooms: whirlpool, fireplace; business services: voice mail, T-1 line; airport limousine transportation; free breakfast and evening cocktails. Rates: $99–650.

10889 N. De Anza Blvd. (just north of I-280), 408/996-7700 or 800/222-4828, fax 408/257-0578, website: www.cupertinoinn.com.

Hilton Garden Inn

Opened August 1998, this is Cupertino's newest hotel, a five-story building conveniently located next to Cupertino Village, which has a large selection of Asian restaurants for dining.

Details: 165 rooms; coffeemaker, refrigerator, microwave, cable TV, hair dryer, iron; some rooms: wet bar; pool, whirlpool, fitness room; business services: private voice mail, high-speed Internet access; free coffee; Great American Grill (breakfast and light dinner) and 24-hour pantry. Rates: $119–299.

10741 N. Wolfe Rd. (just one block north of I-280), 408/777-8787 or 888/771-0741, fax 408/777-8040, website: www.hgi-cupertino.com.

GILROY

Chesbro House B&B

This corn-colored Victorian home with mint-green trim is set in the midst of a mature Gilroy neighborhood along Church St. (appropriately named, given the number of churches on it). It was built in 1890 for Dr. Heaverland Rogers Chesbro, who once served as town mayor. His great granddaughter Elizabeth Barratt, a travel writer, now runs the home as a bed and breakfast with her husband Dick. It's filled with exquisite late-Victorian furniture. One of its guest rooms, decorated with red-flock wallpaper and gilt-framed mirrors, is humorously known as the "bordello room." In winter, fresh-squeezed juice is served at breakfast from the 100-year-old Valencia orange tree growing two stories high in the backyard.

Chesbro House Bed and Breakfast

Details: two rooms; cable TV, VCR; breakfast made with fresh ingredients. Rates: $110–125.

7541 Church St. (two blocks west of Gilroy's downtown), 408/842-3750, website: www.chesbro.gilroy.com.

Country Rose Inn B&B

Cordial innkeeper Rose Hernandez has created a comfortable bed and breakfast in this lovely Dutch colonial manor. Set in the middle of South Valley's wine country, its spacious rooms and serene location have pleased guests such as actress Debbie Reynolds. Every window looks out on a beautiful view that includes magnificent oaks growing around the house. Facilities are available for weddings and small corporate meetings, and special dining can be arranged for groups of about 20 people.

Details: five rooms; some rooms: wood-burning stove, jetted tub; business services: fax; free snacks; breakfast. Rates: $129–239 (higher during special events such as Gilroy Garlic Festival).

455 Fitzgerald Ave. #E, San Martin (from U.S. 101, take Masten Ave. exit, which turns

into Fitzgerald Ave.); mailing address: P.O. Box 2500, Gilroy, CA 95021, 408/842-0441, website: www.bbonline.com/ca/countryrose/.

Forest Park Inn

This three-story motel has close access to U.S. 101 and Gilroy's Outlet Shopping Center. Rooms are comfortable and well kept. It's a convenient place to stay for the Gilroy Garlic Festival.

Details: 78 rooms; cable TV, refrigerator; some rooms: whirlpool, fireplace. Rates: $54–78.

375 Leavesley Rd. (just west of U.S. 101 off Leavesley Rd. exit), 408/848-5144 or 800/237-7846, fax 408/848-1138, website: www.forest-parkinn.com.

LOS GATOS

La Hacienda Inn-Hotel

At first sight, this cozy lodging seems more like a family home than an inn. Built in 1961, the nonsmoking hotel is set amid the quiet of the Santa Cruz Mountain foothills, close to the historic Villa Montalvo estate. Its well-tended flower beds and oak trees provide a relaxing getaway from Silicon Valley's hustle. The adjoining restaurant, built in 1901, is famous among locals for its Sunday champagne brunch.

Details: 20 rooms; cable TV, refrigerator, coffeemaker; some rooms: kitchen; pool, indoor hot tub; business services: private conference facility, fax, photocopier; free breakfast and airport transport; La Hacienda Inn Restaurant. Rates: $130–180.

18840 Saratoga–Los Gatos Rd. (near Austin Way), 408/354-9230 or 800/235-4570, fax 408/354-7590, website: www.lahaciendainn.com.

Los Gatos Lodge

This comfortable two-story hotel built in 1958 is set on 10 acres of lush landscaping overlooking the Los Gatos foothills. Its wedding garden is a popular Silicon Valley locale for weddings and receptions. To help guests unwind, the hotel provides a putting green and boccie ball court as well as close access to the Los Gatos Creek biking/running trail. Five meeting rooms provide facilities for 10 to 200 people.

Details: 128 rooms; coffeemakers; some rooms: kitchen, refrigerator, microwave; pool, whirlpool; business services: dataport; free newspaper; Garden Court Restaurant (California cuisine); allows pets. Rates: $130–205.

50 Los Gatos–Saratoga Rd. (one block east of Hwy. 17), 408/354-3300 or 800/231-8676, fax 408/354-5451.

The Toll House

Named after the historic tollhouse that once served as the turnpike gateway for the Santa Cruz Gap, this charming hotel is within easy walking distance of Los Gatos's downtown area. Its Victorian-style clock tower makes it a distinguished town landmark. Every room has a balcony overlooking the valley, and an extra bonus is the hotel's serving of fresh-baked chocolate-chip cookies and fresh fruit.

Details: 97 rooms; coffeemaker, cable TV, movies; some rooms: refrigerator, microwave; free use of Los Gatos Athletic Club; airport transport to San Jose from 7 A.M.–11 P.M.; free breakfast and newspaper; Clocktower Bar & Grill (California cuisine). Rates: $180–400.

140 S. Santa Cruz Ave. (close to downtown's Plaza Park), 408/395-7070, 800/238-6111, or 800/821-5518, fax 408/395-3730.

MENLO PARK

Menlo Park Inn

Right on El Camino Real and an easy walk to downtown Menlo Park's shopping district, this small motel is clean and relaxing for travelers on a budget. It's conveniently located about 20 minutes from San Francisco International Airport.

Details: 30 rooms; cable TV, coffeemaker, microwave, refrigerator, movies; some rooms: whirlpool; business services: dataport; free breakfast. Rates: $125–145.

1315 El Camino Real (one mile north of Stanford University), 650/326-7530 or 800/327-1315, fax 650/328-7539.

Stanford Park Hotel

A four-diamond lodging close to both Menlo

Park's and Palo Alto's downtown area, the three-story Stanford Park Hotel provides guests with luxurious surroundings in a comfortable home-away-from-home setting. Near the entrance is a playful water fountain surrounded by a canopy of palms, and the spacious lounge area has a nicely carved wood cowboy sculpture in front of the cozy fireplace. The friendly staff make guests feel welcome and will expertly take care of every detail.

Details: 163 rooms; cable TV, robes, voice mail, honor bar; some rooms: coffeemaker, refrigerator, fireplace; sauna, whirlpool; business services: dataport, 24-hour business center; free evening beverages, breakfast, newspaper, and shuttle within three-mile radius; Duck Club (Continental cuisine). Rates: $295–725.

100 El Camino Real (near Stanford Shopping Center), 650/322-1234 or 800/368-2468, fax 650/322-0975, website: www.woodsidehotel.com.

MILPITAS
Embassy Suites

This eight-story luxury hotel with its signature dome has become a well-established landmark for drivers along I-680. Visitors coming inside will find an expansive interior with a jungle-like atrium under a glass roof. The effect is completed with waterfalls and koi fish swimming in ponds, which guests can cross over on footbridges on the way to the glass elevators. Behind the front lobby desk is a breathtaking mural of a horse race along a Monterey beach during California's Mexican era. The pool room also has a beautiful mural. Each of the hotel's 266 suites has a separate living room with a sofa bed and galley kitchen.

Details: 266 rooms; coffeemaker, refrigerator, wet bar, microwave, cable TV; indoor pool, whirlpool, sauna and steam room; Swan Court Restaurant (Continental cuisine). Rates: $169–189.

901 E. Calaveras Blvd. (west just off I-680), 408/942-0400 or 800/362-2779, fax 408/262-8604, website: www.embassy-suites.com/es/milpitas-silicon.

Extended StayAmerica

For travelers planning a long-term visit to Silicon Valley, this is an economical way to create a home away from home. It works much like a studio suite, so it doesn't provide many of the extra services hotels usually provide, such as fancy waiting lounges and swimming pools. The clean and comfortable 300-square-foot rooms include fully equipped kitchens as well as business services such as computer dataports, voice mail, and fax services. Laundry facilities are available 24 hours a day. The Milpitas lodging is conveniently close to I-680.

Details: 146 rooms; full-service kitchen, recliner, desk. Rates: $139 nightly to $649 a week ($79 a night on weekends).

1000 Hillview Ct. (next to Embassy Suites hotel off I-680), 408/941-9977 or 800/326-5651, fax 408/941-9976, website: www.extstay.com.

MORGAN HILL
Best Western Country Inn

A pleasant hotel across the street from an immense soccer park, this hotel provides clean rooms in a rural area that's conveniently close to freeway access. The nearby Golden Oak Restaurant is a good place to relax after-hours.

Details: 84 rooms; coffeemaker, refrigerator; pool, whirlpool; free breakfast; allows small pets. Rates: $101–111.

16525 Condit Rd. (east of U.S. 101 off Tennant Ave.), 408/779-0447 or 800/528-1234, fax 408/778-7170, website: www.bestwestern.com.

Inn at Morgan Hill

This attractive three-story hotel in the heart of South Valley is well worth the 15-minute drive to Silicon Valley. While close to the highway off-ramp, its casual atmosphere is relaxing and quiet. You'll feel a million miles away from the high-tech world with the pleasant views of family-run orchards and the sweeping Diablo Range. The large, luxurious suites are beautiful, and compared with the upscale San Jose and Santa Clara hotels, a real bargain. The staff is friendly, too. Highly recommended.

Details: 101 rooms; cable TV, minibar, coffeemaker, hair dryer, VCR; some rooms: kitchen, gas fireplace, whirlpool; workout room; business services: fax, photocopies; free breakfast, evening snacks, and airport transport. Rates: $109–169.

16115 Condit Rd. (east of U.S. 101 off Tennant Ave.), 408/779-7666 or 800/645-3450, fax 408/779-8757, website: www.innmh.com.

Morgan Hill Inn

For those on a tight budget, this small motel in a neglected section of town is sufficient for a no-frills stay. It's close to the South Valley wine country.

Details: 23 rooms; cable TV, refrigerator, microwave; free coffee. Rates: $75–129.

16250 Monterey Hwy. (one mile north from U.S. 101 off Tennant Ave.), 408/779-1900, fax 408/779-1900.

PALO ALTO

The Cardinal Hotel

Describing itself as a "European-style hotel in the heart of Palo Alto," this historical landmark was built in 1924 and once served as the city's social center. Its Renaissance-inspired architectural design has Spanish overtones, which can be plainly seen in the elegant lobby area complete with an embellished fireplace. Some rooms share a common bathroom.

Details: 60 rooms; cable TV; some rooms: sleeper sofa, microwave, refrigerator, coffeemaker; business services: fax, dataport; free newspaper and coffee; dogs allowed. Rates: $70–205.

235 Hamilton Ave. (corner of Ramona St. one block south of University Ave.), 650/323-5101, fax 650/325-6086, website: www.cardinalhotel.com.

Crowne Plaza Cabaña Hotel

A $20 million overhaul in 1999 revived this stylish hotel, bringing back its former elegance and charm. Its original owner was actress Doris Day, who built it in the 1960s, and its architect went on to create Caesar's Palace in Las Vegas, using many of the same design elements. Past guests have included The Beatles. Its spacious Mediterranean-style dining room features Silicon Valley's largest wine cellar. Service is top-notch.

Details: 200 rooms; cable TV, refrigerator, hair dryer, coffeemaker, iron and ironing board; some rooms: hot tub; pool, whirlpool, fitness center, sauna; business services: business center, dataport, voice mail, personal fax; free newspaper; Bistro du Soleil (Mediterranean cuisine). Rates: $279–329.

4290 El Camino Real (between San Antonio and Arastradero Blvds.), 650/857-0787 or 800/227-6963, fax 650/496-1939, website: www.crowneplaza.com.

Hyatt Rickeys

The exterior of this sprawling hotel is an uninspired chocolate brown, but the rooms recently underwent a $3.5 million renovation. The grounds are well kept and clean, but the ambience feels sluggish and drab.

Details: 344 rooms; coffeemaker, cable TV; some rooms: refrigerator, fireplace, balcony or patio; fitness room, pool; business services: 24-hour center; free video checkout, newspaper, and hotel van within five-mile radius; Hugo's Cafe (California cuisine); pets okay with $50 deposit. Rates: $269–299.

4219 El Camino Real (between San Antonio and Arastradero Blvds.), 650/493-8000 or 800/233-1234, fax 650/424-0836, website: www.hyatt.com.

The Victorian on Lytton

This elegant B&B fronted by a colorful flower garden is within one block of downtown Palo Alto. Originally built in 1895, it was meticulously restored in 1986. Keeping an English sovereign theme, the rooms (all nonsmoking) are named after Queen Victoria's various children and grandchildren. Proprietors Maxwell and Susan Hall even make guests feel regal by serving them breakfast in bed. Lytton Ave. outside is a heavily trafficked street, but inside the house it's surprisingly quiet. There's ample sheltered parking behind the inn.

Details: 10 rooms; cable TV, dataport, private bath; some rooms: handicapped facilities; free newspaper, tea, and coffee. Rates: $183 250.

555 Lytton Ave. (between Webster and Cowper Sts.), 650/322-8555, fax 650/322-7141, website: www.virtualcities.com.

DOWNTOWN SAN JOSE

Arena Hotel

From the street, this lodging's front does resemble a two-story hotel, but with its ample parking lot beyond the driveway, it's obviously a motor inn. Opened in 1990, the architecture is California bland, with tinkling water fountains in the garden. The spacious rooms come with CD stereo systems—a nice touch to make you feel at home. If you're attending a performance or game at the San Jose Arena, stay at the Arena Hotel and take the easy two-block stroll to the stadium. It's also close to the downtown Caltrain station if you want to head up to the Peninsula or San Francisco for the day. San Jose's famous Schura's chocolate factory, an old-fashioned candy store, is across the street.

Details: 89 rooms; efficiencies, cable TV; some rooms: whirlpool; business services; free morning newspaper, breakfast, and parking. Rates: $89–350.

817 The Alameda (near Stockton Ave. west of downtown's San Jose Arena), 408/294-6500 or 800/954-6835, fax 408/294-6585, website: www.pacifichotels.com.

Crowne Plaza

This hotel used to be a seedy Holiday Inn, but in 1997, it underwent a major facelift when Crowne Plaza bought the building. It now has a fresh but unimaginative California look. It's definitely targeted at corporate and business guests attending the McEnery Convention Center across the street. But if you're staying downtown for entertainment, you can take advantage of special weekend packages that let you sample the nightlife or catch a performance at the nearby Center for the Performing Arts. For fitness fiends, the hotel offers a fully equipped gym as well as nearby tennis and racquetball courts. It's conveniently located right next to a Light Rail station.

Details: 239 rooms; coffeemaker, cable TV; some rooms: refrigerator; gym; airport transport; business services; Miro's (Mediterranean and California cuisine). Rates: $119–429.

282 Almaden Blvd. (at San Carlos St.), 408/998-0400 or 800/227-6963, fax 408/289-9081, website: www.crowneplaza.com.

Executive Inn Downtown

For budget-minded travelers, this clean motel is conveniently located near San Jose's downtown action.

Details: 25 rooms; coffeemaker, microwave, cable TV, refrigerator; some rooms: efficiencies, whirlpool; business services; complimentary breakfast. Rates: $109–189.

1215 S. 1st St. (near Alma Ave. south of downtown), 408/280-5300 or 800/509-7666,

LODGING SPLENDOR IN THE MID-19TH CENTURY

In the 19th century, one of the valley's most esteemed lodgings was the Auzerais House, in San Jose's downtown. Brothers Edward and John Auzerais were French immigrants who came to San Jose in the early 1850s and built a successful general merchandise business known as the Mariposa Store. The store brought in the revenue that financed the brothers' purchase of local real estate and establishment of a freight line to ship goods between San Jose and San Francisco. So wealthy did the brothers become that in 1863 they hired local architect Theodore Lenzen to design a hotel which would be one of the grandest in the state.

Built at a cost of about $100,000 and furnished to the tune of an additional $50,000, the Auzerais House opened two years later, a picture of almost unimaginable grandeur (see the banner at the head of this chapter). Modern conveniences included steam heat in every room and bathroom faucets with hot water, which flowed from a tank in the attic. The swank hotel quickly became the gathering spot of choice for the valley's social elite and famous guests, including former President U. S. Grant. But the hotel was razed long ago, and today only a San Jose avenue bears the Auzerais name.

fax 408/280-0569, website: www.executive-inns-suites.com.

Fairmont Hotel

Saunter into the Fairmont, and you'll have no doubt it's *the* grand hotel of Silicon Valley. Greta Garbo would definitely feel at home here. Its spacious lobby is graced with marble columns, fine artwork, and elegant decor. Carrying you back to the sophisticated 1920s, a musician plays Gershwin classics on a grand piano by the lounge bar. From the beginning, the 20-story post-modern hotel quickly grew into an icon for San Jose, serving as the focal point for the redeveloped downtown. When presidents or movie stars such as John Travolta come to town, they stay at the Fairmont. It has a reputation for fine service in elegant surroundings; the friendly and professional staff will go the extra mile to make your stay a pleasant one.

Details: 541 rooms; cable TV; swimming pool, gym; The Fountain (American cuisine), The Grill on the Alley (California cuisine), The Pagoda (Asian cuisine). Rates: $239–1,000.

170 S. Market St., 408/998-1900 or 800/527-4727, fax 408/287-1648, website: www.fairmont.com.

Hensley House

If you desire homey lodgings away from the conventional hotels, this B&B (the only one in downtown San Jose) is a sure bet. The Hensley House is really two houses across the street from each other in San Jose's historical Hensley district. One is a comfortable Victorian built in 1884; the other, a smaller home built in 1906. The lavish decor includes Victorian wallpaper, stained glass windows, antique furniture, and crystal chandeliers hanging over four-poster beds. Innkeepers Ron Evans and Tony Contreras named rooms after famous Californians, including César Chávez and John Frémont. Complimentary snacks fill baskets kept throughout the house. Although the ambience is 19th century, the amenities are definitely high-tech. Every room comes with a computer, fax machine, and modem hookup. Most guests are business travelers, but Hensley

© MARTIN CHEEK

San Jose's Fairmont Hotel

House has facilities for weddings and private parties as well.

Details: nine rooms; cable TV, private bath; some rooms: efficiencies, whirlpool; business services; complimentary breakfast. Rates: $140–300.

456 N. 3rd St. (at Hensley St.), 408/298-3537 or 800/498-3537, fax 408/298-4676, website: www.hensleyhouse.com.

Hotel De Anza

With its rooftop neon sign and 1930s art-deco style, you can't miss the 10-story Hotel De Anza. This historic landmark stands tall and proud at the north end of Almaden Boulevard. If the walls could talk, they'd tell of guests in its early days such as Eleanor Roosevelt, the Du Ponts, and various movie idols. Sadly, by the 1960s the De Anza was neglected and faced eventually being gutted by a wrecking ball. But preservation groups decided to give the old gal a second chance. A major remodeling job started in the late 1980s, and the opulent hotel today has reclaimed its original splendor. It even got back its famous "bathing-suit beauty," a diving woman painted on the outside west wall.

ACCOMMODATIONS

In contrast with some of Silicon Valley's cookie-cutter hotels, the De Anza pampers its guests in intimate surroundings. If you can afford it, enjoy the penthouse, which takes up the entire 10th floor and includes two private balconies, a wood-burning fireplace, and a steam room. The hotel's Hedley Club provides live entertainment, mostly jazz, four nights a week.

Details: 101 rooms; cable TV, complimentary video library for in-room VCR; gym; free newspaper, coffee, and airport transport; La Pastaia (elegant Italian cuisine). Rates: $105–1,300.

233 W. Santa Clara St. (at the north end of Almaden Blvd.), 408/286-1000 or 800/843-3700, fax 408/286-0500, website: www.hoteldeanza.com.

Hyatt Sainte Claire

If you're looking for a European-style hotel in the heart of Silicon Valley, look no farther than the Hyatt Sainte Claire. This registered National Historic Landmark is the essence of elegance. The lobby's lounge design harks back to an era of knights and damsels. You'll think you've stepped into a Gothic hall when you see its immense fireplace and oak-beamed ceiling. Rooms are richly appointed with featherbeds, a European tradition. This being the capital of high-tech, suites come with multimedia workstations, fax machine, printer, and photocopier as well as Internet access. It's within easy walking distance of the McEnery Convention Center and the Civic Auditorium.

"GRANDMA" BASCOM'S HOSPITALITY

Bascom Ave. is a long thoroughfare stretching from Los Gatos to San Jose's Burbank district. It was named after a pioneer family who played an important hospitality role for California's first state legislature.

After a seven-month wagon journey, Louis and Anna Maria Bascom and their seven children arrived in San Jose in 1849 just as the first state legislators started to convene. With the sudden surge in population due to the city becoming the capital, housing was in short supply for the politicians. To help make extra money, the Bascoms turned their San Fernando St. home into a boardinghouse which provided lodging and meals to many legislators.

Anna Maria later came to be known as "Grandma Bascom" and was a colorful character in the 19th century valley. In 1887, she recalled to the *Overland Monthly* magazine her experience running the boardinghouse:

"People began to ask if they couldn't stay with us until they found some other home, and then, somehow, they stayed on. Everybody had to be hospitable. The Legislature was then in session and the town was more than full. The first thing I knew I had 13 boarders—senators and representatives, ministers and teachers. Nobody who came would go away. I could always manage to make people feel at home, and they would all say they would put up with anything an' help in all sorts of ways, if I would only let them stay. Mr. Leek (he was the enrolling clerk of the Legislature) was a wonderful hand at making batter cakes. We got a reputation on batter cakes and our house was dubbed 'Slapjack Hall' by my boy, Al. It stuck to us. Mr. Bradford, of Indiana, could brown coffee to perfection.

"Mr. Orr and Mr. Mullen always brought all the water. They were senators. I used to think they liked the job because there was a pretty girl in the house where they got the water. And that reminds me that several families got water from the same well. It was just a hole in the ground, about eight or ten feet deep and no curb around it. Once a baby was creeping on the ground and fell into it. The mother saw it and ran and jumped in after it. Then she screamed and I ran out. There she was in the well, holding the baby upside down to get water out of its lungs. 'Throw me a rope,' she screamed and I ran for a rope. Then she tied it around the baby and I drew it up. Meanwhile, our cries brought men to the rescue and they drew up the poor woman. We kept the well covered after that."

Details: 170 rooms; cable TV; airport transport; business services; Il Fornaio Cucina (fine Italian cuisine); allows pets. Rates: $99–279.

302 S. Market St. (at San Carlos St.), 408/885-1234 or 800/492-8822, fax 408/977-0403, website: www.hyatt.com.

San Jose Hilton and Tower

The designers of downtown's newest hotel, the San Jose Hilton and Tower, created it with conventioneers in mind. Opened in 1997, it's connected to the west end of McEnery Convention Center, making it a breeze to get to those trade show booths and lectures. For business travelers, the Hilton offers a complete business center, which includes secretarial services and workstation rental. The hotel sits kitty-corner from the Center for the Performing Arts, so after-hours, you can easily catch the San Jose Symphony or the American Musical Theater. A Light Rail station is just outside the hotel.

Details: 355 rooms; cable TV; some rooms: honor bar, whirlpool; swimming pool; free airport transport; The City Bar and Grill (American cuisine); allows pets. Rates: $109–249.

300 Almaden Blvd. (at San Carlos St.), 408/287-2100 or 800/445-8667, fax 408/947-4489, website: www.sjhilton.com.

Travelodge—San Jose Convention Center

If you're looking for a cheap and clean place to stay and don't require fancy frills, this lodging probably makes a good choice.

Details: 26 rooms; cable TV, coffeemaker, free movies, refrigerator; some rooms: microwave, whirlpool; business services; coffee shop. Rates: $120–195.

1415 Monterey Rd., 408/993-1711 or 800/578-7878, fax 408/993-8744, website: www.travelodge.com.

GREATER SAN JOSE
Oakwood Corporate Housing

For travelers looking for extended-stay lodging who don't like the institutional feel of hotels, Oakwood provides an apartment-like place to settle in Silicon Valley. For Asian clients, it provides extra amenities such as rice steamers, woks, and chopsticks.

Details: weekly maid service extra; 782 rooms; kitchen, patio, dining room, living room, separate bedroom; pool, whirlpool, exercise room. Rates: $105–146 (minimum 31-day contract).

700 S. Saratoga Ave., 408/551-6950 or 800/777-4771, fax 408/551-6960, website: www.oakwood.com.

SANTA CLARA
Biltmore Hotel and Suites Silicon Valley

Getting beyond the unattractive front parking lot area, visitors walking into the Biltmore will find a stylishly designed lobby with a friendly staff. The building is divided into two wings separated by the heated pool. The Courtyard Room wing provides standard rooms that are nicely furnished. Rooms in the more expensive Towers Suites wing each contain a separate living room with a sleeper sofa and a working area with a modem connection. The hotel's restaurant serves a traditional Japanese breakfast as well as American fare. It's very much a business traveler–oriented lodging, particularly with Intel and other high-tech companies so close.

Details: 262 rooms; coffeemaker, iron, voice mail, dataport; pool, fitness center; business service center; free newspaper, breakfast, and airport transport; Montague's and Prizmz Sports Bar. Rates: $209–289.

2151 Laurelwood Rd. (intersection of U.S. 101 and Montague Expwy.), 408/988-8411 or 800/255-9925, fax 408/986-9807, website: www.hotelbiltmore.com.

Holiday Inn Great America

Formerly the Days Inn Motel, this lodging underwent a renovation in 1999, modernizing it for today's high-tech travelers. It's conveniently located near the Great America theme park, as well as Mission Community College.

Details: 168 rooms; sofa sleeper, cable TV, coffeemaker, hair dryer, voice mail, in-room checkout; some rooms: microwave, refrigerator;

HISTORIC HAYES MANSION

Near Monterey Hwy. in the Edenvale district of San Jose stands the Hayes Mansion Conference Center, where many of Silicon Valley's businesspeople convene. The conference center and hotel is located on what was once a grand estate built by Mary Hayes-Chynoweth, a 19th-century woman who used her alleged psychic powers to build her family's fortune.

Mary was born in Holland, New York, in 1825, the daughter of a blacksmith and Baptist minister. The ninth of 10 children, she lived in poverty in the early part of her life. At 17, she started working as a schoolteacher and also developed an interest in spiritualism, the belief that if one were in tune with the spiritual realm, the spirits of the dead could offer guidance. At 29, she quit teaching and became a faith-healer and preacher.

At one of her sermons, she charmed a widowed farmer named Anson Hayes (a cousin of President Rutherford B. Hayes). Soon after they met, he proposed marriage and she accepted. They had three sons: Everis, Jay Orley, and Carroll, who died as an infant. In 1873, Anson died of a heart attack.

Everis and Jay Orley graduated with law degrees at the University of Wisconsin and worked as attorneys. Mary moved in with them and, using her psychic powers, advised them on real estate and other investments. The brothers bought shares in Michigan's unproductive Ashland Mine, and Mary used her psychic energy to discover a rich vein of ore. This mine would be the start of the Hayes family's wealth.

Listening to her spirit advisors, Mary and her sons moved to California in 1887. In San Jose, they bought 240 acres of land that once was part of the Bernal Rancho. Here, they began the construction of an extravagant Victorian mansion. Built for $175,000, the four-story, 50-room home had many modern conveniences including electric lightning. Frescoed walls and decorative hardwood furniture made it a lavish place to live. So idyllic was the location that they named it Edenvale after the biblical garden.

Mary provided healing treatment to local residents of the valley through personal visits as well as through letters sent through the mail. She allegedly healed a man named T. B. Chynoweth of blindness, and although he was 21 years her junior, he proposed marriage and she accepted. Unfortunately, T. B. died 10 months after the wedding.

The Edenvale mansion burned down in 1899. Mary hired a local architect named George Page to construct a replacement which would withstand another fire or an earthquake. He designed a three-story, Mediterranean-style villa in the form of a Maltese Cross. This new 62-room mansion was completed in 1905 and was so strongly built, it easily stood up to the 1906 earthquake. Distinguished guests included Teddy Roosevelt, William McKinley, and Herbert Hoover. Mary died shortly after the mansion was completed, but her sons and their families continued to live in the wings until the 1950s.

Everis and Jay Orley Hayes both became prominent men. Everis served in the U.S. House of Representatives from 1904 to 1918. Jay Orley lost his bid for California state governor, but helped to form the Good Government League to fight corruption in San Jose's city council. In 1900, they went into the newspaper business with the purchase of the *San Jose Herald* and, the next year, the *San Jose Mercury.* They would later merge the papers into the *San Jose Mercury News.*

Today, you can take a free self-guided tour of the mansion. And perhaps, if your psychic energy is strong enough, you might feel the presence of the spirit of Mary Hayes-Chynoweth directing you through her beautiful home.

Details: 135 rooms; cable TV; in-room safes, large work desk, dual line phones, iron and ironing board, bathrobes, coffeemaker, business services; Orlo's (fine California cuisine). Rates: $135–395.

200 Edenvale Ave., San Jose, 408/226-3200 or 800/420-3200, website: www.hayesconferencecenter.com; free parking.

pool, whirlpool, exercise room; business services: fax, photocopier, corporate workstation; free newspaper, airport transport, and shuttle within five-mile radius; IHOP (pancake house). Rates: $165–189.

4200 Great America Pkwy. (at Mission College Blvd.), 408/235-8900 or 800/465-4329, fax 408/988-0976, website: www.holidayinn.com.

Madison Street Inn

This bed-and-breakfast targeted at business clientele is set in a Queen Anne Victorian house amid a well-tended, colorful garden. Rooms are named after presidents, such as Jefferson, Madison, and Monroe. A large suite has a Japanese-style tub and shower. Also available are meeting facilities for 4–25 people as well as a garden patio that makes a charming place for wedding receptions.

Details: five rooms (three with private bath, two share a bath); free newspaper; special meals prepared by advance reservation. Rates: $90–150.

1390 Madison St. (from San Jose Airport, drive to Coleman Ave., following it north until it forks to the left and becomes Lewis St.; follow this six blocks to the corner of Lewis and Madison Sts.), 408/249-5541 or 800/491-5541, fax 408/249-6676, website: www.bbinternet.com/santa-clara.

Marriott Hotel

This immense hotel is set in an industrial park containing Intel's headquarters. It's targeted at business travelers, many of whom let their children off at the nearby Great America theme park for the day before they go off to meetings. Built in the 1970s, the hotel's lobby has a casual Spanish Renaissance style with corridor arches and red-glazed brick floor tiles.

Details: 765 rooms; cable TV; pool, tennis courts, basketball court, fitness room, whirlpool, game room; business services: voice mail, dataports; free newspaper and airport transport; Allies American Grille and Characters Sports Bar and Grill; allows small pets. Rates: $99–329.

2700 Mission College Blvd. (near Paramount's Great America theme park), 408/988-1500 or 800/228-9290, fax 408/727-4353, website: www.marriott.com.

The Westin Hotel

Directly attached to the Santa Clara Convention Center, this 14-story hotel is a convenient place for out-of-towners to stay while attending trade shows and conferences. The hotel has a relaxed atmosphere, and the service is friendly. For kids, it's in walking distance of the Great America theme park. For golfers, it's next door to the Santa Clara Golf and Tennis Club, with its par-72 championship golf course. A Light Rail station is near the hotel, allowing guests to get to downtown San Jose or other areas along the N. 1st St. corridor.

Details: 501 rooms; cable TV, on-demand movies; pool, whirlpool spa, fitness center; business services: mobile phones, voice mail, fax, photo processing, audiovisual equipment rental; Tresca (California cuisine with Mediterranean influence); allows small pets. Rates: $159–355.

5101 Great America Pkwy. (north off U.S. 101 at corner of Tasman Dr.), 408/986-0700 or 800/228-3000, fax 408/980-3990, website: www.westin.com.

Woodcrest Hotel

Billing itself as an "executive hotel," this lodging aims at providing personal service to business guests. Its beautifully landscaped courtyard provides a pleasant place to enjoy the Santa Clara sunshine. For small conferences, the hotel has two meeting rooms.

Details: 60 rooms; cable TV, VCR, movie and book library, hair dryer, robes; some rooms: fireplace, wet bar, courtyard view; business services: incoming faxes; free breakfast and deli buffet; free pass to local fitness center. Rates: $99–350.

5415 Stevens Creek Blvd. (off Lawrence Expwy.), 408/446-9636 or 800/862-8282, fax 408/446-9739.

SARATOGA

The Inn at Saratoga

This tasteful hotel with a cozy lobby offers European-style hospitality to its guests. All rooms come with patios and balconies that have floor-to-ceiling French windows overlooking nearby

Wildwood Park and Saratoga Creek. Two suites are named after actresses Olivia de Havilland and Joan Fontaine, who grew up in Saratoga. Bathrooms come with European towel warmers. Excellent restaurants are within easy walking distance in Saratoga Village.

Details: 46 rooms; cable TV, refrigerator, free movies, robes; some rooms: whirlpool; business services: modem ports; free newspaper, breakfast, and evening beverages. Rates: $195–575.

20645 4th St. (north of Big Basin Way in Saratoga Village), 408/867-5020 or 800/543-5020, fax 408/741-0981, website: www.innat-saratoga.com.

Sanborn Park Hostel

Set among the redwoods of Sanborn-Skyline County Park, this hostel provides cheap but beautiful accommodations in the Santa Cruz Mountains. The wood cabin was built in 1908 as a summer home for Judge Welch Hurst. Many international travelers stay here. Occasionally, interpretive programs are scheduled.

Details: Rates: $10 members, $12 nonmembers.

15808 Sanborn Rd. (from Saratoga Village, drive into the mountains along Hwy. 9, take Sanborn Rd. exit), 408/741-9555, website: www.sanbornparkhostel.org.

SUNNYVALE

Maple Tree Inn

A standard lodging with no frills, this hotel is targeted at budget-minded travelers. Service is courteous and professional, and facilities are clean.

Details: 181 rooms; cable TV, video games; some rooms: kitchen, microwave, refrigerator; pool; business services: meeting rooms, audiovisual equipment; free breakfast and passes for nearby fitness center. Rates: $159–180.

711 E. El Camino Real (between Wolfe Rd. and Fair Oaks Rd.), 408/720-9700 or 800/423-0243, fax 408/738-5665, website: www.mapletreeinn.com.

Ramada Silicon Valley

This swank, modern-decor hotel is nestled in the middle of five acres of lush tropical gardens. Service is professionally courteous. The hotel prides itself on its superb restaurants, especially a neon-lit sushi bar that provides tasty Japanese cuisine.

Details: 176 rooms; cable TV, coffeemaker, refrigerator, hair dryer, movies, safe; some rooms: microwave; pool, whirlpool; free newspaper and breakfast; Tobie Tylers (Japanese and American cuisine). Rates: $149–170.

1217 Wildwood Ave. (off Lawrence Expwy. going north), 408/245-5330 or 800/888-3899, fax 408/732-2628, website: www.ramada.com.

Woodfin Suite

Aiming to balance the luxury of a fine hotel with the comforts of a condo, this lodging provides rooms that include fully equipped kitchens and separate living rooms for socializing.

Details: 88 rooms; fireplace, kitchen, stove, dishwasher, microwave, refrigerator, coffeemaker; some rooms: handicapped facilities; business services: personal computers, photocopiers, fax machines; free breakfast, transport to airport and within five-mile radius. Rates: $109–299.

635 E. El Camino Real (exit off U.S. 101 at Fair Oaks and drive 2.5 miles), 408/738-1700 or 800/237-8811, fax 408/738-0840, website: www.woodfinsuitehotels.com.

Wyndham Garden Hotel

Located in an industrial park within walking distance of Sunnyvale Bayland Park, this five-story hotel is entered through a row of palm trees leading to a rock sculpture fountain. In the elegant lounge area, guests can borrow a book from the library and read by the fireplace or gaze out at the well-landscaped garden. Conveniently close to Milpitas just east along Hwy. 237.

Details: 180 rooms; coffeemaker, hair dryer; some rooms: refrigerator; pool, whirlpool, fitness room; business services: meeting room for 10–130 people, fax; free airport transport; Garden Cafe and Lounge (Continental cuisine). Rates: $229–249.

1300 Chesapeake Terrace (off Hwy. 237 and Lawrence Expwy.), 408/747-0999 or 800/996-3426, fax 408/745-0759, website: www.wyndham.com.

Fine Dining, Potables, and Nightlife

San Francisco, an hour's drive to the north, has long received raves as California's culinary capital, but since the early 1980s, Silicon Valley has evolved into a destination also highly respected for good eating. Many of its dining establishments rival the quality of famous San Francisco restaurants without emulating their tourist-gouging prices. From simple vegetarian fare and local burger joints to award-winning, five-star establishments with starched linen and extensive wine lists, the region offers a tremendous variety of eateries for every taste.

Silicon Valley has achieved a small measure of success in its eateries branching out into nationally recognized restaurant chains. Santa Clara's Valley Fair Shopping Mall is the site of the first Fresh Choice restaurant. And until 1999, you could still buy sandwiches at the original Togo's, a small shack at William and 9th Sts. one block south of San Jose State University. Of course, Silicon Valley has its share of Olive Gardens,

Villa Montalvo, Saratoga

Denny's, Burger Kings, KFCs, and McDonald's. But for visitors who want to be more adventurous in their culinary exploration, the area provides a delightful sampling of excellent locally owned restaurants. If you can get on the Internet, visit the website www.dine.com, which will provide you with the latest information on the hottest establishments. The weekly *Metro* and Friday's "Eye" section of the *San Jose Mercury News* also give reviews of the latest restaurant openings. For the most extensive reviewed listing of Silicon Valley eating places—including San Francisco restaurants—the *Good Life Peninsula & Silicon Valley Restaurant Guide* (1998, Good Life Publications, $11.95) is a witty and detailed publication worth picking up.

Most of the region's restaurants are handicapped accessible and, by California law, nonsmoking facilities. Many also have their own websites to log onto and get a menu preview. Most accept major credit cards, but check with your server first if you're uncertain. In keeping with the Silicon Valley lifestyle, dress is generally casual. Prices listed here are for the restaurant's range of entrée items. Several restaurants also have nightclubs where you can party all night long after partaking of a meal. The region's nightclubs offer a variety of entertainment opportunities, from comedy and country music to jazz and top 40 music.

CAMPBELL

Silicon Valley's down-home community has a wide choice of restaurants in its Pruneyard Shopping Center as well as its historic downtown area and busy Winchester Boulevard.

Andy's BBQ

Set in a squat building between Hwy. 17 and Los Gatos Creek, since 1965 the unpretentious Andy's has been famous in Silicon Valley for its choice of barbecued meats slow-cooked over an oak-wood fire. It gets busy here, so while waiting for a table, enjoy a drink at the bar before heading into the somewhat cramped dining area. Observe the collection of barbecue sauce bottles from around the United States lining a high shelf along the room's ceiling.

700 E. Campbell Ave. (next to Hwy. 17 overpass), 408/378-2838, website: www.andysbbq.com; dinner $6–21; open Mon.–Sat. 11 A.M.–10 P.M.

El Burro

Step back into the graceful era of old California in this authentically decorated restaurant reflecting the Santa Clara Valley's pre-gringo days. This Mexican eatery (a personal favorite) serves generous portions and plenty of chips and salsa. On sunny days, sit outside in the patio area and enjoy your enchilada and a margarita.

1875 S. Bascom Ave. (in the Pruneyard Shopping Center), 408/371-5800; lunch $5–8, dinner $7–13; open daily 11 A.M.–10 P.M.

Hawgs Seafood Bar

This friendly neighborhood restaurant has quickly grown into a popular Silicon Valley destination for seafood. It got its unusual moniker from co-owner Steven Hardin's childhood nickname of "Hawg." The decor is kept unpretentious, with only a few swordfish mounted on the walls. Executive Chef German (HER-man) Amaya has fun coming up with new recipe creations such as the creamy "Newhatten" clam chowder, and everything comes in generous portions. For dessert, try the mouth-watering Hawgs Creme Brulee or the frozen lemon meringue pie (both $4.50). (A second Hawgs Seafood Bar is located in downtown San Jose in the same building as the Repertory Theatre.)

1700 W. Campbell Ave. (in the Kirkwood Shopping Center at San Tomas Aquino Rd.), 408/379-9555; lunch and dinner $11.75–14.75; open daily 11 A.M.–9 P.M.

Other Choices

Good beer and American-style cuisine pack the crowds in at the **Rock Bottom Brewery,** 1875 S. Bascom Ave. in the Pruneyard, 408/377-0707. Downtown Campbell's **Shebele,** 422 E. Campbell Ave., 408/378-3131, serves well-flavored Ethiopian foods. A good selection of Italian dishes with a French accent are served at **Giuseppe Restau-**

rant, 33 S. Central Ave. (in a renovated prune shed), 408/370-7705. Wood-fired pizzas and excellent pastas are made at **Palermo Pizza,** 915 S. San Tomas Aquino Rd., 408/374-1800. The economical **Russian Cafe & Deli,** 1712 Winchester Blvd., 408/379-6680, serves traditional dishes such as borscht and cabbage rolls in a homey kitchen atmosphere. **Kazoo Sushi Boat,** 10 E. Hamilton Ave., 408/871-1250, provides guests with a selection of 33 Japanese appetizers as well as sushi. Friendly Italian bistro **Buca La Pastaia,** 2081 S. Winchester Blvd., 408/871-3135, is an intimate place to have dinner.

CUPERTINO

In Apple Computer land, you'll find a large number of Asian restaurants as well as down-home diners serving traditional American cuisine.

Hamasushi

For those into authentic Japanese cuisine, this well-run place vastly surpasses the usual sushi establishment. Since its opening in 1978, it has been awarded "Best Sushi in the Bay Area" many times. It has a sleek, modern sushi bar area, as well as traditional Japanese rooms. A karaoke lounge is popular with regulars ($25 weekdays, $10 Sat.).

20030 Stevens Creek Blvd. (between De Anza Blvd. and Blaney Ave.), 408/446-4262, website: www.hamasushi.com; lunch $6–11.50, dinner $11–16; open Mon.–Fri. 11:30 A.M.–2 P.M., 5:30–10:30 P.M., Sat. 5–10 P.M., Sun. 5–9:30 P.M.

Hobee's

With its diverse country-style menu and genuinely friendly service, Hobee's has become a beloved local institution—especially for breakfast. On your visit to Silicon Valley, it's well worth trying out their world-famous blueberry coffee cake. Started by Paul Taber in Mountain View in March 1974, the restaurant struggled for a few years until the California health craze kicked into gear and shot it to success. Its moniker is meant to convey a fun and convivial attitude. Hobee's has grown into a popular chain with several locations throughout the valley. You'll see families dining

next to corporate executives making major high-tech deals. (The Cupertino restaurant even got onto the front page of *The Wall Street Journal* when it was revealed that an illegal secret meeting between Apple and Microsoft officials took place here.) All Hobee's restaurants serve breakfast and lunch, and those open late serve dinner as well. And, of course, with its rise in popularity, the restaurant also hawks merchandise such as T-shirts, mugs, and herbal teas. Breakfast $5–7.50, lunch and dinner $5–11.

In Campbell at 1875 S. Bascom Ave. (in the Pruneyard Shopping Center), 408/369-0575; open Mon.–Wed. 6:30 A.M.–9 P.M., Thurs.–Fri. 6:30 A.M.–10 P.M., Sat. 7:30 A.M.–10 P.M., Sun. 7:30 A.M.–9:30 P.M.

In Cupertino at 21267 Stevens Creek Blvd. (across from De Anza College in the Oaks Shopping Mall), 408/255-6010; open Mon.–Thurs. 6:30 A.M.–9:30 P.M., Fri. 6:30 A.M.–10 P.M., Sat. 7:30 A.M.–10 P.M., Sun. 7:30 A.M.–9 P.M.

In Mountain View at 2237 Central Expwy. (off Rengstorff Ave.), 650/968-6050; open Mon.–Fri. 6:30 A.M.–2:30 P.M., weekends 7:30 A.M.–2:30 P.M.

In San Jose at 680 River Oaks Pkwy. (at Montague Expwy.), 408/232-0190; open Mon.–Fri. 6:30 A.M.–2:30 P.M., weekends 8 A.M.–2:30 P.M.

In San Jose at 920 Town & Country Village (at Stevens Creek and Winchester Blvds.), 408/244-5212; open Mon. 7 A.M.–2:30 P.M., Tues.–Fri. 7 A.M.–9 P.M., Sat. 8 A.M.–9 P.M., Sun. 8 A.M.–3 P.M.

Near Stanford at 67 Town & Country Village (El Camino Real and Embarcadero Rd.), 650/327-4111; Mon.–Fri. 7 A.M.–9 P.M., Sat.–Sun. 8 A.M.–9 P.M.

In Palo Alto at 4224 El Camino Real (Charleston and San Antonio Rds.), 650/856-6124; Mon. 7 A.M.–2:30 P.M., Tues.–Fri 7 A.M.–9 P.M., Sat. 7:30 A.M.–9 P.M., Sun. 8 A.M.–2:30 P.M.

In Sunnyvale at 800 Ahwanee Ave. (at Mathilda Ave. near U.S. 101), 408/524-3580; open Mon.–Fri. 7 A.M.–2:30 P.M., weekends 8 A.M.–3 P.M., website: www.hobees.com.

Santa Barbara Grill

It's a little tricky winding your way through the

M

FINE DINING

maze of a Cupertino industrial park to the entrance of this popular eatery, but it's worth the effort to reach Chef Patrick Clark's prime American regional cuisine using the freshest ingredients. Clark cooked at San Francisco's Ritz-Carlton and the Cliff House before opening this popular grill just across the street from Apple Computer's headquarters. Jazz music plays in the background, and the decor is playfully colorful, with avant-garde glass sculptures accenting its windows. Try the award-winning gumbo for lunch. Dinner reservations recommended.

10745 N. De Anza Blvd. (just south of I-280 on De Anza, turn right at Valley Green Dr. and follow the sign), 408/253-2233, website: www.santabarbaragrill.com; lunch $7–18, dinner $9–18; open Mon.–Fri. 11:30 A.M.–10 P.M., weekends 4–10 P.M.

Other Choices

If you're in the mood for traditional British pub fare, try the **Duke of Edinburgh,** 10801 N. Wolfe Rd., 408/446-3853. **Canton Delight,** 10125 Bandley Dr., 408/777-9888, serves authentic Macao cuisine, including a number of vegetarian dishes. **Jade Tree Restaurant,** 10074 E. Estates Dr., 408/996-2999, serves good Chinese dishes in a neighborhood setting. Szechuan and Yangzhou foods as well as an excellent weekend dim sum brunch are served at **Silver Wing,** 10885 N. Wolfe Rd., 408/873-7228. Those adventurous enough to sample reasonably priced and delicious Nepalese food will want to try out **Kathmandu West,** 20916 Homestead Rd., 408/996-0940. For the budget-minded interested in a cafeteria serving a range of meals, from seafood and steaks to curry and chow mein, try the **Wolfe Cafe,** 10851 N. Wolfe Rd. in Cupertino Village, 408/777-9398. Cuisine from India's northern Punjab region is served at **Bombay Oven,** 20803 Stevens Creek Blvd., 408/252-0520.

LOS ALTOS

Although relatively sparse in eateries compared with other Silicon Valley communities, Los Altos has its share of quality bistros and restaurants to

GILROY'S PRECIOUS PUNGENT ROSE

Whatever you may think, garlic is not a spice, an herb, or a vegetable. It is a pungent bulb known as *alium sativum,* a member of the lily family. Two major varieties of garlic grow in California. One, called California Early, is covered with a white skin. Planted in November, it's ready for harvest in June. The other, California Late, is smaller, and the skin has a purple-bluish color. It's planted in December and harvested in midsummer.

Gilroy is known as "Garlic Capital of the World" not because it grows the greatest quantities of this bulb, but because its three companies—Gilroy Foods, Rogers Foods, and Basic Vegetables—process about 90 percent of the United States' supply of dehydrated garlic. Only about 500 to 700 acres of garlic are grown in the fields around Gilroy. But an additional 15,000 acres are grown in the San Joaquin Valley, then hauled over Pacheco Pass to the South Valley city. At the height of the season, Gilroy Foods processes more than one million pounds of raw garlic per day. In what is mostly an automated process, the bulbs are skinned, washed, and dehydrated in large ovens. Finally, they are put into powerful mills, which grind them into garlic powder. Drivers along Hwy. 152 near Pacheco Pass can often get a strong whiff of the delicious odor.

While visiting downtown Gilroy, an enjoyable place to get high-quality garlic gifts is the Garlic Festival Store and Gallery at 7526 Monterey St., 408/842-7081, website: www.garlicfestival.com.

enjoy lunch or dinner after a couple hours of shopping in the quaint downtown.

Chef Chu's

For more than three decades, Owner-Chef Lawrence C. C. Chu has focused on using only the freshest ingredients and cooking with traditional Chinese methods, making his establishment the premier Bay Area Chinese restaurant. In 1995, the American Academy of Restaurant & Hospitality Sciences gave it the Gold Award, making it one of the Top Ten Restaurants in the United States for its category. Pictures on the wall show such famous patrons as George Bush, Margaret Thatcher, and John F. Kennedy Jr. Try the Crispy Flounder in Pepper-Salt. The classic Peking duck is good but requires four hours' notice. For health-conscious patrons, no MSG is used, and dishes can be ordered with no meat and no oil. Delivery is provided for groups of 20 or more diners.

1067 N. San Antonio Rd. (at El Camino Real), 650/948-2696; lunch $7–11, dinner $4.50–20; open Mon.–Fri. 11:30 A.M.–9:30 P.M., Sat. noon–10 P.M., Sun. noon–9:30 P.M.

Other Choices

The upscale American grill **Bandera,** 233 3rd St., 650/948-3524, serves dinner only, cooked over a wood-flame fire. Japanese cuisine is colorfully prepared at **Akane,** 250 3rd St., 650/941-8150. For fine Continental dining on seafood and healthy game, go to **Beauséjour,** 170 State St., 650/948-1382. Classic Italian cuisine in a swank setting is the specialty of **I Fratelli,** 388 Main St., 650/941-9636. The friendly **Maltby's,** 101 Plaza North, 650/917-8777, is a downtown restaurant serving grilled sandwiches, steaks, fish, and burgers. Creekside fine dining, including a Sunday brunch, can be enjoyed at **The Echo,** 1579 Miramonte Ave. at Foothill Expwy., 650/967-0969.

LOS GATOS

The town of the cats is a favorite place for Silicon Valley residents to go for a special meal in a friendly community setting. The majority of eateries are located in the downtown district.

C. B. Hannegan's Restaurant

This California-style Irish pub is a long-established Los Gatos institution serving an ample selection of beers and stouts. It's still run by founders Chris Benson and John Hannegan. The casual decor features an antique bottle collection and San Francisco 49er team memorabilia, such as a jersey signed by Jerry Rice on the ceiling. The eclectic menu includes tacos, grilled and cold sandwiches, salads, and pizza. The Thursday night special is corned beef and cabbage.

208 Bachman Ave. (off N. Santa Cruz Ave.), 408/395-1233, website: www.cbhannegans.com; lunch and dinner $5.75–15; open daily 11:30 A.M.–2 A.M.

The Chart House

Set in the Coggeshall-Place Mansion, a Queen Anne Victorian built in 1891 (which served as a mortuary from 1920 to 1974), this distinctive restaurant is separated from bustling downtown Los Gatos by an attractive garden. Known for its slow-roasted prime rib, seafood, and steaks, the Chart House only serves dinner, and reservations are recommended.

115 N. Santa Cruz Ave. (between Nicholson and Bean Sts.), 408/354-1737, website: www.chart-house.com; dinner $15–40; open Sun.–Thurs. 5–10 P.M., Fri.–Sat. 5–11 P.M.

Mary's Patio Cafe

This small diner (a favorite of Los Gatos cops) serves good food in a well-presented style. Hostess Mary Masouris, a native of Corinthias, Greece, warmly welcomes guests, while husband Dino serves as chef.

337 N. Santa Cruz Ave. (just south of Hwy. 9), 408/395-0711; breakfast $4–7, lunch $5–9, dinner $8–14; open Mon.–Sat. 6 A.M.–10 P.M., Sun. 7 A.M.–10 P.M.

Tapestry: A California Bistro

This sophisticated restaurant set in a century-old bungalow provides a spacious and comfortable setting decorated with bold artwork. The outside patio is a pleasant place to enjoy your meal. Co-owners Gary and Vickie Messick and Carol

FINE DINING

and Joe Hargett brainstormed to come up with the name, meant to convey a "weaving of good food, good atmosphere, and good wine." Award-winning Chef Gary serves up visually stunning dishes such as his specialty, grilled filet mignon, while Vickie comes up with delicious pastry creations.

11 College Ave. (just off Main St.), 408/395-2808; lunch $8.50–11; dinner $13.50–20; open Tues.–Sat. 11:30 A.M.–2:30 P.M., Mon.–Sat. 5:30–10 P.M.

Other Choices

Beautiful mountaintop vistas along with flavorful American food can be taken in at **Lindsey's at the Summit,** 23123 Hwy. 17, 408/353-5679. For quality tandoor Indian food in an easygoing setting, try **Mount Everest,** 412 N. Santa Cruz Ave., 408/354-2427. **La Maison du Cafe,** 14103-C Winchester Blvd., 408/378-2233, serves country French cooking in a romantic environment. A Los Gatos institution, **The Cats,** 17533 Hwy. 17, 408/354-4020, is a popular hangout for those seeking steaks and chicken grilled over an oakwood fire. **The Los Gatos Bar & Grill,** 151 N. Santa Cruz Ave., 408/399-5424, is located next to the lively Mountain Charlie's. French bistro **Pigalle,** 27 N. Santa Cruz Ave., 408/395-7924, serves robust lunches and dinners as well as an exceptional Sunday breakfast. Popular seafood eatery **Steamers,** 31 University Ave., 408/395-2722, features a spacious enclosed patio in the quaint Old Town Shopping Center. Some of Silicon Valley's best pizza can be enjoyed at **Willow Street Wood-Fire Pizza,** 20 S. Santa Cruz Ave., 408/354-5566. **I Gatti,** 25 E. Main St., 408/399-5180, is a boisterous neighborhood Italian bistro known for its grilled veal chops.

MENLO PARK

Appealing to the wallets of the city's many venture capitalists, many of Menlo Park's restaurants show off a sophistication in their menus, but there are also choices for more budget-minded diners.

British Bankers Club

The party place for Menlo Park, this traditional Victorian pub set in a historic building is also a good spot to drop in for traditional grub such as English bangers, shepherd's pie, and fish and chips. Live music is performed Fri. and Sat. nights.

1090 El Camino Real (at Santa Cruz Ave.), 650/327-8769; entrées $7.95, sandwiches $7.50; open daily 11 A.M.–2 A.M.

Draeger's Bistro

Upscale supermarket Draeger's is a fun place to browse for specialized ingredients or kitchen tools. The bistro and coffee bar upstairs makes it a good destination for breakfast, lunch, or a quick latte. If you have a sweet tooth, try the old-fashioned milkshakes ($3.75) made with Häagen-Dazs ice cream, or if you're more health-conscious, enjoy a refreshing fresh-fruit smoothie ($2.95). Brunch is served weekends 8 A.M.–2:30 P.M.

1010 University Dr. (between Santa Cruz Ave. and Menlo St.), 650/688-0677; breakfast $7.50–9.50, lunch $8–13.75; open daily 7 A.M.–2:30 P.M.

Flea Street Cafe

This bistro's moniker has fun with the unusual Spanish name for the street it's located on. It's run by well-liked Chef Jesse Cool, who believes in serving her guests food prepared with organic, pesticide-free ingredients, including free-range poultry and meat. The restaurant's various rooms are elegantly decorated with mirrors and floral wallpaper. Reservations recommended.

3607 Alameda de las Pulgas (on Avy Ave.), 650/854-1226, website: www.fleast.com; lunch $9–15, dinner $17–24; open Tues.–Fri. 11:30 A.M.–2 P.M., 5:30–9:30 P.M., Sat. 5:30–9:30 P.M., Sun. 10 A.M.–2 P.M., 5:30–9 P.M.

Wild Hare

This restaurant's stunning wood decor and high, intricately beamed ceilings suggests a ski lodge. Executive Chef Joey Altman aims to provide diners "cuisine without border," and his menu gives a nod to Silicon Valley's diverse ethnicity. For example, starters include "Thai Sticks" as well as

FINE DINING

seared Hudson Valley foie gras with caramelized pears and ginger. As a dinner entrée, you could choose the Wild Hare pot pie, about which the menu claims, "We'd tell you what's in it, but we'd have to kill you."

1029 El Camino Real (between Santa Cruz Ave. and Menlo St.), 650/327-4273, website: www.wildharerestaurant.com; lunch $5–15, dinner $6–26; open weekdays 11:30 A.M.–2:30 P.M., Mon.–Thurs. 5:30–10 P.M., Fri.–Sat. 5:30–11 P.M., Sun. 5–9:30 P.M.

Other Choices

Trattoria Buon Gusto, 651 Maloney Ln., 650/328-2778, is a friendly neighborhood restaurant serving southern Italian cuisine. The intimate **Scala Mia House of Garlic,** 820 Santa Cruz Ave., 650/323-3665, provides guests with a wide selection of traditional Italian dishes. **Acorn,** 1906 El Camino Real, 650/322-6201, serves Continental food with a Greek influence. The pricey **Dal Baffo,** 878 Santa Cruz Ave., 650/325-1588, serves quality European cuisine inclined toward Italian. For a quick trip to the City of Light, try out **Left Bank,** 635 Santa Cruz Ave., 650/473-6543, very much like a traditional Parisian street cafe. **Gaylord,** 1706 El Camino Real, 650/326-8761, serves northern Indian dishes cooked in a mesquite-fired tandoori oven. Gourmet pizza can be sampled downtown at **Applewood Inn,** 1001 El Camino Real, 650/324-3486.

MILPITAS

Silicon Valley's industrial city boasts a large Asian population, which is reflected in the number of restaurants serving Oriental cuisine.

Hot Pot City

This all-you-can-eat Asian restaurant has a spartan ambience but provides an interesting outing for culinary adventurers. Select from a buffet of raw meats, including lamb and squid, and grill these with vegetables at your own table-side Korean hot pot. It's a good way to taste an eclectic mix of Oriental cuisine, such as Japanese *shabu shabu*. The dessert bar has 16 offerings, including shaved ice.

500 Barber Ln. (in Milpitas Square Shopping Center), 408/428-0988, website: www.hotpotcity.com; lunch $8.99 (Mon.–Fri.), $11.99 (Sat.), $12.99 (Sun.); dinner $11.99 (Mon.–Thurs.), $12.99 (Fri.–Sun.); open daily 11 A.M.–10 P.M.

Other Choices

Minh's Restaurant, 1422 Dempsey Rd., 408/956-1000, serves tasty northern Vietnamese cuisine, including vermicelli rice noodle dishes. Reasonably priced, generous servings of seafood, chicken, and beef entrées can be found at the Filipino-American eatery **Bahay Ihawan,** 100 Dixon Rd., 408/945-9055. Guests can taste a wide variety of traditional Indian cuisine at **Swagat,** 68 S. Abel St., 408/262-1128. A reasonably priced fusion of Thai and Vietnamese food is available at **Tam Restaurant,** 1720 N. Milpitas Blvd., 408/934-3970. Vegetarians frequent Chinese restaurant **Lu Lai Garden,** 210 Barber Ct., 408/526-9888. For Continental and Mediterranean food, **Brandon's Restaurant,** 1800 Barber Ln., 408/432-6311, is a good bet. A hint of the Bavarian Alps can be found at the German restaurant **Gasthaus Zum Goldenen Adler,** 1380 S. Main St., 408/946-6141.

MOUNTAIN VIEW

The charming Castro Street downtown district contains a diverse selection of Asian and Indian eateries, and a number of quality restaurants can also be found along El Camino Real.

Kapp's Pizza Bar and Grill

Originally a lumber and hardware store, this upscale pizza restaurant is decorated with historic photos of old Mountain View. The menu includes sandwiches and calzone, but definitely come for the pizza, such as the "Wild West," which is topped with barbecued chicken.

191 Castro St. (at Villa St.), 650/961-1491, website: www.kappspizza.com; lunch and dinner $4.65–6.60, pizzas $10.25–21.45 depending on size and combination; open Mon.–Thurs. 11:30 A.M.–9:30 P.M., Fri. 11:30 A.M.–11 P.M., weekends 4–10 P.M.

The Rio Grande

With its signature outside sign of a cowboy on a bucking horse, this combination restaurant and country nightclub serves American food ranging from burgers to grilled 18-ounce New York steaks. It was probably rare for a chuck wagon to serve skewered quail with cornbread-sausage stuffing during a Texas cattle drive. The location is a former movie palace that underwent a multimillion-dollar renovation, the highlight of which is the breathtaking Southwestern wall murals. Western dance lessons are given Tues. and Thurs. nights at 7:30 P.M., and live country music is performed Thurs.–Sat. nights.

228 Castro St. (between Dana and Villa Sts.), 650/988-6700; lunch and dinner $8–22; open Tues.–Sat. 11 A.M.–10 P.M.

Other Choices

Pho To Chau, 853 Villa St. in the downtown area, 650/961-8069, serves spicy Vietnamese noodle dishes. **Mei Long,** 867 E. El Camino Real, 650/961-4030, serves terrific Shanghai, Szechuan, and Yangzhou Chinese dishes in creative presentations. For high-tech-minded eaters, **Global Village Cafe,** 209 Castro St., 650/965-4821, is an innovative bistro incorporating computers into the decor. Reasonably priced Indian food can be enjoyed at **Maharaja,** 236 Castro St., 650/961-7382. If you're hankering for some old-fashioned Texas barbecue, try out unpretentious **Austin's,** 1616 W. El Camino Real, 650/969-9191. With its Lone Star decor, **El Paso Cafe,** 1407 W. El Camino Real, 650/961-8858, is a must for Texas-philes who want to try out its Tex-Mex dishes. A bit pricey, French restaurant **Chez TJ,** 938 Villa St., 650/964-7466, serves a seasonal menu that changes monthly. For a taste of Central America, try out the Salvadoran foods at **El Calderon,** 699 Calderon Ave., 650/940-9533. With its exceptional Mexican menu, **La Fiesta,** 240 Villa St., 650/968-1364, has been pleasing regulars since 1977. For Persian cuisine, including a healthy selection of tasty vegetarian dishes, try **Paradise,** 1350 Grant Rd. No. 15B, 650/968-5949.

PALO ALTO

This Peninsula city that originated from Leland Stanford's university is a gold mine of exceptional restaurants ranging from swank, eat-to-be-seen bistros to friendly Jamaican and Cuban cafés that care more about fun than status.

La Bodeguita del Medio

The liveliest place along placid California Ave., this Cuban bar and restaurant takes its name and theme from the original La Bodeguita in Havana, a famous Hemingway hangout. The name means "little bar in the middle of the block." Food includes Cuban fare such as the delicious Chicken à la Plancha as well as fresh fish and seafood. The enclosed divan in back is a good place to enjoy rum cocktails and hand-rolled cigars. Look for the cheesy wood cutout of Papa Hemingway in front holding a fish with a menu plastered on it.

463 California Ave. (off El Camino Real near Page Mill Rd.), 650/326-7762, website: www.labodeguita.com; lunch $6–11, dinner $6–20; open Mon.–Fri. 11:30 A.M.–2:30 P.M., Sat. noon–2:30 P.M., Mon.–Thurs. 5–9:30 P.M., Fri.–Sat. 5–10 P.M.

Peninsula Fountain & Grill

A Palo Alto institution since 1923, this old-fashioned diner was originally started by the Peninsula Dairy and still serves the best shakes in Silicon Valley. (Owner Robert Fischer's business card describes him as a "certified shake-ologist.") The diverse menu includes Belgian waffles, New York steak and eggs, Southern fried chicken salad, and Yankee pot roast. If you're celebrating a major venture capital deal, try the Bubbly Burger ($110.95—but that does include a chilled bottle of Dom Perignon).

566 Emerson St. (at Hamilton St. one block south of University Ave.), 650/323-3131; breakfast $4.50–9.50, lunch $5–9, dinner $9.50–13; open Mon.–Wed. 7 A.M.–10 P.M., Thurs. 7 A.M.–11 P.M., Fri. 7 A.M.–midnight, Sat. 8 A.M.–midnight, Sun. 8 A.M.–10 P.M.

University Coffee Café

A casual place to enjoy breakfast or a light midday lunch, this café offers good coffee, "health-smart" food, and a relaxed atmosphere. You'll see many Stanford students here, poring over textbooks at the small tables. On warm days, the glass doors are pushed aside to open the café to the bustling University Avenue. The menu's basics include pasta, salad, bruschettas, and burgers.

271 University Ave. (between Bryant and Ramona Sts.), 650/322-5301; breakfast $5–8.50; lunch and dinner $4–8; open Sun.–Thurs. 7 A.M.–11 P.M.; Fri.–Sat. 7 A.M.–midnight.

Other Choices

NOLA, 535 Ramona St., 650/328-2722, is a fun Cajun eatery serving good-quality gumbos and jambalayas. Upscale **Spago Palo Alto,** 265 Lytton Ave., 650/833-1000, run by celebrity chef Wolfgang Puck, serves California cuisine. For some "nouvelle Hellenic" dishes of Greece, try **Evvia,** 420 Emerson St., 650/326-0983. German cuisine, including an exceptional goulash, are served at the intimate **Elbe,** 117 University Ave., 650/321-3319. You've got to try out the garlic fries with a burger at sports bar **The Old Pro,** 2865 El Camino Real, 650/325-2070. A little rambunctious at times when it gets crowded, **Zibibbo,** 430 Kipling St., 650/328-6722, serves Mediterranean dishes cooked over a wood fire. **Compadres,** 3877 El Camino Real, 650/858-1141, serves generous margaritas and good-quality Mexican food. **Straits Cafe,** 3295 El Camino Real, 650/494-7168, presents guests with a colorful blending of dishes from Singapore. Southern-style foods such as grilled catfish and spoon bread are given a quality Silicon Valley touch at the **Blue Chalk Cafe,** 630 Ramona St. (across from city hall), 650/326-1020. Those looking for inexpensive Asian eats in downtown Palo Alto should try out **ZAO Noodles,** 261 University Ave., 650/328-1988. Reasonably priced Italian-American food such as gourmet sandwiches are sold at **Mike's Cafe,** 2680 Middlefield Rd, 650/473-6453. Visually-stunning **Cafe Maremonti,** 201 California Ave., 650/322-8586, is a bistro with Mediterranean-style cuisine.

SAN JOSE

If you can't find a restaurant you love in San Jose, you just can't be looking. The city has many high-quality, family-run eateries that reflect the diverse ethnic heritage of its citizens. Downtown San Jose has an abundance along every street, but many neighborhood restaurants are hidden in the strip malls found throughout the sprawling geography.

Bella Mia

Step into this popular restaurant and bar, and you'll feel warmly welcomed. Its stated philosophy is: "There are no strangers here . . . just friends you haven't met." The young staff provides energetic, cordial service. The kitchen creates regional Italian cuisine with flair. Bella Mia's decor is a mixture of Victorian and modern, with walls reaching upward in cathedral splendor, embellished with imperial green wallpaper. The 1st floor holds comfortable booths for casual dining, while the 2nd floor is more formal, including a superbly decorated banquet room with a skylight. Jazz is played Fri. and Sat. nights. Reservations recommended for Fri. nights.

58 S. 1st St. (between San Fernando and Santa Clara Sts.), 408/280-1993, website: www.bellamia.com; lunch $6–17, dinner $9–22; open Mon.–Thurs. 11 A.M.–9:30 P.M., Fri.–Sat. 11 A.M.–10 P.M., Sun. 10 A.M.–9 P.M.

Blake's

Blake's is downtown San Jose's best steakhouse, but its classic American grill also offers a fine menu of fresh fish, chicken, and pasta as well as vegetarian dishes. In the midst of lively San Pedro Square, Blake's caters to a suburban clientele. A large bar in the center of the restaurant serves fine wines and cocktails. The ambience is light and spacious, with a large wall mural titled "The Valley of Heart's Delight" showing the area in its agricultural days. A whimsical touch is the various clocks on the wall showing the time at such locations as King Ranch, Texas. Service is experienced and professional. Dinner reservations recommended.

17 N. San Pedro (off Santa Clara St.), 408/298-9221, website: www.blakessteakhouse.com; lunch $8–15, dinner $12–25; open Mon.–Fri. 11:30 A.M.–2 P.M., daily 5–10 P.M.

Emile's

Definitely for the crowd that demands excellence in a sophisticated European menu. Open since 1973, Emile's is a five-star restaurant with a cultivated attitude. Chef Emile Mooser was trained in classic French cuisine, and his philosophy is to make the best use of peak season ingredients. *Condé Nast* magazine ranks Emile's "one of the top 100 restaurants in the U.S." The decor is elegant, with fresh flowers decorating each exquisitely set table, and hand-sculptured brass works hanging overhead. The service is excellent, which you should expect at these prices. Reservations recommended. Off-site theme dinners are held on special occasions.

545 S. 2nd St. (between William and Reed Sts.), 408/289-1960, website: www.emiles.com; dinner $25–34; open Tues.–Sat. 6 P.M.–10 P.M.

Eulipia's

A "global fusion" menu is served at this well-respected restaurant in the heart of the downtown's SoFA district. It's a successful combination of international cuisines, including Asian, Mexican, and Caribbean. The service and decor are polished and unpretentious, aiming to create a relaxed atmosphere for diners. Renaissance-style artwork creates a graceful Mediterranean look and feel. The restaurant's name was inspired by saxophonist Rahsaan Roland Kirk's "Theme for the Eulipians." It's next door to Camera One, so you can enjoy an art flick after dinner.

374 S. 1st St. (between San Carlos and William Sts.), 408/280-6161, website: www.eulipia.com; lunch $12, dinner $10–20; open Tues.–Fri. 11:30 A.M.–2 P.M., Tues.–Sat. 5:30–10 P.M., Sun. 4:30–9 P.M.

Juicy Burger

Patrons call this the best burger joint in Silicon Valley—period. If you're looking for something beyond bland food pitched by clowns, this family-run place is a good bet, with a menu

offering interesting specialties such as guacamole cheeseburgers.

1597 Meridian Ave. (at Hamilton Ave.), 408/723-5484; lunch and dinner $3–5; open Tues.–Sat. 10 A.M.–10 P.M., Sun.–Mon. 10 A.M.–9 P.M.

94th Aero Squadron

Named after the first U.S. air squadron to see action on the Western front, this fun restaurant has a not-overly kitschy World War I ambience. Set in a faux French château with a triplane parked in front, it's located along the western boundary of the San Jose International Airport so you can watch airplanes land as you enjoy your meal. Entrées range from sandwiches and salads to chicken and London broil. Try the excellent Sunday brunch for $19.95.

1160 Coleman Ave. (near Airport Blvd.), 408/287-6150; lunch $7–12, dinner $11–23; open Mon.–Sat. 11:30 A.M.–3 P.M., 4–10 P.M., Sun. 9:30 A.M.–9 P.M.

O'Brien's Candy Store

A San Jose institution for almost nine decades, this soda fountain restaurant got its start in 1868 when Irish immigrant Maurice O'Brien started selling candy in the doorway of downtown's now-gone Pacific Hotel. So popular was his little business that he set up a candy store that also sold sandwiches and ice-cream snacks (it was the first place west of Detroit to sell ice cream sodas). Called "the prettiest and most attractive candy store on the Pacific Coast," it became a popular spot for locals hungry for a bite to eat after an evening's theater. Richard Nixon once remarked that this old-fashioned soda fountain was one of his favorite places to eat. The original O'Brien's closed in January 1956, but you can visit (and eat at) a replica of the store inside the San Jose Historical Museum's reconstruction of the Pacific Hotel. Complete with marble-top fountain counters and candy displays (some sweet treats even still going for a price-time-forgot of $.10), it's well worth an afternoon's outing.

1600 Senter Rd. in Kelley Park (across the street from Municipal Stadium), 408/918-1058. Parking costs $4 on weekends. Lunch runs about

$4. Museum admission costs $6 for adults, $5 for seniors, $4 for youths 6–17, and free for children 5 and under. Open Tues.–Sun. noon–5 P.M.

Original Joe's

You've gotta come here. Original Joe's (or "O.J.'s," as regulars call it) has been a San Jose tradition since 1956. Simply put, it's a fun place to eat. The cuisine is fine Italian and charcoal broiler, and it'll take you a while to select from the menu of more than 100 entrées. The excellent food is served in generous quantities by tuxedoed waiters with Italian accents who love to banter playfully with customers.

Original Joe's

Sit at one of the two counters and watch the chef in a white stovepipe cook's hat prepare your meal. The decor is definitive '50s style, with immense fake Chinese vases, palm plants, and subdued red neon accenting ceiling edges. It's easy to imagine Frank Sinatra walking in for a bite with the Rat Pack. Reservations are not taken.

301 S. 1st St. (at San Carlos St.), 408/292-7030, website: www.originaljoes.com; breakfast (served all day) $4–6, lunch $7–8, dinner $9–13.50; open daily 11 A.M.–1:30 A.M.

Picasso's

This authentic Spanish restaurant specializes in tapas and paellas. The menu provides a wide selection of traditional cuisine, including seafood specialties such as stewed calamari cooked in their ink. The light and airy decor will make you believe you've left Silicon Valley and journeyed to the Costa del Sol. Reproductions of Picasso masterpieces hang on the walls. Owner Julio Garcia welcomes all guests with an outgoing manner and a delightful Spanish accent, while his wife prepares the meals. They stock a fine selection of Spanish wines. This cordial restaurant makes a great escape from ordinary eateries. A flamenco guitarist entertains on Fri. and Sat. nights. Special dinners on Spanish holidays.

380 S. 2nd St. (between San Carlos and William Sts.), 408/298-4400; lunch $7 10, dinner $10–15; open Tues.–Fri. 11:30 A.M.–2 P.M., Tues.–Thurs. 5–9 P.M., Fri. 5–10 P.M., Sat.–Sun. 5–9:30 P.M.

Scott's

Situated on the 6th floor, Scott's Seafood Grill provides a panoramic vista of downtown San Jose and the Santa Cruz Mountains. Besides seafood (Scott's is famous for its calamari), the California-style menu features steaks, chicken, and pasta, with an emphasis on freshness and variety. The understated decor doesn't distract from the view. Owner-managers Erin and John Barclay make sure guests receive warm and comfortable service. Located near the Center for the Performing Arts, Scott's draws in theater- and symphony-goers.

185 Park Ave. (between Almaden Blvd. and S. Market St.), 408/971-1700, website: www. scottsseafoodsj.com; lunch $10–18, dinner $14–21; open Mon.–Fri. 11:30 A.M.–2 P.M., Mon.–Sat. 5 P.M.–9:30 P.M., Sun. 4:30–9 P.M.

Sushi Masa

A favorite of rock star and KFOX disc jockey Greg Kihn, this restaurant serves traditional Japanese cuisine in a quiet country inn–style setting. Its wide selection of seafood appetizers includes fried octopus and squid teriyaki.

5363 Camden Ave. (at the Avanti Shopping Center about one mile south of Hwy. 85), 408/265-3232; lunch $5.25–10.25, dinner $6–17; open Tues.–Fri. 11:30 A.M.–1:45 P.M.,

Sun.–Thurs. 5–9:30 P.M., Fri. 5–10 P.M., Sat. 5–9:45 P.M.

Vung Tau

This is a favorite restaurant of San Jose's large Vietnamese-American population because it's highly respected for serving traditional cuisine. Named after the owner's hometown in Vietnam, Vung Tau is a family-oriented place—noisy, fun, and carefree. Come for the food, not the decor, a hodgepodge of Asian knickknacks. Enjoy generous servings at low prices. Try the sautéed prawns, and if you're in for some culinary exploration, the clay pot catfish and Thai soup make good choices.

535 E. Santa Clara St. (at 12th St.), 408/288-9055; lunch $5–8, dinner $6–19; open Sun.–Thurs. 9 A.M.–9 P.M., Fri.–Sat. 9 A.M.–10 P.M.

Waves Smokehouse & Saloon

Waves is well on its way to becoming a San Jose institution. Its Texas barbecue is great, some of the best outside of Amarillo, and the service is family-friendly. This colorful restaurant and bar is also a mother lode of local history. Since the two-

© MARTIN CHEEK

Waves Smokehouse & Saloon

story Italianate Victorian's construction in 1873, it has served as a brothel, a boardinghouse, and a bar. (Take a look at the "spitter gutter" spittoon on the floor by the entrance.) Spirits abound at Waves, and not just in bottles. Its owners claim a female ghost haunts the 2nd floor, whispering the names of diners in their ears. On the ground level, an Irish specter named Blackie supposedly pokes unsuspecting customers in the back. The downstairs bar is a magnificent mahogany and stained-glass creation, a perfect place to enjoy its great selection of beers while exchanging ghost stories with the friendly barkeep. You can also relax on the roof patio while dining under the stars by a wood fire. Live reggae and jazz music is played on Sat. and Fri. nights.

65 Post St. (off S. Market St.), 408/885-9283, website: www.waves-smokehouse.com; lunch $6–10, dinner $8–15; open Mon.–Sat. 11 A.M.–11 P.M., Sun. noon–10 P.M.

White Lotus

Strictly for vegetarians, this Vietnamese restaurant opened in 1991 offers a wide selection of dishes. It provides the same meatless and eggless menu for both lunch and dinner. Restaurant review website www.dine.com selected it as "Best Vietnamese Restaurant in San Jose." The simple and elegant decor lends it more of a classic Mediterranean feel than Oriental, but the family-run service is polite and professional. White Lotus is right around the corner from historic St. James Park.

80 N. Market St. (between Santa Clara and St. John Sts.), 408/977-0540; lunch $6.50, dinner $6.50; open Mon.–Thurs. 11 A.M.–2:30 P.M. and 5:30–9 P.M., Fri.–Sat. 11 A.M.–9:30 P.M.

Other Choices

The contemporary Italian **Paolo's,** 333 W. San Carlos St., 408/294-2558, is a downtown institution—baseball slugger Joe DiMaggio often came here for its blue-ribbon cheesecake (local legend says the eatery's founder Jack Allen tricked a New York chef out of the recipe). In Willow Glen, try out **John's XLNT Foods,** 1238 Lincoln Ave., 408/998-1440, a friendly American cuisine restaurant serving breakfast, lunch, and dinner. Sandwich shop **Amato's,** 1162 Saratoga Ave., 408/246-4007, boasts it makes "the best cheese steak in the world." Near the Rosicrucian Egyptian Museum, the hospitable **Gervais Restaurant Francais,** 1798 Park Ave., 408/275-8631, serves a diverse Continental menu. **Lou's Village,** 1465 W. San Carlos St., 408/293-4570, is a seafood house that has grown into a banquet hall institution in its more than 50 years. **Cafe Primavera,** 1365 Lincoln Ave., 408/297-7929, is a popular Willow Glen restaurant serving good seafood and pasta. When visiting charming Alviso, have lunch or dinner at **Vahl's Restaurant,** at the end of 1st St., 408/262-0731, for old-fashioned American food. Before a game or concert at the downtown Arena, try the barbecue at **Henry's World Famous Hi-Life,** 301 W. St. John St., 408/295-5414, a local landmark. **Sam's Bar-B-Que,** 1110 S. Bascom Ave., 408/297-9151, serves exceptional chicken and baby-back ribs while entertaining diners with a model train set. Inexpensive Ethiopian cuisine, particularly vegetarian dishes, is the specialty at **Red Sea Restaurant,** 684 N. 1st St., 408/993-1990. A bit pricey but with a nice quiet setting, **Le Papillon,** 410 Saratoga Ave., 408/296-3730, is locally famous for its quality Continental cuisine. The **Cardinal Coffee Shop & Lounge,** 3197 Meridian Ave., 408/269-7891, serves generous plates of good American food 24 hours a day, every day. You wouldn't be surprised if a leather-jacketed Fonzie happened to wander into **City Diner,** 1160 Blossom Hill Rd., 408/269-5490, a fun place caught in a '50s time warp that serves good burgers and shakes. Since 1968, steak and lobster have been the specialty of the **Bold Knight,** 1600 Monterey Rd., 408/293-7700. Good American cooking in San Jose's Eastside can be found at the **White Rock Cafe,** 3116 Alum Rock Ave., 408/729-4843. For fish and chips and a wide selection of imported British ales and beers, try the **Britannia Arms of Almaden,** 5027 Almaden Expwy., 408/266-0550. A San Jose institution since 1946, **Garden City,** 360 S. Saratoga Ave., 408/244-4443, serves steaks and fresh seafood as well as provides jazz and casino entertainment. In San Jose's Japantown, a splendid choice is **Okayama,** 565-A N. 6th St.,

408/289-9508, for traditional tempura, teriyaki, and sukiyaki. **Habana-Cuba,** 238 Race St., 408/998-2822, is an authentic family-run Cuban restaurant with reasonable prices, friendly service and excellent food.

SANTA CLARA

In the center of Silicon Valley, Santa Clara's restaurants are often filled with high-tech workers at lunch. The busy El Camino Real provides a gauntlet of eateries, including many serving Asian cuisine.

Birk's

Stop at this restaurant and you might see some of the San Francisco 49er team members; they often eat here after a practice at their nearby training facility. This upscale grill is known for its steaks cooked over a sizzling red oak fire. The decor of wood, brass, marble, and glass was tastefully designed by Pat Kuleto, an award-winning restaurant architect. It's convenient to the Santa Clara Convention Center as well as many corporations, such as Intel. Reservations recommended.

3955 Freedom Circle (near Mission College Blvd. north of U.S. 101), 408/980-6400, website: www.birksrestaurant.com; lunch $8–20, dinner $11–28; open Mon.–Fri. 11:15 A.M.–2:30 P.M., daily 5–10 P.M.

Coleman Still

This darkly lit restaurant set in an industrial part of Santa Clara has a rustic ambience that includes 19th-century farm tools, mining equipment, and wagon wheels. Its standard American fare includes burgers and sandwiches, fish, steaks, and pasta.

1240 Coleman Ave. (near Brokaw Ave.), 408/727-4670; breakfast $4–6.75, lunch $6.25–11, dinner $6–16; open daily 9 A.M.–10 P.M.

Mondo Burrito

Silicon Valley's best burritos—period. This family-run restaurant uses only top-quality ingredients to produce its savory Mexican food. It's immensely popular with Santa Clara University students as well as the techies who work in the area. Stop by after visiting the nearby Santa Clara Mission and enjoy lunch on the patio.

3300 The Alameda (corner of Benton St. one block north of SCU), 408/260-9596; lunch and dinner $1.99–6.99; open Mon.–Fri. 11 A.M.–9 P.M., Sat. 11:30 A.M.–9 P.M.

Other Choices

For all-you-can-eat Asian barbecue, try **Su's Mongolian BBQ,** 1111 El Camino Real, 408/985-2958. Moderately priced Indian food can be found at **Pasands,** 3701 El Camino Real, 408/241-5150, or at **Shilpa,** 3530 El Camino Real, 408/243-6737. Sushi lovers should drop by **Kobe International Japanese Restaurant,** 2086 El Camino Real (in the Mervyn's shopping center), 408/984-5623. Pizza aficionados will want to try out **Pizz'a Chicago,** 1576 Halford Ave., 408/244-2246. In the Moonlite Shopping Center, **La Galleria,** 2798 El Camino Real, 408/296-6800, serves northern Italian food influenced by the Swiss, Italian, and French. For superb steak and seafood, try **Arthur's,** 2875 Lakeside Dr., 408/980-1666. Quality barbecue steaks, ribs, and chicken along with cocktails can be enjoyed at **Mr. Steer Steak House,** 2367 El Camino Real, 408/243-1545.

SARATOGA

Saratoga is Silicon Valley's premier place to enjoy a fine dinner. A wide selection of the area's best restaurants, particularly French cuisine, can be found in upscale Saratoga Village.

Bella Saratoga

A well-liked Italian restaurant in the Village, it's run by congenial Saratoga locals Bill and Ellen Cooper. You can eat inside this quaint Victorian, but on sunny days it's more pleasant to enjoy the street-side patio. Dishes range from pizza and sandwiches to fresh fish, chicken, and pasta. The dessert menu features a mouth-watering selection, including delectable tiramisu and sinfully rich cappuccino mud pie. Sunday brunch often features jazz music.

14503 Big Basin Way (between 3rd and 4th Sts.), 408/741-5115, website: www.saratoga-ca.com/bella; lunch $4–18, dinner $4.75–22; open Mon.–Thurs. 11:30 A.M.–9:30 P.M., Fri. 11:30 A.M.–11 P.M.; Sat. 10 A.M.–10 P.M., Sun. 10 A.M.–9 P.M.

La Fondue

This fondue-specialty restaurant is definitely a treat. Walk in and you'll be transported to a whimsical medieval setting of crown-like chandeliers, court jester chairs, sweeping draperies, and gilded sunburst faces hanging from the ceiling. Try the chocolate fondue for dessert. Reservations recommended.

14510 Big Basin Way, Ste. 3 (between 3rd and 4th Sts.), 408/867-3332, website: www.lafondue.com; two-person dinner menu $54–88, à la carte menu $18–50; open Mon.–Thurs. 5–9:30 P.M., Fri. 5–11 P.M., Sat. 4–11 P.M., Sun. 4–9:30 P.M.

Vienna Woods

Under the oak tree canopy of the Plaza del Roble, you'll find this European-style restaurant and deli, which provides a welcome relief from the hoity-toity eateries of Saratoga Village. Hot and cold sandwiches can be eaten in the outside patio, or enjoy a dinner of knackwurst or bratwurst. Breakfast is also available.

14567 Big Basin Way (between 4th and 5th Sts.), 408/867-2410; breakfast $2.25–7, lunch $4.50–5, dinner $5–6.25; open Mon.–Sat. 9 A.M.–6 P.M., Sun. 11 A.M.–4 P.M.

Other Choices

Viaggio Ristorante Mediterraneo, 14550 Big Basin Way, 408/741-5300, is well respected for its good service and terrific Mediterranean cuisine. For a classic French menu, go to **La Mere Michelle,** 14467 Big Basin Way, 408/867-5272. For contemporary French dishes with a California influence, try **Restaurant Sent Soví,** 14583 Big Basin Way, 408/867-3110, which has gained national recognition for the quality of its cuisine. For country French, the **Plumed Horse Restaurant,** 14555 Big Basin Way, 408/867-4711, is an excellent choice.

VALLEY OF HEART'S DELIGHT: THE DESSERT

First served at the Duck Club restaurant in Menlo Park's Stanford Park Hotel on September 15, 1999, the Valley of Heart's Delight is a fruit-based dessert confected specifically for *Silicon Valley Handbook*. Many of its ingredients have a connection with the region's past. The honey used in the crust commemorates the valley as the location where California's honey industry was started (a historical marker just outside Terminal C at the San Jose International Airport describes the original honeybee farm site). The brandy honors General Naglee's superb Burgundy Brandy, which received a perfect score of 100 from wine expert Professor Eugene Hilgard at the Centennial Exposition. Other ingredients, such as walnuts, strawberries, pears, apples, apricots, peaches, cherries, oranges, and, of course, prunes have all been commercially grown in the valley. Instead of *silicon* wafers, manufactured here by the area's chip-makers (the recipe works better if you avoid using these), *vanilla* wafers are used in the crust, forming the "valley." Fresh fruit is highly recommended, but canned fruit can also be used for convenience or if ingredients are out of season. (After all, this area *was* once famous for its canning industry, too.)

Crust

1.5 cups finely crushed vanilla wafers (about 40 wafers)
2 tablespoons honey
1/3 cup melted butter
6 finely chopped walnuts

Filling

1.5 cups cold water

1 packet gelatin
1/2 cup sugar (or to taste)
1/2 cup diced unpeeled Bartlett pears
1/2 cup diced unpeeled apples
1 cup halved apricots
1/2 cup seedless grapes
1/2 cup fresh pitted cherries (use a sweet variety)
1/2 teaspoon cinnamon
8 dried prunes
3 tablespoons brandy (optional)

Garnish

1 large peach
12 strawberries
1 orange

For **crust,** add crushed vanilla wafers, honey, and walnuts to melted butter and mix well. Spread the mixture across a 9-inch pie plate and onto bottom and side to form an even crust. Bake at 375°F for 8–10 minutes or until edge turns golden. Cool.

For **filling,** mix gelatin with water in a saucepan and bring to a boil. Add sugar, diced apples, and pears. Boil one minute. Turn heat to simmer and add apricots, grapes, and cherries. Simmer about five minutes, occasionally stirring mixture. Add cinnamon. Take off heat and let cool for 10 minutes. Halve the dried prunes and place on bottom of crust. Pour fruit filling over prunes. Sprinkle top with brandy. Place in refrigerator two hours or until set.

Garnish with peach and orange slices and strawberries before serving.

SOUTH VALLEY

Still retaining much of its rural atmosphere, the South Valley region attracts many visitors to its wineries and slower-paced lifestyle. Morgan Hill's Mushroom Mardi Gras and the famous Gilroy Garlic Festival showcase much of this area's culinary excellence.

Harvest Time

Located in the former Milias Hotel built in 1929, this downtown Gilroy restaurant follows its philosophy of "Where old friends and new friends meet." Past satisfied patrons have included John Wayne, Will Rogers, and Tennessee Ernie Ford. Today's restaurant has an elegant decor, with crystal chandeliers hanging from high ceilings and a swank bar decorated with a Budweiser neon sign in the shape of a garlic clove. The menu features pasta, seafood, chicken, veal, steak, and pork. As an appetizer, try out the savory garlic mushrooms. Breakfast on weekends includes free champagne.

7397 Monterey St., Gilroy (at 4th St., kitty-corner from the town clock), 408/842-7575; lunch and dinner $7–16; open daily 11:30 A.M.–2 P.M., Sun.–Thurs. 5–9 P.M., Fri.–Sat. 5–10 P.M.

Sinaloa Cafe

Morgan Hill locals pack into this family-oriented Mexican diner located in the Madrone district, about a mile north of downtown. The plain decor and food can't really be described as exceptional, but patrons rave about the margaritas. Specialties include chimichangas (a crisp flour tortilla stuffed with meat, beans, and cheese), the spicy menudo, and taco salad; special kids' items run $2 each. Weekend nights are very busy, so expect a wait. Parking is limited.

19210 Monterey Rd., Morgan Hill (at Peebles Ave. just north of Cochrane Rd.), 408/779-9740; lunch and dinner, $3.50–9; Tues.–Fri. 11:30 A.M.–9 P.M., weekends noon–9 P.M.

Other Choices

For fine wines and dining in a quiet country atmosphere looking out at the Diablo Mountains, try the **Golden Oak Restaurant,** 16695 Condit Rd. in Morgan Hill, 408/779-8085. **Giancarlo's Ristorante,** 16180 Monterey Rd. in Morgan Hill, 408/776-2995, serves fine Italian lunches and dinners as well as offers classes to aspiring chefs. **Great Wall Imperial,** 16135 Monterey Rd. in Morgan Hill, 408/776-7780, serves a Chinese lunch buffet as well as traditional cuisine. Eat seafood, steak, fowl, or lamb in a pseudo-medieval castle at the **Camelot Restaurant and Lounge,** 275 E. Dunne Ave. in Morgan Hill, 408/782-2525. To get a taste of exceptional seasonal dishes, drop into **Le Bistro,** 207 W. Main Ave. in Morgan Hill, 408/782-2505.

SUNNYVALE

Town founder Martin Murphy Jr. would scarcely recognize the industrial city built on what was once his farm, but he would certainly feel welcome at the multitude of Irish pubs along downtown Murphy Ave., a thoroughfare named after him. The city's various ethnic restaurants testify to its cultural diversity.

Il Postale

The term "going postal" takes on a totally different meaning in this small, congenial Italian bistro. The site was once Sunnyvale's post office, explaining how this romantic restaurant got its name and the pictures of Italian postage stamps decorating the walls. Although famous for its martinis, the restaurant also has a good selection of California and Italian wines.

127 W. Washington St. (between Mathilda and Murphy Aves.), 408/733-9600; lunch $4.25–12.50, dinner $4.25–17.50; open Mon.–Thurs. 11 A.M.–10 P.M., Fri. 11 A.M.–11 P.M., Sat. 5–11 P.M., Sun. 5–9:30 P.M.

The Palace

The old Palace movie theater in historic downtown Sunnyvale has been recast into a dreamscape of a restaurant with an almost mystical ambience. Columns, mirrors, and demure colors and lighting create an almost surreal effect. Its adventurous cuisine was developed by Executive Chef Dennis Ickowski (also in charge of the Rio Grande in Mountain View). Desserts include such savory delights as rum-soaked fruitcake and bourbon-pecan pie with cinnamon ice cream. Live jazz combos entertain diners Tues.–Sat. nights.

146 S. Murphy Ave. (between Washington and Evelyn Sts.), 408/739-5179, website: www.thepalacerestaurant.com; dinner $17–22; open for dinner Tues.–Sat. 6–10 P.M., nightclub open Fri.–Sat. 10 P.M.–2 A.M.

Pezzella's Villa Napoli

You'll be greeted with a smile as warm as an Italian summer day when you walk into this friendly, family-run restaurant. Pezzella's has been a Sunnyvale favorite since its founding in 1957, serving a varied menu including chicken, seafood, pasta, and pizza. Just outside along the street, look for a replica of an El Camino Real bell.

1025 W. El Camino Real (between Mary and Bernardo Aves.), 408/738-2400; lunch $6–18.50, dinner $7–18.50; open Tues.–Fri. 11:30 A.M.–2:30 P.M., Tues.–Sat. 5–10:30 P.M.

Other Choices

Real Irish beer and food including Irish stew can be savored at the historic downtown's **Fibbar Magee's Irish Pub & Restaurant,** 156 S. Murphy Ave., 408/749-8373. To sample Egyptian and eastern Mediterranean dishes, try the inexpensive **Sahari Restaurant,** 126 E. Fremont Ave., 408/245-1448. **Tarragon,** 140 S. Murphy Ave., 408/737-8003, is a good downtown choice for California and Pacific Rim cuisine. For tasty kebabs and other ethnic delights, try out the unique menu of the **Armenian Gourmet,** 929 E. Duane Ave., 408/732-3910. **Afghani House,** 1103 El Camino Real, 408/248-5088, also serves good kebabs as well as many Persian rice dishes. The inexpensive **Country Gourmet,** 1314 S. Mary Ave., 408/733-9446, serves breakfast, lunch, and dinner as well as a scrumptious Sunday brunch.

Wineries, Brewpubs, and Nightclubs

The Santa Clara Valley is Northern California's oldest wine district. To make sacramental wines, Franciscan priests introduced vineyards at Mission Santa Clara de Asis in 1777, almost half a century before wine grapes were planted in Sonoma. In the mid-1800s to the 1880s, hundreds of acres of redwood trees were cut in the Santa Cruz Mountains to provide timber for San Francisco and other growing cities in the region. Many Gold Rush immigrants coming into the area saw this cleared land as a perfect place to turn into vineyards. The region's first commercial vineyard was planted by a John Burns in 1853, who named his winery and the nearby mountain Ben Lomond after a wine-growing district in his native Scotland.

In the late 1890s, an aphid root louse called *phylloxera* destroyed many of the vines in the region, hurting the valley's wine industry. A more resistant rootstock was planted, and the turn of the 19th century saw wineries prosper again until Prohibition was passed in 1922. The post–World War II years saw the loss of much of Santa Clara Valley's fertile vineyard land as developers constructed vast housing tracts here. As property here became more valuable, many of the area's larger wineries such as Paul Masson, Almaden, and Mirassou moved their vineyards south to San Benito County and the Salinas Valley.

Although the county doesn't have the vast number of wineries it had at the turn of the 19th century, it's still home to many small, high-quality wineries that welcome visitors for tastings. Instead of heading up to Napa, residents and visitors to Silicon Valley often stop at these local wineries for a taste from their vintage. Many of these beautiful estates set amid the valley's rolling hills are also ideal for weddings and small company parties. Several, such as Byington and Emilio Guglielmo wineries, hold special holiday festivities during Dec. weekends, making a relaxing outing for buying gifts. Many small wineries normally closed to the public open their doors on "Passport Days," a special program operated by the Santa Cruz Mountain Winegrowers Association. For a onetime fee of $15, participants

FINE DINING

can buy a passport that allows them to visit member wineries on the third Sat. of Jan., Apr., July, and November. For wine lovers, it's a great way to see some interesting family-run vineyards.

For beer connoisseurs, a number of brewpubs, such as the Tied House and Gordon Biersch, started throughout the region during the 1980s. These are popular with techies, who often hang out at these places after working hours. Although better known for its wineries than its breweries, the area had a reputation for the suds in the 19th century. San Jose's Fredericksburg Brewery once was one of the largest beer-making facilities west of the Rocky Mountains. The massive brick buildings, constructed in 1869, later became the Falstaff Brewery, and a portion of its original building now serves as the tasting room for the J. Lohr Winery. Whether you're into grapes or hops, there's something for everyone's taste here.

WINERIES

You don't have to be an enologist to enjoy a Silicon Valley wine-tasting tour. But an understanding of the basics of sampling wine will certainly enhance your experience.

California wines come in two categories. **Generic** wines are those that have come to be associated with certain well-known wine-producing regions of Europe such as Chablis, Rhine, and Burgundy. **Varietal** wines, on the other hand, are made from a predominant grape variety that constitutes as much as 75 percent of the contents. Examples of these include cabernet, sauvignon blanc, chenin blanc, and johannisberg riesling. A further specific is the **vintage.** Unlike many wines, vintage selections use only grapes grown entirely within a particular year (this is shown on the bottle's label).

Although individual wineries may use slightly different methods, the overall process of making wine is much the same for all production. The grapes are harvested at the peak of their ripeness and pressed to squeeze out their juice. Yeast colonies digest the juice sugars, converting it into alcohol and carbon dioxide in a process called fermentation. The fermenting grape juice is called "must." A machine called a juice separator is used to cull the skins and seeds from this must. After fermenting, the wine is placed in large vats of stainless steel or wood. (Wine stored in oak barrels absorbs flavors from the wood and is usually costlier.) In these containers, the wines are aged over a certain period in order to achieve the flavor the winemaster thinks is best for the final product.

Tasting wine doesn't have to be a major production. You'll develop a better taste for wines the more you sample. If you have questions, don't be afraid to ask the tasting room personnel—most will be glad to share their knowledge. Remember to hold your wine glass by the stem instead of the bowl—you don't want the warmth of your hand to heat up the wine, which can affect its taste.

Perhaps most important, if you're planning on doing a lot of wine-tasting, select a designated driver beforehand—especially if you're going to be visiting many of Silicon Valley's mountain wineries, which are located on curving roads. Wine-tasting is most fun when it's done responsibly.

Byington Winery and Vineyard

Byington is a newcomer as far as Santa Clara Valley wineries go. The Byington family planted their vines in 1987 and opened the eight-acre grounds in June 1990. A magnificent Italian-style château set amid mountain redwood trees is used for wine-tasting and small corporate events. For intimate wedding ceremonies, a knoll set among the vines overlooks Monterey Bay. Byington's wines do well in *Wine Spectator* magazine, receiving scores of 89 or better, and they've won several gold medals at state fairs.

21850 Bear Creek Rd., Los Gatos (take Bear Creek Rd. exit from Hwy. 17 near Lexington Reservoir, drive 5.5 miles), 408/354-1111, website: www.byington.com; winemaster: Don Blackburn; produces a wide variety of chardonnay and cabernet wines; gift shop, facilities for weddings, private parties, and seminars; tours and tasting; open daily 11 A.M.–5 P.M.

Cinnabar Vineyards and Winery

Named after the cinnabar ore found near this

PAUL MASSON'S MOUNTAIN WINERY

Paul Masson is best known, perhaps, for the famous commercials featuring Orson Welles orotundly intoning the rather down-market vintage's slogan, "Old Paul Masson himself said it nearly a century ago: We will sell no wine before its time." The real Paul Masson grew up in the Burgundy region of France, attended Paris's Sorbonne University for a short while, and came to California in 1878 to attend San Jose's University of the Pacific. He never attended this college, but instead got a job sweeping the floors at fellow Frenchman Charles Le Franc's Almaden Winery, the largest wine-making operation in the valley at that time. Masson soon made his way into the office and worked his way up the management line.

In 1888, after Le Franc's tragic death from being trampled by runaway horses the year before, Masson married his former boss's daughter Louise. While honeymooning in France, he took cuttings of champagne grapes and brought them back to the Santa Clara Valley. Soon after, he bought land from Allesandro Rondoni in the Saratoga foothills along Pierce Road. Here, he started his La Cresta Vineyard, affectionately calling it his "Little Vineyard in the Sky." The vineyard would eventually become known as Paul Masson's Mountain Winery, and it would produce some of the world's best bottles of sparkling wine. In 1914, Paul Masson won the Gran Prix in Saint Louis, France—the first for any American champagne.

The 1906 earthquake devastated San Jose's St. Patrick's Church, which had a Romanesque stone portal originally brought around Cape Horn from Spain. Masson purchased this medieval entryway and used it in his own stone winery building. During Prohibition in the 1920s, Masson kept himself in business by making sacramental wine as well as selling grape juice. During this decade, he built himself a mansion on his Saratoga estate designed after one in his boyhood Burgundy. He called it Chateau La Cresta, and here he entertained many of California's most prestigious people with lavish parties. His teetotaling wife Louise is said never to have set foot in the house, preferring to stay in their S. 13th St. home in San Jose's Naglee Park area. But actress Anna Held took a champagne bath in the stately dwelling, a titillating story that received wide publicity in the press.

Masson died on October 22, 1940, but his name lives on as a popular brand of wine. In the late 1950s, the Mountain Winery became the scene of a well-known summer concert series called Music in the Vineyard. Now run by the Villa Montalvo Association and holding more than 100 concerts a year, it has become Silicon Valley's most prestigious music series. Famous performers of popular, classical, jazz, and country music have played at the intimate venue, with the famous St. Patrick's Church portal as a backdrop. Wine is no longer made here, but the historic facilities are popular for weddings, corporate and private events, and concerts.

14831 Pierce Rd. (about a mile up the hill on your left from Hwy. 9); opening hours vary according to concert schedule; 408/741-0763; website: www.chateaulacresta.com.

FINE DINING

vineyard, this winery was started in 1983 by Tom Mudd, a former laser spectroscopy research engineer at SRI in Menlo Park. And like the medieval alchemists who used the mercury in cinnabar to attempt to change lead into gold, Mudd considers himself a modern alchemist transforming rainwater into wine. The vineyard spreads across 30 acres of hillside in the mountains near Saratoga. To achieve a more intensely flavored wine, the vineyard uses dry farming techniques.

23000 Congress Springs Rd., Saratoga (about 2.5 miles from Saratoga Village), 408/741-5858, website: www.cinnabar.org; winemaster: Tom Mudd; produces cabernet sauvignon, merlot, chardonnay, and pinot noir; facilities for business meetings and special events; open only on Passport Days.

Cooper-Garrod Vineyards

The Cooper family has farmed this 21-acre property for more than 100 years, originally growing apricot and prune orchards here amid the rolling Saratoga hills. To keep active after retirement, George Cooper began his wine-making business, planting his first vines in 1972. The vineyard keeps its production to 3,000 cases per year, and French oak barrels are used to ferment and age its excellent estate-grown chardonnay. The facility also has a riding stable, so after sampling the vino, visitors can rent a horse for a ride along a scenic Santa Cruz Mountain trail.

22600 Mt. Eden Rd., Saratoga (off Pierce Rd.), 408/741-8094, website: www.cgv.com; winemaster: George Cooper; produces cabernet sauvignon, cabernet franc, and chardonnay, among others; gift shop; facilities available for weddings and corporate events; tasting only; open Wed.–Fri. 1–5 P.M., weekends 11 A.M.–5 P.M., or by appointment.

David Bruce Winery

Started in 1964 by David Bruce, a former San Jose dermatologist, this mountain winery in a panoramic setting near Los Gatos has views of Monterey Bay. Two banquet rooms provide facilities for special dinners and functions. The winery's specialty is its much-awarded pinot noir.

Buy a case of wine and automatically become a Private Cellars Club member, receiving special discounts and other benefits. The winery also makes a terrific spot for picnickers.

21439 Bear Creek Rd. (off Hwy. 17, five miles from Lexington Reservoir), 408/354-4214 or 408/295-2739, website: www.davidbrucewinery.com; winemaker: David Bruce; produces chardonnay, cabernet sauvignon, zinfandel, petite syrah, and pinot noir; facilities for corporate events; tasting; open daily noon–5 P.M.

Emilio Guglielmo Winery

Founder Emilio Guglielmo (gool-YELL-mo) brought his wine-making skills from northern Italy and started this Morgan Hill winery in 1925. Villa Emile is set among 80 beautiful acres of estate vineyards among South Valley's hills. The family's third generation produces its hand-crafted private reserve in limited releases. Its one of only two California wineries producing the rare grignolino red wine. The winery's Guglielmo Wine Group is a club providing members with special discounts and other benefits. The winery's grounds have an Old California ambience and are available for weddings and events of up to 300 people. Special events throughout the year include La Dolce Vita festival in June.

1480 E. Main Ave., Morgan Hill (across from Live Oak High School), 408/779-2145, website: www.guglielmowinery.com; winemaster: George Guglielmo; produces chardonnay, red zinfandel, merlot, cabernet sauvignon, and petite sirah, among others; gift shop; tasting; open daily 10 A.M.–5 P.M.; tours by appointment.

Fortino Winery

Formerly the Cassa Brothers' winery, which produced bulk wines, Ernest Fortino bought the Hecker Pass facilities in 1970 and focused on producing 16 varietal wines, strongly emphasizing premium reds. The Fortino family came from southern Italy and made wine in the Calabria area before reaching the Golden State. Their 120-acre vineyard enjoys the warm South Valley climate at this friendly winery, which produces 30,000 cases a year. A redwood terrace provides a beautiful outdoor facility for up to 300 guests, and an indoor barrel room can house 120 guests.

4525 Hecker Pass Rd., Gilroy (west of the city along Hwy. 152), 408/842-3305, website: www.scvwga.com/Fortino; winemaster: Gino Fortino; produces cabernet sauvignon, zinfandel, and petite syrah, among others; gift shop; picnic facilities; tasting and tours; open daily 10 A.M.–5 P.M.; tours by appointment; also has sales room at the Gilroy Outlet Center, open 10 A.M.–8 P.M.

Hecker Pass Winery

This winery grows grapes on 14 scenic acres in the Hecker Pass area and produces about 4,000 cases annually. It is run by Mario Fortino, who bought the vineyard in 1970 and has received more than 70 awards from state and national wine competitions.

4605 Hecker Pass Hwy., Gilroy (west of the city along Hwy. 152), 408/842-9799, website: www.scvwga.com/heckerpass; winemaster: Mario Fortino; produces petite sirah, zinfandel, chianti, port, and sherry, among others; gift shop; picnic facilities; tasting daily 9 A.M.–5 P.M.; tours by appointment.

J. Lohr Winery

The former Fredericksburg Brewery houses the J. Lohr tasting room, and its location just off The Alameda near downtown San Jose places this winery truly in the heart of Silicon Valley. Founded by Stanford engineering student Jerry Lohr, the winery sold its first wines in 1974. It has grown to become Santa Clara County's largest winery, producing about 370,000 cases a year. Its grapes come from vineyards in the Monterey and Paso Robles regions, and has consistently received top ratings from *Wine Spectator* and *Wine Enthusiast* magazines. It recently introduced a line of nonalcoholic wines under the Ariel label.

1000 Lenzen Ave., San Jose (just east of The Alameda near where it curves at Race St.), 408/288-5057, website: www.jlohr.com; winemaster: Jeff Meier; produces cabernet sauvignon, merlot, chardonnay, and petite syrah; price range: $6–28; tasting; open daily 10 A.M.–5 P.M.; tours on weekends.

Kirigin Cellars

Previously the Bonesio Winery and acquired in 1976 by Nikola Kirigin, a native of Croatia, this winery grows its crops on 50 scenic acres. The land once belonged to the Solis Rancho grant, and one of its historic buildings dates from 1827. Try out the winery's delicate and slightly sweet wine called Malvasia Bianca.

11550 Watsonville Rd., Gilroy (turn north from Hecker Pass Rd.), 408/847-8827, website: www.scvwga.com/kirigin; winemaster: Nikola Kirigin; produces zinfandel, cabernet sauvignon, sauvignon blanc, and chardonnay, among others; picnic facilities; tasting; open daily 10 A.M.–5 P.M.; tours by appointment.

Mirassou Champagne Cellars

To celebrate its centennial of wine-making in 1954, Edmund and Norbert Mirassou made the family's first sparkling wine. The winery still produces champagne at Los Gatos's former Novitiate Winery, which provides a breathtaking vista of Silicon Valley on clear days.

300 College Ave., Los Gatos (from E. Main St., follow College Ave. up the hill and turn right at the entrance gate), 408/395-3790, website: www.mirassou.com; champagne master: Sean Lin; produces various brut-style champagnes; tasting Wed.–Sun. noon–5 P.M.; tours on weekends, 2 P.M.

Mount Eden Vineyards

Set among the redwoods of the Santa Cruz Mountains, this vineyard was first planted in 1942 by Martin Ray, who took grape cuttings from the MacGregor Vineyards in Edna Valley. It became known as Mount Eden in 1972.

22020 Mt. Eden Rd., Saratoga (off Pierce Rd.), 408/867-5832; winemaster: Jeffrey Patterson; produces chardonnay, cabernet sauvignon, and pinot noir; no tasting room; open only by appointment.

Pedrizzetti Winery

In 1945, John Pedrizzetti from Italy's Piedmont wine district purchased this lovely Morgan Hill vineyard, which has been a winery since 1913. His son Ed continues the family tradition today,

FINE DINING

MIRASSOU: THE VALLEY'S FIRST FINE WINERY

In the Evergreen district in San Jose's eastern foothills stands a winery run by America's oldest wine-making family. The Mirassou Winery was founded in 1854 by Pierre Pellier, who came to California's goldfields from France. Eventually, he found his way to the Santa Clara Valley, where, impressed by the fertile soil and the mild climate, he used cuttings from his homeland to start his vineyard. Pellier's winery was the first in California to produce a pinot noir.

In 1881, Pellier's oldest daughter, Henrietta, married a neighboring vintner named Pierre Huste Mirassou. The am-

Mirassou Winery

bitious Mirassou joined with his father-in-law to produce some of Northern California's finest wines—rivaling even those of France. The family faced setbacks, however. Along with most of California's vintners, their vineyards were hit in 1894 by an outbreak of *phylloxera,* an infestation that attacks the vine roots and kills the plant. In 1919, Prohibition also affected Mirassou's operation (along with that of the rest of the American wine industry), but the vineyard managed to survive until the amendment's repeal.

In 1961, Mirassou began planting vines in Monterey County near the Salinas Valley town of Soledad. This is one of the world's premier winegrowing regions, and the vineyard recognized the location's prestige by being the first to put the name "Monterey" on its labels. In the 1960s, the company also pioneered the use of mechanical harvest, which used machines to pick grapes by vigorously shaking the vines—allowing only the ripe bunches to fall.

Today, the Mirassou name is one of the most highly respected in Silicon Valley wines. The family's fifth generation still produces wine (under the supervision of winemaster Tom Stutz) at the Aborn Road site, whose cozy tasting room is one of the most hospitable in Northern California.

3000 Aborn Rd., San Jose (take Capitol Expwy. from U.S. 101, and turn east on Aborn, drive into the foothills). Tasting room open Mon.–Sat. noon–5 P.M., Sun. noon–4 P.M.; 408/274-4000, website: www.mirassou.com.

producing wines in its charming estate. The covered patio surrounded by lawns, evergreens, and arbors creates a friendly setting for visitors. The facility is available for weddings and business events.

1645 San Pedro Ave., Morgan Hill (off Murphy Ave., by the soccer field near Golden Oaks Restaurant), 408/779-7389, website: www.scvwga.com/pedrizzetti; winemaster: Ed Pedrizzetti; produces chardonnay, petite sirah, and barbera, a red wine made from Italy's Piedmont district's barbera vines; tasting; open daily 10 A.M.–5 P.M.; tours by appointment.

Rapazzini Winery

This hospitable winery established in 1962 is unique in that—fitting for Gilroy—it produces California's only garlic wine, an interesting vintage called "Chateau de Garlic." For those connoisseurs with more mainstream tastes, it produces a nice johannisberg riesling and a tasty chardonnay among its other wines. The winery produces about 10,500 cases annually and holds several popular events throughout the year, including a spring wine fair and a harvest festival in the fall.

4350 Monterey Rd., Gilroy (along U.S. 101 close to Hwy. 25 overpass), 408/842-5649, website: www.scvwga.com/rapazzini; winemaker: Jon Rapazzini; produces cabernet and zinfandel from grapes purchased in Mendocino and San Luis Obispo; gift shop; tasting; open daily 9 A.M.–6 P.M.; tours by appointment.

Ridge Vineyards

Established in 1885 by San Francisco doctor Osea Perrone, this pleasant winery along Cupertino's Monte Bello Ridge became his scenic summer home, known as the Monte Bello Winery. Incorporated as Ridge Vineyards in 1967, the winery was restored to its original prestige by Stanford philosophy graduate Paul Draper, and it now produces more than 50,000 cases a year.

17100 Montebello Rd., Cupertino (from I-280, take Foothill Blvd. south three miles, turn right on Montebello Rd. and drive 4.4 miles), 408/867-3233, website: www.ridgewine.com;

winemaker: Paul Draper; produces cabernet, zinfandel, chardonnay, merlot, mataro, and petite sirah; tasting; open weekends 11 A.M.–3 P.M.

Sarah's Vineyard

Established in 1978 in a redwood building among Gilroy's foothills, this nine-acre vineyard is run by "life adventurer" Marilyn Clark. Ask her the origin of the name and she'll tell you, "I just dreamed it up!" and it's best to let her personally explain how "Sarah" symbolizes the essence of Clark's own personality. She went into the winemaking business after a philosopher told her, "Wine will be your teacher." The vineyard produces about 2,000 cases a year.

4005 Hecker Pass, Gilroy (west of the city along Hwy. 152), 408/842-4278, website: www.scvwga.com/Sarah; winemaster: Marilyn Clark; produces chardonnay, pinot noir, and merlot; facilities for private and corporate events; tasting; open Sat. noon–4 P.M.; tours by appointment.

Savannah-Chanel Vineyards

Wine grapes have grown on this 14-acre mountain vineyard since 1892, when French immigrants planted their original cuttings. Some zinfandel vines from 1910 are still producing. The Ballard family bought the property in 1996 and named the vineyards after their two daughters. The historic Villa Monmartre built here in 1923 is a Mediterranean-style château looking out over the valley. Visitors can sample wine in a 1912 redwood tasting room.

23600 Congress Springs Rd., Saratoga (3.3 miles along Hwy. 9 from Saratoga Village), 408/741-2930, website: www.savannahchanel.com; winemaster: Michael McNeill; produces cabernet franc, chardonnay, and zinfandel, among others; facilities for business seminars, weddings, and picnics; tasting; open daily 11 A.M.–5 P.M.

Solis Winery

The Hecker Pass region's most beautiful winery has a pavilion-style wine-tasting facility looking out at vineyards growing along the base of the Gabilan Range. Vineyards have grown in the area since the Bertero Winery originally was established here in 1917. The Vanni family bought the property in 1980 and named their winery after the Solis Ranch, a Mexican-era land grant the property once was part of. Paintings and photographs from local artists decorate the tasting room walls. The winery produces about 5,000 cases a year and holds special music and tasting events, such as its popular Wine & Pasta Open House that takes place the first weekend of May.

3920 Hecker Pass, Gilroy (west of the city along Hwy. 152), 408/847-6306, website: www.soliswinery.com; winemaster: David Vanni; produces zchardonnay, merlot, johannisberg riesling, and zinfandel, among others; gift shop; tasting; open Wed.–Sun. 11 A.M.–5 P.M.; tours by appointment.

Sycamore Creek Vineyards

This winery, set in the scenic Uvas Canyon west of Morgan Hill, was founded in 1906 but was later closed due to Prohibition. The 14-acre property was acquired in 1975 by Terry and Mary Kay Parks, who reopened it as a winery. In 1989, it was acquired by the Morita family. It produces about 3,500 cases of varietal wines a year.

12775 Uvas Rd., Morgan Hill (off Watsonville Rd.), 408/779-4738, website: www.scvwga.com/SycamoreCreek; winemaster: Masao Inoue; produces chardonnay and cabernet sauvignon; picnic facilities; tasting; open weekends 11:30 A.M.–5 P.M.

Thomas Kruse Winery

While working as a financial analyst, Chicago native Thomas Kruse started making wine as a hobby and soon discovered it was his life's calling. He came out to California, and in 1971 bought the abandoned Roffinella Winery, which once operated in Gilroy's Hecker Pass foothills during the turn of the 19th century. There, he started his one-acre vineyard growing French Colombard vines. Santa Clara County's smallest winery, it annually produces about 2,500 cases of dry varietal table wines and sparkling wines.

4390 Hecker Pass Rd., Gilroy (west of the city on Hwy. 152), 408/842-7016, website: www.scvwga.com/ThomasKruse; winemaster: Thomas Kruse; produces zinfandel, chardonnay,

© MARTIN CHEEK

Scruffy Murphy's Irish Pub & Restaurant

and cabernet; tasting and picnic facilities; open daily noon–5 P.M.; tours by appointment.

BREWPUBS

Since the 1980s, trendy microbrewery restaurants have popped up throughout Silicon Valley. These gathering places quickly have become popular spots for local engineers and marketers wanting to try out custom-made ales, stouts, lagers, and even fruit beers. The California cuisine served in these places is usually just as good as the beer. A few of these microbreweries provide musical entertainment on weekend nights.

Rock Bottom Brewery, 1875 S. Bascom Ave., Campbell (in the Pruneyard Shopping Center), 408/377-0707; open daily from 11 A.M.–midnight or 1 A.M.

Los Gatos Brewing Company, 130 N. Santa Cruz Ave., Los Gatos (on Grays St.), 408/395-9929; open Sun.–Thurs. 11:30 A.M.–3 P.M. and 5–10 P.M., Fri.–Sat. 11:30 A.M.–3 P.M. and 5–11 P.M.

Stoddard's Brewhouse, 111 S. Murphy Ave., Sunnyvale (off Evelyn Ave.), 408/733-7824, website: www.stoddardsbrew.com; open Mon.–Thurs. 11:30 A.M.–2:30 P.M., 5:30–10 P.M., Fri. 11:30

A.M.–2:30 P.M., 5–11 P.M., Sat. 11 A.M.–3 P.M., 5–10 P.M., Sun. noon–3 P.M., 5–9 P.M.

The Tied House, two locations: downtown San Jose, 65 N. San Pedro St. (in San Pedro Square), 408/295-2739; open Sun.–Thurs. 11:30 A.M.–9 P.M., Fri.–Sat. 11:30 A.M.–10 P.M.; also in downtown Mountain View, 954 Villa St. (between Franklin and Bryant Sts.), 650/965-2739, website: www.tiedhouse.com; open Mon.–Thurs. 11:30 A.M.–10 P.M., Fri. 11:30 A.M.–11 P.M., Sat. 11:30 A.M.–10 P.M., Sun. 11:30 A.M.–9:30 P.M.

Gordon Biersch Brewing Company; two locations: 640 Emerson St. (between Hamilton and Forest Sts.), 650/323-7723; open Sun.–Wed. 11 A.M.–11 P.M., Thurs. 11 A.M.–midnight, Fri.–Sat. 11 A.M.–1 A.M.; also at 33 E. San Fernando St., San Jose (between 1st and 2nd Sts.), 408/294-6785; website: www.gordonbiersch.com; open Sun.–Thurs. 11:30 A.M.–10 P.M., Fri.–Sat. 11:30 A.M.–11 P.M.

NIGHTCLUBS

Silicon Valley has a variety of nightclubs and bars suitable for every taste. For most of these establishments, the front-door cover ranges from free to about $10, depending on the night and which band is playing. Several, such as the Saddle Rack, give free dancing lessons during the week. Some, like the Agenda Lounge, play various musical styles, depending on the day of the week. The valley also has some adult clubs where topless dancers perform.

Comedy

Comedy Sportz, 3428 El Camino Real, Santa Clara, 408/985-5233

Rooster T. Feathers, 157 W. El Camino Real, Sunnyvale, 408/736-0921

The Rose and Crown, (Mon. at 8:30 P.M.), 547 Emerson St., Palo Alto, 650/327-7673

Country

Gaslighter's Music Hall, 7430 Monterey St., Gilroy, 408/848-3488

Kacey Jones, 8337 Church St., Gilroy, 408/847-0333

The Saddle Rack, 1310 Auzerais Ave., San Jose, 408/286-3393

Celtic and Folk

King's Head Pub and Restaurant, 201 Orchard City Dr., Campbell, 408/871-2499

Jazz and Blues

Bathtub Gin and Blues 1131 Lawrence Expwy., Sunnyvale, 408/734-2500

French Quarter Cabaret, 193 S. Murphy Ave., Sunnyvale, 408/773-8700

Garden City Casino (also known for its casino and restaurant), 360 S. Saratoga Ave., San Jose, 408/244-4443

Hedley Club (in Hotel De Anza), 233 W. Santa Clara St., San Jose, 408/286-1000

J.J.'s Blues, 3439 Stevens Creek Blvd., Santa Clara, 408/243-6441

#1 Broadway, 102 S. Santa Cruz Ave., Los Gatos, 408/354-4303

Quarter Note, 1214 Apollo Way, Sunnyvale, 408/732-2110

Wave's Smokehouse & Saloon, 65 Post St., San Jose, 408/885-9283

Latin and Salsa

Club Caribe, 1001 1st St., San Jose, 408/297-7272

Club Miami, 177 W. Santa Clara St., San Jose, 408/279-3670

King of Clubs, 893 Leong Dr., Mountain View, 650/968-6366

Latin Village, 1897 Alum Rock Ave., San Jose, 408/259-7712

Starlight Ballroom, 1160 N. Fair Oaks Blvd., Sunnyvale, 408/745-7827

Tropicana, 47 Notre Dame Ave., San Jose, 408/279-2340

Rock/Top 40/Various

Agenda Lounge, 399 S. 1st St., San Jose, 408/287-4087

A.P. Stump's, 163 W. Santa Clara St., San Jose, 408/292-9928

Backbeat, 777 Lawrence Expwy., Santa Clara, 408/241-0777

Bay 101, 1801 Bering Dr., San Jose, 408/451-8888

Boswell's, 1875 S. Bascom Ave., Campbell, 408/371-4404

Britannia Arms Cupertino, 1087 Saratoga-Sunnyvale Rd., Cupertino, 408/252-7262

FINE DINING

Cactus Club, 417 S. 1st St., San Jose, 408/491-9300

Cardinal Lounge, 3197 Meridian Ave., San Jose, 408/269-7891

Club Ibex, 55 S. Market St., San Jose, 408/971-4239

Club 369, 369 S. 1st St., San Jose, 408/275-8828

Club Max, 2050 Gateway Pl., San Jose (inside Doubletree Hotel), 408/437-2167

Club Wild, 175 N. San Pedro St., San Jose, 408/298-9983

Coyote Inn, 102 Monterey Rd., San Jose (in Coyote Valley), 408/463-0970

El Rodeo Club, 610 Coleman Ave., San Jose, 408/279-8515

Fibbar Magee's, 156 Murphy Ave., Sunnyvale, 408/749-8373

Fuel, 44 S. Almaden Ave., San Jose, 408/295-7374

The Lime Light Restaurant and Club, 228 Castro St., Mountain View, 650/903-4830

Galaxy, 134 S. Main St., Milpitas, 408/262-1123

Mountain Charley's, 15 N. Santa Cruz Ave., Los Gatos, 408/395-8880

Polly Esther's Culture Club, 396 S. 1st St., San Jose, 408/280-1977

Toon's, 52 E. Santa Clara St., San Jose, 408/292-7464

The Usual, 400 S. 1st St., San Jose, 408/535-0330

VooDoo Lounge, 14 S. 2nd, San Jose, 408/286-8636

Adult Entertainment

AJ's, 393 Lincoln Ave., San Jose, 408/292-3445

The Brass Rail, 160 Persian Dr., Sunnyvale, 408/734-1454

Candid Club, 1053 E. El Camino Real, Sunnyvale, 408/246-3624

The Hiphugger, 948 W. El Camino Real, Sunnyvale, 408/736-8585

Kit Kat Club, 907 E. Arques Ave., Sunnyvale, 408/733-2628

T's Cabaret 1984 Old Oakland Rd., San Jose, 408/435-3066

Resources

Suggested Reading

HISTORY

Arbuckle, Clyde. *History of San Jose.* San Jose: Smith McKay Printing, 1986. Considered the definitive San Jose history, this work by the official city historian chronicles in well-researched detail San Jose's lively past.

Beilharz, Edwin A., and Donald O. DeMers Jr. *San Jose: California's First City.* Tulsa, OK: Continental Heritage Press, 1980. Published before San Jose's redevelopment started in earnest, this city profile contains a number of anecdotes and historic photographs that make it an excellent browsing book.

Brutz, George G. *History of Los Gatos: Gem of the Foothills.* Fresno, CA: Valley Publications, 1971. Local tales include how cowboy star–producer "Bronco Billy" Anderson used Los Gatos as a Western town movie set in 1906.

Butler, Phyllis Filiberti. *Old Santa Clara Valley: A Guide to Historic Buildings from Palo Alto to Gilroy.* San Carlos, CA: Wide World Publishing, 1991. Architecture, history, and biography are woven together in a book that celebrates the region's structures.

Christensen, Terry, et al. *Reflections of the Past: An Anthology of San Jose.* Encinitas, CA: Heritage Media, 1996. Eight historical essays written by local writers describe how San Jose became the capital of Silicon Valley.

Douglas, Jack. *Historical Footnotes of Santa Clara Valley.* San Jose: San Jose Historical Museum Association, 1993. History is brought vividly to life in this fascinating book giving the inside scoop on many of the valley's colorful characters.

Farrell, Harry. *San Jose and Other Famous Places: The Lore and Lure of the South Bay.* San Jose: San Jose Historical Museum Association, 1983. Farrell worked as a reporter for the *San Jose Mercury News,* and his memories of the area are tinged with humanity and humor.

Farrell, Harry. *Swift Justice: Murder and Vengeance in a California Town.* New York: St. Martin's Press, 1992. Gripping and well documented, this is the definitive book about the brutal killing of San Jose's Brooke Hart and the mob lynching of the murderers in St. James Park.

Goodell, Jeff. *Sunnyvale: The Rise and Fall of a Silicon Valley Family.* New York: Villard Books, 2000. The author's memoir is a touching look at growing up in the industrial city during the start of the digital revolution.

Gullard, Pamela, and Nancy Lund. *History of Palo Alto: The Early Years.* San Francisco: Scottwall Association, 1989. From the Ohlones to World War II, this book gives a glimpse of life in the Palo Alto area.

Jacobson, Yvonne. *Passing Farms, Enduring Values: California's Santa Clara Valley.* Los Altos, CA: William Kaufmann, 1984. Wallace Stegner provides the foreword to this beautifully written book that paints an intimate portrait of the agricultural life of the valley's past. Well stocked with historic photos.

Loomis, Patricia. *Signposts.* San Jose: San Jose Historical Museum Association, 1982. From Agnew Rd. to White Rd., this slim book introduces the people behind many of Silicon Valley's thoroughfares.

McEnery, Thomas. *The New City-State: Change and Renewal in America's Cities.* Niwot, CO: Roberts Rinehart Publishers, 1994. Written by a former San Jose mayor, this positive portrayal of running a modern city uses McEnery's experience in revitalizing the "Capital of Silicon Valley" as a case study for urban renewal.

McKay, Leonard, and Nestor Wahlberg. *A Postcard History of San Jose*. San Jose: San Jose Historical Museum Association, 1992. Peer at San Jose's past through penny postcards that include colorful views of Sarah Winchester's mansion and Alum Rock Park.

Nagel, Gunther. *Iron Will: The Life and Letters of Jane Stanford*. Stanford, CA: Stanford Alumni Association, 1985. The story of Leland Stanford's wife and the fascinating times she lived through, as witnessed through her personal correspondence.

Payne, Stephen M. *Santa Clara County: Harvest of Change*. Northridge, CA: Windsor Publications, 1987. The first section chronicling the valley's history is filled with superb historic photos highlighting interesting text. Skip the dull profiles of business sponsors at the end of the book.

Peck, Willys I. *Saratoga Stereopticon: A Magic Lantern of Memory*. Cupertino, CA: California History Center Foundation, 1998. A collection of columns written for the *Saratoga News* has been turned into a folksy memoir of the valley's bygone years.

Rambo, Ralph. *Pen and Inklings: Nostalgic Views of Santa Clara Valley*. San Jose: San Jose Historical Museum Association, 1981. Rambo's multidimensional talents as a local historian, poet, artist, and short-story writer make this a truly fun book to browse through, especially with its collection of outhouse misadventures and an "Ode to the Prune."

Regnery, Dorothy F. *The Battle of Santa Clara*. San Jose: Smith and McKay Printing, 1978. Although the text can get dry, this book is a well-researched history of the only Northern California campaign in the Mexican-American War.

Sawyer, Eugene T. *History of Santa Clara County, California*. Los Angeles: Historic Record Company, 1922. A fascinating and thorough story of the valley's early days. It contains biographical sketches of local residents both famous and infamous.

Schneider, Jimmie. *Quicksilver: The Complete History of Santa Clara County's New Almaden Mine*. San Jose: Zella Schneider, 1992. Schneider, whose interest in the mines started as a boy, provides a richly textured view of life at the mines as well as their vital importance to the Union during the Civil War.

Watson, Jeanette. *Campbell: The Orchard City*. Campbell, CA: Campbell Historical Museum Association, 1989. This Campbell chronicle shows how a small agricultural village grew into a Silicon Valley city.

Young, John V. *Ghost Towns of the Santa Cruz Mountains*. Santa Cruz, CA: Western Tanager Press, 1984. A pleasurable browsing book, filled with wild tales of the frontier days of the mountains.

COMPUTER CULTURE

Bronson, Po. *The Nudist on the Late Shift and Other True Tales of Silicon Valley*. New York: Random House, 1999. Rich and weird—that's what everyone thinks of the folks in Silicon Valley. This book supports that interpretation with profiles of some of the eccentrics who live and work here.

Bunnell, David. *Making the Cisco Connection: The Story Behind the Real Internet Superpower*. New York: John Wiley & Sons, 2000. A behind-the-scenes look at the people who have made Cisco the bedrock company of the Internet. Full of engrossing anecdotes.

Carlton, Jim. *Apple: The Inside Story of Intrigue, Egomania, and Business Blunders*. New York: Times Books, 1997. For more than a decade, authors have been writing Apple's obituary, and yet the Cupertino firm keeps proving it's the "Comeback Kid" of computer companies. This is yet another book providing a look at the poor decisions and personnel problems plaguing the company.

Cringely, Robert X. *Accidental Empires: How the Boys of Silicon Valley Make Their Millions, Battle Foreign Competition, and Still Can't Get a Date.* Menlo Park: Addison-Wesley Publishing, 1992. The famous *InfoWorld* columnist uses his satirical wit to take shots at some of the valley's high-tech gurus. A fast, honest, and informative read.

Hall, Mark, and John Barry. *Sunburst: The Ascent of Sun Microsystems.* Chicago: Contemporary Books, 1990. Although it gives a slanted view of Sun's rise, this book provides a good introduction to the Silicon Valley style of business.

Hanson, Dirk. *The New Alchemists: Silicon Valley and the Microelectronics Revolution.* Boston: Little, Brown and Company, 1982. Lacking imaginative text, this is nonetheless an adequate overview of the sorcery behind Silicon Valley's electronics industry.

Hayes, Dennis. *Behind the Silicon Curtain: The Seduction of Work in a Lonely Era.* Boston: South End Press, 1989. Hayes's exposé reveals the dark underside of Silicon Valley's work world, including computer hackers, drugs, and the dehumanization in various corporate cultures.

Jackson, Tim. *Inside Intel: Andy Grove and the Rise of the World's Most Powerful Chip Company.* New York: Dutton Books, 1997. A behind-the-scenes look at the successes, failures, and personalities of one of the computer industry's most competitive players.

Kaplan, David A. *The Silicon Boys and Their Valley of Dreams.* New York: William Morrow & Company, 1999. This very amusing book generated a lot of buzz in the area—especially in the affluent town of Woodside, where the author describes, among other things, an annual fundraising event that raised $439,000 for the local high school (not your usual bingo night or bake sale).

Kaplan, Jerry. *Startup: A Silicon Valley Adventure.* New York: Houghton Mifflin, 1995. A brutally honest take on the rise and fall of an ambitious company. The founder of GO Corporation, a failed pen computing firm, gives a vivid and lively account of what went wrong.

Lewis, Michael. *The New New Thing.* New York: Norton, 1999. The wry author of the best-seller *Liar's Poker* takes a look at Silicon Valley's unique style of business, using as an exemplar Jim Clark, founder of billion-dollar firms Silicon Graphics, Netscape, and Healtheon, and owner of an extremely large yacht, which Lewis puts to metaphoric use.

Mahon, Thomas. *Charged Bodies: People, Power and Paradox in Silicon Valley.* New York: New American Library, 1985. This collection of interviews includes Intel's Robert Noyce and kingmaker venture capitalist Arthur Rock. It covers the valley's metamorphosis up until the mid-1980s.

Malone, Michael S. *The Big Score: The Billion-Dollar Story of Silicon Valley.* Garden City, New York: Doubleday & Company, 1985. Writing with a top-notch novelist's imagination, local TV talk-show host Malone gives a vibrant account of the computer industry's all-too-human side.

McLaughlin, John, and Ward Winslow. *The Making of Silicon Valley: A One Hundred Year Renaissance.* Palo Alto: Santa Clara Valley Historical Association, 1995. An excellent history of high-tech discoveries in the region that portrays the human side of the valley's companies.

Packard, David. *The HP Way: How Bill Hewlett and I Built Our Company.* New York: HarperCollins, 1995. This likable, clearly written memoir relates the ups and downs of creating Hewlett-Packard.

Rogers, Everett M., and Judith K. Larsen. *Silicon Valley Fever: Growth of High-Technology Cul-*

ture. New York: Basic Books, 1984. Although somewhat dated in its views now, this book gives a comprehensive analysis of the business components that built Silicon Valley.

Rose, Fran. *West of Eden: The End of Innocence at Apple Computer.* New York: Viking, 1989. A candid look not just at how upstart Apple slid into the big business mentality, but also of the Silicon Valley phenomenon.

GUIDES

Peninsula & Silicon Valley Restaurant Guide. Good Life Publications, 1998. A slim paperback listed for $11, this 224-page guide gives overviews of restaurants in Santa Clara, Alameda, and San Mateo Counties.

Taber, Tom. *The Santa Cruz Mountains Trail Book.* San Mateo, CA: The Oak Valley Press, 1998. Revised every few years, the guide provides hikers with details and maps for over 1,000 miles of trails cutting through the Santa Cruz Mountains which border Silicon Valley.

Weir, Kim. *Moon Handbooks: Northern California.* Emeryville, CA: Avalon Travel Publishing, 2000. Over 900 pages long and packed full of fascinating detail of Northern California. The coverage of Silicon Valley is 20 pages long, but buy it for details on day trips in the Bay Area and beyond.

FICTION

Bronson, Po. *The First $20 Million Is Always the Hardest.* New York: Random House, 1997. Light fluff, this whimsical book, in which a start-up attempts to develop the ultimate network computer, takes satirical swipes at Silicon Valley's power mongers.

Busch, Niven. *The Titan Game.* New York: Random House, 1989. The author of the classic *Duel in the Sun*—who lived on a ranch near Hollister for many years—takes an early, somewhat wide-eyed stab at the high-tech thriller. The beginning of the book is set in Silicon Valley, and the intrigue focuses on the development of a robotic weapons system. Lots of sex and violence without much emotion.

Chapman, Sally. *Hardwired: A Silicon Valley Mystery.* New York: St. Martin's Press, 1997. One of a series of Silicon Valley detective novels, including *Cyberkiss.* They're all quick reads with little emotional depth.

Coates, Lawrence. *The Blossom Festival.* Las Vegas: University of Nevada Press, 1999. This novel details life in the Santa Clara Valley's orchards from the turn of the 19th century to World War II. *San Jose Mercury News* book reviewer Jill Wolfson wrote of Coates, "There is an old-fashioned quality to his writing, and his descriptions take on an echo of Steinbeck."

Dillon, Pat. *The Last Best Thing: A Classic Tale of Greed, Deception, and Mayhem in Silicon Valley.* New York: Simon & Schuster, 1996. Originally serialized in the *San Jose Mercury News,* this comical potboiler about startup Infinity Computers was written by a two-time Pulitzer Prize–winning reporter. It's a Vonnegut-like satire of the weirdness of Silicon Valley.

Houston, James D. *Snow Mountain Passage.* New York: Knopf, 2001. A fictional account of the tragic Donner Party that focuses on its leader James Frazier Reed, who settled in San Jose.

Hutsko, Joe. *The Deal.* New York: Forge Books, 1999. Think of this as *Primary Colors* Silicon Valley–style. It's a brisk read that parallels Apple founder Steve Jobs's power struggle with his hand-picked Apple CEO, John Sculley.

McNamara, Joseph. *Code 211 Blue.* New York: Ballantine Books, 1996. McNamara—former San Jose chief of police, former Stegner creative writing fellow, and current fellow at Stanford's Hoover Institute—is sort of Silicon Valley's answer to L.A.'s Joseph Wambaugh. But this novel, and McNamara's three other crime and cop thrillers (*Fatal Command, First Directive,* and *Blue Mirage,* now out of print but available at libraries and used bookstores), can be an entertaining way of getting a feel for the area.

Stegner, Wallace. *Angle of Repose.* New York: Penguin Books, 1971. This Pulitzer Prize–winning novel passionately portrays San Jose's New Almaden region.

COFFEE-TABLE BOOKS

Di Salvo, Chris. *San Jose & Silicon Valley: Primed for the 21st Century.* Montgomery, AL: Community Communications, 1997. The text lacks flair and sounds like a visitor's bureau pamphlet, but it's the high-quality photos showing active people of the valley that makes this book worth browsing through.

Sexton, Jean Deitz. *Silicon Valley: Inventing the Future.* Chatsworth, CA: Windsor Publications, 1992. The writing is smart, but the drab layout of the stock photos lacks creativity.

PUBLICATIONS

The Silicon Valley/ San Jose Business Journal
Silicon Valley's version of *The Wall Street Journal,* this weekly provides news and inside gossip on the region's business front. One of a series of papers run by American City Business Journals, it does an excellent job targeting all business developments in the valley, not just high-tech. Website: www.amcity.com/sanjose.

Gentry
Based in Menlo Park since 1993, this is a high-quality magazine targeted at the upscale society along the Peninsula. It really knows its readership, providing a good array of articles showing that it's in touch with the region's affluent lifestyle. The bimonthly costs $4. Email address: gentrymag@aol.com.

Metro
A hip and smart-aleck freebie that comes out every Thursday in fire-engine red newsstands across the valley. Unlike the staid and conservative *Mercury,* the *Metro* gives readers an in-your-face style of writing that isn't afraid to describe the emperor's new clothing when it comes to local politicians. Pick it up for its restaurant and entertainment reviews. Unless you're prudish, you'll get some good laughs from the spicy personals section making up the last third of the tabloid. Website: www.metroactive.com.

San Jose Magazine
Distributed in major cities throughout the U.S., this newcomer aims to make its presence felt not just in San Jose but nationally. The photos in this beautifully designed, glossy publication easily please the eye. Despite calling itself "the magazine for Silicon Valley," it still needs to develop a stronger local connection—many of its articles focus on nonregional topics. At $2.95, this bimonthly magazine is worth picking up at local newsstands for its profiles of interesting Silicon Valley personalities. Website: www.sanjosemagazine.com.

San Jose Mercury News
The *"Merc"* is the powerhouse of Silicon Valley's news publications. The daily is owned by Knight-Ridder and has won Pulitzer Prizes for photography and reporting, including an investigative series on the Philippines's Ferdinand Marcos that helped bring about the dictator's fall. As should be expected in a place where money is a driving force, the business section provides well-analyzed articles, particularly about stocks and finance. Friday's paper contains an entertainment supplement called "Eye," which is a wanna-be *Metro.* Compared with other metropolitan newspapers, the Sunday section tends to be lean, padded with a lot of ad inserts. Overall, the paper does an excellent job covering the area's human and high-tech news. It costs $.35 daily, $1.25 Sunday. Website: www.mercurycenter.com.

LOCALIZED PUBLICATIONS

The *"Merc"* and *Metro* aren't the only sources of news in Silicon Valley. The region contains numerous small hometown papers that give a focused look at the issues and stories in the communities and neighborhoods they target. Reading these publications can give you a feel for the human aspects of Silicon Valley.

Almaden Times, 408/494-7000
Blossom Valley Times, 408/494-7000
Cambrian Times, 408/494-7000
Campbell Express, 408/374-9700
Campbell Times, 408/494-7000
Country News, Morgan Hill, 408/778-2317
Cupertino Courier, 408/255-7500
El Mensajero (Bay Area's #1 Latino weekly), 888/724-4627

Evergreen Times, 408/494-7000
Gilroy Dispatch, 408/842-6400
Los Altos Town Crier, 650/948-9000
Los Gatos Weekly Times, 408/354-3110
Milpitas Post Newspaper, 408/262-2454
Morgan Hill Times, 408/779-4106
Mountain View Voice, 510/964-6300
Palo Alto Daily News, 650/327-6397
Palo Alto Weekly Times, 650/326-8210
San Jose City Times, 408/298-8000
Santa Clara Weekly, 408/243-2000
Santa Teresa Times, 408/494-7000
Saratoga News, 408/867-6397
The Sun (Sunnyvale), 408/481-0170
Valley Scene (Silicon Valley society paper), 408/271-9047
Willow Glen Resident, 408/298-8000
Willow Glen Times, 408/494-7000

Suggested Reading

Internet Resources

Local News Sites

Several websites give daily and weekly updates on local news and issues relating to Silicon Valley. They also provide entertainment options:

Business Journal (www.sanjose.bcentral.com/sanjose/)

Mercury Center (www.siliconvalley.com)

Metro Active (www.metroactive.com)

Entertainment Sites

If you're looking for websites showcasing local restaurants, entertainment, nightlife, and maps, try these:

San Jose Downtown Association (www.sj-downtown.com/)

San Jose/Silicon Valley Convention and Visitors Bureau (www.sanjose.org)

Dining (www.dine.com)

University Sites

Silicon Valley's three major universities offer visitors a variety of entertainment options including theater and sports. To check out what's happening on campus, try:

San Jose State University (www.sjsu.edu)

Santa Clara University (www.scu.edu)

Stanford University (www.stanford.edu)

Official City Sites

The official city government sites provide a wealth of information for each individual Silicon Valley community. You can find out about the city's history, entertainment, sports and recreation, businesses, arts and entertainment, festivals, weather, demographics, and organizations. Some of these sites also provide local weather and road camera video.

Campbell (www.ci.campbell.ca.us/)

Cupertino (www.cupertino.org)

Gilroy (www.ci.gilroy.ca.us/)

Los Altos (www.ci.los-altos.ca.us/)

Los Altos Hills (www.losaltoshills.ca.gov/)

Los Gatos (www.losgatosweb.com/)

Menlo Park (www.ci.menlo-park.ca.us/)

Milpitas (www.ci.milpitas.ca.us/)

Morgan Hill (www.morgan-hill.ca.gov/)

Mountain View (www.ci.mtview.ca.us/)

Palo Alto (www.city.palo-alto.ca.us/)

San Jose (www.ci.san-jose.ca.us/)

San Martin (www.sanmartin.com)

Santa Clara (www.ci.santa-clara.ca.us/)

Saratoga (www.saratoga.ca.us/)

Sunnyvale (www.ci.sunnyvale.ca.us/)

Chambers of Commerce

Campbell
1628 W. Campbell Ave.
(in the Kirkwood Shopping Plaza)
408/378-1666

Cupertino
20455 Silverado Ave.
408/252-7054
www.cupertino-chamber.org

Gilroy
7471 Monterey St.
408/842-6437
www.gilroy.org

Los Altos and Los Altos Hills
321 University Ave.
650/948-1455
www.losaltoschamber.org

Los Gatos
349 N. Santa Cruz Ave.
408/354-9300
www.losgatosweb.com

Menlo Park
1100 Merrill St. (CalTrain depot)
650/325-2818
www.mpchamber.com

Milpitas
138 N. Milpitas Blvd.
408/262-2613
www.milpitas-chamber.com

Morgan Hill
25 W. 1st St.

408/779-9444
www.morganhill.org/mhcc

Mountain View
580 Castro St.
650/968-8378
www.chambermv.org

Palo Alto
325 Forest Ave.
650/324-3121
www.batnet.com/pacc

San Jose-Silicon Valley
310 S. 1st St.
408/291-5250
www.sjchamber.com

San Jose Convention and Visitors Bureau
Information office: 150 W. San Carlos (inside
McEnery Convention Center)
408/977-0900 or 800/800-7522
www.sanjose.org

Santa Clara
1850 Warburton Ave.
408/244-8244
www.santaclara.org

Saratoga
20460 Saratoga–Los Gatos Rd.
408/867-0753
www.saratoga-ca.com

Sunnyvale
494 S. Murphy Ave.
408/736-4971

Accommodations Index

Restaurant Index

Restaurant Index

General Index

Gardens

General Index

General Index

General Index

U.S.~METRIC CONVERSION

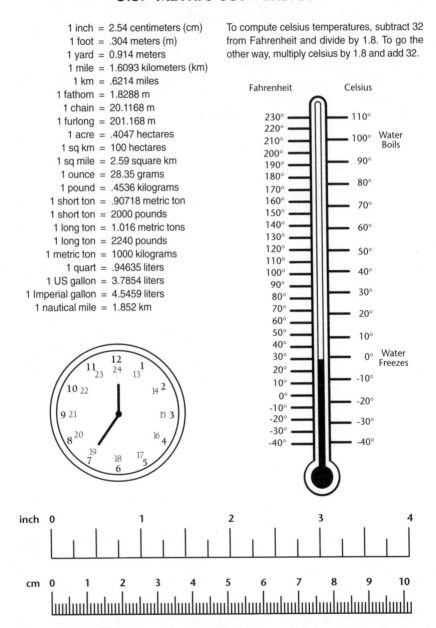

1 inch = 2.54 centimeters (cm)	
1 foot = .304 meters (m)	
1 yard = 0.914 meters	
1 mile = 1.6093 kilometers (km)	
1 km = .6214 miles	
1 fathom = 1.8288 m	
1 chain = 20.1168 m	
1 furlong = 201.168 m	
1 acre = .4047 hectares	
1 sq km = 100 hectares	
1 sq mile = 2.59 square km	
1 ounce = 28.35 grams	
1 pound = .4536 kilograms	
1 short ton = .90718 metric ton	
1 short ton = 2000 pounds	
1 long ton = 1.016 metric tons	
1 long ton = 2240 pounds	
1 metric ton = 1000 kilograms	
1 quart = .94635 liters	
1 US gallon = 3.7854 liters	
1 Imperial gallon = 4.5459 liters	
1 nautical mile = 1.852 km	

To compute celsius temperatures, subtract 32 from Fahrenheit and divide by 1.8. To go the other way, multiply celsius by 1.8 and add 32.

AVALON
TRAVEL
publishing

How far will our travel guides take you? As far as you want.

Discover a rhumba-fueled nightspot in Old Havana, explore prehistoric tombs in Ireland, hike beneath California's centuries-old redwoods, or embark on a classic road trip along Route 66. Our guidebooks deliver solidly researched, trip-tested information—minus any generic froth—to help globetrotters or weekend warriors create an adventure uniquely their own.

And we're not just about the printed page. Public television viewers are tuning in to Rick Steves' new travel series, *Rick Steves' Europe*. On the Web, readers can cruise the virtual black top with *Road Trip USA* author Jamie Jensen and learn travel industry secrets from Edward Hasbrouck of *The Practical Nomad*.

In print. On TV. On the Internet.

We supply the information. The rest is up to you.

Avalon Travel Publishing

Something for everyone

www.travelmatters.com

Avalon Travel Publishing guides are available at your favorite book or travel store.

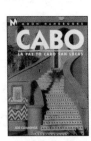

FOGHORN OUTDOORS guides are for campers, hikers, boaters, anglers, bikers, and golfers of all levels of daring and skill. Each guide focuses on a specific U.S. region and contains site descriptions and ratings, driving directions, facilities and fees information,and easy-to-read maps that leave only the task of deciding where to go.

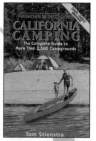

"Foghorn Outdoors has established an ecological conservation standard unmatched by any other publisher."
~Sierra Club

WWW.FOGHORN.COM

TRAVEL SMART guidebooks are accessible, route-based driving guides focusing on regions throughout the United States and Canada. Special interest tours provide the most practical routes for family fun, outdoor activities, or regional history for a trip of anywhere from two to 22 days. Travel Smarts take the guesswork out of planning a trip by recommending only the most interesting places to eat, stay, and visit.

"One of the few travel series that rates sightseeing attractions. That's a handy feature. It helps to have some guidance so that every minute counts."
~San Diego Union-Tribune

CiTY·SMaRT™ guides are written by local authors with hometown perspectives who have personally selected the best places to eat, shop, sightsee, and simply hang out. The honest, lively, and opinionated advice is perfect for business travelers looking to relax with the locals or for longtime residents looking for something new to do Saturday night.

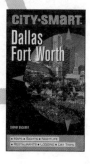

Will you have enough stories to tell your grandchildren?

Yahoo! Travel

©2001 Yahoo! Inc.